Global Capital Markets: Integration, Crisis, and Growth

This book presents an economic history of international capital mobility since the late nineteenth century. A preamble introduces the major issues and examines developments in the eighteenth century and before, the important historical preconditions that set the stage for a global market in the nineteenth century. Theory and empirical evidence are used to evaluate the evolution of globalization in financial markets. A discussion of institutional developments focuses on policies toward capital controls and on the pursuit of domestic policy objectives in the context of changing monetary regimes. Governments face a fundamental *macroeconomic policy trilemma*, which forces them to trade off among their conflicting goals, with natural implications for capital mobility. Understood in this way, the present era of globalization can be seen, in part, as the resumption of a liberal world order that was established in the years from 1880 to 1914. Much has changed along the way. Marking a reaction against the old order, the Great Depression emerges as the key turning point in the recent history of international capital markets and offers important insights for contemporary policy debates. Today's return to a world of globalized capital is marked by great unevenness in outcomes, in terms of both participation in capital-market integration and in the distribution of risks and rewards. More than in the past, foreign investment flows largely from rich countries to other rich countries. Yet the burden of financial crises falls most harshly on developing countries, with costs for everyone. After a century in which markets closed and then reopened, this book brings together what we have learned about the dynamics of the international macroeconomic order.

MAURICE OBSTFELD is Class of 1958 Professor of Economics at the University of California, Berkeley, a Research Associate of the National Bureau of Economic Research, and a Research Fellow of the Centre for Economic Policy Research.

ALAN M. TAYLOR is Professor of Economics at the University of California, Davis, a Research Associate of the National Bureau of Economic Research, and a Research Fellow of the Centre for Economic Policy Research.

Global Capital Markets

Integration, Crisis, and Growth

MAURICE OBSTFELD
ALAN M. TAYLOR

CAMBRIDGE
UNIVERSITY PRESS

CAMBRIDGE UNIVERSITY PRESS
Cambridge, New York, Melbourne, Madrid, Cape Town, Singapore, São Paulo

Cambridge University Press
40 West 20th Street, New York, NY 10011-4211, USA

www.cambridge.org
Information on this title: www.cambridge.org/9780521633178

First published 2004
Reprinted 2004, 2005
First paperback edition 2005

Printed in the United States of America

A catalog record for this publication is available from the British Library.

Library of Congress Cataloging in Publication Data

Obstfeld, Maurice
Global capital markets : integration, crisis, and growth / Maurice Obstfeld, Alan M. Taylor.
    p.   cm. – (Japan-U.S. Center Sanwa monographs on international financial markets)
Includes bibliographical references and index.
ISBN 0-521-63317-6
1. International finance – History.   2. Capital market – History.   3. International economic
relations – History.   I. Taylor, Alan M., 1964–   II. Title.   III. Series.
HG3881.02633   2004
332′.042–dc21   2004051477

ISBN-13   978-0-521-63317-8 hardback
ISBN-10   0-521-63317-6 hardback

ISBN-13   978-0-521-67179-8 paperback
ISBN-10   0-521-67179-5 paperback

To Leslie Ann, Eli, Clara, and Zachary
M. O.

To Claire and Olivia
A. M. T.

Contents

List of Tables

List of Figures

Acknowledgments

This book reflects more than six years of research and writing on the evolution of global capital markets and an even longer period spent thinking about the topic. The culmination of the project allows us to recall how much we owe to the many people and institutions that have helped to make our work possible. Various kinds of financial and logistical support facilitated our collaboration, especially when we were working at long distance. Equally important were the intellectual and personal debts we accrued, which can be counted among every author's greatest assets.

We are sincerely obliged to Sanwa Bank (now UFJ Bank) for their generous endowment, which established this monograph series and the associated prize to encourage research on international finance. This initiative has been all the more successful thanks to the oversight of the Japan-U.S. Center at New York University and, in particular, Professors Ryuzo Sato and Rama Ramachandran. On several occasions we received helpful comments on the manuscript from the prize selection committee, which, in the initial stages of the project, included Richard Zeckhauser, the late Merton Miller, and the late James Tobin.

The long gestation of our book has also been helpfully sustained by other sources of material assistance. Obstfeld gratefully acknowledges support from the U.S. National Science Foundation, through grants to the National Bureau of Economic Research (NBER), and from the Class of 1958 Chair at the University of California, Berkeley. Taylor gratefully acknowledges the support of the National Fellowship at the Hoover Institution, Stanford University, and the Chancellor's Fellowship at the University of California, Davis.

We are indebted to a great many of our fellow scholars. On account of his role in shaping our research, we would first like to thank our colleague, Jay Shambaugh – for making it a pleasure to research and write with him and for permission to draw on our joint work in this book. We are also grateful to our research assistants, who have been closely involved in the endeavor since the beginning. Haru Connolly, Julian di Giovanni, Ryan Edwards, Miguel Angel Fuentes, David Jacks, Matthew Jones, and Marc Muendler all provided superb help and useful suggestions, while retaining the good humor that is essential when working with historical records. They bear no responsibility for the final work, of course, and neither do the many scholars who gave constructive criticism or assisted us in tracking down data and details. For their help we thank Ronald Albers, Pranab Bardhan, Luis Bértola, Ben Bernanke, Michael Bordo, Guillermo Bózzoli, Charles Calomiris, Kevin Carey, Gregory Clark, Michael Clemens, Nicholas Crafts, Lance Davis, Gerardo della Paolera, the late Rudi Dornbusch, Michael Edelstein, Barry Eichengreen, Graham Elliott, Niall Ferguson, Albert Fishlow, Marc Flandreau, Jeffrey Frankel, Jeffry Frieden, Stephen Haber, Timothy Hatton, Peter Henry, Douglas Irwin, Michael Jansson, Matthew Jones, Joost Jonker, Graciela Kaminsky, Michael Klein, Jan Tore Klovland, Michael Knetter, Philip Lane, David Leblang, Peter Lindert, James Lothian, Paolo Mauro, Ian McLean, Satyen Mehta, Christopher Meissner, Gian Maria Milesi-Ferretti, Joel Mokyr, Larry Neal, Lawrence Officer, Kevin O'Rourke, Şevket Pamuk, Peter Pedroni, Richard Portes, Leandro Prados de la Escosura, Dennis Quinn, Carmen Reinhart, Vincent Reinhart, Jaime Reis, Hugh Rockoff, Peter Rousseau, Sergio Schmukler, Pierre Sicsic, James Stock, Nathan Sussman, Lars Svensson, Richard Sylla, Mark Taylor, Michael Tomz, Gail Triner, Michael Twomey, Jürgen von Hagen, Frank Warnock, Mark Watson, Marc Weidenmier, Michael Wickens, Jeffrey Williamson, Yishay Yafeh, and Tarik Yousef.

We have also had the benefit of presenting our work to numerous audiences around the world and we would like to thank them for their helpful comments. We gave related papers to the following conferences: Econometric Society Seventh World Congress, Tokyo, Japan, August 1995; NBER, Development of the American Economy, Cambridge, Mass., March 1996; NBER, Exchange Rates, Cambridge, Mass., May 1996; NBER, The Defining Moment: The Great Depression and the American Economy in the Twentieth Century, Kiawah Island, S.C., October 1996; UC Berkeley–Federal Reserve Bank of San Francisco International Finance Summer Camp, Berkeley and San Francisco, Calif., July 1998; Latin American and Caribbean Economic Association Meetings, Buenos Aires, Argentina, October 1998; American Economic Association Meetings, New York, January 1999; Colloquium on Globalization, University of California at Los Angeles, Los Angeles, Calif., November 1999; Canadian Network in Economic History Meeting, Stratford, Ont., Canada, October 2000; Centre for Economic Policy Research, Analysis of International Capital Markets: Understanding Europe's Role in the Global Economy Workshop, Tel Aviv, Israel, November 2000; NBER, Globalization in Historical Perspective, Santa Barbara, Calif., May 2001; Globalization, Trade, and Development, Inter-American Development Bank and Brookings Institution, Washington, D.C., May 2001; International Financial Conference, University of Rome, Tor Vergata, Rome, Italy, December 2001; International Monetary Fund, Institute High-Level Seminar, Washington, D.C., August 2002; European Historical Economics Society, ESF Conference on Political Economy of Globalization, Dublin, Ireland, August 2002; Money, Macro, and Finance Research Group and ESRC Understanding the Evolving Macroeconomy Programme Conference, University of Warwick, U.K., September 2002; NBER, International Finance and Macroeconomics, Cambridge, Mass., October 2002; Global Linkages and Economic Performance, De Nederlandsche Bank, Amsterdam, The Netherlands, November 2002; American Economic Association Meetings, Washington, D.C., January 2003; The History of Financial Innovation, Yale School of Management, New Haven, Conn., March 2003. We also made presentations at the following: Banco Central del Uruguay; Bank of Japan; Centre for History and Economics, King's College, Cambridge; Columbia University; De Paul University; Fundação Getulio Vargas; Georgetown University; Harvard University; Indiana University; Massachusetts Institute of Technology; New York University; Queen's University; Stanford University; Universidad Argentina de la Empresa; Universidad Torcuato Di Tella; Universitat Pompeu Fabra; University of California, Berkeley; University of California, Davis; University of California, Los Angeles; University of California, San Diego; University of California, Santa Cruz; University of Chicago; University of Hawaii; University of Toronto; University of Virginia; University of Wisconsin; and the Washington, D.C., Area Economic History Workshop.

Certain parts of this book draw on some of our previously published work and we gratefully acknowledge the permission we were granted to quote from the following: "The Global Capital Market: Benefactor or Menace?" *Journal of Economic Perspectives* 12 (1998): 9–30; "The Great Depression as a Watershed: International Capital Mobility in the Long Run," in *The Defining Moment: The Great Depression and the American Economy in the Twentieth Century*, edited by Michael D. Bordo, Claudia D. Goldin, and Eugene N. White (Chicago: University of Chicago Press, 1998), ©1998 National Bureau of Economic Research, all rights reserved; "A Century of Current Account Dynamics," *Journal of International Money and Finance* 21 (2002): 725–48; "A Century of Purchasing Power Parity," *Review of Economics and Statistics* 84 (2002): 139–50; "Globalization and Capital Markets," in *Globalization in Historical Perspec-*

tive, edited by Michael D. Bordo, Alan M. Taylor, and Jeffrey G. Williamson (Chicago: University of Chicago Press, 2003) ©2003 National Bureau of Economic Research, all rights reserved; and "Sovereign Risk, Credibility, and the Gold Standard: 1870–1913 versus 1925–31," *Economic Journal* 113 (2003): 1–35.

Getting from an idea to a manuscript to a book is a lengthy, laborious trek and for encouragement along the way we thank our patient and persistent editor, Scott Parris. His colleague at the Press, Shari Chappell, made the production process as smooth as possible, even for two authors foolish enough to typeset their own manuscript. Sara Black copyedited the ever-changing flurry of paper with great skill and Ernie Haim kept the manuscript moving through the hoops.

Our deepest thanks go to our families for their support. They know what an investment this has been.

M. O. & A. M. T.
Berkeley and Davis, California
September 2003

Part one

Preamble

This first part of the book introduces the main argument. An overview of the functions of an international capital market, the problems it raises, and the historical development of capital mobility through the nineteenth century sets the scene for our study. We then move to a summary of developments in the twentieth century and look ahead to the economic and institutional history that follows in the next part of the book.

1

Global Capital Markets: Overview and Origins

At the turn of the twenty-first century, the merits of international financial integration are under more forceful attack than at any time since the 1940s. Even mainstream academic proponents of free multilateral commodity trade, such as Jagdish Bhagwati, argue that the risks of global financial integration outweigh the benefits. Critics from the left such as Lord Eatwell, more wary even of the case for free trade on current account, claim that since the 1960s "free international capital flows" have been "associated with a deterioration in economic efficiency (as measured by growth and unemployment)."[1]

Such a resurgence of concerns about international financial integration is understandable in light of the multiple crises seen since the early 1990s in Western Europe, Latin America, East Asia, Russia, and elsewhere. Supporters of free trade in tangible goods have long recognized that its net benefits to countries typically are distributed unevenly, creating domestic winners and losers. Recent international financial crises, however, have submerged entire economies and threatened their trading partners, inflicting losses all around. International financial transactions rely inherently on the expectation that counterparties will fulfill future contractual commitments; they therefore place confidence and possibly volatile expectations at center stage.[2] These same factors are present in

---

[1] See Bhagwati (1998) and Eatwell (1997, 2). For alternative skeptical perspectives on the prospects for different facets of international economic integration, see Rodrik (2000) and Stiglitz (2002). More recently, the economically liberal *Economist* newspaper has endorsed the use of capital controls in some circumstances (see "A place for capital controls," May 3, 2003). The position of the International Monetary Fund (IMF) has also moved in this direction (see *IMF Survey*, "Opening up to capital flows? Be prepared before plunging in," May 19, 2003). Prior to the financial turbulence of the late 1990s, which we discuss further below, the IMF had considered amending its Articles of Agreement so as to promote the further easing of capital-account restrictions among its members. See Fischer (1998).

[2] The vast majority of commodity trades also involve an element of intertemporal exchange, via deferred or advance payment for goods, but the unwinding of the resulting cross-border obligations tends to be more predictable than for assets, and transaction volumes are smaller.

purely intranational financial trades, of course, but the relatively higher costs of trading goods and assets internationally make the adjustments to market shocks more costly. Furthermore, problems of oversight, adjudication, and enforcement all are orders of magnitude more difficult among sovereign nations with distinct national currencies than within a single national jurisdiction. And because there exists no natural world lender of last resort, international crises are intrinsically harder to head off and contain than are purely domestic ones. Factors other than the threat of crises, such as the power of capital markets to constrain domestically oriented economic policies, also have sparked concerns over greater financial openness.

Yet we must be careful not to allow the potential risks to obscure the potential benefits. In this introductory chapter we will outline the efficiency gains that international financial integration offers in theory; to a great extent these correspond to those attainable through financial markets even within a closed economy, although the scope is global. We will then turn to the practical problems that arise in trying to realize the gains from asset trading at the level of the global economy. To place theory in a historical context, we conclude the chapter with a brief survey of the evolution of modern international capital markets starting in the late middle ages.

Our goal in this chapter is to set out the core themes of the book. The ebb and flow of international capital since the nineteenth century illustrates recurring difficulties, as well as the alternative perspectives from which policymakers have tried to confront them. Subsequent chapters are devoted to documenting these vicissitudes quantitatively and explaining them. We believe that economic theory and economic history together can provide useful insights into events of the past and deliver relevant lessons for today.

1.1 Theoretical benefits

Economic theory leaves no doubt about the potential advantages of global financial trading. International financial markets allow residents of different countries to pool various risks, achieving more effective insurance than purely domestic arrangements would allow. Furthermore, a country suffering a temporary recession or natural disaster can borrow abroad. Developing countries with little capital can borrow to finance investment, thereby promoting economic growth without sharp increases in saving rates. At the global level, the international capital market channels world savings to their most productive uses, irrespective of location. The other main potential role of international capital markets is to discipline policymakers who might be tempted to exploit a captive domestic capital market. Unsound policies – for example, excessive government borrowing or inadequate bank regulation – would spark speculative capital outflows and higher domestic interest rates under conditions of financial openness. In theory, at least, a government's fear of these effects should make rash behavior less attractive.

1.1.1 International risk sharing

A basic function of a world capital market is to allow countries with imperfectly correlated income risks to trade them, thereby reducing the global cross-sectional variability in per capita consumption levels. In a world of two economies, for example, a pure terms-of-trade change redistributes world income away from the country whose exports cheapen and, in equal measure, toward its trading partner. If the countries exchange equity shares in each other's industries, however, the redistributive effect of terms-of-trade fluctuations is dampened. Both countries benefit from the exchange because both can enjoy consumption streams that are less variable after trade. This pooling of risks can be accomplished through a diversity of financial instruments: stock shares, foreign direct investments, insurance contracts, or even nominally noncontingent securities whose real values are subject to exchange-rate risk. In addition, many derivative securities based on some of these underlying assets are also traded internationally.

As a simple example that conveys the intuition behind the risk-pooling function of a global capital market, imagine a one-period world endowment economy made up of N countries, each populated by a representative individual. Every country or individual i has a random output Y_i of a single perishable world consumption good; for all i, Y_i has mean μ and variance σ^2, and national outputs are uncorrelated. If there is no trade in assets, the representative individual from country i has a consumption level of $C_i = Y_i$, and thus a consumption variance of σ^2. In contrast, suppose that there is an international asset market in which people from different countries can trade claims to national outputs at the start of the period, prior to the realization of the random national outputs. Then the resident of country i, say, will sell off a fraction $(N-1)/N$ of his claim on the domestic output process to residents of other countries, while using the proceeds to purchase a fractional claim $1/N$ of Y_j, for all $j \neq i$. This leaves everyone in the world holding the same global mutual fund with payoff $\sum_{i=1}^{N} Y_i/N$. This payoff, in turn, equals C_i for *all* countries i, but now the variance of this consumption level for each individual or country is only σ^2/N, far below the variance σ^2 of autarky consumption.

For analytical purposes, economists often think of uncertainty as representable by a set of possible "states of the world" on every date, one of which will be randomly chosen by Nature. In that setting, the most basic type of contingent contract is an Arrow-Debreu security that pays off 1 unit of consumption in a specified state of the world, but 0 in all other states. Asset markets are said to be "complete" when a full set of such Arrow-Debreu contracts, one for each possible state on every date, is traded. Under a hypothetical complete-markets regime with free international asset trade, agents the world over can pool risks to the utmost (technologically feasible) extent. The relative prices of Arrow-Debreu securities are common to all countries, and everyone trades so as to equate his or her marginal rate of substitution between consumption in different states to a common relative-price ratio. This process fully exhausts all potential gains that existed prior to trade. Figure 1.1 displays an efficient, post-trade allocation in an economy with two agents (think of them as countries) and two goods, the "goods" being consumption in the two states of nature. In Figure 1.1, the length of the Edgeworth box's horizontal edge measures the total world output available in state 1, that of the vertical edge total state 2 output. We have drawn the box to have horizontal and vertical edges of equal length, meaning that there is no *systematic* uncertainty about world output, only *idiosyncratic* uncertainty about national output shares. Thus, the "contract curve" of Pareto optimal allocations is the linear diagonal connecting the domestic and foreign origins O^H and O^F. Given the absence of systematic risk, the equilibrium price of the two Arrow-Debreu assets is unity and agents trade at that price from an initial endowment point such as E to the equilibrium consumption allocation at C.[3]

The effect of global asset markets on *production* decisions may offer even greater gains than their function in allocating exogenous consumption risks more efficiently. As Arrow observes, "the mere trading of risks, taken as given, is only part of the story and in many respects the less interesting part. The possibility of shifting risks, of insurance in the broadest sense, permits individuals to engage in risky activities that they would not otherwise undertake."[4] In one economic model, the ability to lay off risks in a global market induces investors to shift their capital toward riskier but, on average, more profitable activities. The result is a rise in the average growth rate of world output and, possibly, high welfare gains.[5]

[3] See Obstfeld and Rogoff (1996, chap. 5).
[4] See Arrow (1971, 137).
[5] Obstfeld (1994a).

Fig. 1.1. Asset trade in an economy with two agents and two goods

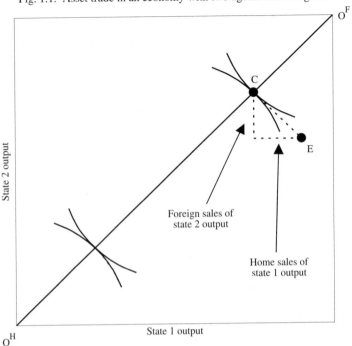

Notes: As shown in this Edgeworth box, identical agents home (H) and foreign (F) have different endowments of the state-contingent output in a two-state world. They can trade Arrow-Debreu state-contingent output claims on the two goods shown in the diagram, consumpiton in state 1 and consumption in state 2. Agents' allocations are measured from their respective origins (home up and right from the lower left, foreign down and left from the upper right). Trade allows them to shift allocations from endowment point E to consumption point C via the trade triangle (broken line); it thus raises the utility of both agents (iso-utility lines are solid curves). We have illustrated the case of no systematic (or aggregate) uncertainty: the box's edges are of equal length.

1.1.2 Intertemporal trade

The risk-sharing function of capital markets is to improve the allocation of resources across different random states of the world. That function, conceived in the abstract, need have no dynamic dimension; but capital markets also reallocate resources over time in ways that can raise efficiency. In principle, this second function of intertemporal reallocation can be understood without reference to uncertainty. So we temporarily abstract from it and imagine a world of perfect foresight. In such a world, an international capital market allows countries to smooth out over time the dynamic consumption effects of predictable income fluctuations. A country whose output is temporarily low, for example, can borrow to support consumption, repaying the loans later after the anticipated output increase. The borrowing opportunity allows a less variable consumption path than would be available in autarky.

As in the case of risk sharing, purely intertemporal trading opportunities will also affect the production activities that agents undertake, contributing further to efficiency in the absence of distortions. A country that has rich investment opportunities, but that generates little saving of its own, can tap the international capital market to exploit its investment potential without massive short-run consumption cutbacks. Conversely, countries with abundant savings but more limited investment prospects at home can earn higher returns to wealth than they would domestically. Both borrowers and lenders gain as capital flows to its most productive uses worldwide. In particular, developing countries can invest more than they could if closed, while simultaneously enjoying higher consumption and wages. The process of economic convergence is hastened by capital flows from rich to poor countries.

Under conditions of uncertainty, even trades of noncontingent assets (that is, consumption-indexed loans) can help countries mitigate the effects of the risks that they face. Countries that suffer random but temporary income shortfalls, such as crop failures, can blunt their impacts by borrowing abroad until better fortune returns. The capacity of loans to substitute partially for an absence of risk-sharing markets simply reflects the fact that the economy faces ongoing uncertainty. However, the degree of risk shifting that loan markets permit is generally far inferior to what truly complete asset markets would allow. In the complete-markets case, countries would lay off all idiosyncratic output risk in world insurance markets, and an idiosyncratic shock to national *output* therefore would not affect national *income* at all (and would induce no international borrowing or lending response). Of course, international trades involving assets with random payoffs, such as foreign direct investments, can also serve to exploit the gains from intertemporal trade. In reality, the scope of world asset trade is intermediate between the cases of noncontingent loans and complete markets, though still probably closer to the former, as we shall see.

1.1.3 Discipline

An open capital market can impose discipline upon governments that might otherwise pursue overexpansionary fiscal or monetary policies or tolerate lax financial practices by domestic financial intermediaries. The prospect of rising interest rates and capital flight may discourage large public-sector deficits; the sharp reaction of exchange rates to investor expectations and interest rates may restrain inflationary monetary moves. Tirole (2002) puts discipline effects at the heart of his framework for analyzing proposed international financial reforms.

There is considerable evidence that during the period up to 1914, countries that adhered to the international gold standard were rewarded by lower costs of borrowing from abroad. Countries with lower public debts were similarly rewarded during the years of the restored interwar gold standard, 1925–31. In more recent data, developing countries' external borrowing spreads reflect, at least partially, certain macro fundamentals.[6] Markets seem to try, as well, to divine the economic implications of national foreign policy moves. In 1998, for example, Moody's and Standard and Poor's downgraded India as an investment destination in reaction to the country's controversial announcement of nuclear tests. As Thomas L. Friedman wrote in the *New York Times*, "This is far more important than any U.S. sanctions, because it will raise the cost of borrowing for every Indian company and state government seeking funds from abroad."[7]

Unfortunately, market discipline often seems insufficient to deter misbehavior. Capital markets may tolerate inconsistent policies too long and then abruptly reverse course, inflicting punishments far harsher than the underlying policy "crimes" would seem to warrant. And in some cases, capital-market openness has constrained the official pursuit of arguably desirable economic goals. These problems and others are critical to understanding both perception and reality in the historical evolution of the modern global capital market.

1.2 Problems of supranational capital markets in practice

In a world of multiple sovereign states, an integrated world capital market necessarily straddles several distinct political jurisdictions that may differ in economic infrastructure, legal institutions, and commercial culture, as well as in the trade-generating factors (endowments, technologies, preferences) stressed in textbooks. The existence of political entities smaller than the market itself can limit the market's effectiveness and even render market linkages counterproductive. Any overall assessment of the net gains conferred by the global capital market must therefore account for the market's extent over a number of sovereign states.[8]

---

[6] We discuss the evidence on the pre-1914 and interwar gold standards in Chapter 6 of this book. On more recent developing-country borrowing, see, for example, Edwards (1986). See Haque et al. (1996) for an analysis of credit ratings.

[7] See Friedman, "What goes around...," *New York Times*, June 23, 1998, A21.

[8] Considerations of space allow only brief mention of a topic as important as it is vast. For an authoritative recent survey, see Bryant (2003).

1.2.1 Enforcement of contracts and informational problems

An obvious first problem is the enforcement of financial contracts. The gains from financial trade are, from an analytical point of view, formally indistinguishable from those that result from static commodity trade when contracts can be costlessly verified and enforced. All that is involved in demonstrating this equivalence is to redefine goods available on different dates, or contingent upon different states of nature, as distinct commodities. Static trade gains, however (at least in a hypothetical world without shipping time or trade credit), do not require payment today in return for expected payment tomorrow. Thus, the question of *confidence*, which is central to financial transactions in reality, need not arise. In dynamic real-world financial markets, though, the problem is a dominating one. The contracting party who is the first to receive payment may have little motivation to fulfill his or her part of the deal later on.

The problem of enforcement is that of ensuring sufficient incentives to fulfill contractual obligations. While enforceability is pivotal even in a closed economy, it becomes even more problematic in contracts between residents of different countries. If one party to the contract is a sovereign, legal remedies in cases of breach of contract may be limited. Even when all contracting parties are private agents, it can be comparatively difficult to pursue legal actions in foreign courts or to impose domestic legal judgments on foreigners. Sometimes, governments will assume the troubled debts of their domestic private sectors, turning private-sector debt problems into sovereign debt problems. In general, as Tirole (2002) emphasizes, actions of the sovereign can affect private residents' willingness or ability to fulfill contracts with foreigners.

The efficiency of contracts is limited further by informational asymmetries, which again are more severe in an international setting than within a single nation's borders. Cross-border monitoring can be more difficult than in a domestic context because of differences in accounting standards, legal systems, government efficiency, governance mechanisms, and other factors. Both enforcement limitations and informational asymmetries reduce the gains that can feasibly be reaped from international trade, without necessarily eliminating them.[9]

1.2.2 Loss of policy autonomy

Politicians, states, rulers, and – in democratic polities – voters prize the ability to make sovereign, independent policy choices. That is, they wish to decide the particular goals of domestic policy, as well as the policies that will shape

[9] See Obstfeld and Rogoff (1996, chap. 6) for a survey.

the future of the nation, state, or regional entity. Such desires often come into conflict with supranational markets that extend beyond the polity's borders. Financial openness, in particular, may compromise the ability of fiscal and monetary policy to attain various national goals.

Why might the constraints of financial openness pose a dilemma for fiscal policy? If capital is free to emigrate in the face of taxes, then either the burden of providing social services must be shifted toward labor, or those services must be scaled back (or, alternatively, some capital emigrates, wages fall in equilibrium, and the burden is shifted by another means). Tax competition could lead to a global downward leveling of capital taxes below the politically desirable levels. In short, footloose capital confronts governments with a harsher tradeoff between the size of the public sector and an equitable functional distribution of income. Because capital mobility can substitute for trade, as stressed by Mundell, and thus can have effects on the income distribution similar to those of trade, a reduction in the government's ability to attain distributional goals could be all the more damaging to social cohesion when capital is mobile.[10]

Financial openness also constricts governments' choices over monetary policies. As we shall discuss at greater length in Section 1.4, governments cannot simultaneously maintain an open capital account, a fixed exchange rate, and a domestically oriented monetary policy for any substantial length of time. They can combine at most two elements from this list of three. This *macroeconomic policy trilemma* is central to understanding how the global capital market has evolved over time. The trilemma is also central to the aspect of the global capital market that arguably has generated the most concern over the years: its susceptibility to crisis and even collapse.

1.2.3 International aspects of capital-market crises

In the 1990s, foreign-exchange crises disrupted exchange markets across the globe. These recent events sharpened debate over two opposing views on the causes of crises. One claim is that otherwise successful economies have been victims of greedy market operators, usually foreign ones. This view is especially popular with government ministers in the afflicted countries. The opposing view is that such crises are largely home-grown, and that the global

---

[10] See Mundell (1957). The downward pressure on taxes and spending induced by the threat of capital flight is often termed a "race to the bottom." Yet again, exactly the same concerns can arise *within* certain political units, as in federal states. For research on the implications of U.S. federalism on fiscal outcomes and social programs at the state level see, for example, Ferejohn and Weingast (1997). For an early comparison of issues raised by intranational and international mobility, see Cooper (1974).

capital market is simply performing a valuable and needed role in disciplining imprudent government policies.

Recent thinking on crises would argue that neither view is universally correct. Currency crises do not occur any time market whims dictate; but they may not represent, either, an inevitable punishment for unsustainable government policies. Instead, there may be extensive "gray areas" in which unwise policies or adverse economic shocks make countries vulnerable to crises, but in which a crisis is not inevitable and might in fact not occur without the impetus of a sudden capital-flow reversal. For example, a government with a large domestic-currency public debt of short maturity may be induced to devalue by very high short-term interest rates, which themselves reflect a rational expectation of devaluation. The government's motivation in devaluing is to debase its debt in real terms so as to limit future tax burdens. On the other hand, there can be a second equilibrium in which markets do not expect devaluation, interest rates are low, and the government's pain therefore is not so great as to induce a devaluation. A jump from the second equilibrium to the first – due to an essentially exogenous shock to expectations – generates a sudden crisis.[11]

As a result, currency crises, like bank runs, may contain a self-fulfilling element that can generate multiple market equilibria and render the timing of crises somewhat indeterminate. What we see in these cases is a sharp break from an essentially tranquil equilibrium to a crisis state, rather than a gradual deterioration in domestic interest rates and other market-based indicators. This scenario helps to explain why capital markets can appear to impose too little discipline before the crisis arrives and too harsh a discipline afterwards.

A national solvency crisis need not be related to a currency collapse, and could occur even in a country that uses a foreign currency such as the U.S. dollar as its money. Thus, the exchange-rate channel is not central in theory, though it often has been in practice. If lenders refuse to roll over a country's maturing dollar debts, and if it lacks the liquid resources – foreign reserves and credit lines – with which to meet its obligations, a crisis ensues. Here we have a close analogy with the case of a banking panic. Willing rollover would preclude panic, whereas a market fear that others will flee makes it optimal for each individual lender to flee as well. In many recent cases, indeed, banking

---

[11] See Obstfeld, (1994b, 1996) for details. More recent crisis models, such as that of Morris and Shin (1998), focus on possible restoration of a unique equilibrium when market actors have asymmetric information. But these models do not deliver good news for fixed exchange rates, as the unique equilibrium is the one in which speculators attack a currency whenever there is a sufficiently good chance that the attack will succeed. Subsequent research has tended to restore multiplicities; see, for example, Angeletos et al. (2003) and Chamley (2003).

and currency crises have coincided, worsening the pain inflicted by both. At times, national solvency has come into question as a result.

The European countries that devalued in the 1992 crises of the Exchange Rate Mechanism did not subsequently fall into solvency crises, which is why their forced devaluations did not impair growth (indeed, they probably helped it). But in some crisis countries (notably some of the Nordic countries), bank-sector weakness enhanced economic vulnerability. In general, exchange-rate, financial-sector, and national-solvency crises can interact in explosive ways. The attempt to ensure pegged exchange rates (or a preannounced ceiling on exchange depreciation) can lead to the very vulnerabilities that raise the possibility of a national solvency crisis. When domestic banks and corporate borrowers are (over)confident in a peg, they may borrow dollars or yen without adequately hedging against the risk that the domestic currency will be devalued, sharply raising the ratio of their domestic-currency liabilities to their assets. They may believe that even if a crisis occurs, the government's promise to peg the exchange rate represents an implicit promise that they will be bailed out in one way or another. Such beliefs introduce an element of moral hazard. Borrowers may face little risk of personal loss even if a bailout does not materialize because they have little capital of their own at stake. When confidence in the peg evaporates, however, the government is placed in an impossible bind: an aggressive interest-rate defense will damage domestic actors with maturity mismatches, while currency depreciation will damage those with currency mismatches.

Such problems have been especially acute in developing countries, where (typically) prudential regulation is looser, financial institutions are weaker, borrowing from foreigners generally is denominated in foreign currency, and the government's credit may be shaky. As market sentiment turns against an exchange-rate peg, the government is effectively forced to assume the short foreign-currency positions in some way – or else to allow a cascade of domestic bankruptcies. Because the government at the same time has used its foreign-exchange reserves (in a vain attempt to defend the peg), may have sold dollars extensively in forward markets, and cannot borrow more in world credit markets, national default becomes imminent. As a result, the "crisis triplets" of currency, banking, and public credit collapse have been witnessed in numerous historical crises.[12]

The international nature of capital movements makes it harder to exercise prudential regulation and to institute other safeguards – deposit insurance, lender of last resort facilities, and the like – that have proven useful in imparting greater

---

[12] Krugman and Obstfeld (2000, chap. 22); James (2001).

stability to the domestic credit markets of the industrial countries. There are certainly distortions on the supply as well as on the demand side of the market.[13] In addition, there is a major source of systemic risk not present in the closed-economy context: the exchange rate itself. Even among industrial countries, concerns over gaps in prudential oversight have motivated the Basel Committee for more than a quarter century to seek enhanced international regulatory cooperation. In the late 1990s, the same concerns for oversight became a major focus of the International Monetary Fund (IMF) in its responses to crises. For a time, the Fund espoused a Sovereign Debt Restructuring Mechanism (SDRM) meant to provide a set of bankruptcy procedures for sovereign debtors. But the proposal proved unpopular with borrowers and lenders alike, who now seem likely to settle instead on alternative market-based solutions that will encourage orderly workouts, such as collective-action clauses.[14]

1.3 The emergence of world capital markets

The Asian financial turmoil of 1997–8 started as a seemingly localized tremor in far-off Thailand but then swelled into a crisis with massive repercussions in financial markets on every continent. Both the international lending institutions, led by the International Monetary Fund, and national governments joined in the policy response.

At the time, the broad repercussions of the Asian crisis seemed extraordinary. Such turns of events would have been inconceivable, say, during the 1950s and 1960s. During those years, most countries' domestic financial systems labored under extensive government restraint and were cut off from international influences by official firewalls. Yet, despite those restrictions, which were a legacy of the Great Depression and World War Two, international financial crises occurred from time to time. Between 1945 and 1970, however, their effects tended to be localized, with little discernible impact on Wall Street, let alone Main Street.

Given the supposed benefits of a global capital market, why was the market still so fragmented and limited in scope a full generation after the end of World War Two? Following the setback of World War One and a brief comeback between 1925 and 1931, international finance withered in the Great Depression. Governments everywhere limited the scope of domestic financial markets

---

[13] These are stressed by Dobson and Hufbauer (2001).

[14] See Basel Committee (1997) and IMF (1998). Krueger (2002) discusses the SDRM as well as other reforms espoused by the Fund. On the retreat from the SDRM approach, see *Economist*, "Dealing with default," May 10, 2003.

as well, imposing tighter regulation and prohibiting myriad activities outright. World War Two cemented the demise of the global capital market. In the early 1950s, the world's major economies remained linked only by the most rudimentary, and typically bilateral, trade and financial arrangements. Only in the 1960s did private capital movements start to return on any scale, but in the 1970s they grew rapidly. In the 1980s, that growth accelerated (though global capital largely bypassed the developing countries mired in the decade's debt crisis). Periodic crises in emerging financial markets have continued occasionally to hamper developing countries' access to capital flows from abroad. On the whole, however, a worldwide trend of financial opening after the 1980s has begun to restore a degree of international capital mobility that has not been seen for almost a century.

Prior to World War One, a vibrant, free-wheeling capital market linked financial centers in Europe, the Western Hemisphere, Oceania, Africa, and the Far East. A nineteenth-century reader of the *Economist* newspaper could track investments in American railroads, South African gold mines, Egyptian government debt, Peruvian guano, and much more. The big communications advance of the era was perhaps more significant than anything that has been achieved since. The laying of the trans-Atlantic cable in 1866 reduced the settlement time for intercontinental transactions from roughly ten days (the duration of a steamship voyage between Liverpool and New York) to only hours. A flourishing world capital market had already evolved in the years between the mid-nineteenth century and 1914. But despite a revival following the hiatus of World War One, the market collapsed as a result of the worldwide Great Depression. The middle third of the twentieth century, was marked by a sharp reaction against global markets, especially the financial market.

The core of this book will document the quantitative and institutional history of that market over the last century or more: how the market functioned in its golden age, its subsequent destruction, and the recent attempts to rebuild another, even more comprehensive, global market. We will use that historical analysis to ask what lessons the evolutionary story of the world capital market offers for today. Before we begin, it remains to consider how the first global market emerged. It was built over centuries, starting in Europe during the late middle ages. It rose in importance and efficiency in the Renaissance. In the seventeenth and eighteenth centuries, in Amsterdam and London, it began to assume a form that we recognize today. The world capital market embraced other European centers, Latin America, and the United States by the early nineteenth century. By the mid-nineteenth century, it stood poised to bring the entire global economy into its reach.

1.3.1 Early modern financial development

As we have indicated, the growth of modern world financial markets has distant origins. Identification of any single starting point is necessarily arbitrary, yet we certainly discern beginnings in the commerce centered on medieval fairs. International credit was in widespread use by the latter thirteenth century. One impetus for this use of credit was long-distance trade, where the purchase of goods by importers and traders might be separated from their sale for profit by long journeys and considerable time.

On the increasingly busy overland trade routes of Europe a key commercial nexus developed at the Champagne fairs: the four fair towns were an important place of intermodal exchange and arbitrage, but they are best remembered for seminal financial developments in the twelfth century. Using specie as a limited liquidity buffer, medieval merchants could always try to buy and sell goods in a more or less balanced way, but this was not always possible or desirable. The "letters of fair" were a response to this problem: an early form of commercial credit, these were paper assets that could permit trade imbalances to exist over time. Net sellers could leave the fair with a credit on their account and net buyers with a debit, balances which the authorities would carry over until the next fair convened. It was in Champagne, then, that we find the first recorded intertemporal deficits and surpluses in interregional trade, certainly a landmark in the evolution of the global economy.[15]

By the first half of the fourteenth century, Italian houses with agents or correspondents throughout the Atlantic seaboard of Europe and the Mediterranean were the center of a credit network based on nonnegotiable bills of exchange. These bills usually took the form of instructions to pay the bearer a specified currency in a specified locale on the bill's due date.[16] These bills greatly economized on the need to ship specie between financial centers, a costly and sometimes perilous enterprise. Interestingly, the dominance of foreign currency bills derived from the need to circumvent the Church's usury doctrine. Because bills payable in foreign currency involved an element of exchange risk, church doctrine did not forbid their discounting. The evolution of the credit market in the middle ages thus furnishes an early example of financial regulation driving transactions offshore.[17]

---

[15] Cameron (1993; 65, 67).

[16] Italian lenders' operations included sovereign lending, such as the underwriting of English king Edward III's invasion of France (a very unwise investment, as it turned out).

[17] See De Roover (1948, chap. 4). Even though fiat currencies were not in use, exchange rates between centers could vary because of "(1) changes in the monetary standard at home or abroad, (2) disturbances in the balance of payments between any two places, and (3) speculation based on the expectations of the exchange-dealers or on the criminal attempts of manipulators who

By the late sixteenth century, Antwerp emerged as a major international trading and financial center and the *negotiable* foreign bill of exchange was in widespread use in this "multilingual, multinational marketplace of the emerging world economy."[18] Although some domestic financial instruments had been developed with similar transferability characteristics in the Low Countries, this was the first instrument used in any significant way to permit international transactions. The bills were provided with a space on the back for a series of endorsements, making them negotiable and allowing a trade in these bills to develop. The bills served as a form of foreign exchange in complement to local currency in port cities.

The pre-1600 development of the bill market is seen by most observers as the beginning of the "financial revolution" at the international level. The institution behind it was the merchant bank. With correspondent banks in Antwerp, London, and Amsterdam in constant communication, the merchant banks managed the flow of credit and payments associated with the bills, as physical goods and payments circulated contrariwise around this embryonic international market system. The system was further perfected, and its center moved to Amsterdam, with the founding of the celebrated Amsterdam Wisselbank in 1609, a clearing-house organization for various merchant bankers who held accounts there denominated in bank money (banco).[19]

The cosmopolitan nature of this trading world derived in large part from the ever-extending network of European trade. In the major financial centers, just as goods flowed in from around the Mediterranean, then from the East, and then from the Americas, so too did people, ideas, and customs. Many such immigrants, some refugees from persecution and expulsion, brought information about the economies they had left, human capital and skills for engaging in trade or commerce, or financial capital with which to start their own enterprises. In this context, the emergence of a new financial services sector was a true novelty and thus a challenge to the established order. But the bill of exchange and the emerging merchant credit operations were just the start of things to come. The development of joint-stock companies, and the consequent growth of securities markets in the seventeenth century, represented yet another huge leap in financial development.[20]

---

sometimes tried to corner the money market. To this list one should perhaps add the disturbing effects of regulations enacted by the public authorities" (De Roover 1948, 63).

[18] See Neal (1990, 5). Neal supplies a clear explanation of the workings of the negotiable bill of exchange as a financial instrument. On Antwerp see van der Wee (1963).

[19] See Neal (1990, 7).

[20] See Neal (1990, 2000).

1.3.2 Technological and institutional changes

Looking at the frenetic pace and charged atmosphere of today's world stock markets, the reader might imagine that modern finance would be unable to function without coffee. This could be true in more ways than one.

Four hundred years ago coffee was, on the one hand, a typical "exotic" product, one of the many new consumption goods introduced to Europe as colonial expansion took European powers into new trading regions in the Americas and the Orient. And, on the other hand, the original java was, of course, brought from the East by the fleet of that earliest of joint-stock companies, the Dutch East India company. It was in 1609 that Dutch East India company stock began to trade broadly in Amsterdam and the other five cities that controlled the company. The stocks took the form of easily transferable securities that could be owned by domestic and foreign investors alike. Soon an active secondary market in these and other securities developed on the Amsterdam Beurs (Bourse), the first modern stock exchange.[21]

Subsequently, in London, similar transactions in various domestic securities began to be regularized at customary times and places. Eventually the market settled down in the cozy confines of the latest, trendy places-to-be-seen: the coffeehouses. In London, the prime coffeehouse trading locations included Garraway's, Jonathan's, Sam's, Powell's, and the Rainbow. The first two in particular, on Exchange Alley, near the Royal Exchange itself, soon became the center of the trade, and, in a classic demonstration of network externalities, eventually only one became the place-to-be for trading (if not the brew), and that was Jonathan's. Despite being destroyed and rebuilt after fire in 1748, Jonathan's still flourished, so much so that a move to newer and larger premises on Threadneedle Street was necessary in 1773, at Sweeting's Alley, and again in 1801 at Capel Court. These new establishments were called the "Stock Exchange." Vestiges of the original Jonathan's survive to this day in the Old Stock Exchange complex.[22]

Though far from modern, these early stock markets were in no sense primitive, and their features would be instantly recognizable to today's observer. In 1688 Josef Penso de la Vega, a Portuguese Jew living in Amsterdam, published his remarkable work *Confusion de Confusiones*.[23] Like the countless financial self-help guides to be found at airport bookstands nowadays, Penso de la Vega's tract aimed at educating the stock-market neophytes of his day. He described not only trading in derivative securities, such as put and call options, but also

---

[21] See Neal (1990).
[22] See Dickson (1967, 490 et seq.).
[23] Penso de la Vega (1688).

all manner of incidents and events, such as attempts to manipulate the market, panics, crashes, and bull and bear markets.

Almost identical developments were witnessed in London as chronicled by John Houghton in his 1681 pamphlet *A Collection for the Improvement of Husbandry and Trade*. The correspondence in timing between the English and Dutch markets should come as no surprise: the two markets had long been intertwined by the evolving markets for bills of exchange and other instruments, so information flowed between them very rapidly, and institutional developments were easily imitated. The diffusion of ideas between the two centers was all the more fluid after the Glorious Revolution of 1688 brought William of Orange to the English throne and a host of his courtiers, advisers, and financiers into London.[24]

Such developments arose in an already maturing British market for domestic credit, itself founded on an expanding and liquid market for government debt. This had been, and was still to be, a trump card in the British military ascendancy of the seventeenth and eighteenth centuries, notwithstanding formidable foes such as the French with superior manpower, natural resources, and technology. From the beginning, the idea was to imitate the Dutch model and so create a liquid market where money would be "cheap" – that is, where government bonds could be floated at lower interest rates (say 3 to 4 percent, versus 8 percent or more). Interest costs could greatly multiply the burden of wartime deficits, so the state financiers well understood the benefits of creating such a market and lowering their debt servicing costs. Coupled with emerging British dominance in international financial markets, and a rapidly growing market for sterling bills of exchange increasingly centered on London, this also helped the British finance and wage wars more effectively – and, eventually, to do so on a global scale. In this manner, the British state – as much as the private-sector companies such as the Bank of England, the (British) East India Company, or the Royal African Company – came to find itself increasingly a beneficiary of the new financial markets.[25]

These were heady days for finance. The sector expanded in novel and unpredictable ways. It offered new opportunities, but it unsettled traditional arrangements. It crossed national boundaries and had its own lingua franca. New financial products and services emerged that confused and bewildered many. A new class of entrepreneurs, many of them immigrants and foreigners, held great sway in this new form of enterprise. Both the private sector and governments increasingly fell under its influence. From this mix, new and difficult tensions

[24] See Neal (1990, 16–17) and Neal (2000, 123–4).
[25] See Dickson (1967); Brewer (1989); Ferguson (2001, 2003b).

began to surface in the late seventeenth and early eighteenth centuries, and a possible backlash loomed, even as the benefits of an expanding capital market seemed apparent.

Thus, although today's debates about financial integration may generate plenty of heat, the fires being stoked have been smoldering for a very long time. Indeed, even in the most favorable circumstances, capital markets have caused some consternation: Amsterdam and London might be celebrated today as the progenitors – and exemplars – in the Anglo-Saxon world of prudently managed, modern financial markets, but their precocious activities still could not escape scrutiny. Just as it does today, the complex and volatile securities market alarmed many observers and inclined policymakers to intervene either to regulate or to close the market. The esoteric world of financial derivatives was a common target.

As early as 1609 in Amsterdam, the futures market was threatened when the board of the Dutch East India Company, perhaps motivated by concerns about dealings in the company's shares, lobbied the Estates of Holland to ban all futures trading. The local stockbrokers promptly petitioned the government, pointing out that such an action would be as ineffective as it was inequitable. Their rejoinder took the form of a memorandum in which they highlighted various flaws in the proposed ban.

Three main arguments were advanced by the brokers. First, contrary to the board's position, the brokers claimed that futures trading did not tend to depress share prices. On the contrary, they noted, the evidence showed that Amsterdam shares traded higher than those in the outlying bourses where there was no futures trade. Second, they argued for an equitable application of the principles of free trade – including futures trading, which had always been allowed in the Dutch commodities markets, most notably in those for uncaught herring and unharvested grain. Finally, the brokers warned that the proposed regulation was futile in any event. Should the freedom of securities trade be restricted, the business would simply move elsewhere, as there were already active markets opening in such potential rival financial centers as Middelburg, Hamburg, Frankfurt, Cologne, and Rouen.[26]

Arguments against financial activity were very common in early modern times – as they have been ever since. Sometimes objections were based on claims about welfare, efficiency, equity, and so on – but all too often they could degenerate into baser forms of misunderstanding, suspicion, rumor, or envy, with an undercurrent of racism. London was not spared these concerns

---

[26] See Dillen (1930, 50–57). We thank Joost Jonker for bringing these events to our attention.

either, though eventually the arguments in favor of free and transparent financial
markets prevailed:

> The main criticisms of these developments followed obvious lines: objections to Jews,
> foreigners, and men of low origins; to novel ways of getting rich quickly; to new and
> outlandish techniques and vocabulary; to bearish manipulation of prices. Against this
> it could be argued that the evolution of the market was an essential counterpart to
> government borrowing, and that its operations helped provide a flow of new capital for
> war loans. It could also be argued that the daily valuation of the government's credit on
> the floor of Jonathan's was, like the popular press, one of the features of England's "open"
> form of government in the eighteenth century; and that this form, despite the risks it
> involved, was to prove more secure in the long run, because more firmly based on public
> discussion and evaluation, than the closed and supposedly more efficient bureaucratic
> governments of France and other European powers.[27]

Then, as now, the critics could be influential. From time to time, attempts
were made to rein in the London market. Exchange Alley came in for tough
regulation at times. On occasion, outright bans were imposed on the trading
of derivative securities such as calls ("refuses") and puts. The government
sometimes attempted to coerce the market to maintain good prices on public
debt instruments so as to preserve the appearance of a good reputation. Brokers
were required to be licensed for operations. Most of these measures were
temporary or ineffective. An exception was the Bubble Act of 1720, a response
to the mania and panic of the infamous South Sea Bubble, when shares of that
company soared tenfold only to crash after a few months. This act did make
the formation of joint stock companies more difficult and limited the growth of
the market to some degree for a century or more.

Yet by the late 1700s, the climate had changed: for the most part, the stock
exchange and the financial services sector as a whole were by then left to regulate
themselves. Faith in government intervention in the market had been replaced
to a great extent by a laissez-faire belief that "the wealth of nations could only
increase if controls on enterprise were reduced."[28] These developments set the
stage for an even more impressive two-stage growth in the London financial
market in the nineteenth century, during the century of comparative European
peace that lasted from the Congress of Vienna (1815) until the outbreak of
World War One (1914). The first stage went hand in hand with the Industrial
Revolution and raised the profile of international finance. The second stage,
after 1850, put international finance center stage and laid the foundation for the
first truly global market in the era from 1870 to 1914.

[27] Dickson (1967, 516).
[28] Dickson (1967, 516–20); Neal (1990); Muller (2002).

1.3.3 The rise of global finance

Prior to the nineteenth century, the reach of international finance remained relatively limited. London and Amsterdam were the key centers, and their currencies and financial instruments were the principal focus of market players. As the Industrial Revolution gathered steam in Britain, and as the Napoleonic Wars raged on, the importance of international financial markets became apparent in both public and private spheres. Research now suggests that continental savings helped augment British budget constraints in an era when war finance and industrialization threatened to exhaust the domestic supply of savings, and when military crises could require extensive short-term financing.[29] Yet, viewed with hindsight, or from a global perspective, these and other fledgling markets were still quite isolated and the capital flows between them were very small relative to economic activity in general.

In due course, the range of this trade extended to other centers that developed the markets and institutions capable of supporting international financial transactions, and whose governments were not hostile to such developments. On the United States's eastern seaboard, a range of centers including Boston, Philadelphia, and Baltimore gave way to what became the dominant American center of national and international finance, New York. France and Germany had developed sophisticated and expanding capital markets that became well integrated into the widening networks of global finance.

After 1870, these developments progressed even further. Elsewhere in Europe and the New World similar markets evolved from an embryonic stage, and eventually financial trading spread to places as far afield as Melbourne and Buenos Aires.[30] With the world starting to converge on the gold standard as a monetary system, and with technological developments in shipping (for example, steamships replacing sail, the Panama Canal) and communications (the telegraph, transoceanic cables) coming online, the construction of the first global marketplace in capital, as well as in goods and labor, took hold in an era of undisputed liberalism and virtual laissez faire.

Finance also advanced through the development of a broader array of private debt and equity instruments, through the expansion of insurance activities, and through international trade in government bonds. By 1900, the key currencies

[29] See Neal (1990, chap. 10); Oppers (1993); Brezis (1995).
[30] On the United States, see Davis (1965) and Sylla (1975; 1998). On Europe, see Kindleberger (1984). For a comprehensive discussion of the historical and institutional developments in some key countries where international financial markets made an impact at this time – the United Kingdom, the United States, Australia, Argentina, and Canada – see Davis and Gallman's (2001) volume in this series. For a long-run perspective on comparative financial deepening and sophistication, see Goldsmith (1985).

and instruments were known everywhere and formed the basis for an expanding world commercial network, whose rise was equally meteoric. Bills of exchange, bond finance, equity issues, foreign direct investments, and many other types of transaction were by then quite common among the core countries, and among a growing number of nations at the periphery.

More and more day-to-day activities came into the orbit of finance via the growth and development of banking systems in many countries. This in turn raised the question of whether banking supervision would be done by the banks themselves or the government authorities, with solutions including free banking and "wildcat" banks (as in the United States), and changing over time to include governmental supervisory functions, often as part of a broader central monetary authority, the central bank. From what was once an esoteric sector of the economy, the financial sector grew locally and globally to touch increasingly more areas of activity.

Thus, the scope for capital markets to do good – or harm – loomed larger as time went by. Who stood to gain or be hurt? What policies would emerge as government objectives evolved? Would global capital markets be allowed to proceed unfettered or not?

From the turn of the twentieth century, the unfolding of this history of the international capital market has been of enormous import. It has undoubtedly shaped the course of national and international economic development and swayed political interests in all manner of directions at various times. In terms of distribution and equality, it has produced winners and losers, though so often is it misunderstood that the winners and losers – at the national and the global level – are often unclear.

The aim of this book is to tell the history of what became a truly *global* capital market at the dawn of the twentieth century and to explore how it has shaped and been shaped by events ever since.

1.3.4 Stylized facts for the nineteenth and twentieth centuries

Notwithstanding the undisputed record of technological advancement and economic growth over the long run, we must reject the temptations of a simple linear history as we examine international capital markets and their evolution. It has not been a record of ever-more-perfectly-functioning markets with ever-lower transaction costs and ever-expanding scope. As we have noted, the global capital market collapsed during the middle third of the twentieth century. The market became fragmented as governments strove to resist the effects of the Great Depression, and as both public opinion and policy reacted against financial markets' perceived role in the onset of global crisis. Echoes of this same antimarket reaction can be heard once again in public debate at the start of the twenty-first century.

What do we already know about the evolution of global capital mobility in the last century or more? Very few previous studies exist for the entire period and covering a sufficiently comprehensive cross section of countries; but many authors have focused on individual countries and particular epochs, and from their work we can piece together a working set of hypotheses that might be termed the conventional wisdom concerning the evolution of international capital mobility in the post-1870 era. The story comes in four parts, corresponding – not coincidentally – to the division of the twentieth century into distinct international monetary regimes.[31]

The first period in our classification ends in 1914. Between 1870 and World War One, the first age of globalization sprang forth. An increasing share of the world economy came into the orbit of the classical gold standard, and a global capital market with London as its nerve center. The trends are clearly seen in Figure 1.2. By 1880, many countries were on gold; by 1900, a large majority. This fixed-exchange-rate system was for most countries a stable and credible regime that functioned as a disciplining or commitment device. Accordingly, interest rates across countries tended to converge, and capital flows surged. Many peripheral countries, not to mention the New World offshoots of Western Europe, increasingly took part in a globalized trade not only in capital, but also in goods and labor.[32]

In the second period, from 1914 to 1945, this global economy was destroyed. Two world wars and the intervening Great Depression accompanied a rise in nationalism and increasingly noncooperative economic policymaking. With gold-standard credibility broken by World War One, monetary policy became subject to different political goals, in the first instance as a way to help finance wartime deficits. Later, monetary policy was used as a tool to stabilize domestic economic activity under more flexible exchange rates. As a guard against currency crises and to protect gold, capital controls became widespread. The

---

[31] On this division of history, see, in particular, Eichengreen (1996). Earlier surveys of the progress of financial-market globalization since the nineteenth century include Obstfeld and Taylor (1998), Bordo, Eichengreen, and Kim (1999), and Flandreau and Rivière (1999). For an even longer quantitative perspective see Lothian (2002).

[32] On the gold-standard regime and late-nineteenth-century capital markets, see, inter alia, Edelstein (1982), Eichengreen (1996), Eichengreen and Flandreau (1996), Bordo and Kydland (1995), and Bordo and Rockoff (1996). On this first era of globalization in goods and factor markets, see Green and Urquhart (1976), Sachs and Warner (1995), Williamson (1996), Taylor and Williamson (1997), O'Rourke and Williamson (1999), and the volume edited by Bordo, Taylor, and Williamson (2003).

Fig. 1.2. Adherence to the gold standard, 1870–1939
Percentage of countries

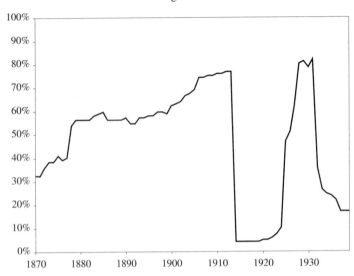

Source: Estevadeordal, Frantz, and Taylor (2003).

world economy went from globalized to almost autarkic in the space of a few decades. Private capital flows dried up, international investment was regarded with suspicion, and international prices and interest rates fell completely out of synchronization. Global capital (along with finance in general) was demonized and seen as a principal cause of the world depression of the 1930s.[33]

In the third period, the Bretton Woods era (1945–71), an attempt to rebuild the global economy took shape. Trade flows accomplished a remarkable expansion and world economic growth began its most rapid spurt in history. Yet the fears of global capital that had been formed in the interwar period were not easily dispelled. The IMF, designed at Bretton Woods, New Hampshire, in 1944, initially sanctioned capital controls as a means to prevent speculative attacks on currency pegs. Controls lent some domestic policy autonomy to governments, both by providing more room for activist monetary policy and by facilitating relatively orderly occasional adjustments in the official exchange rates against the U.S. dollar. For 25 years, this prevailing philosophy held firm; and although

[33] See Eichengreen (1992; 1996) and Temin (1989). In labor markets migrations collapsed, and in goods markets trade barriers multiplied (Kindleberger 1986; Williamson 1995; James 2001).

capital markets recovered, they did so only slowly. But by the late 1960s, with international trade expanding rapidly, global capital could no longer be held in check so easily. Its workings were eventually to break the network of fixed-but-adjustable exchange rates at the core of the Bretton Woods system.[34]

In the fourth and final period, the post–Bretton Woods era of mostly floating industrial-country exchange rates, a different trend has been evident. Fixed dollar exchange-rates were given up by the developed countries, and over the twentieth century's final three decades, capital account restrictions were widely eliminated or reduced. Broadly speaking, industrial-country governments no longer needed capital controls as a tool to help preserve a mandatory fixed exchange-rate peg, since the peg was gone. Because a floating rate could accommodate market developments, controls could be lifted. European countries, on the other hand, gave up monetary autonomy but jettisoned capital controls in embracing monetary unification. In both cases the dismantlement of controls encouraged the flow of capital. In many developing countries, economic reforms reduced the transaction costs and risks of foreign investment, and capital flows grew there too – at least until the emerging-market crises of the 1990s reminded investors of the unreliably fixed exchange rates and fragile financial infrastructures that had tended to persist on the periphery. Increasingly, the smaller developing countries that desired fixed exchange rates looked to give up domestic monetary policy autonomy credibly through some form of "hard peg" (such as a currency board or even dollarization), whereas larger developing countries such as Mexico, Chile, and Brazil opted for exchange-rate flexibility coupled with inflation targeting.

In the 1990s, the term "globalization" became a catch-all to describe the phenomenon of an increasingly integrated and interdependent world economy, one that exhibits supposedly free flows of goods, services, and capital, albeit not of labor. Yet for all the hype, economic history suggests that we be cautious in assessing how novel this development really is. We will show that a period of impressive global integration was witnessed before, at least for capital markets, at the turn of the twentieth century, over a hundred years ago. Of course, that earlier epoch of globalization did not endure. As the preceding discussion suggests, if we were roughly to sketch out the implied movements in capital mobility, we would chart an upswing from 1880 to 1914. This would be followed by a collapse through 1945, interrupted by a limited recovery during the brief reconstruction of the gold standard in the 1920s, a transient interlude between the autarky of World War One and the Depression. We would then envision a

---

[34] On Bretton Woods, see, for example, Bordo and Eichengreen (1993) and Eichengreen (1996).

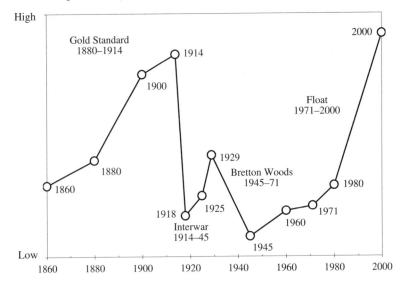

Fig. 1.3. A stylized view of capital mobility in modern history

Source: Introspection.

gradual rise in mobility after 1945, one that accelerates after the demise of the Bretton Woods system in the early 1970s.

For illustrative purposes, let us make the fanciful assumption that international capital mobility or global capital market integration *could* be measured in a single parameter. Suppose we could plot that parameter over time for the last century or so. We would then expect to see a time path something like the one shown in Figure 1.3, where the vertical axis carries the mobility or integration measure. Given the histories of various subperiods and certain countries, as contained in numerous fragments of the historical literature, it seems reasonable to speak of capital mobility increasing or decreasing at the times we have noted. Based on this largely narrative evidence, the pattern of a nineteenth-century rise followed by a twentieth-century U-shape that we have depicted in the figure is probably correct.

Without further quantification, however, the usefulness of this stylized view remains unclear. For one thing, we would like to know if it accords with various empirical measures of capital mobility. Moreover, even if we know the direction of changes in the mobility of capital at various times, we cannot measure the extent of those changes. Without such evidence, we cannot assess whether the

U-shaped trend path is complete: that is, have we now reached a degree of capital mobility that is above, or still below, that seen in the years before 1914? To address these questions requires more formal empirical testing, and that is one of the motivations for the quantitative analysis that follows.

1.4 Trilemma: Capital mobility, the exchange rate, and monetary policy

This book not only offers evidence in support of the stylized description of global capital market evolution, it also provides an organizing framework for understanding that evolution and the forces that shaped the international economy of the late nineteenth and twentieth centuries. What explains the long stretch of high capital mobility that prevailed before 1914, the subsequent breakdown in the interwar period, and the very slow postwar reconstruction of the world financial system? The answer is tied up with one of the central and most visible areas in which openness to the world capital market constrains government power: the choice of an exchange-rate regime.[35]

It is a trite but true assertion of international monetary economics that the exchange rate is an open economy's most important price. Exchange rate movements therefore have widespread repercussions even in the very large U.S. economy, and have increasingly become a cause for public and official concern. Because of its pivotal importance, the exchange rate is, in most of the world's economies, a key instrument or target for monetary policy. At the very least, it is a prime policy indicator.

An open capital market, however, deprives a country's government of the ability simultaneously to target its exchange rate and to use monetary policy in pursuit of other economic objectives. To take a simple example, look at a country such as Denmark, which pegs the exchange rate between its currency, the krone, and the euro. Since market participants understand that the exchange rate will not change by much, nominal interest rates in Denmark must closely match those in the euro zone. (The rates are kept in line by arbitrageurs who would massively borrow at the low rate and lend at the high rate, confident that their gains cannot be erased by an exchange-rate movement.) But this equality of interest rates also means that Denmark cannot conduct a monetary

---

[35] This section's discussion of the open-economy macroeconomic policy "trilemma" draws on Obstfeld and Taylor (1998), who first invoked the term, and on Obstfeld (1998). Intimately related is the idea of the "inconsistent quartet," the fourth element being free trade, as famously set out in the context of European monetary unification by Padoa-Schioppa (1988). Trade restrictions furnish an awkward stabilization tool for a number of reasons, and meaningful capital mobility presupposes some openness to trade. We therefore take the level of trade openness as given and focus on the trio consisting of the other three quartet members.

policy independent of the European Central Bank's; both the exchange rate and the interest rate, the two conduits for monetary-policy effects, are exogenously determined. Since Denmark (and not the European Central Bank) is pegging the exchange rate, the Danish central bank has only one monetary role, to vary its liabilities so as to offset any incipient change in the krone's exchange value against the euro.

In theory (if not in practice, given European Union treaties), Denmark could regain an independent monetary policy in two ways. If it could prohibit any cross-border financial transactions, Denmark would decouple its interest rate from the euro zone's but could still maintain the fixed exchange rate. In that case, Denmark might unilaterally lower its interest rates, for example, but investors no longer would have the right to move funds from Copenhagen to Frankfurt in response to the resulting return differential. Pressures in the foreign exchange market would be limited to euro demands from Danish importers and from exporters to Denmark wishing to convert their krone earnings into euros. Any exchange-rate effects of these trade-driven demands for euros (which are far smaller than the potential demands associated with international financial flows) could normally be offset by sales of Danish official euro reserves. Alternatively, Denmark could maintain freedom of private capital movement but allow the krone-euro rate to float. In that case, Denmark would be free to lower its interest rates, but the krone would depreciate against the euro as a result. Both developments would tend to spur aggregate demand for Danish output.

Secular movements in the scope for international lending and borrowing may be understood, we shall argue, in terms of a fundamental *macroeconomic policy trilemma* that all national policymakers face. In brief, the chosen macroeconomic policy regime can include at most two elements of the "inconsistent trinity" of three policy goals:

(i) full freedom of cross-border capital movements;
(ii) a fixed exchange rate; and
(iii) an independent monetary policy oriented toward domestic objectives.

The implications of the trilemma are straightforward yet stark. If capital movements are prohibited, in the case where element (i) is ruled out, then a country with a fixed exchange rate can break ranks with foreign interest rates and thereby run an independent monetary policy. Similarly a floating exchange rate, in the case where element (ii) is ruled out, reconciles freedom of international capital movements with monetary-policy effectiveness (at least when some nominal domestic prices are sticky). But monetary policy is powerless to achieve domestic goals when the exchange rate is fixed and capital movements are free.

In that case, element (iii) is ruled out because interventions in support of the exchange parity then entail capital flows that exactly offset any monetary-policy actions threatening to alter domestic interest rates.[36]

This conflict among rival policy choices, the trilemma, structures our discussion of the historical evolution of world capital markets in the pages that follow, and helps make sense of the ebb and flow of capital mobility in the long run and in the broader political-economy context. Our central proposition is that secular movements in the scope for international lending and borrowing over the course of history may be understood in terms of the trilemma. Capital mobility has prevailed and expanded under circumstances of widespread political support either for an exchange-rate-subordinated monetary regime (for example, the gold standard), or for a monetary regime geared mainly toward domestic objectives at the expense of exchange-rate stability (for example, the recent float). The middle ground in which countries attempt simultaneously to hit exchange-rate targets and domestic policy goals has, almost as a logical consequence, entailed exchange controls or other harsh constraints on international transactions.[37]

---

[36] The choice between fixed and floating exchange rates should not be viewed as dichotomous; nor should it be assumed that the choice of a floating-rate regime necessarily leads to a useful degree of monetary-policy flexibility. In reality, the degree of exchange-rate flexibility lies on a continuum, with exchange-rate target zones, crawling pegs, crawling zones, and managed floats of various other kinds residing between the extremes of irrevocably fixed and freely floating. The greater the attention given to the exchange rate, the more constrained monetary policy is in pursuing other objectives. Indeed, the notion of a "free" float is an abstraction with little empirical content, as few governments are willing to set monetary policy without some considerations of its exchange-rate effects. If exchange rates are subject to pure speculative shocks unrelated to economic fundamentals, and if policymakers are concerned to counter these movements, then monetary control will be compromised. This scenario motivated James Tobin's proposal for a tax on capital flows – the "Tobin tax" – although, as Tobin recognized, a tax with teeth would have to apply to all foreign exchange transactions. Debate on Tobin's proposal continues, but the major industrial countries that maintain floating rates seem to view it as an extremely costly route to highly uncertain gains.

[37] Our interpretation is consistent with the view in the political science literature that purposeful government control is the key factor determining the degree of international financial integration. See, for example, Helleiner (1994) and Kapstein (1994), and the references they list. Also relevant to our analysis is the paper by Epstein and Schor (1992), who link the existence of controls to the balance of power between labor-oriented interests favoring Keynesian macroeconomic policies and financially-oriented interests favoring inflation containment. We stop short of a formal econometric analysis of the determinants of capital controls. Alesina, Grilli, and Milesi-Ferretti (1994) and Grilli and Milesi-Ferretti (1995) carry out panel studies of the incidence of capital controls (for 20 industrial countries over the years 1950 to 1989, and for 61 industrial and developing countries over the years 1966 to 1989). Consistent with our interpretation, they find that more flexible exchange rate regimes and greater central-bank independence lower the probability of capital controls. For OECD countries, Posen (1995) argues empirically that stronger financial-sector influence leads to both greater central-bank independence and lower inflation. Campillo and Miron (1997) question the role of financial-sector influence in explaining more recent inflation performance.

Of course, the trilemma is only a proximate explanation, in the sense that deeper institutional and socio-political forces explain the relative dominance of some policy targets over others. Cohen (1996, 274–5) usefully distinguishes four potential categories of explanation concerning the evolution of international financial integration. We paraphrase his categories by distinguishing four different explanations based upon:

(i) the impacts of technological innovation, including in addition any associated increases in market competition;

(ii) the results of policy competition among governments that seek to advance "state interest," somehow defined;

(iii) the forces of domestic institutions and politics, including partisan rivalry and interest-group lobbying; and

(iv) the influences of ideology and advances in economic knowledge.

We view explanations based on technology as secondary for the period of interest to us (starting in the latter nineteenth century), as it follows the deployment of transoceanic cable technology.[38] The precise definition of "state interest" may well reflect the domestic political power structure, so explanations of classes (ii) and (iii) need not be disjoint. Yet there may be situations in which there is a broad domestic consensus regarding certain policies as furthering the national interest. Similarly, ideology and the state of knowledge can determine the policies that states pursue in seeking a given perceived national interest. As will become clear in what follows, we regard explanations along the lines of (ii) and especially (iii) as the "deep factors" behind movements in international financial integration, with a supporting role for (iv) as well.[39] The pivotal force of the trilemma is to constrain the choice set within which the deep factors can play their roles.

We likewise view these deeper factors as ultimate determinants – perhaps *the* ultimate determinants – of economic performance, in that they underlie government behavior across the entire spectrum of policies (Tommasi 2002).

---

[38] We recognize, however, that technologically driven changes in the extent of goods-market integration might affect aspects of financial integration, as in the analysis of Obstfeld and Rogoff (2000). The decline in real freight rates for shipping from 1870 to 1914 remains unparalleled. This trend slowed or even, by some measures, reversed, in the interwar period: see Isserlis (1938) and Shah Mohammed and Williamson (2003). Government imposed trade barriers spiked upward during the interwar period, of course. On the impact of these transaction cost trends on world trade, see Estevadeordal, Frantz, and Taylor (2003).

[39] Rajan and Zingales (2003) place interest-group politics at center stage in their theory of domestic financial-market liberalization. They find a U-shaped evolution in domestic financial markets reminiscent of the pattern for international integration that we document in this book. We return to domestic liberalization briefly at the end of Chapter 4.

If a country's weak institutional underpinnings lead to chronic incursions on private property rights, for example, then no resolution of the trilemma will produce favorable outcomes.[40] Given a government's propensity toward ill-advised policy interventions, however, it remains true that combining open capital markets with fixed rather than flexible exchange rates assures an even steeper descent into financial chaos.

1.4.1 A brief narrative

This introductory chapter began by drawing on economic theory to review the potential benefits and costs of international capital mobility for the national participants. Clearly, the ability to lend or borrow represents, trivially, a loosening of constraints relative to those faced by a perfectly closed economy. In this dimension, at least, open trade in financial markets offers unambiguous gains relative to a closed economy. Such trades permit insurance and the smoothing of shocks, and allow capital to seek out its highest rewards, implying the usual gains-from-trade results.

In other ways, however, international financial mobility raises concerns, particularly for policymakers pursuing objectives that may be inconsistent with the free flow of capital across international boundaries. In addition, the risks of financial and balance of payments crises – some of them self-fulfilling crises fueled by pure expectations effects interacting with weak "fundamentals" – may represent further obstacles to the adoption of free capital markets.

Although these are very much contemporary questions of policy debate, the issues they raise can be traced back the early history of international financial markets. Then, too, advanced forms of financial asset trade developed very quickly, yet, as we have seen, they were subject to suspicion from various quarters, both public and private. The markets saw bubbles, panics, and crises. In consequence, calls for the regulation and restriction of such financial market activity have been with us from the start.

We have already noted that, despite these fears, a succession of technological breakthroughs and a gradual institutional evolution had contributed to the emergence of a wide-reaching international capital market by the late nineteenth century. This network of nations embraced modern financial practices and instruments and operated virtually free of controls on the part of governments. Under the generalized gold-standard monetary regime, a flourishing global market for capital developed and reached its peak in the decades just before World War One.

[40] Obstfeld (2002); Calvo and Mishkin (2003).

Subsequent history, as we have also noted, showed that this seemingly linear path toward ever more technological progress and institutional sophistication in a liberal world order could indeed be upset. Two global wars and a long, deep depression pushed the world near to autarky. Conflicting policy goals and political imperatives often put the interests of global capital at a low premium relative to other objectives. Activist governments used capital controls to sidestep the discipline of external markets, and thereby freed monetary policy for use (or abuse) as a tool of macroeconomic control. Only over the half century following World War Two did the world capital market eventually re-emerge with a vibrancy rivaling its pre-1914 incarnation.

These broad trends and cycles in the world capital market reflect changing responses to the fundamental trilemma. Before 1914, each of the world's major economies pegged its currency's price in terms of gold, and thus, implicitly, maintained a fixed rate of exchange against every other major country's currency. Financial interests prevailed in the world of of the classical gold standard and financial orthodoxy saw no alternative mode of sound finance.[41] Thus, the gold-standard system met the trilemma by opting for fixed exchange rates and capital mobility, sometimes at the expense of domestic macroeconomic objectives that would be paramount today. Between 1891 and 1897, for example, the United States endured a harsh deflation in the face of persistent speculation on the dollar's departure from gold. These policies were hotly debated; the Populist movement agitated forcefully against gold, but lost.[42]

The balance of political power began to shift only with the First World War, which brought a sea change in the social contract underlying the industrial democracies.[43] For a sample of industrial countries, Figure 1.4 shows the Polity IV coding for "institutional democracy" as it evolved over the period bracketing World War One (the coding ranges from 0 to 11; see Marshall and Jaggers 2002 for details). Apart from the United States (which has a constant score of 10 throughout the sample period, and is omitted from the figure), there is clear evidence of a discrete increase in political openness in the decade or so after 1918.[44] Organized labor emerged as a political power, a counterweight to

---

[41] See Bordo and Schwartz (1984) and Eichengreen (1996).

[42] Frieden's (1997) econometric evidence shows how financial interests promoted U.S. adherence to gold, whereas those who would have gained from currency depreciation favored silver. A similar debate over the monetary regime arose in Germany, where the Prussian agricultural nobility lobbied in vain for relaxing the restraints of the gold standard (though they were successful in getting tariff protection instead). See Gerschenkron (1943, 57, n. 62).

[43] See Polanyi (1944); Temin (1989); Eichengreen (1992, 1996); Obstfeld and Taylor (1998). For a recent elaboration, see Tortella (2003).

[44] The institutional democracy variable is composed of separate codings for the "competitiveness of political participation," the "openness and competitiveness of executive recruitment," and

Fig. 1.4. Institutional democracy, Polity IV scores
Index on a scale of 0 to 11

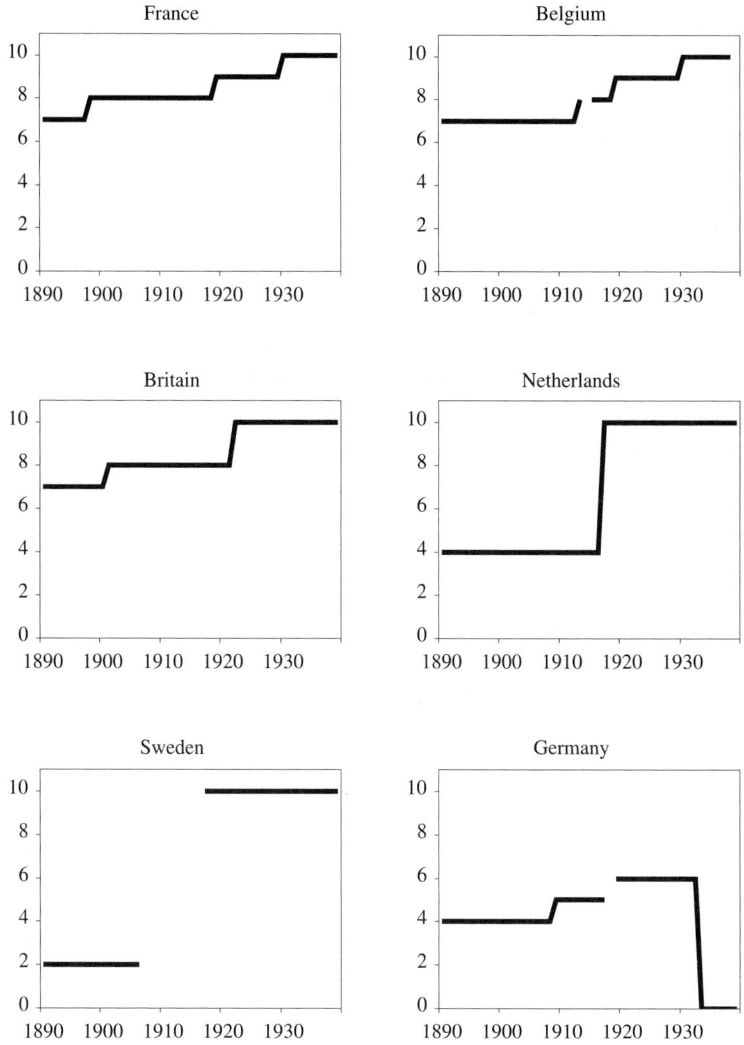

France

Belgium

Britain

Netherlands

Sweden

Germany

Source: Marshall and Jaggers (2002).

Fig. 1.5. The rise of social spending
Percent of GDP

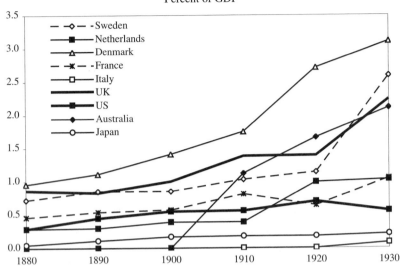

Notes and Source: Lindert (2004, chap. 1). Includes transfers for welfare and unemployment, pensions, health, and housing. Excludes public education.

the interests of capital, as seen in the British labor unrest of the 1920s, which culminated in the General Strike.

Consistent with the new social contract was a distinct rise in the shares of national income devoted to social transfers. Figure 1.5, which is drawn from Lindert (2004), illustrates the extent of the rise in transfer payments starting in the early twentieth century in nine countries. As Lindert has noted:

Democracy was a more important influence on the timing of the rise of the welfare state [than was economic development]. The rise of voting rights helps explain the greater redistributions after World War One, while the incompleteness of voter participation in the interwar elections helps explain why the rich were not soaked further before World War Two. Social insurance through government was favored more strongly in the kinds of democracies that gave women the vote.[45]

Britain's return to gold in 1925 may have led the way to a restored international gold standard and a limited resurgence of international finance, but weaknesses in the rebuilt system helped propagate a global depression after

"constraints on the chief executive." We do not plot the variable during periods of political interruption or transition.

[45] Lindert (1994, 34).

the 1929 U.S. downturn. Following (and in some cases anticipating) Britain's example, many countries abandoned the gold standard in the late 1920s and the early 1930s and depreciated their currencies; many also resorted to trade and capital controls in order to manage independently their exchange rates and domestic policies. Those countries in the "gold bloc," which stubbornly clung to gold through the mid-1930s, showed the steepest output and price-level declines. James's (2001, 189–97) account of French policymakers' vacillation between controls and devaluation well illustrates the interaction between political pressures and the constraints of the trilemma. Eventually in the 1930s, all countries jettisoned rigid exchange-rate targets and/or open capital markets in favor of domestic macroeconomic goals, leading to the demise of the gold standard seen earlier in Figure 1.2.[46]

These decisions reflected the shift in political power solidified after the First World War. They also signaled the beginnings of a new consensus on the role of economic policy that would endure through the inflationary 1970s. As an immediate consequence, however, the Great Depression discredited gold-standard orthodoxy and brought Keynesian ideas about macroeconomic management to the fore. It also made financial markets and financial practitioners unpopular. Their supposed excesses and attachment to gold became identified in the public mind as causes of the economic calamity. In the United States, the New Deal brought a Jacksonian hostility toward Eastern (read: New York) high finance back to Washington. Financial markets were more closely regulated, and the Federal Reserve was brought under heavier Treasury influence. Similar reactions occurred in other countries.

Changed attitudes toward financial activities and economic management underlay the new postwar economic order negotiated at Bretton Woods in July 1944. Forty-four allied countries set up a system based on fixed but adjustable exchange parities. They did so in the belief that floating exchange rates would exhibit instability and damage international trade. At the center of the system was the International Monetary Fund. The IMF's prime function was as a source of hard-currency loans to governments that might otherwise have to put their economies into recession to maintain a fixed exchange rate. Countries experiencing permanent balance-of-payments problems had the option of realigning their currencies, subject to IMF approval.

Importantly, the IMF's founders viewed its lending capability as primarily a substitute for, not a complement to, private capital inflows. Interwar experience had given the latter a reputation as unreliable at best and, at worst, a

---

[46] See Díaz Alejandro (1983), Eichengreen and Sachs (1985), Temin (1989), Campa (1990), Eichengreen (1992), Romer (1992), Bernanke and Carey (1996), and Obstfeld and Taylor (1998).

dangerous source of disturbances. Broad, encompassing controls over private capital movement, perfected in wartime, were expected to continue. The IMF's Articles of Agreement explicitly empowered countries to impose new capital controls. Articles VIII and XIV of the IMF agreement did demand that countries' currencies eventually be made convertible – in effect, freely saleable to the issuing central bank, at the official exchange parity, for dollars or gold. But this privilege was to be extended only if the country's currency had been earned through current-account transactions. Convertibility on capital account, as opposed to current-account convertibility, was not viewed by the IMF at this time as either mandatory or desirable.

Unfortunately, a wide extent even of current-account convertibility took many years to achieve, and even then it was often restricted to nonresidents. In the interim, countries resorted to bilateral trade deals that required balanced or nearly balanced trade between every pair of trading partners. If France had an export surplus with Britain, and Britain had a surplus with Germany, Britain could not use its excess marks to obtain dollars with which to pay France. Germany had very few dollars and guarded them jealously for critical imports from the Americas. Instead, each country would try to divert import demand toward countries with high demand for its goods, and to direct its exports toward countries whose goods were favored domestically.

Convertibility gridlock in Europe and its dependencies was ended through a regional multilateral clearing scheme, the European Payments Union (EPU). The clearing scheme was set up in 1950 and some countries reached de facto convertibility by mid-decade. But it was not until December 27, 1958, that Europe officially embraced convertibility and ended the EPU. Although most European countries still chose to retain extensive capital controls (Germany being the main exception), the return to convertibility, important as it was in promoting multilateral trade growth, also increased the opportunities for disguised capital movements. These might take the form, for example, of misinvoicing, or of accelerated or delayed merchandise payments. Buoyant growth encouraged some countries in further financial liberalization, although the United States, worried about its gold losses, raised progressively higher barriers to capital outflow over the 1960s. Eventually, the Bretton Woods system's very successes hastened its collapse by resurrecting the trilemma.[47]

Key countries in the system, notably the United States (fearful of slower growth) and Germany (fearful of higher inflation), proved unwilling to accept the domestic policy implications of maintaining fixed rates. Even the limited

---

[47] See Triffin (1957), Einzig (1968), and Bordo and Eichengreen (2001).

capital mobility of the early 1970s proved sufficient to allow furious speculative attacks on the major currencies, and after vain attempts to restore fixed dollar exchange rates, the industrial countries retreated to floating rates early in 1973. Although viewed at the time as a temporary emergency measure, the floating-dollar-rate regime is still with us more than 30 years later.

Floating dollar exchange-rates have allowed the explosion in international financial markets experienced over the same three decades. Freed from one element of the trilemma – fixed exchange rates – countries have been able to open their capital markets while still retaining the flexibility to deploy monetary policy in pursuit of national objectives. No doubt the experience gained after the inflationary 1970s in anchoring monetary policy to avoid price instability has helped to promote ongoing financial integration. Formal inflation targeting has been adopted in a number of countries. Perhaps for the first time in history, countries have learned how to keep inflation in check under fiat monies and floating exchange rates.

There remain several potentially valid reasons, however, for countries still to fix their exchange rates – for example, to keep a better lid on inflation or to counter exchange-rate instability arising from financial-market shocks. Such arguments may find particular resonance, of course, in developing countries. But few countries that have tried to fix have succeeded for long. Eventually, exchange-rate stability comes into conflict with other policy objectives, the capital markets catch on to the government's predicament, and a crisis adds enough economic pain to make the authorities give in. In recent years, only a very few major countries have observed the discipline of fixed rates for as long as five years, and most of those can be considered rather special cases.[48]

The European Union (EU) members that successfully maintained mutually fixed rates prior to January 1999 were aided by market confidence in their own planned solution to the trilemma, an imminent currency merger. A number of non-European Union countries have taken a different approach and adopted extreme straitjackets for monetary policy in order to peg an exchange rate. The developing countries following this route have not generally fared so well. Even Hong Kong, which operates a currency board supposedly subordinated to maintaining the Hong Kong-U.S. dollar peg, suffered repeated speculative attacks in the Asian crisis period. Another currency-board experiment, Argentina, held to its 1 : 1 dollar exchange rate from April 1991 for a remarkable stint of more than 10 years. To accomplish that feat, the country relied on help from international financial institutions and, despite episodes of growth, endured levels

---

[48] See Obstfeld and Rogoff (1995).

Table 1.1. *The trilemma and major phases of capital mobility*

| Era | Resolution of trilemma? Countries choose to sacrifice: | | | Notes |
	Activist policies	Capital mobility	Fixed exchange rate	
Gold standard	Most	Few	Few	Broad consensus.
Interwar (when off gold)	Few	Several	Most	Capital controls, especially in Central Europe and Latin America.
Bretton Woods	Few	Most	Few	Broad consensus.
Float	Few	Few	Many	Some consensus except for hard pegs (currency boards, dollarization, etc.).

of unemployment higher than many countries could tolerate. It suffered especially acutely after Brazil moved to a float in January 1999. Three years later Argentina's political and economic arrangements disintegrated in the face of external default (December 2001) and currency collapse (January–February 2002). Both Argentina's tenacity in maintaining convertibility for over a decade and the chaos following its collapse illustrate domestic institutional weaknesses of that country, which make a low-inflation fiat regime hard to sustain.[49]

For most larger countries, the trend toward greater financial openness has been accompanied – almost inevitably, we would argue – by a declining reliance on pegged exchange rates in favor of greater exchange-rate flexibility. If monetary policy is geared toward domestic considerations, capital mobility or the exchange-rate target must go. If, instead, fixed exchange rates and integration into the global capital market are the primary desiderata, monetary policy must be subjugated to those ends.

The details of this argument form the core of this book, based on empirical evidence and the historical record, but we can already pinpoint the key turning points (see Table 1.1). The Great Depression stands as the watershed here, in that it was caused by an ill-advised subordination of monetary policy to an exchange-rate constraint (the gold standard), which led to a chaotic time of troubles in which countries experimented, typically noncooperatively, with alternative modes of addressing the fundamental trilemma. Interwar experience, in turn, discredited the gold standard and led to a new and fairly universal policy

[49] Once again, see Tommasi (2002).

consensus. The new consensus shaped the more cooperative postwar international economic order fashioned at Bretton Woods by Harry Dexter White and John Maynard Keynes, but implanted within that order the seeds of its own eventual destruction a quarter century later. The global financial nexus that has evolved since then rests on a solution to the basic open-economy trilemma quite different than that envisioned by Keynes or White – one that allows considerable freedom for capital movements, gives the major currency areas freedom to pursue internal goals, but largely leaves their mutual exchange rates as the equilibrating residual.

This brief overview demonstrates the centrality of the macroeconomic policy trilemma in any account of the ups and downs of the global capital market's evolution. In what follows, we match the stylized facts in Table 1.1 with some of the quantitative record, so as to document more carefully the course of events. It is a remarkable history without which today's economic, financial, political, and institutional landscape cannot be fully understood.

Part two

Global Capital in Modern Historical Perspective

In this part of the book we survey the development of global capital markets over the late nineteenth and twentieth centuries. Two empirical chapters use quantity and price evidence to examine quantitatively the evolution of capital mobility. For most of the measures of market integration that we examine, international capital mobility advanced in the late nineteenth century, only to follow a U-shape pattern over the course of the twentieth century. Starting from the height reached on the eve of World War One, integration declined sharply through the Great Depression and World War Two, recovering only gradually in the first postwar decades before beginning a steeper ascent in the final decades before the present century.

2

Globalization in Capital Markets:
Quantity Evidence

In theory and practice, the extent of international capital mobility can have profound implications for the operation of individual economies and the global economy. With respect to theory, the applicability of various classes of macroeconomic models rests on many assumptions, and not the least important of these are axioms linked to the closure of the model in the capital market. The predictions of a theory and its usefulness for policy debates can revolve critically on this part of the structure.

The importance of these issues for policy is equally clear. Capital mobility can drastically alter the efficacy of a range of policy interventions, from capital taxation to domestic monetary management. Thus, the feasibility and relevance of key policy actions cannot be judged absent some informed position on the extent to which local economic conditions are in any way separable from global ones. This implies that an empirical measure of market integration is implicitly, though rarely explicitly, a necessary adjunct to any policy discussion. Although recent globalization trends have brought this issue to the fore, this book illustrates how the experience of longer run macroeconomic history can clarify and inform these debates.

In attacking the problem of measuring market integration, economists have no universally recognized criterion to turn to. For example, imagine the simple expedient of examining price differentials. Prices could be identical in two identical neighboring economies, being determined in each by the identical structures of tastes, technologies, and endowments. But if the two markets were physically separated by a prohibitively high transaction-cost barrier, one would hardly describe them as being integrated into a single market. Rather, the equality of prices would be a mere chance event. Or consider using the size of flows between two markets as a gauge of mobility. This is a similarly flawed criterion, for suppose we simply destroy the assumed barrier between the two identical economies just described, reducing trade costs to zero. We would then truly have a single integrated market, but, with prices identical in autarky, there would be no incentive for any good or factor to move after the barrier disappeared. Intramarket flows would be nil, notwithstanding full international economic integration.

Thus, convergence of prices and movements of goods are not in general unambiguous indicators of market integration. One could run through any number of other putative criteria for market integration, examining perhaps the levels or correlations of prices or quantities, and find essentially the same kind of weakness: all such tests may be able to evaluate market integration, but only as a joint hypothesis test where some auxiliary maintained assumptions are needed to make the test meaningful.[1]

Given this impasse, an historical study such as the present one is potentially valuable in two respects. First, we can use a very large array of data sources covering different aspects of international capital mobility over more than one hundred years. Without being wedded to a single criterion, we can attempt to make inferences about the path of global capital mobility with a battery of tests, using both quantity and price evidence of various kinds. As long as important caveats are kept in mind about each method, especially the auxiliary assumptions required for meaningful inference, we can essay a broad-based approach to the evidence. If a range of different methodologies point to similar conclusions about the long swings in international financial integration, we can have greater confidence in our interpretation than if we relied on a single test, resting on one particular set of maintained assumptions that might be difficult to confirm or refute.

Historical work offers a second benefit, in that it provides a natural set of benchmarks for our understanding of today's situation. In addition to the many competing tests for capital mobility, we also confront the problem that almost every test is usually a matter of degree, of interpreting a parameter or a measure of dispersion or some other variable or coefficient. Hence, we face the typical empirical conundrums (how big is big? or how fast is fast?) in trying to place an absolute meaning on these measures. An historical perspective, however, can allow a more nuanced view because it places all such inferences in a relative context. When we find that some parameter, estimate, or measure of capital mobility is big, it is easier to interpret if we can say that by this we mean bigger than a similar parameter, estimate, or measure taken a decade or a century ago. The historical focus of this chapter will be directed at addressing just such

---

[1] See Bayoumi (1997) for a complementary discussion.

comparative concerns.[2] Our empirical goal is to examine the broadest range of data available for the last one-hundred-plus years to see what has happened to the degree of capital mobility in a cross section of countries over the long run.[3]

This chapter employs quantity data on the stocks and flows of capital between countries to examine how the extent of capital mobility has changed since the late nineteenth century. We first discuss the size of foreign investment stocks and flows. Ceteris paribus, a greater degree of capital mobility should lead to larger flows and, with cumulation over time, larger stocks of foreign investment. We then relate the size of flows to saving and investment patterns, to see to what extent external flows mattered in terms of the overall composition of saving and investment. We finally consider the statistical relation between saving and investment rates, an oft-employed metric that asks whether saving and investment activities lean toward being delinked, as could occur theoretically for a fully open economy, or instead tend toward equality, as in a closed economy. An important discussion of caveats ends this section.

The next chapter then focuses on price-based criteria for capital-market integration, and looks at three international price relationships: covered nominal interest parity or exchange-risk-free interest parity, real interest-rate convergence, and purchasing power parity. In principle, all three relations should come closer to equality the more integrated markets are. Purchasing power parity pertains in the first instance to goods markets, not financial markets, but imperfect integration of goods markets can also segment financial markets along several dimensions, so we view purchasing power parity as very relevant.[4] An examination of long-run price and interest-rate series since the late nineteenth century yields information on the changing nature of the three price relationships between countries. Once again, an important section details caveats associated with these price measures.

---

[2] But note that, again, auxiliary assumptions will be necessary, and caveats will be considered along the way. For example, what if neighboring economies became exogenously more or less similar over time, but no more or less integrated in terms of transaction costs? The advantage of using a broad battery of empirical criteria becomes clear in this example. If two economies are becoming more alike rather than more integrated over time, we would not simultaneously observe price convergence *and* a higher volume of trade flows between them. The same pattern of joint price and quantity behavior also contradicts an interpretation of the higher flow volume as the result of increasing structural divergence, with no true increase in the degree of international market integration.

[3] Given the limitations of the data, we will frequently be restricted to looking at between a dozen and 20 countries for which long-run macroeconomic statistics are available, and this sample will be dominated by today's developed countries, including most of the OECD economies. However, we also have long data series for some developing countries such as Argentina, Brazil, and Mexico; and for some criteria, such as our opening look at the evolution of the stock of foreign investments, we can examine a much broader sample.

[4] Obstfeld and Rogoff (2000).

2.1 The stocks of foreign capital

The extant data on foreign capital stocks can give some sense of the evolution of the global market. We seek a measure of the size of worldwide foreign investment that is appropriately scaled and consistent over time.

Although the concept is simple, the measurement is not. Perhaps the simplest measure of the activity in the global capital market is obtained by looking at the total stock of overseas investment at a point in time. Suppose that the total asset stock in country or region i that is owned by country or region j at time t is denoted A_{ijt}. This notation covers the domestically owned capital stock, A_{iit}. Of interest are two concepts. What assets of country j reside overseas? And what liabilities of country i are held overseas?

Note that here we are concerned also to identify the extent to which the *net* wealth of a country is held in its own versus others' portfolios. There is, then, a potential complication to our measures, since, over the long-run timescales we are dealing with, there has been a vast multiplication in the ratio of total assets to net wealth and total assets to gross domestic product (GDP). This is because financial development, and the increasing sophistication of national capital markets, has allowed the capital stock of each economy to be packaged and repackaged in various asset bundles, which may be held as a chain of assets and liabilities by various financial intermediaries between the physical asset itself and the ultimate net wealth owner. At the international level, we also need to keep the net wealth question in perspective, but the problem is somewhat simpler in the sense that all net foreign claims are true net claims on a national economy: should all creditors show up demanding payment, then, even after a country liquidates its own foreign holdings, it will still need to hand over an amount of its own net wealth equal to the net claim. In that sense, net foreign liabilities represent a claim on an economy's net wealth.[5]

A relatively easy hurdle to surmount concerns normalization of the data; foreign investment stocks are commonly measured at a point in time in current nominal terms, in most cases U.S. dollars. Obviously, the growth of both the national and international economies might be associated with an increase in such a nominal quantity, as would any long-run inflation. These trends would have nothing to do with market integration per se. To overcome this problem, we chose to normalize foreign capital at each point in time by some measure of the size of the world economy, dividing through by a denominator in the form of a nominal size index.

A seemingly ideal denominator, given that the numerator is the stock of

---

[5] For cross-country evidence on the evolution of financial assets as a fraction of output, see Goldsmith (1985).

foreign-owned capital, would probably be the total stock of capital, whether financial or real. The problem with using financial capital measures is that they have greatly multiplied over the long run as financial development has expanded the number of balance sheets in the economy, thanks to the rise of numerous financial intermediaries.[6] This trend, in principle, could happen at any point in time without any underlying change in the extent of foreign asset holdings. The problem with using real capital stocks is that the construction of such data series is fraught with difficulty.[7]

Given these problems we chose a simpler and more readily available measure of the size of an economy, namely the level of output Y measured in current prices in a common currency unit.[8] Over short horizons, unless the capital-output ratio were to move dramatically, the ratio of foreign capital to output should be adequate as a proxy measure of the penetration of foreign capital in any economy. Over the long run, difficulties might arise if the capital-output ratio has changed significantly over time – but we have little firm evidence to suggest that it has.[9] Thus, as a result of these long-run data constraints, our analysis focuses on capital-to-GDP ratios of the form

$$\text{Foreign assets-to-GDP ratio}_{it} = \sum_{j \neq i} A_{jit}/Y_{it}; \qquad (2.1)$$

$$\text{Foreign liabilities-to-GDP ratio}_{it} = \sum_{j \neq i} A_{ijt}/Y_{it}. \qquad (2.2)$$

Even with the concept established, however, an irksome empirical problem still arises for the numerator. It is in fact very difficult to discover the extent of

---

[6] See Goldsmith (1985).

[7] Only a few countries have reliable data from which to estimate capital stocks. Most of these estimates are accurate only at benchmark censuses, and in between census dates they rely on combinations of interpolation and estimation based on investment flow data and depreciation assumptions. Most of these estimates are calculated in real (constant price) rather than nominal (current price) terms, which makes them incommensurate with the nominally measured foreign capital data. At the end of the day, we would be unlikely to find more than a handful of countries for which this technique would be feasible for the entire twentieth century, and certainly nothing like global coverage would be possible even for recent years.

[8] For the GDP data we rely on Maddison's (1995) constant price 1990 U.S. dollar estimates of output for the period from 1820. These figures are then "reflated" using a U.S. price deflator to obtain estimates of nominal U.S. dollar "World" GDP at each benchmark date. This approach is crude, since, in particular, it relies on a PPP assumption. Ideally we would want historical series on nominal GDP and exchange rates, to estimate a common (U.S. dollar) GDP figure at various historical dates.

[9] But for exactly the reasons just mentioned, since we have no capital stock data for many countries, it is hard to form a sample of capital-output ratios to see how these differ across time and space. The conventional wisdom is that the capital-output ratio ranges from 3 to 4 for most countries, although it is perhaps lower in capital-scarce developing countries.

foreign capital in an economy using both contemporary and historical data. For example, the International Monetary Fund (IMF) has always reported balance-of-payments flow transactions in its *International Financial Statistics*. It is straightforward for most of the recent postwar period to recover the annual *flows* of equity, debt, or other forms of capital-account transactions from these figures. Conversely, it was only in 1997 that the IMF began reporting the corresponding *stock* data, namely, the international investment position of each country. These data are also more sparse, beginning in 1980 for less than a dozen countries, and expanding to about 30 countries by the mid-1990s, and over 60 countries by the year 2000.

The paucity of data is understandable, as the collection burden for these data is much more significant. Knowing the size of a bond issue in a single year reveals the flow transaction size; knowing the implications for future stocks requires, for example, tracking each debt and equity item and its fluctuating market value over time. The stock data are not simply a temporal aggregate of flows: the stock value depends on past flows, capital gains and losses, any retirements of principal or buybacks of equity, defaults and reschedulings, and a host of other factors. Not surprisingly accurate data of this type are hard to assemble.[10] Just as the IMF has had difficulty doing so, so too have economic historians. Looking back over the nineteenth and twentieth centuries, an exhaustive search across many different sources yields only a handful of benchmark years in which estimates have been made, an effort that draws on the work of dozens of scholars in official institutions and numerous other individual efforts.[11]

2.1.1 The recovery of gross stocks

Based on these efforts, we can put together a fragmentary, but still potentially illuminating, historical description in Table 2.1 and Figure 2.1. Displayed here are nominal foreign investment and output data for major countries and regions, grouped according to assets and liabilities. Many cells are empty because data are unavailable, but where possible we have derived summary data to illustrate the ratio of foreign-owned capital to output, and the share of various countries in foreign investment activity.

What do the data show? On the asset side, it is immediately apparent that for all of the nineteenth century, and until the interwar period, the British were

---

[10] An important new source, however, is Lane and Milesi-Ferretti (2001a). See the discussion that follows.

[11] See, for example, Paish (1914), Feis (1931), Lewis (1938; 1945), Rippy (1959), Woodruff (1967), and Twomey (2000). Twomey, following Feinstein (1990), favors the estimates of Paish versus the downward revisions to pre-1914 British overseas investment proposed by Platt (1986).

Table 2.1. *Foreign capital stocks*

Gross foreign investment, current U.S. $ billion

	1825	1855	1870	1900	1914	1930	1938	1945
Assets								
United Kingdom	0.5^a	0.7^a	4.9^a	12.1^a	19.5^a	18.2^a	22.9^c	14.2^a
France	0.1^a	—	2.5^a	5.2^a	8.6^a	3.5^a	3.9^c	—
Germany	—	—	—	4.8^a	6.7^a	1.1^a	0.7^c	—
Netherlands	0.3^a	0.2^a	0.3^a	1.1^a	1.2^a	2.3^a	4.8^c	3.7^a
United States	0.0^a	0.0^a	0.0^a	0.5^a	2.5^a	14.7^a	11.5^c	15.3^a
Canada	—	—	—	0.1^a	0.2^a	1.3^a	1.9^c	—
Japan	—	—	—	—	—	—	1.2^c	—
Other Europe	—	—	—	—	—	—	4.6^c	—
Other	—	—	—	—	—	—	6.0^c	2.0^a
All	0.9^a	0.9^a	7.7^a	23.8^a	38.7^a	41.1^a	52.8^c	35.2^a
World GDP	—	—	111^b	128^b	221^b	491^b	491^b	722^b
Sample GDP	—	—	16^f	43^f	76^f	149^f	182^f	273^f
Sample size	—	—	4^f	7^f	7^f	7^f	7^f	7^f
Assets/sample GDP	—	—	0.47	0.55	0.51	0.28	0.26	0.12
Assets/world GDP	—	—	0.07	0.19	0.18	0.08	0.11	0.05
U.K./all	0.56	0.78	0.64	0.51	0.50	0.44	0.43	0.40
U.S./all	0.00	0.00	0.00	0.02	0.06	0.36	0.22	0.43
Liabilities								
Europe	—	—	—	5.4^a	12.0^a	—	10.3^a	—
North America	—	—	—	2.6^a	11.1^a	—	13.7^a	—
Australia & N.Z.	—	—	—	1.6^a	2.0^a	—	4.5^a	—
Japan	—	—	—	0.1^a	1.0^a	—	0.6^a	—
Latin America	—	—	—	2.9^g	8.9^g	—	11.3^g	—
Asia (excl. Japan)	—	—	—	2.4^g	6.8^g	—	10.6^g	—
Africa	—	—	—	3.0^g	4.1^g	—	4.0^g	—
Developing countries	—	—	—	6.0^g	13.0^g	—	25.9^g	—
All	—	—	—	18.0^a	45.5^a	—	55.0^a	—
World GDP	—	—	111^b	128^b	221^b	491^b	491^b	722^b
Sample GDP	—	—	—	—	—	—	—	—
Sample size	—	—	—	—	—	—	—	—
Liabilities/sample GDP	—	—	—	—	—	—	—	—
Liabilities/world GDP	—	—	—	0.14	0.21	—	0.11	—
Developing countries/all	—	—	—	0.33	0.29	—	0.47	—

Table 2.1 (continued)
Gross foreign investment, current U.S. $ billion

	1960	1980	1985	1990	1995	2000
Assets						
United Kingdom	26.4[a]	551[d]	857[d]	1,760[d]	2,490[d]	4,450[d]
France	—	268[d]	428[d]	736[d]	1,100[d]	2,430[d]
Germany	1.2[a]	257[d]	342[d]	1,100[d]	1,670[d]	2,600[d]
Netherlands	27.6[a]	99[d]	178[d]	418[d]	712[d]	1,140[d]
United States	63.6[a]	775[d]	1,300[d]	2,180[d]	3,350[d]	7,350[d]
Canada	—	92[d]	129[d]	227[d]	302[d]	546[d]
Japan	—	160[d]	437[d]	1,860[d]	2,720[d]	2,970[d]
Other Europe	—	503[d]	715[d]	1,777[d]	2,855[d]	4,999[d]
Other	5.9[a]	94[d]	123[d]	214[d]	337[d]	2,499[d]
All	124.7[a]	2,800[d]	4,508[d]	10,272[d]	15,536[d]	28,984[d]
World GDP	1,942[b]	11,118[e]	12,455[e]	21,141[e]	25,110[e]	31,499[e]
Sample GDP	671f	7,806[d]	9,705[d]	17,250[d]	21,956[d]	25,785[d]
Sample size	7f	26[d]	26[d]	26[d]	26[d]	63[d]
Assets/sample GDP	0.18	0.36	0.46	0.60	0.71	1.12
Assets/world GDP	0.06	0.25	0.36	0.49	0.62	0.92
U.K./all	0.21	0.20	0.19	0.17	0.16	0.15
U.S./all	0.51	0.28	0.29	0.21	0.22	0.25
Liabilities						
Europe	7.6[a]	1,457[d]	2,248[d]	5,406[d]	8,592[d]	14,509[d]
North America	12.5[a]	684[d]	1,412[d]	2,830[d]	4,681[d]	9,611[d]
Australia & N.Z.	2.2[a]	71[d]	118[d]	216[d]	318[d]	494[d]
Japan	0.3a	147[d]	307[d]	1,530[d]	1,970[d]	1,810[d]
Latin America	9.2[a]	250[g]	—	505[g]	768[g]	490[d]
Asia (excl. Japan)	2.7[a]	129[g]	—	524[g]	960[g]	132[d]
Africa	2.2[a]	124[g]	—	306[g]	353[g]	155[d]
Developing ountries	14.1[a]	506[g]	—	1,338[g]	2,086[g]	3,595[d]
All	39.9[a]	3,368[d g]	—	12,655[d g]	19,728[d g]	30,020[d]
World GDP	1,942[b]	11,118[e]	12,455[e]	21,141[e]	25,110[e]	31,499[e]
Sample GDP	—	9,508[d]	—	19,294[d]	25,043[d]	25,785[d]
Sample size	—	65[d g]	—	65[d g]	65[d g]	63[d]
Liabilities/sample GDP	—	0.35	—	0.66	0.79	1.16
Liabilities/world GDP	0.02	0.30	—	0.60	0.79	0.95
Developing countries/all	0.35	0.15	—	0.11	0.11	0.12

Notes and Sources: Units for foreign investment and GDP are billions of current U.S. dollars. [a] From Woodruff(1967, 150–9). [b] From Maddison (1995); sample of 199 countries; 1990 U.S. dollars converted to current dollars using U.S. GDP deflator; some interpolation. [c] From Lewis (1945, 292–7). [d] From IMF, *International Financial Statistics*, various years; 1980–95 sample of 26 countries, fixed sample, trend interpolation on missing data; 2000 sample of 63 countries. [e] From World Bank, *World Development Indicators*, various years. [f] Excludes "Other Europe" and "Other"; GDP data from appendix. [g] From Twomey (1998; unpublished worksheets).

Fig. 2.1. Foreign capital stocks

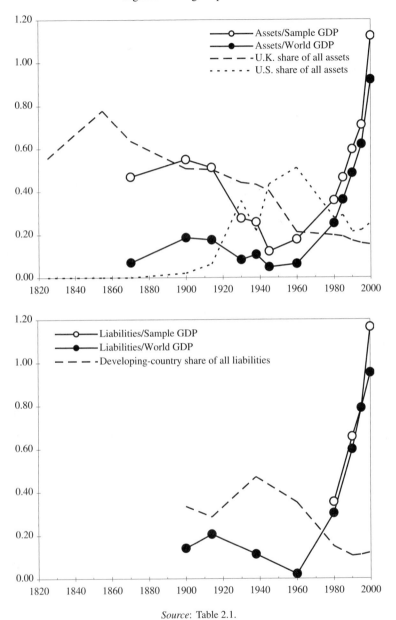

Source: Table 2.1.

rightly termed the "bankers to the world." At its peak, the British share of total global foreign investment was almost 80 percent. This is far above the recent U.S. share of global foreign assets, a "mere" 25 percent in 2000, and still higher than the maximum U.S. share of 50 percent circa 1960. The only rivals to the British in the early nineteenth century were the Dutch, who according to these figures held perhaps 30 percent of global foreign assets in 1825. This comes as no surprise given what we know of Amsterdam's early preeminence as the first global financial center before London's rise to dominance in the eighteenth and nineteenth centuries. By the late nineteenth century, both Paris and Berlin had also emerged as major financial centers, and, as the French and German economies grew and industrialized, their holdings of foreign capital rose significantly, both eclipsing the Dutch position until World War One.

In this era, the United States was a net debtor nation and was only starting to emerge as a major lender and foreign asset holder after 1900. European borrowing from the United States in World War One suddenly made the country a big creditor. This change came at a time when the U.S. was ready, if not altogether willing, to assume the mantle of "banker to the world," following Britain's abdication of this position under the burden of war and recovery in the 1910s and 1920s.[12] But the dislocations of the interwar years were to postpone the United States' rise as a foreign creditor, and New York's pivotal role as a financial center. After 1945, however, the United States decisively surpassed Britain as the major international asset holder, a position that has never since been challenged.[13]

How big were nineteenth century holdings of foreign assets? In 1870, we estimate that foreign assets were just 7 percent of world GDP; but this figure rose quickly, to just below 20 percent in the years 1900–14 at the zenith of the classical gold standard. During the interwar period, the collapse was swift, and foreign assets were only 8 percent of world output by 1930, 11 percent in 1938, and just 5 percent in 1945. Since this low point, the ratio climbed slowly to 6 percent in 1960, then dramatically to 25 percent in 1980, 49 percent in 1990, and 92 percent in 2000. Thus, the 1900–14 ratio of foreign investment to output in the world economy was not equaled again until 1980 and has now been approximately quintupled.[14]

---

[12] This Anglo-American transfer of hegemonic power is discussed by Kindleberger (1986) and by Bordo, Edelstein, and Rockoff (1999). Gallarotti (1995) challenges the view that Britain acted as a monetary hegemon up to 1914.

[13] Of course, this is the gross foreign investment position, not the net position. The United States is also now the world's number one debtor nation, in both gross and net terms, having become a net debtor in the late 1980s for the first time since the First World War.

[14] Even then, however, we cannot necessarily infer that there has been an increase in the extent of

An alternative measure recognizes the incompleteness of the data sources: for many countries we have no information on foreign investments at all, so a zero has been placed in the numerator, although that country's output has been included in the denominator as part of the world GDP estimate. This is an unfortunate aspect of our estimation procedure and makes the preceding asset-to-GDP ratio a likely underestimate, or lower bound, for the true ratio of foreign assets to output. One way to correct this is to include in the denominator only the countries for which we actually have data on foreign investment in the numerator.[15] This procedure yields an estimate that we term the ratio of foreign assets to sample GDP. This is likely an overestimate, or upper bound, of the true ratio, largely because in the historical data, if not in contemporary sources, scholars' attention in the collection of foreign investment data has usually focused on the principal players, that is, the countries that have the most substantial foreign-asset holdings.[16]

Given all these concerns, does the ratio to sample GDP evolve in a very different way? Not in the post–World War Two data. From 1870 to 1914, however, the sample of seven countries had a foreign asset-to-GDP ratio of around 50 percent, far above the "world" figure of 7 to 20 percent. By this measure we only surpassed the 1914 ratio as recently as 1990, and have since exceed it by a factor of two.

Is the picture similar for liabilities as well as assets? Essentially, yes. The data are more fragmentary here, and essentially nonexistent for the nineteenth century, when the information for the key creditor nations was simpler to collect than data for a multitude of debtors. Even so, we have some estimates from

foreign ownership of underlying national capital stocks. The asset-to-GDP ratio within countries has risen throughout the twentieth century with financial development (Goldsmith 1985), and the evolving complex structure of financial intermediation increasingly crosses national boundaries. This is not problem if we can view all foreign assets as direct claims on capital; but while that might be a reasonable approximation for the nineteenth century, it would be much more misleading now. In the past, most asset-liability positions were one-way at the national level (example: Britain circa 1900), but today the net flows are much less than the gross flows (example: most OECD countries today). Imagine that investors in country *A* buy an intermediary in *B* that then buys the physical capital in *A*. In this example, the ratio of foreign claims on *A* to *A*'s capital stock rises, yet there is no true increase in the foreign ownership of *A*'s capital. Given the type of aggregate data we are dealing with here, however, the resolution of this kind of issue seems impractical.

[15] That sample of countries is much smaller than the entire world, as we have noted. Until 1960, it includes only the seven major creditor countries noted in Table 2.1. Starting in 1980, the IMF sample progressively broadens the scope of this measure.

[16] That is, we are probably restricted in these samples to countries with individually high ratios of foreign assets to GDP. For example, in the rest of Europe circa 1914, we would be unlikely to find countries with portfolios as diversified internationally as the British, French, Germans, and Dutch. If we included those other countries it would probably bring our estimated ratio down. However, in the 1980s and 1990s IMF data, the problem is much less severe since we observe many more countries and both large and small asset holders.

1900 to the present at a few key dates. The ratio of liabilities to world GDP follows a path very much like that of the asset ratio, which is reassuring: these are each approximations built from different data sources, though, in principle, with ideal data, they should be equal. Again, the ratio reaches a local maximum in 1914 of 21 percent, collapsing in the interwar period to 11 percent in 1938, and just 2 percent in 1960. By 1980, the ratio had exceeded its 1914 level and stood at 30 percent. By 2000, the ratio was 95 percent.

2.1.2 The equity home bias

In the late nineteenth century, the major creditors tracked in Table 2.1 and Figure 2.1 held internationally diversified asset portfolios in a way that no group of countries does today. One dimension in which modern international financial integration remains incomplete, despite the impressive growth in gross foreign asset holdings, is that equity holders continue to concentrate their attention on home shares. Between 1980 and 2000, the share of foreign stocks in United States equity portfolios rose from about 1 percent to about 12 percent, an impressive rate of increase. However, the share of U.S. equities in the world portfolio remained steady at about 50 percent, so U.S. equity holdings remain far below what full diversification would imply in a world of literally perfect global asset-market integration. The puzzle applies to other countries, not only the United States, to different degrees. Japan holds relatively fewer foreign equities, the United Kingdom more, than the United States. Because a number of studies imply substantial gains to further diversification, the prevalence of home bias is a puzzle. Potential explanations range from information asymmetries to goods-market frictions, but a definitive resolution awaits further research.[17]

2.2 The size of net international flows

In contrast to the previous discussion of stocks, this section now attempts an analogous historical survey of global foreign investment flows since the late nineteenth century. The stock data suggested a marked diminution of foreign investment activity in the middle of the twentieth century, with recovery to the 1900–14 levels only seen as recently as the 1980s or even the 1990s. Do the flow data reveal a similar historical evolution?

Some basic definitions and notation will now prove useful. A country's gross domestic product, Q, is the value of goods produced there; GDP, together with

---

[17] The cited figures are from Warnock (2002). Lewis (1999) surveys the literature. Obstfeld and Rogoff (2000) show how international trade costs can limit international portfolio diversification.

imports M, may be allocated to private consumption C, public consumption G, investment I, or export X, so that $Q + M = C + I + G + X$. Rearranging, we see that GDP is given by

$$\text{GDP} \equiv Q = C + I + G + NX, \tag{2.3}$$

where $NX = X - M$ is net exports. If the country's net credit (debt) position vis-à-vis the rest of the world is B $(-B)$, and these claims (debts) earn (pay) interest at a world rate r^*, then gross national product is GDP plus (minus) this net factor income from (to) the rest of the world,

$$\text{GNP} \equiv Y = Q + r^*B = C + I + G + NX + rB. \tag{2.4}$$

The net balance on current account is

$$CA \equiv NX + r^*B = (Y - C - G) - I = S - I, \tag{2.5}$$

where $S \equiv Y - C - G$ is gross national saving. Finally, the dynamic structure of the current account and the national net credit position is given by the equality of the current account surplus (CA) and the capital (or financial) account deficit $(-KA)$, so that

$$\Delta B_{t+1} = B_{t+1} - B_t \equiv CA_t = -KA_t. \tag{2.6}$$

We now focus on the patterns of saving (S), investment (I), and the current account (CA) as previously defined. The basic identity (2.5), $CA = S - I$, is central to the analysis. In terms of historical data collection, it proves essential to utilize the identity to measure saving residually, as $S = I + CA$, because no national accounts before the 1940s supply independent saving estimates; rather, we have access only to investment and current account data.

A sense of the changing patterns of international financial flows can be gleaned by examining their trends and cycles. However, a normalization is again needed. Measurement traditionally focuses on the size of the current account balance CA, equal to net foreign investment, as a fraction of national income Y. Thus, $(CA/Y)_{it}$ becomes the variable of interest, for country i in period t, a convention we follow here. Table 2.2 presents some basic trends in foreign capital flows. We can measure the extent of capital flows with the cross-sectional mean absolute value $\mu_{|CA/Y|,t}$. The average size of capital flows in this sample was often as high as 4 to 5 percent of national income before World War One, as the quinquennial averages in Figure 2.2 illustrate. At its first peak, it reached 5.1 percent in the overseas investment boom of the late 1880s. This fell to around 3 percent in the depression of the 1890s. The figure approached 4 percent again in 1905–14, and wartime lending pushed the figure

Table 2.2. Current accounts relative to GDP
Mean absolute value

	ARG	AUS	CAN	DNK	FIN	FRA	DEU	ITA
1870–1889	.187	.097	.072	.018	.062	.029	.019	.012
1890–1913	.062	.063	.076	.027	.059	.023	.014	.019
1914–1918	.027	.076	.035	.054	.142	.031	—	.117
1919–1926	.049	.088	.023	.012	.039	.117	.022	.043
1927–1931	.037	.128	.036	.007	.029	.037	.018	.015
1932–1939	.016	.037	.016	.008	.029	.025	.004	.007
1940–1946	.048	.071	.065	.024	.069	.018	—	.034
1947–1959	.031	.034	.023	.014	.014	.015	.020	.014
1960–1973	.010	.023	.012	.019	.017	.006	.010	.021
1974–1989	.017	.037	.026	.032	.022	.008	.019	.014
1989–2000	.029	.045	.023	.016	.042	.011	.013	.019
	JPN	NLD	NOR	ESP	SWE	GBR	USA	All
1870–1889	.005	.060	.016	.010	.031	.045	.015	.040
1890–1913	.022	.053	.041	.014	.023	.045	.008	.037
1914–1918	.066	—	.043	.033	.063	.029	.035	.058
1919–1926	.021	—	.069	.027	.020	.029	.017	.039
1927–1931	.006	.004	.019	.018	.016	.020	.008	.027
1932–1939	.011	.018	.013	.012	.015	.011	.006	.015
1940–1946	.010	—	.049	.013	.019	.073	.010	.039
1947–1959	.013	.038	.031	.023	.011	.012	.006	.020
1960–1973	.010	.013	.024	.012	.007	.008	.005	.013
1974–1989	.020	.025	.050	.020	.014	.014	.013	.022
1989–2000	.023	.042	.046	.018	.023	.019	.018	.026

Notes and Sources: See text and appendix.

over 6 percent in 1915–19. Flows diminished in size in the 1920s, however, and international capital flows were less than 2 percent of national income in the late 1930s. Again, wartime loans raised the figure in the 1940s, but in the 1950s and 1960s, the size of international capital flows in this sample declined to an all-time low, around 1.3 percent of national income. Only starting in the late 1970s did flows increase, though not nearly to levels comparable to those of a century ago. Figure 2.2 presents an additional series that gauges the extent of capital flows, the cross-sectional standard deviation $\sigma_{CA/Y,t}$. The general picture is the same whichever yardstick is used.

Individual country data supply some detail to fill in this general picture. Some countries were clearly very dependent on foreign capital inflows before 1914, including the well-known cases of the settler economies – Argentina, Australia, and Canada. Many of these countries had typical capital inflows in excess of 5 percent of GDP, and in some years inflows were in excess of 10 percent. The Argentine figure before 1890 is inaccurate and surely an overstatement, as it

Fig. 2.2. Current accounts relative to GDP
Mean absolute value and standard deviation

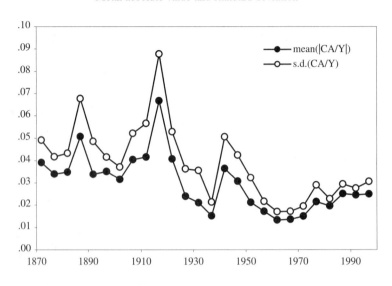

Notes and Sources: See text and appendix. 15 countries, quinquennial samples.

derives from the rather poor-quality data from that era. Even so, it reveals the
extent to which foreign finance was willing to fuel an investment boom before
the Baring crash in 1890. Also, note that, unlike the settler economies, the
U.S. economy had matured by the turn of the century and was on the verge of
becoming a capital exporter, with saving and investment almost in balance.

The major capital exporter was Britain, with 4.5 percent of GDP devoted
to overseas investment in a typical year between 1870 and 1914 – that figure
rising as high as 8–10 percent during lending booms. This massive capital
export coincided with the years of so-called "Edwardian failure" at home, and
the increasingly promising ventures for capital within and beyond the empire.[18]
This extraordinary net flow of capital as a share of output has never been matched
since by any overseas investing country. All countries shared in the collapse of
capital flows in the interwar period, and few have recovered the pre-1914 level
of flows as a share of output.[19]

Given that the size of flows is still smaller then a century ago, we would

[18] See Edelstein (1982) and Hall (1968) for more on this phenomenon of British capital outflow.
[19] This is true with the exception of brief upsurges during and after the wartime periods when
credits, especially from the United States to Europe, inflated the size of international transactions.

have to take these data as indicative of an incomplete recovery of global capital markets relative to their level of integration in 1914. There still could be other explanations for this path of capital flows over time, but, as in the caveats for the stock data, we would have to posit some large shock that made countries more alike for a time, reducing the incipient flows after 1914. This is potentially plausible *within* the group of most developed OECD (Organization for Economic Cooperation and Development) countries where productivity convergence has taken place; but it still leaves out the potential flows *between* core and periphery that one might expect, given the still-large development gap between rich and poor countries today. This is a major problem, deserving a thorough analysis of its own, and we return to it in the concluding part of the book.

Of course, mere flow data, as a quantity criterion, serve only as weak evidence of changing market integration. However, these basic descriptive tables and figures do illustrate the record of capital flows and offer prima facie evidence that the globalization of the capital market has been subject to major dislocations, most notably in the interwar period, with a dramatic contraction of flows seen in the Depression of the 1930s. Moreover, this low level in the volume of flows persisted long into the postwar era, and possibly persists even today. We now turn to more formal tests to see whether this description, and the conventional historiography of world markets that points to the Depression as an era of disintegration, receives broader support from the statistical record.

2.3 The saving-investment relationship

The presence of capital flows is neither a necessary nor sufficient condition for market integration. A small autarkic country with a rate of return no different from the "world" market may exhibit no incipient net flows upon opening its capital market. Conversely, countries with substantial barriers to capital mobility may nonetheless experience capital flows of some sort provided international rate-of-return differentials are sufficiently large. Still, despite shortcomings, a substantial literature has evolved using quantity evidence for evaluating capital mobility. An influential contribution was that of Feldstein and Horioka (FH) (1980), which used data for the 1960s and early 1970s on national saving and domestic investment rates to assess whether incremental savings were retained in the home country or else entered the global capital market seeking out the highest return. The FH "puzzle" was the surprisingly high correlation of saving and investment, or, put another way, the very small size of current accounts.

In the wartime quinquennia (1914–18 and 1940–46), furthermore, the averages are based on incomplete samples.

2.3.1 The Feldstein-Horioka puzzle over time

Feldstein and Horioka (1980) proposed cross-country saving-investment correlations as a measure of international capital mobility. They reasoned that, in a
world of perfectly mobile capital, national savings would seek out the highest
returns in the world capital market independent of local investment demand,
and, by the same token, the world capital market would cater to domestic investment needs independent of the national savings supply. They therefore
expected to find low correlations of saving and investment rates among developed countries, given the widespread view at the time that international capital
markets had become reasonably well integrated at least a decade before. In a
provocative and somewhat surprising result, however, they discovered a high
and significant slope coefficient in cross-sectional regressions of investment
rates on saving rates, with coefficients typically close to unity for the OECD
country sample. It appeared that changes in national saving passed through almost fully into domestic investment, suggesting highly imperfect international
capital mobility. That inference was hard for many researchers to accept in view
of the apparently high degree of international arbitrage of risk-free returns by
the mid-1970s – for example, between the Eurodollar market and onshore U.S.
certificates of deposits (Marston 1995).

Feldstein and Horioka coined the term "savings-retention coefficient" to
describe the regression coefficient b in the regression equation $I/Y = a + b(S/Y) + \epsilon$. Their finding has been replicated many times, so much so as to
be now considered a stylized but very robust fact.[20] Obviously, if capital flows
are small, the FH coefficient is bound to be close to unity. For illustration, the
FH test applied to the panel data produces the results shown in Figures 2.3 and
2.4. Figure 2.3 displays the FH coefficient for both five-year and ten-year averaged data. Figure 2.4 shows Sinn's (1992) cross-sectional coefficient calculated
using annual data.[21]

A substantial literature has evolved following Feldstein and Horioka to assess
whether incremental savings were retained in the home country or else entered
the global capital market seeking out the highest return. But as is well known,
the same literature has criticized the FH methodology on both theoretical and

---

[20] See Feldstein and Bacchetta (1991), Frankel (1991), Obstfeld (1986, 1995), Tesar (1991), Sinn
(1992), and Obstfeld and Rogoff (2000). For historical analyses see Obstfeld (1986), Bayoumi
(1990), Eichengreen (1990), Zevin (1992), and Jones and Obstfeld (2001). Our statistical tests
have enhanced power compared to other historical studies, since we have increased the sample
size: we use annual data for the full period 1850 to the present, and we increase the cross-
sectional size from the usual 9 or 10 up to 15, by adding various countries that were missing
from earlier studies.

[21] After 1870 the sample always includes between 12 and 15 countries – not a huge sample, but
comparable in size to Blanchard and Giavazzi's (2002) samples of euro zone and EU countries.

Fig. 2.3. Cross-sectional savings-retention coefficient ± 2 standard errors

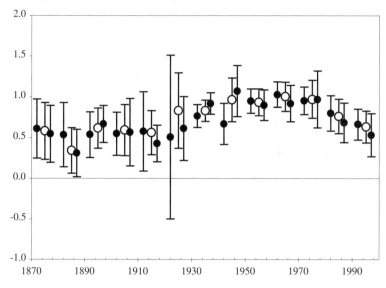

Notes and Sources: See text and appendix. 15 countries, quinquennial and decadal samples.

empirical grounds. The theoretical question revolves around the endogeneity of saving. Since saving and investment are jointly determined variables, common underlying shocks may induce a high saving-investment correlation even with perfectly mobile capital. Many researchers have attempted to identify and control for such common shocks, starting with Feldstein and Horioka themselves, but have had little success in explaining saving-investment correlations econometrically. Furthermore, regional saving and investment data from within individual countries, where they are available, do not reflect the FH correlation, which also seems to have declined dramatically among the group of EU countries in recent years.[22] Thus, while some correlation between saving and investment might be expected even under high capital mobility, and while structural changes in the pattern of economic shocks could themselves alter that correlation, large secular swings in the propensity for saving and investment to diverge seem likely to reflect at least some variation in the degree of international capital mobility. (They might also reflect changes in goods-market integration, of course, as Obstfeld and Rogoff 2000 discuss.)

[22] On regional data, see Obstfeld (1995). On recent developments in the European Union and euro zone, see Blanchard and Giavazzi (2002).

Fig. 2.4. Sinn's cross-sectional coefficient ± 2 standard errors

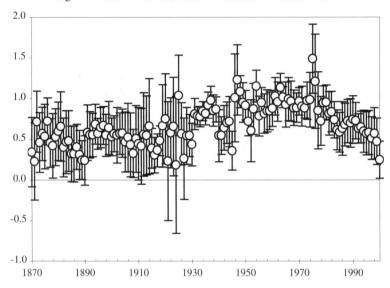

Notes and Sources: See text and appendix. 15 countries, annual samples.

With these caveats, we return to Figures 2.3 and 2.4 and note that both are broadly consistent with the idea of a ∪-shape pattern in the evolution of capital mobility since World War One. In both figures one discerns an inverted ∪-shape in the cross-sectional saving-investment coefficient post-1914, as the coefficient rises from about 0.5 to near 1.0 and then declines starting in the early 1970s.

The preceding purely cross-sectional results do not throw any light on the pure time-series correlation between saving and investment – the between-country covariation of saving and investment is displayed but the within-country covariation is ignored. Capital mobility will affect the short-term time-series comovements of saving and investment, however. To also investigate the latter, we can estimate a cross-sectional time-series system of the form $(I/Y)_{it} = a_i + b(S/Y)_{it} + \epsilon_{it}$ on annual data for a sample of 15 countries covering approximately the period 1870 to the present (Argentina, Australia, Canada, Denmark, Finland, France, Germany, Italy, Japan, the Netherlands, Norway, Spain, Sweden, the United Kingdom, and the United States).[23]

This framework allows a unified treatment of four alternative estimators. The *pooled* estimator takes $a_i = a$ (as well as imposing a common slope b)

[23] Feldstein (1983) presented such estimates in a follow-up to the first FH study.

for all countries i. The *between* estimator regresses the long-run country mean investment rates $\overline{(I/Y)}_i$ on the mean saving rates $\overline{(S/Y)}_i$, as in the original FH regressions. The within (or *fixed effects*) estimator allows for a country-specific intercept a_i. Finally, the *random effects* estimator treats a_i as a random variable uncorrelated with saving and uses generalized least squares (whereas fixed effects in essence subtracts out the country-specific means prior to estimation of b). As is well known, in the fixed-effects framework a_i can be interpreted as a random variable possibly correlated with saving. For example, a_i could be a demographic variable that raises a country's long-run investment rate while simultaneously augmenting national saving, in which case least-squares estimates of b would exaggerate the seeming influence of an "exogenous" saving shift on investment. Following Corbin (2001), we compare the fixed and random effects estimates via a Hausman (1978) test to ascertain whether any long-run country-specific shocks to investment (the fixed effects) can be regarded as independent of saving.[24]

Table 2.3 compares the different estimators over five epochs: pre–World War One (1870–1913), the early interwar period (1921–30), the late interwar period (1931–8), the Bretton Woods period (1946–72), and the modern floating–exchange rate era (1973–2000). The pooled regression is, in all cases, resoundingly rejected in favor of either fixed or random effects and we do not bother to report the relevant test statistics. In all epochs, the between estimate of b tends to be highest, followed by the pooled estimate and then the fixed- and random-effects estimates, though in some cases (1931–8 or 1973–2000) the differences are slight. Only for Bretton Woods does the Hausman test indicate a preference for fixed over random effects, indicating the presence of an unspecified determinant of national investment that is correlated with domestic saving. Also for that period, the between estimate of b suggests the long-run retention of *all* national saving.

In contrast, the pre–World War One and early interwar between estimates are lower (0.53 and 0.67, respectively), while the fixed- and random-effects estimates are lower still. Those numbers suggest that, on average in our sample, a country that increased saving by 1 percent of output in a year before 1930 saw its investment rise by 0.4 to 0.44 percent in that same year. This looks like a substantial degree of capital mobility. After 1930 and through 1972, these coefficients rise sharply, such that 80 to 85 percent of any increase in saving is

---

[24] Again we must urge caution in interpreting the panel estimates, since in this case the regressor (the saving rate) cannot be regarded as exogenous with respect to the equation errors. For example, if private agents (but not the econometrician) can partially forecast future investment opportunities, saving may well be correlated with future investment shocks.

Table 2.3. *Panel estimates of the savings-retention coefficient, 1870–2000*

		1870–1913	1921–1930	1931–1938	1946–1972	1973–2000
Pooled	b	0.50	0.50	0.85	0.92	0.78
		(0.02)	(0.06)	(0.03)	(0.02)	(0.03)
	R^2	0.41	0.31	0.90	0.82	0.69
Between	b	0.53	0.67	0.87	1.03	0.81
		(0.15)	(0.22)	(0.05)	(0.07)	(0.10)
	R^2	0.49	0.27	0.78	0.94	0.83
Fixed effects	b	0.44	0.40	0.79	0.83	0.75
		(0.03)	(0.06)	(0.04)	(0.03)	(0.04)
	R^2	0.33	0.27	0.78	0.73	0.54
Random effects	b	0.44	0.42	0.82	0.85	0.75
		(0.02)	(0.06)	(0.03)	(0.02)	(0.04)
	R^2	0.33	0.27	0.78	0.73	0.54
Hausman test	χ_1^2	0.38	1.30	1.48	7.96	0.31
(Fixed versus random)	p	[0.54]	[0.25]	[0.22]	[0.00]	[0.58]

Notes and Sources: See text. Standard errors in parentheses.

estimated to remain at home in the short run. For 1973–2000, all the coefficients decline, but not nearly back to the levels seen before the Great Depression. On average, only about 25 percent of an increase in saving flows abroad within a year. Thus, while the results in Table 2.3 are broadly consistent with a ∪-shaped development of capital mobility, they agree with the raw data on current-account balances in depicting a level of financial integration apparently lower than that attained before 1914. The 1973–2000 estimate of b seems surprisingly high, though it can be attenuated by expanding the country sample, and as we have noted, it has fallen sharply in recent years within the European Union.

A problem that may bias these panel estimates is that short-run saving-investment correlations are actually quite heterogeneous across countries, as noted by Obstfeld (1986, 1995) and Jansen (1996). There is some tendency for the correlation to be lower for smaller economies, though that tendency is by no means uniform. Kraay and Ventura (2000) and Ventura (2002) have proposed an inherently stochastic model of the current account that allows for such heterogeneity. Their underlying framework also portrays the saving-investment correlation, not as a decreasing function of the international mobility of risk-free lending, but as a decreasing function of the extent of foreign diversification of national wealth. This feature ties the Feldstein-Horioka puzzle to the equity-home-bias puzzle.

In the standard deterministic intertemporal current account model (as in Obstfeld and Rogoff 1996, chap. 1), there are diminishing returns to domestic investment, which proceeds until the marginal product of capital equals a world rate of return. In that setting, exogenous saving shocks may have little or no investment effect: additional savings tend to flow abroad, implying an FH effect near zero. In the Kraay-Ventura setup, in common with the standard intertemporal model, there is free international trade in risk-free securities. Contrary to the standard model, however, Kraay and Ventura posit that domestic and foreign capital are risky, internationally traded assets, and that there are constant expected returns to domestic capital accumulation. With intertemporally homothetic preferences, the portfolio shares of domestic capital and foreign assets do not depend on the level of domestic wealth or on the domestic capital stock, and so saving shocks feed into domestic investment with a coefficient equal to the share of home capital in domestic wealth. An interesting implication is that the FH coefficient can vary across countries. Countries with substantial foreign asset shares in wealth (often times smaller countries) will have low FH coefficients, whereas countries showing more extreme portfolio home biases (the United States, Japan) will have large FH coefficients. Countries that have negative net foreign assets will tend to run current account deficits when national saving rises.

The Kraay-Ventura model itself does not explain the degree of home bias in country portfolios. With complete international asset markets superimposed onto the Kraay-Ventura framework, a small country with purely idiosyncratic investment risk would exhibit a zero saving-investment correlation. The model is important, however, in giving a new interpretation of the FH coefficient's bearing on international financial integration. The coefficient may say little about the mobility of risk-free loans, but instead indicate the extent to which countries' diversification into foreign assets is incomplete. In support of their model, Kraay and Ventura (2000) and Ventura (2002) show that regressions of OECD current accounts on saving interacted with the foreign asset share yield coefficients not too different from unity.

2.3.2 Intertemporal budget balance and current-account dynamics

Here we extend the historical application of saving-investment analysis and seek to extend its theoretical and empirical scope in several ways. Methodologically, the main contribution is to go beyond the traditional cross-sectional or panel

FH test and to offer an alternative time-series approach based on a more explicit dynamic model. At low frequencies, we expect saving and investment to be highly correlated simply because every country must abide by a long-run version of current-account balance in order to satisfy its intertemporal national long-run budget constraint (LRBC).[25]

We next develop an applied LRBC framework as a tool for assessing capital mobility in a comparative historical setting. Applying the approach to data from the last century, we find results consistent with the stylized facts summarized previously. We also can make sense of the common FH finding, since the "high" correlation of saving and investment emerges as a natural implication of the LRBC.

We believe that the results do tell us something of interest about the changing degree of integration in global capital markets over time. Because our focus is the LRBC condition, our empirical approach is designed to reveal the changing ability of economies to employ net capital inflows and outflows to escape closed-economy saving-investment constraints.

Earlier studies, such as those by Trehan and Walsh (1991), Hakkio and Rush (1991), and Wickens and Uctum (1993), focus on a transversality condition for a country's external debt as indicating adherence to its intertemporal budget constraint. Such a criterion cannot be definitive, however, because a debt process that satisfies the transversality condition mechanically need not be consistent with nonnegative values of consumption and feasible levels of disinvestment. Here we take a simpler approach. Our basic finding is that a feasible intertemporal budget balance requires the ratio of the current account to output to be a stationary random variable.

Recall that external asset accumulation equals the current account surplus,

$$B_{t+1} - B_t = CA_t. \tag{2.7}$$

Normalizing by income Y_t (one could alternatively use output), and defining the gross growth rate of output by $g_t = Y_t/Y_{t-1}$, we may write

$$\frac{B_{t+1}}{Y_{t+1}} = \left(\frac{1}{g_{t+1}}\right)\frac{B_t}{Y_t} + \frac{CA_t}{Y_t}. \tag{2.8}$$

We may note from this expression that if CA/Y is nonstationary then B/Y will also be nonstationary. This would mean, in particular, that B/Y could drift downward indefinitely – it would pierce any lower bound in finite time with

---

[25] For application of this idea to the FH puzzle, see Obstfeld (1986, 73, n. 17), Jansen (1996), Jansen and Schulze (1996), Miller (1988), and Vikøren (1991). Later we draw on the methodology in Taylor (2002a).

probability 1. But the LRBC must preclude levels of external debt (in relation to GDP) so negative that they exceed the present value of national output. As a result, CA/Y is necessarily stationary.

An important corollary now follows from the identity $CA = S - I$. Even if S/Y and I/Y appear to be individually nonstationary, they must be cointegrated with cointegrating coefficient -1, so that $CA/Y = (S/Y) - (I/Y)$ is stationary. Thus, we would expect S/Y and I/Y to have a long-run tendency to move together. This result suggests that the FH regularity should always appear in very long-run data. In reality, one would not expect S/Y and I/Y literally to be nonstationary, yet as we shall see, they both appear quite persistent in the data, much more so than the current account ratio to GDP. In light of this, our analysis and interpretation will focus on the speed with which saving-investment gaps have been eliminated in different historical epochs.

Capital flows and the LRBC in two centuries

To investigate the time-series implications of the LRBC, we use our basic data sample on 15 countries since 1870, adding information on saving ratios, S/Y, and investment ratios, I/Y, to our observations of current account ratios, CA/Y. We ask whether the new tests lend broader support to the conventional historiography of world markets, which points to the Great Depression as an era of international disintegration. Our initial question is whether the data contradict the LRBC condition. To check this we test for stationarity of CA/Y, using the full time dimension of our data, at least 100 years in all cases.

Table 2.4 shows the results of applying the augmented Dickey-Fuller test, with a constant but no time trend, to the series S/Y, I/Y, and CA/Y for each country in our data set.[26] Whereas the saving and investment ratios often do not strongly contradict the hypothesis that they are nonstationary, the current account-to-GDP ratio is stationary for all countries in the raw data. That is, using the present test, there is no indication that any country in our sample violates its long-run budget constraint in the long sweep of history from the late nineteenth century to the present.

This is not to say that, in some periods, countries were unable to run "unsustainable" current account deficits, which were occasionally disrupted by crises, real adjustments, or defaults. Episodes in some countries during the 1890s, 1930s, or 1980s could fit this description, but in the long-run analysis we find that such short-run explosive tendencies have been, in general, too limited in

---

[26] Regarding lag selection, the Lagrange Multiplier (LM) test for serial correlation suggested 0 lags in most cases, with 1 lag on only two occasions. The results with 1 lag are similar to those presented here.

Table 2.4. *Stationarity tests: Current accounts*

Series	S/Y	I/Y	CA/Y	T
Argentina	−2.65*	−1.90	−4.30***	108
Australia	−3.63***	−3.58***	−6.02***	132
Canada	−2.05	−2.32	−2.61*	123
Denmark	−1.91	−1.81	−5.05***	113
Finland	−2.44	−2.18	−4.86***	133
France	−3.39**	−3.71***	−8.31***	134
Germany	−2.50	−4.23***	−5.33***	99
Italy	−3.02**	−3.29**	−3.67***	132
Japan	−1.87	−1.68	−5.03***	107
Netherlands	−4.18***	−2.56	−4.66***	119
Norway	−2.93**	−3.72***	−5.14***	122
Spain	−1.86	−1.31	−5.51***	143
Sweden	−2.33	−2.13	−4.91***	132
United Kingdom	−2.75*	−3.30**	−3.43***	124
United States	−3.76**	−1.25	−3.31***	143

Notes and Sources: See text, appendix, and Taylor (2002a). Augmented Dickey-Fuller t-test. No lags, no time trend, constant term in all cases. T is sample size. * denotes significant at 10 percent level, ** at 5 percent level, and *** at 1 percent level.

duration or amplitude to cause a globally nonstationary current account-to-GDP ratio or protracted Ponzi-like behavior of foreign debt.

Accordingly, our strategy will be to treat such shocks to creditworthiness, ability to pay, country risk, and so on, as a part of the perturbation dynamics of the system, along with all other real shocks. In modeling, we will aim to partition the system's behavior between such perturbations and the endogenous dynamics. Because the preceding results do not contradict the view that these economies have obeyed the LRBC, we next consider what intertemporal solvency implies for the dynamics of the current account, saving, and investment, and how we use those implications as a tool for measuring of capital mobility.

Current account dynamics and capital mobility

We can do more than just verify that CA/Y is stationary. In fact, the dynamics of CA/Y can tell us a great deal about capital mobility, so we investigate the adjustment speed of CA/Y back toward its equilibrium or steady-state value. To do this we implement simple AR(1) regressions of the form

$$\Delta(CA/Y)_t = \alpha + \beta(CA/Y)_{t-1} + \epsilon_t, \tag{2.9}$$

where stationarity leads us to expect that $\beta < 0$. We examine the convergence speed $-\beta$ and error variance σ^2 in each case. We do this four ways: with pooling across space, for each of the 15 individual countries, for pooling across time, and for four subperiods.

We will find later that the AR(1) model is an adequate and parsimonious specification for these purposes. Using the LM test, higher lag orders are not required so that all the internal dynamics of the model are summarized in the coefficient β, and the shocks ϵ are random and serially uncorrelated (nonpersistent). Thus, interpretation of the dynamic model is relatively simple.

How should we interpret the model parameters? If β is small (close to zero), we would infer that the country has a flexible current account and the capacity to run persistent deficits or surpluses. Conversely, if β is high (close to one), the country has a more rigid current account constraint where deviations from long-run equilibrium are hard to sustain. In this framework, we might consider the former to be evidence of high capital mobility as compared to the latter.[27]

Hence, we take the strong view that β is a summary statistic, derivable from the dynamic processes of saving and investment (which we consider in a moment), and pertinent to the ability of countries externally to smooth shocks to saving and investment. We take these parameters to be related to the true, underlying transaction costs that might impede perfect capital mobility – where costs are broadly construed to include distortions and barriers arising from policies, institutions, and underdevelopment that impinge on the efficient workings of external capital markets.

How should we interpret the shocks ϵ_t? These can be construed as shocks to the open economy resulting from a variety of sources: technology, tastes, monetary or fiscal policy, world interest rates, and so on. These will be considered the forcing terms for the equation, and for the present purposes, they are assumed to be exogenous. If the error variance σ^2 is high, it indicates a large range of shocks to the current account. Conversely, a small variance indicates more tranquil times.

The parameter β and shocks ϵ_t clearly have a direct bearing on the FH puzzle. Now that we have a dynamic AR(1) model of the current account, we see that the long-run or asymptotic variance of CA/Y (for a one-country sample, in the time dimension) is simply

$$\text{Var}(CA/Y) = \frac{\sigma^2}{1 - \rho^2}, \qquad (2.10)$$

---

[27] We view the long run current-account ratio as determined by the economy's trend growth rate and the long-run net foreign asset ratio to GDP, where the latter is a function of demographics, fiscal variables, and other factors. For empirical evidence on the determinants of net foreign asset positions, see Lane and Milesi-Ferretti (2001b).

Table 2.5. *Current-account dynamics*
Pooled sample with fixed effects

Country sample	Periods	β	σ	R^2	T	Specification tests No lags	Pooling periods	Pooling countries
All	All	−0.31 (0.02)	0.028	.16	1840	.00	.00	.00
All	Gold std.	−0.34 (0.03)	0.027	.17	498	.00		.07
All	Interwar	−0.41 (0.04)	0.037	.22	417	.00		.01
All	B. Woods	−0.74 (0.04)	0.021	.45	376	.29		.01
All	Float	−0.32 (0.04)	0.017	.16	315	.00		.89

Notes and sources: See text, appendix, and Taylor (2002a). "No lags" tests for up to 6 lags; "Pooling periods," for common structure across periods; "Pooling countries," for common structure across countries. All tests are F-tests. All specifications include country fixed effects.

where $\rho = 1 + \beta < 1$ is a persistence parameter. Hence, as is intuitively obvious, countries will have large current accounts (according to this variance measure used in Figure 2.2) only if their dynamics allow it: if shocks are large or if the convergence speed is slow (that is, persistence is high).

This intuition generalizes to AR(p) processes with p lags, provided that they are linear processes, since the variance of the left-hand side of equation 2.10 is separable into the effects of the internal dynamics of the system (a function of the coefficients) and the variance of the error term (which must enter linearly into the variance of the left-hand side). Thus, one way to throw light on the FH puzzle is to see exactly what kind of sustained current-account imbalances the dynamics do in fact permit.

Table 2.5 shows the results for the simple AR(1) model, with country fixed effects included but a common adjustment speed β imposed across countries. These results are very striking in that they confirm, in a *dynamic* model of current-account adjustment, the stylized facts of the historical literature concerning capital mobility.

Looking at the results in Table 2.5 in more detail, we see that the convergence speed $(-\beta)$ was very low in the pre-1914 era, about 34 percent per annum. That is, current account deviations had a half-life of about 1.5 years, suggesting considerable flexibility to smooth shocks over medium to long horizons. This freedom to adjust was reduced in the interwar period, as the convergence speed rose to about 41 percent per annum, implying a half-life of about 1.2 years. It was curtailed yet further under the Bretton Woods era when the convergence speed rose again to 74 percent, with a half-life now well under one year. Only in the recent floating period has flexibility returned to the current account in this sample, with a convergence speed of 32 percent, not significantly different from the pre-1914 estimate.

These findings accord with the notion that the Bretton Woods redesign of the international financial architecture, as it sought to avoid a repeat of volatile interwar foreign-exchange conditions, had as its intent a significant curtailment of international capital markets, and apparently it was very successful in achieving that end. We also find that the contemporary period looks little different from the gold-standard period of a century ago in terms of the extent of current-account flexibility.

A brief look at the error variance (σ) reveals no surprises given our historical priors. Shocks were largest during the turbulent interwar years, just as flexibility started to be lost – despite large shocks measured by σ, the lack of flexibility as measured by β prevented large flows from developing. Shocks were smallest in both post–World War Two periods, both during and after Bretton Woods.

The pre-1914 years saw shocks larger than those of the post–World War Two years, yet the gold standard system had more flexibility in terms of capital flows. Shocks under the gold standard were nonetheless substantially smaller than those of the interwar years. Thus, the Bretton Woods redesign was based on a valid premise – high volatility in international capital markets during the interwar period. However, the immediate post–World War Two solution was based, not on a return to market-based smoothing of shocks as in the pre-1914 gold-standard era, but rather on an attempt to shut down both the flows and the shocks themselves.

Cross-country variation and the stylized facts

Are such inferences valid in all countries? The trouble with the preceding estimates is that they may not be reasonable given the implied restriction that all countries adjust at the same rate. As Table 2.5 shows, it is easy to reject the uniformity of β across countries, at the 10 percent level or below in all cases except during the float. The table also shows that the simple specification with no lags of $\Delta(CA/Y)_t$ looks doubtful, given a specification test on the inclusion of additional (up to 6) lags. With country-by-country estimation, however, the absence of a complex lag structure is usually accepted.

Loosening up the specification in this way, whilst allowing us to admit different dynamics for each country, does not significantly alter our historical interpretation overall, though it does reveal some interesting heterogeneity of experience. In Figure 2.5, we see that for most countries the peak in the adjustment speed is experienced in the Bretton Woods period (9 out of 15 cases). Denmark, France, and Italy are fairly close, which leaves three other cases. Germany has its peak in the interwar period, which is as expected given the severe constraints on borrowing imposed after 1919, and only briefly eased by the Dawes plan. Japan has a much larger peak in the pre-1914 period, which is no surprise given the then-recent advent of the Meiji reforms. Spain's pre-1914 peak might be reasonable given that it was a country on the periphery at that time and somewhat isolated from the group of well-integrated gold standard countries by dint of its preference for silver money. Even so, given wide standard errors, none of these cases present examples where having a peak in the Bretton Woods era can be definitively rejected.

The error variances also accord well with the pooled results, with peak volatility in the interwar period again in 11 out of 15 cases. Unsurprisingly, volatility is much larger for the smaller economies: the U.S. variance is very small indeed as compared to those characterizing small countries such as Argentina, Australia, Finland, and Norway. The Danish case is also too close to call, and there are three exceptions to worry about once more. Argentina has its biggest error variance before 1914, which is no news to anyone familiar with the massive disruptions that caused, and then were caused by, the Baring crisis of 1890: a massive herding in of foreign capital, giving way to a sharp reversal and several years of austerity and outflows to settle debts. Even so, Argentina's interwar variance is still very high by world standards. Japan and the Netherlands also have high current-account error variances before 1914. We have fragile data for each country in this period, so that is one possible source of noise – as is also true of Argentina. The Dutch were big players relative to country size at this time, as capital exporters in the global capital market, which also argues for a volatile external balance. Newly opened Japan, like Argentina, might similarly have been exposed to turbulence as an emerging market. The one other unusual spike in error variance outside the interwar period – Norway in the floating-rate era – is clearly related to resource shocks following the discovery of North Sea oil, an episode that has by now become a textbook example of intertemporal current-account dynamics.

One would not wish to claim that an historical account of this sort can, nor would we desire that it should, say why each and every parameter has the value it does at each particular moment in time. There is an obvious danger of overexplanation. It is merely worth noting at this juncture that estimates from a simple dynamic model of the current account seems to corroborate priors derived from historical sources.

Fig. 2.5. Current-account adjustment speeds and error variances

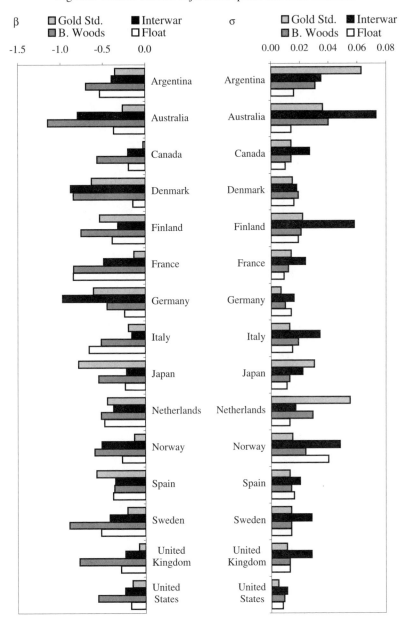

Notes and Sources: See text, appendix, and Taylor (2002a).

A vector error-correction model of saving and investment

We have shown that the current account ratio CA/Y is stationary. It immediately follows that the saving and investment ratios, S/Y and I/Y, if $I(1)$, must be cointegrated, since $CA/Y = S/Y - I/Y$ is an identity. Hence, without loss of generality, we can adopt a vector error-correction representation as a dynamic model of saving and investment. Let $s = S/Y$ and $i = I/Y$, and let $z = CA/Y$ be the cointegrating term. Under these conditions the dynamics of s and i take the form,

$$
\begin{pmatrix} \Delta s_t \\ \Delta i_t \end{pmatrix} = \begin{pmatrix} \alpha_s \\ \alpha_i \end{pmatrix} + \sum_{j=1}^{p} \begin{pmatrix} \beta_{ssj} & \beta_{sij} \\ \beta_{isj} & \beta_{iij} \end{pmatrix} \begin{pmatrix} \Delta s_{t-j} \\ \Delta i_{t-j} \end{pmatrix}
$$
$$
+ \begin{pmatrix} \gamma_s \\ \gamma_i \end{pmatrix} z_{t-1} + \begin{pmatrix} \epsilon_{st} \\ \epsilon_{it} \end{pmatrix}, \tag{2.11}
$$

where we expect $\gamma_s < 0$ and $\gamma_i > 0$, implying that current account deficits (surpluses) bring about adjustment via savings increases (decreases) and investment decreases (increases).

The vector error-correction model (VECM) presented here has a very general lag structure, and it is clear that it implies a more general dynamic model for $z = CA/Y$ than we saw in the previous section. If we subtract row two from row one in equation 2.11, we find that

$$
\Delta z_t = \alpha_z + \sum_{j=1}^{p} (\beta_{sj} \Delta s_{t-j} + \beta_{ij} \Delta i_{t-j}) + \gamma_z z_{t-1} + \epsilon_{zt}, \tag{2.12}
$$

where $\alpha_z = \alpha_s - \alpha_i$, $\beta_{sj} = \beta_{ssj} - \beta_{isj}$, $\beta_{ij} = \beta_{sij} - \beta_{iij}$, $\gamma_z = \gamma_s - \gamma_i$, and $\epsilon_z = \epsilon_s - \epsilon_i$. Only under certain restrictions would a pure AR representation of CA/Y obtain, independent of lagged S/Y and I/Y, and this would depend on having identical β coefficients in each row of equation 2.11.

The dynamic saving and investment model avoids some of the pitfalls of the FH approach. The model is not ad hoc, being based on the LRBC. And it gives us a way of comparing flexibility in the current account to saving and investment dynamics. In particular, changes in the adjustment coefficients $\gamma_s < 0$ and $\gamma_i > 0$ will directly affect the current account adjustment coefficient, $\gamma_z = \gamma_s - \gamma_i < 0$. And changes in the saving-investment vector error variance, $\text{Var}(\epsilon_t)$, will affect the current-account error variance, $\text{Var}(\epsilon_z) = \text{Var}(\epsilon_s - \epsilon_i) = \text{Var}(\epsilon_s) - 2\text{Cov}(\epsilon_s, \epsilon_i) + \text{Var}(\epsilon_i)$.

Dynamic model parameters and FH regression implications

We have a dynamic model of s, i, and $z = s - i$, and we can interpret adjustment speeds and error variances as telling us something about current-account flexibility and volatility. How do these time-series parameters relate to the FH cross-sectional results? Is there any relationship between capital-market integration as measured by the dynamic parameters and the estimated FH savings-retention coefficient?

To assess this link, we undertook the following simulation exercise. First, we fitted the model to actual data, allowing for individual country fixed effects but imposing a common lag structure across countries. Next, we simulated 100 years of data from a 1900 starting point for all 15 countries. Then we took the simulated 1990–9 data and performed cross-sectional or "between" FH regressions on long-run time-averages. We found the b (FH) coefficient for each simulation and repeated it for 1,000 simulations. This yielded the distribution of the estimated b coefficient, allowing us to calculate the mean value of the b estimate.[28]

Next, we repeated the whole exercise for different adjustment speeds $\gamma_z = \gamma_s - \gamma_i$ and different error variances $\text{Var}(\epsilon_z) = \text{Var}(\epsilon_s - \epsilon_i)$. How did we choose a range of parameters? We took the base calibration of the (s, i) model and left the lag structure and its parameters unchanged. But we did change convergence coefficients and error variances through a simple scaling of the base calibration. We replaced γ_z with $\phi_\gamma \gamma_z$ for various multipliers ϕ_γ, and similarly we replaced the variance-covariance (VCV) matrix $\text{Var}(\epsilon)$ with $\phi_\epsilon \text{Var}(\epsilon)$ for various multipliers ϕ_ϵ.

Finally, we tabulated the results to see how changes in the underlying dynamic parameters of the (s, i) VECM model – namely, γ_z and $\text{Var}(\epsilon)$, the parameters we take as our basic measures of the underlying mobility of capital – affected the mean value of b, the estimated cross-sectional FH coefficient.[29]

---

[28] The fitted model had

$$\begin{pmatrix} \gamma_s \\ \gamma_i \end{pmatrix} = \begin{pmatrix} -0.12 \\ 0.08 \end{pmatrix}, \text{Var} \begin{pmatrix} \epsilon_s \\ \epsilon_i \end{pmatrix} = \begin{pmatrix} 0.00100 & 0.00046 \\ 0.00046 & 0.00065 \end{pmatrix},$$

implying that γ_s and γ_i had the expected signs, $\gamma_z = -0.20$, and $\text{Var}(\epsilon_z) = 0.00073$.

[29] The first draft of this material (Taylor 1996b) approached the dynamic modeling exercise with a single-equation error-correction model (ECM) following Jansen and Schulze (1996). The vector error-correction model model developed here is much more general and does not require a weak-exogeneity assumption for saving. Using the single-equation ECM framework, in independent work, Jansen (1997) used a simulation approach to show how parameter shifts in the ECM could affect the cross-sectional implied FH coefficient. Our exercise is in the same vein, but it is calibrated to actual historical processes, whereas Jansen used ad hoc parameter choices to make an artificial cross section of countries. We also do not assume a random walk for saving as he did, but instead model saving as part of a VECM process.

Table 2.6. *Simulated savings-retention coefficients*

Multiplier Adjustment speed	VCV matrix	Mean FH regression coefficient					
		Annual		5-year		10-year	
0.01	1.00	0.48	(0.19)	0.51	(0.16)	0.48	(0.16)
0.05	1.00	0.56	(0.16)	0.61	(0.15)	0.59	(0.17)
0.10	1.00	0.71	(0.12)	0.70	(0.13)	0.72	(0.14)
0.20	1.00	0.81	(0.14)	0.82	(0.11)	0.84	(0.11)
0.50	1.00	0.91	(0.09)	0.91	(0.07)	0.94	(0.07)
1.00	1.00	0.96	(0.07)	0.97	(0.05)	0.97	(0.05)
2.00	1.00	0.97	(0.06)	0.98	(0.04)	0.99	(0.03)
5.00	1.00	0.98	(0.06)	1.00	(0.02)	1.00	(0.01)
1.00	0.01	1.00	(0.02)	1.00	(0.01)	1.00	(0.01)
1.00	0.05	0.98	(0.04)	0.99	(0.03)	0.99	(0.03)
1.00	0.10	0.97	(0.05)	0.97	(0.04)	0.98	(0.04)
1.00	0.20	0.96	(0.06)	0.97	(0.05)	0.97	(0.05)
1.00	0.50	0.96	(0.06)	0.97	(0.06)	0.97	(0.04)
1.00	1.00	0.94	(0.07)	0.97	(0.06)	0.97	(0.05)
1.00	2.00	0.94	(0.06)	0.96	(0.06)	0.97	(0.06)
1.00	5.00	0.95	(0.07)	0.95	(0.06)	0.97	(0.05)
1.00	10.00	0.94	(0.07)	0.96	(0.06)	0.96	(0.05)
1.00	20.00	0.94	(0.07)	0.96	(0.06)	0.97	(0.05)
1.00	50.00	0.94	(0.07)	0.96	(0.06)	0.96	(0.05)

Notes and Sources: See text, appendix, and Taylor (2002a).

Table 2.6 shows results for changes in one set of parameters at a time. Holding the error variance fixed and rescaling the convergence coefficients in the (s, i) model show that larger convergence coefficients (of s, i, and, hence, z) are associated with larger FH coefficients, and the whole range runs from a low of $b = 0.5$ (when the convergence coefficient is cut by a factor of $\phi_\gamma = 0.01$) to a high of $b = 1$ (for $\phi_\gamma = 5$).[30] This is intuitive: if the current account adjusts very quickly back to zero, then for a given distribution of shocks, we will very rarely see saving and investment taking on unequal values and would expect a high b estimate.

In an alternative experiment we can hold the convergence coefficients fixed and rescale the size of the error shocks, again using the real data for the base calibration. When we perform this experiment, there is a monotonic relationship of sorts, but the magnitude of the changes in b are very small as the rescaling of shocks ranges over a multiplicative factor of $0.02 \le \phi_\epsilon \le 50$. This is a very wide range over which to see practically no variation in the FH savings-retention coefficient (with $0.96 < b < 1$).

[30] When $\phi_\gamma > 5$, the convergence coefficient $\phi_\gamma \gamma_z$ exceeds 1 and the model implies unrealistic oscillations. These results therefore are not reported.

Fig. 2.6. Simulated savings-retention coefficients

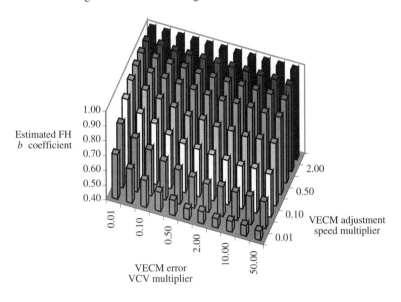

Notes and Sources: See text, appendix, and Taylor (2002a).

In Table 2.6, though, the small response of b to $\text{Var}(\epsilon_z)$ might be the result of holding γ_z fixed at a given level; the response could be bigger at other values of γ_z. We would really like to know what happens to the FH coefficient when both parameters $(\phi_\gamma, \phi_\epsilon)$ vary simultaneously and over a wider range. On this question, the display format of Table 2.6 appears inadequate for the task of clearly showing the mapping from these underlying parameters to the b statistic. Accordingly, we turn to a three-dimensional graphical display. While it requires careful interpretation, it better illustrates the range of results possible in this framework.

Figure 2.6 plots the mapping from various imposed $(\phi_\gamma, \phi_\epsilon)$ pairs on the horizontal plane to the implied average estimate of b on the vertical axis. The figure confirms that with smaller convergence coefficients (smaller levels of ϕ_γ), higher volatility (larger ϕ_ϵ) translates into a lower value of b, the FH coefficient. This is also an intuitive finding: bigger disturbances in the (s, i) model should, holding the convergence coefficient constant, lead to bigger differences between saving and investment levels in each country and, hence, a lower correlation of s and i in cross section.[31]

Thus, we find that simulated data from the dynamic model generate a range of FH coefficients between 0.5 and 1, an interval that encompasses most of the actual range seen in published FH tests. This finding explains why truly small FH parameters (close to zero) are unlikely ever to be seen in practice. A meaningful, albeit deformed, yardstick for the FH tests can be based on these simulations. *Very* low convergence coefficients can push b as low as about 0.5 (but rarely lower), so this is a plausible lower extreme on the scale. Conversely, high convergence coefficients soon push b close to 1, the plausible high extreme on the scale. This provides a useful barometer by which to evaluate our earlier results on the saving-investment correlation.

Are the conclusions limited and model-specific? They should not be. The LRBC must be a common feature of all useful models in international finance, with or without growth, whether deterministic or stochastic. From the LRBC restriction, certain implied time-series dynamics for debts and the current account must follow – dynamics that must resemble the models estimated here.

2.4 Variations in the types of capital flows

The study of disaggregated capital flows is a vast field, and it is beyond the scope of the book to make a comprehensive study of portfolio equity flows, foreign direct investment (FDI), bank finance, and bond issues by both public and private sectors. It is of interest, however, to mention two large-scale features of the data on disaggregated investment over the last century and a half for which some data exist – features which tend to corroborate our basic characterization of the evolution of capital markets and the role of public policy.

First, if we study the evolution of capital flows to public and private recipients over time, a clear pattern in the distribution of flows can be seen that parallels the magnitude of flows. Here, flows to public entities reach national or subnational governments and take the form of debt finance. Private flows, on the other hand, consist of the debt and equity finance of all private firms including FDI, portfolio equity, bonds, and bank loans. As can be seen in Figure 2.7, the shares of international capital flows going to public and private entities have varied over time, and with a pattern that looks quite familiar given its resemblance to our depiction of the stylized facts on the evolution of overall international capital mobility.

---

[31] Figure 2.6 shows only the results for 10-year-averaged samples. The results are similar for 1- and 5-year averaging.

Fig. 2.7. Foreign capital flows to private-sector recipients, 1870–2000
Private flows as a share of total flows, percent

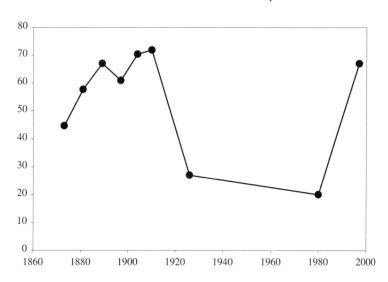

Sources: 1870–1913 from Stone (1999) as elaborated by Clemens and Williamson (2002);
1921–97 from World Bank (2000) as elaborated by Bordo and Eichengreen (2002).

As global capital markets developed during the late nineteenth century, an ever-greater share (of an ever-increasing pie) took the form of flows to private-sector recipients. Once the market took a more autarkic turn after World War One, capital flows went increasingly to governments: the private sector took a smaller and smaller share (of a rapidly shrinking pie). The World Bank data we use are patchy for the postwar period. But we can see that after the 1980s, this pattern reversed itself again, and when aggregate capital flows surged, so too did the share going to private-sector recipients. We think this large-scale correlation is highly suggestive. It indicates that the same forces that limited total capital flows during the relatively autarkic mid-twentieth century also tended disproportionately to inhibit flows to private-sector activity. For sure, an important factor in the rise of public-sector borrowing after 1914 was the growth in the public sector itself as a share of total economic activity, as one can document by looking at the ratio of government outlays to GDP. Larger governments often have a concomitant need for larger doses of finance. Yet, as the recovery of private-sector borrowing after 1980 shows, this cannot be the whole story, for government sector activity has hardly receded in the last

Table 2.7. *Foreign investment in core and periphery*

Outward investment from core countries Index (1938=100)	1913	1929	1938	1960	1971	1980	1990	1995
FDI/GDP	121	—	100	49	56	58	108	143
FI/GDP[1]	196	108	100	69	—	138	231	273
FDI/FI	62	—	100	71	—	42	47	52
Inward investment in developing countries Percent	1914	1930s		1950s	1970			1995
FDI/GDP	40	51		30	13			18
FI/GDP	94	96		53	32			86
FDI/FI	43	53		57	41			21

Source: Twomey (2000, tables 3.3, 3.4, and 7.1) except [1] from Table 2.1.

two decades. Instead, the small share of private-sector finance activity from the 1920s to the 1970s is, to our way of thinking, another manifestation of policy choices in the regulation of international finance – that is, another result of the political economy of the trilemma and the inward turn of states against markets.

Another way to examine the changing composition of flows is to examine the variation in FDI against other forms of foreign investment (FI). Table 2.7 shows how the ratios of FDI and FI to GDP, and to each other, have evolved in the long run. It is clear that the main source countries for FDI, the core OECD countries, have experienced very different trends in their asset composition as compared to an important set of recipient countries, the developing countries, and their respective liability composition.

This table shows, first and foremost, the familiar U-shape in the evolution of overall foreign investment during the last century. This needs little further elaboration, given our earlier discussion. Second, the table also shows that this pattern is common to both FI and FDI for core countries' outward investments, but is only true for FI in the recipient developing countries. Why? The table indicates that in the interwar period, the fall in FDI was much less pronounced than that of total FI. We can understand this result as a manifestation of political economy forces. Recall that policymakers, confronted with the trilemma, sought to close down the flows of "hot money" – thus controls would tend to dissuade the more mobile forms of capital such as tradable debt and equity instruments. In contrast, FDI was not hot at all – direct ownership of plant and equipment tended to be a longer-run investment.

Such an explanation, though tempting, remains conjectural, given its ceteris paribus assumptions. There are many other possible explanations for changes in FDI intensity (Feenstra 2004, chap. 11). In the postwar period, other autarkic

Table 2.8. *Foreign direct investment flows, 1986–99*
Billions of U.S. dollars, annual averages

	1986–90	1991–5	1996–9
World	160.9	229.1	641.8
Developed	133.0	149.8	459.7
All developing	27.9	79.3	182.2
Least developed	0.6	1.8	3.6

Source: International Monetary Fund, *World Economic Outlook*, October 2001, 159.

policies, such as trade restrictions, tended to encourage tariff hopping FDI as a means for multinational firms to evade import controls and sell in the local market. These possible biases in favor of FDI were to endure long into the postwar period, and affected outward FDI to all countries. With the recent return to more liberal trade policies in developing countries, the tariff hopping motive for so-called "horizontal FDI" has somewhat abated. What has arguably taken its place is so-called "vertical FDI," where firms outsource across space to take advantage of more competitive low-wage/low-skill locations for certain parts of the production process. This fragmentation of production stages is responsible for an ever growing share of FDI and of trade itself (Feenstra 1998). Yet, at least through 1995, FDI had not been the major factor in the recovery of developing-country FI inflows toward 1914 levels.

The failure of the postwar FDI/GDP ratio fully to rebound in most developing countries prompts alternate hypotheses that deserve further research. It is well know that poor countries today are characterized by poor-quality institutions and weak property rights (a topic to which we return in Chapter 7). In an era of increased political uncertainty for these countries, foreign investors could well avoid FDI, noting that foreign plants are not immune from expropriation, hold-up problems, or capricious taxes, whereas opportunities to acquire portfolio investments, which are potentially more liquid, have expanded. Although there seems to be only a recent and minor recovery evident in these data through 1995, a continued FDI boom in the late 1990s suggests that this trend may have turned (Table 2.8), with FDI to poor countries increasing in magnitude and, importantly, reaching a more widely dispersed group of recipient countries.

2.5 Caveats: Quantity criteria

We have spent many pages reviewing quantity evidence from the nineteenth and twentieth centuries. An obvious objection to quantity criteria is that they may be poor indicators of market integration, for reasons we have spelled out.

In particular, changes in economic structure in the markets under consideration could induce quantity changes without any shift in the underlying costs of arbitrage, and hence with no change in the true degree of integration. For this reason, some argue, one should really work with price data and eschew quantity criteria. However, we make three responses to this critique. First, we *will* examine historical price data in the very next chapter. Second, a moment's thought will convince the reader that price evidence is not necessarily easier to interpret: structural shifts in markets could just as easily lead to price convergence as to quantity movements, making inferences about underlying shifts in mobility just as difficult to discern. Third, the joint consideration of price and quantity data can narrow the range of possibilities with which the data are consistent.

Given the evidence presented here, and what is about to follow, our belief is that changes in mobility do dominate the picture for the twentieth century. We base this view on a conjecture, and on the consistent weight of evidence in various tests. The conjecture is that a rival explanation based on long-term structural developments would have to propose some implausible changes in the world economy to generate the patterns seen, given a constant degree of capital mobility. We would have to posit some technological or endowment changes in the interwar period that rendered economies more similar (with less incentive for capital movements between them), followed by a prompt reversal of these shocks in the postwar period.

It is not easy to think what these shocks could be. With respect to population trends, very large gaps opened up between rich and poor countries this century, as demographic transitions drew to a close in the core and were only just begun at the periphery. At the same time, capital accumulation and technological progress raced ahead in the core and stagnated at the periphery. All of these shocks have had predictable implications for living standards, what economic historians have termed the "Great Diveregence," as shown in Table 2.9. To the extent that this divergence was driven by a relative increase in capital-labor ratios in the core, incipient capital flows ought to have been in the direction of the capital-scarce periphery, and with an increasing intensity. Clearly, the absence of such flows poses problems for the simple frictionless neoclassical model, as noted by many observers.[32] However, to the extent that productivity has advanced more rapidly in the core, such incipient flows could be neutralized, even reversed, with capital inclined to remain in, or flow towards, the core countries. This much is clear, but from a historical standpoint there is as yet

---

[32] See, for example, Lucas (1990).

Table 2.9. *The "Great Divergence"*
Levels of GDP per capita in 1990 international dollars

	1820	1870	1913	1950	1973	1998
Western offshoots	1,201	2,431	5,257	9,288	16,172	26,146
Western Europe	1,232	1,974	3,473	4,594	11,534	17,921
Japan	669	737	1,387	1,926	11,439	20,413
Latin America	665	698	1,511	2,554	4,531	5,795
Eastern Europe & former U.S.S.R.	667	917	1,501	2,601	5,729	4,534
Asia (excluding Japan)	575	543	640	635	1,231	2,936
Africa	418	444	585	852	1,365	1,368
World	667	867	1,510	2,114	4,104	5,709
Interregional spreads	3:1	5:1	9:1	15:1	13:1	19:1

Notes: The four "Western offshoots" are Australia, Canada, New Zealand, and the United States.
Source: Maddison (2001, Table 3-1b).

no indication over the course of the last century or more that these types of deep structural changes differed systematically between periods of small and large global capital movements. As we shall see in the final part of the book, the divergence in national living standards witnessed in the twentieth century appears to have its origins in both capital *and* productivity shortfalls in the developing countries, but this process has been in seemingly inexorable motion since (at least) the nineteenth century, albeit with some signs of reversal in recent decades.[33]

Absent any reasonable alternative explanations, and given the corroborating evidence from price criteria that we discuss in the next chapter, we can gain further confidence from what is a fairly consistent picture delivered by a variety of quantity criteria. All told, almost every quantity measure we have proposed has illustrated the kind of stylized ∪-shape postulated by conventional wisdom. Had this not been the case, our interpretation would have to be more nuanced,

---

[33] See Chapter 7 below. On recent trends in global inequality and some historical perspective, see Lindert and Williamson (2003) and Sala-i-Martin (2002). In addition to physical capital, there is also the question of whether *human* capital is an important explanatory variable in the Great Divergence, since if it is complementary to physical capital, its scarcity in poorer countries will discourage capital inflows. This effect has been proposed in growth theory for the recent postwar period (Lucas 1990). However, the historical data before 1945 are so poor on schooling and literacy that we have little idea how much divergence or convergence in human capital endowments could have accounted for the behavior of capital flows. Note again that an (exhaustive) explanation based on human capital would require some implausible reversals: a convergence in human capital levels before 1913, then a divergence, and then a convergence once again in the recent decades. No study we know has made such a claim for global schooling and literacy patterns. This is not to deny that schooling was important as a growth determinant in more distant eras. On late nineteenth-century schooling and catch-up, see O'Rourke and Williamson (1995). Nor do we deny that for some countries, at some critical junctures, human capital and investment in research might have made a very big difference. On how the United States kept its technological lead at mid-century, see Nelson and Wright (1992).

but the fact that many signs point in the same direction is surely an important result – all the more so because there is, in reality, no single measure of capital mobility. All depends on the kind of mobility one wants to measure. It is reassuring for our interpretative schema that, in most dimensions, the evidence appears to be leading the same way.

Given these caveats, what do the quantity data say about capital mobility? In few areas is it obvious that the contemporary world vastly dominates the pre-1914 era in terms of market efficiency. Net flows of foreign capital today are no larger than during the last golden age on the eve of World War One. The ability of countries today to to sustain current account imbalances, thereby decoupling saving and investment, seems to be no greater than a century ago. We are ahead today in gross two-way asset positions among the industrial countries, but diversification still remains low as compared to a hypothetical complete-integration optimum, as the persistent home-equity bias indicates. Meanwhile, developing countries appear to be playing a much smaller role in today's so-called global capital market than they did before World War One.

3

Globalization in Capital Markets: Price Evidence

Having examined quantity criteria for market integration in the previous chapter, the next stage of our empirical discussion moves on to price criteria. Here we will encounter some venerable parity tests from the international finance literature: exchange-risk-free interest parity, real interest parity, and purchasing power parity. Compared to quantity criteria, such tests offer a seemingly more direct way to assess market integration. For reasons already given, however, changes in price differentials between two locations will track changes in market integration only if certain auxiliary assumptions hold true. These problems will be faced when we sum up our findings and encounter another set of caveats.

3.1 Exchange-risk-free nominal interest parity

Perhaps the most unambiguous indicator of capital mobility is the relationship between interest rates on identical assets located in different financial centers.[1,2] The great advantage of comparing onshore and offshore interest rates such as these is that relative rates of return are not affected by pure currency risk. In principle, therefore, such interest differentials (when they exceed normal market transaction costs) represent pure arbitrage opportunities, absent some impediments to free international capital flow.[3]

[1] See the discussion in Obstfeld (1995), for example.
[2] This section draws on Obstfeld and Taylor (1998) for the case of Britain but adds new data on Germany for comparison. After our 1998 paper was published, we became aware of a similar 1889–1909 U.S.-U.K. interest rate comparison in Calomiris and Hubbard (1996).
[3] Eichengreen (1991) presents similar data for the interwar period, as does Marston (1995) for the postwar period. Under a fixed-exchange-rate regime such as the gold standard, another arbitrage-like test of financial-market integration asks whether nominal interest differentials in different currencies are consistent with the maximal allowable exchange-rate fluctuation band (Goschen 1861; Weill 1903; Morgenstern 1959; Officer 1996). Such a test relies on the maintained hypothesis that the exchange-rate band is credible (though not on uncovered interest

For much of the period we study here, a direct offshore-onshore comparison is impossible. However, the existence of forward exchange instruments allows us to construct roughly equivalent measures of the return to currency-risk-free international arbitrage operations.

For the period stretching from 1921 until the first half of 2003, we have monthly data on forward exchange rates, spot exchange rates, and nominal interest rates. We therefore can assess the degree of international financial-market integration by calculating the return to covered interest arbitrage between financial centers. For example, a London resident could earn the gross sterling interest rate $1 + i_t^*$ on a London loan of one pound sterling. Alternatively, he or she could invest the same currency unit in New York, simultaneously covering the exchange risk by selling dollars forward. He or she would do this in three steps: buy e_t dollars in the spot exchange market (where e_t is the spot price of sterling in dollar terms); next, invest the proceeds and earn a total of $e_t(1 + i_t)$ dollars (where i_t is the nominal dollar interest rate); and, finally, sell that sum of dollars forward for $e_t(1 + i_t)/f_t$ in sterling (where f_t, the forward exchange rate, is the price of forward sterling in terms of forward dollars). The net gain from borrowing in London and investing in New York,

$$\frac{e_t}{f_t}(1 + i_t) - (1 + i_t^*), \tag{3.1}$$

is zero when capital mobility is perfect and the interest rates and forward rate are free of default risk. The left-hand side of expression 3.1 represents a price of present pounds sterling in terms of future pounds sterling (i.e., of sterling dated t in terms of sterling dated $t + 1$), but it can be viewed as the relative price prevailing in the New York market, that is, as reflecting a kind of offshore sterling interest rate. Thus, our test, in effect, examines the equality of the onshore sterling interest rate i^* with the offshore New York rate so defined. We perform a similar calculation for mark interest differentials between London (considered as the offshore center) and Germany (onshore), thereby gauging the difference between implicit mark interest rates in London and the rates prevailing near the same time in Germany.

For pre-1920 data, we examine a related but distinct measure based on current New York prices of sterling for (two-months) future delivery, as in Obstfeld and Taylor (1998). The parallel London-Germany arbitrage calculation before 1920, corresponding to the preceding New York-London comparison, is based on London prices for marks to be delivered three months in the future. Forward

parity), and more recently has been interpreted as a test of the credibility of an exchange-rate target band, assuming full financial integration (Svensson 1991a; Giovannini 1993; Marston 1995, chap. 5; Hallwood, MacDonald, and Marsh 1996).

exchange contracts of the kind common after 1920 were not prevalent before then (except in some exceptional financial centers, see Einzig 1937), so we instead base our pre-1920 comparison of onshore and offshore interest rates on the most widely traded instrument, one for which prices were regularly quoted in the major financial centers' markets, the long bill of exchange. Long bills could be used to cover the exchange risk that might otherwise be involved in interest-rate arbitrage.[4]

To see how such a transaction would work, let b_t denote the date-t dollar price in New York of £1 deliverable in London after 60 days, and e_t the spot New York price of sterling.[5] One way to purchase a future pound deliverable in London would be through a straight sterling loan, at price $1/(1 + i_t^*)$, where i_t^* is the London 60-day discount rate. An alternative would be to purchase in New York a bill on London, at a price in terms of current sterling of b_t/e_t. With perfect and costless international arbitrage, these two prices of £1 to be delivered in London in the future should be the same.

Perkins (1978) observed that the series $(e/b) - 1$ defines the sterling interest rate in American financial markets, that is, the offshore sterling rate in the United States. This series may be compared with the London rate i^* to gauge the degree of cross-border financial integration. That is, we calculate the differential

$$\frac{e_t}{b_t} - (1 + i_t^*) \tag{3.2}$$

before 1920.

Perkins's (1978) primary aim was to modify earlier series of dollar-sterling spot rates derived by Davis and Hughes (1960), who applied U.S. rather than U.K. interest rates to the dollar prices of long sterling bills in order to infer a series of sight exchange rates. Perkins argued that the sight bill rate should be derived by multiplying the (lower) long bill rate by a sterling, not a dollar, interest factor (that is, by $1 + i^*$). Subsequent scholars have followed him; see, for example, the judgment of Officer (1996, 69). From a theoretical point of view, the verdict is clear: the relative price of current and future sterling defines a sterling nominal interest rate, in the present case, the offshore New York rate that we compare to London rates.

The upper panel of Figure 3.1 is based on monthly differences between sterling rates in New York and in London from 1870 to 2001, where we simply splice together the 1870–1920 numbers based on time bill rates with the

---

[4] Margraff (1908, 37) speaks explicitly of the need to "cover" interest arbitrage through the exchange market.

[5] In fact, such long bills were payable after 63 days due to a legal "grace period" of three days, an institutional fact we account for in the following calculations (Haupt 1894, 429).

Fig. 3.1. Exchange-risk free nominal interest differentials since 1870
U.S.-U.K. and U.K.-Germany

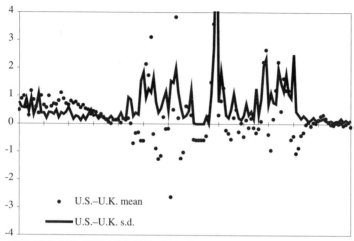

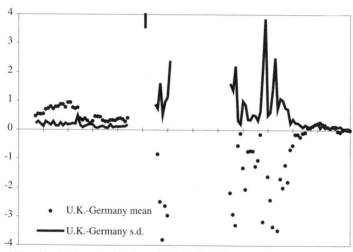

Notes and Sources: Annual samples of monthly data, percent per annum. See text.

subsequently available covered interest differentials. Differential returns are calculated as annual percentage rates of accrual. Data sources are documented in the appendix.

The U.S.-U.K. evidence broadly supports other indicators of the ∪-shaped evolution of capital mobility since the late nineteenth century. Differentials were relatively small and steady under the pre-1914 gold standard but started to open up during World War One. They stay quite large in the early 1920s. Differentials diminished briefly in the late 1920s but widened sharply in the early 1930s. There were some big arbitrage gaps in the late 1940s through the mid-1950s – including a spike in volatility at the time of the 1956 Suez crisis.[6] But these gaps shrunk in the late 1950s and early 1960s, only to open up again in the late 1960s as sterling's 1967 devaluation initiated a period of foreign exchange turmoil, culminating in the unraveling of the Bretton Woods system in the early 1970s. Interest differentials have become small once again since the disappearance of U.K. capital controls around 1980. The differentials appear even smaller now than they were before 1914.[7]

Indeed, for the 1870–1914 data we observe a tendency, quite systematic albeit declining over time, for New York sterling rates to exceed London rates. In arguing in favor of a sterling discount rate for valuing long sterling bills traded in the United States, Perkins (1978) demonstrated a tendency for the implicit offshore sterling interest rate $(e/b) - 1$ to converge toward Bank Rate toward the end of the nineteenth century (see his figure 2, p. 399). Our Figure 3.1, however, compares the New York offshore sterling interest rate with the London money-market rate of discount, which tended to be somewhat below Bank Rate. Were we to use Bank Rate as the London interest rate in the figure, much of the pre-1914 gap would be eliminated. Given that the U.S. data consist of prices of high-quality paper (such as bank bills), however, comparisons with Bank Rate are probably inappropriate. As Spalding (1915, 49) observes: "Bank Rate, as

---

[6] See Klug and Smith (1999) for a fascinating empirical study of the Suez crisis. The paper includes a discussion of daily covered arbitrage differentials during the crisis, from June 1, 1956, to January 31, 1957.

[7] We alert the reader to several potential problems with our calculations and data. First, as we have stressed already and indeed stressed quite clearly in Obstfeld and Taylor (1998), the two measures of market integration that we calculate refer to different arbitrage possibilities before and after 1920. Second, some forward transactions appear at different maturities in our data set. Third, most data are observed at or near the end of the month, but some data are averages of weekly numbers. Averaging has the effect of dampening measured volatility. Fourth, data from World War Two reflect rigidly administered prices and have no capital-mobility implications. Fifth, the data used are not closely aligned for time of day (and even differ as to day in some cases), so that some deviations from parity may be exaggerated. The purpose of the exercise, however, is merely to convey a broad sense of the trend in integration, not to pursue a detailed hunt for small arbitrage possibilities.

is well known, is usually higher than market rate; therefore if ordinary trade bills are remitted [to London] from [abroad], to find the long exchange, interest will be calculated at our Bank Rate, as trade paper is not considered such a good security as bank bills."[8] Officer (1996, 69) concurs, though on different grounds: "Whereas the Bank Rate was set by the Bank of England, the money-market rate was a true competitive price....The money-market rate of discount is the better measure..."

If it is impermissible to compare the sterling interest rate in New York with Bank Rate in London, how, then, can we explain the systematic positive interest gap in favor of New York before 1914? Much if not all of the gap can be explained as an artifact of the procedure we have used to extract the "offshore" interest rate from the observations on sight and time bill prices.

Continuing our focus on the New York-London comparison of sterling interest rates, we notice that the published money-market discount rate for London is quoted as a "pure" relative price of future in terms of present sterling. In contrast, as practitioners' textbooks of the period make amply clear, in determining the price to be paid for a long bill of exchange on London, purchasers would factor in not only the spot exchange rate and the London market discount rate, but, in addition, commissions, profit margins, and, importantly, the stamp duty (0.05 percent of the bill's face value) payable to the British government. These factors made bill prices lower than they would have been if they simply were equal to the spot exchange rate discounted by the pure New York sterling rate of interest.

Margraff (1908, 121) estimates that for a 90-day bill, the total of such factors amounted to 0.125 percent of face value. For a 60-day bill, that charge would represent about 75 basis points in annualized form; Escher (1918, 81–2), published a decade later, cites a very slightly smaller number. If we were to subtract that "tax" from the pre-1914 differentials plotted in the top of Figure 3.1, we would find that the apparent average excess return in New York would disappear.

Indeed, the implied average excess return becomes negative for 1890–1914, so that 75 basis points in additional costs may well be an overestimate for the entire prewar period. Suggestive of declining costs is the tendency shown in the figure for the average bias to decline over time. Perkins (1978, 400–1) argues that U.S. foreign exchange dealers of the period were able to exploit market power to inflate their commissions. Certainly such market power declined through 1914 as markets evolved, and Officer's (1996, 75) data on brokers'

---

[8] See also the summary table in Margraff (1908, 112).

commissions supports this view.[9] Of course, a process of market integration increases competition and drives commissions down. Thus, we would argue that, leaving aside the portion resulting from the stamp tax, the size of the New York-London discrepancy is to some degree a reflection of financial market segmentation, and its secular decline looks like evidence of a process of progressive integration.

The lower panel of Figure 3.1 shows the difference between the implicit mark interest rate in London and the one prevailing in Germany. Again, the now-familiar U-shaped pattern in the evolution of capital mobility is suggested over our entire sample period. Before 1914, the former, offshore, rate is calculated on the basis of 90-day prime bills of exchange on Berlin traded in London. The results are remarkably consistent with those for New York-London.

In particular, we again observe a systematic but secularly declining excess return in London prior to 1914. The explanation is essentially the same as in the preceding New York-London comparison. Germany levied a stamp duty on bills at the same rate as Britain's (0.05 percent; see Haupt 1894, 164, or Margraff 1908, 133). Margraff's estimates of concomitant costs suggest that for a 90-day bill on Berlin, about 40 basis points should be subtracted from the annualized sight bill premium $4 \times [(e/b) - 1]$ to ascertain the true London mark interest rate. On the assumption that some costs decline over time, with 40 basis points an average for the prewar period as whole, that cost adjustment brings the offshore and onshore mark rates roughly into line.[10]

Even though the cost and tax considerations we have described potentially eliminate the pre-1914 upward bias in our estimated series of offshore interest rates, other financial transaction costs would, as usual, create no-arbitrage bands around the point of offshore-onshore interest rate equality. One way to evaluate the evolution of capital mobility through time would be to estimate over different eras what Einzig (1937, 25) calls "transfer points" (i.e., the minimum return differential necessary to induce arbitrage operations). Keynes and Einzig agreed that during the interwar period, at least a 50 basis-point covered differential would be needed to induce arbitrage. That is, they suggested a no-arbitrage band of ±50 basis points. Applying nonlinear estimation techniques including a

---

[9] Country risk type arguments cannot easily rationalize the pre-1920 interest differential in favor of New York, as we pointed out in Obstfeld and Taylor (1998, 361, n. 6). The reason is that the two transactions we compare both entail future promised payments by agents located in the same place, London. This is not necessarily the case in the post-1920 covered interest arbitrage calculations.

[10] Flandreau and Rivière (1999) focus on a London-Paris comparison for 1900–14. Their results are entirely consistent with the patterns that we show in Figure 3.1, including a systematic excess of the London franc interest rate over that in Paris. Their rationale for the differential is apparently different from ours, although they do not include details of their derivation.

threshold autoregressive (TAR) methodology to weekly interwar data on dollar-sterling covered return differentials, Peel and Taylor (2002) confirm that a no-arbitrage band close to ±50 basis points did appear to prevail, as Keynes and Einzig claimed. Only outside of this range did arbitrage forces push spot and forward exchange rates toward conformity with the band.

A detailed investigation is beyond the scope of this chapter, but a first pass at the data using the TAR methodology of Obstfeld and Taylor (1997) is sugges-tive. For the dollar-sterling exchange between June 1925 and June 1931, we calculate a band of inaction of ±60 basis points, very close to the Peel-Taylor estimate given that we are using coarser, monthly data. For the corresponding interwar sterling-mark exchange our estimated band is ±91 basis points wide. On 1880–1914 differentials, in contrast, we find (after subtracting a constant mean differential) bands of only ±19 basis points for New York-London and ±35 basis points for London-Berlin.

Could such bands be considered large? By way of comparison, Clinton (1988) suggests that covered interest differentials in the mid-1980s needed to reach just ±6 basis points to become economically significant. Balke and Wohar (1998) produce an estimate 50 percent higher for the 1974–93 period. We suspect that a more careful analysis of pre-1914 differentials, one taking account of the upward trend in market integration, would reduce our estimated transaction cost bands for the early twentieth century.

Accordingly, the degree of integration among core money markets achieved under the classical gold standard must be judged as truly impressive compared to conditions over the following half century or more. The Great Depression, perhaps as part of a much broader interwar phase of disintegration, therefore stands out as an event that transformed the world capital market and left interest arbitrage differentials higher and more volatile than ever before.

The data in Figure 3.2 throw additional light on the recent progress of finan-cial integration in developed countries. For four industrial economies – France, Italy, the Netherlands, and Japan – the data show the difference between the three-month interbank interest rate (the onshore rate) and the three-month Lon-don Interbank Offered Rate measured in the same currency (the offshore rate). The three European economies show a high degree of recent convergence that intensifies markedly after the introduction of the single European currency in January 1999. This phenomenon is related to the creation of a centralized EU euro payments system. In Japan the convergence process is also apparent, but somewhat more uneven. Some discrepancies in the late 1990s are related to the troubled state of Japan's financial system.

Fig. 3.2. Onshore-offshore interest differentials

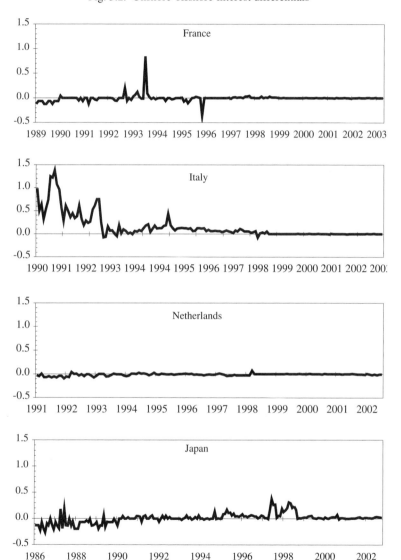

Notes and Sources: End-of-month annualized rates of accrual (in percent), onshore from Global Financial Data, offshore from Datastream. See text.

3.2 Real interest-rate convergence

A fundamental property of fully integrated international capital markets is that investors are indifferent on the margin between any two activities to which they allocate capital, regardless of national location. The international equality of national real interest rates holds in the long run in a world where capital moves freely across borders and technological diffusion tends to drive a rapid convergence process for national production possibilities.[11]

One basic indication of internationally integrated financial markets therefore might be the statistical stationarity of real long-term interest-rate differentials. We focus on real *long-term* bond yields because these are most directly related to financing costs for long-lived capital investments and, hence, to the expected marginal return on investment. It is the latter variable that we would like to be able to measure directly in order to evaluate the international mobility of capital based on deviations from the law of one price. In the absence of adequate data, however, we take an indirect route that focuses on real domestic borrowing costs. In examining long-term interest rates over more than a century, we are essentially restricted to instruments denominated in domestic currency, because for a number of subperiods, it is hard if not impossible to construct measures of exchange-risk free international return differences.[12]

For a bond rate i_t, we use the monthly Global Financial Data series on long-term government bond yields, which apply to bonds of maturities of 7 years or longer. In principle, inflation π_{t+1} should be the annualized percent rise in the price level over the term of the bond (although we use a different measure in practice, as detailed shortly). The ex post real interest rate is then calculated as $r_t = i_t - \pi_{t+1}$, and we make the standard assumption that this is equal to the ex ante real rate plus a white-noise stationary forecast error.

We consider three countries in our sample, relative to the United States as a base country. They are Britain, France, and Germany. We should note that the interest-rate series are as consistent as possible, given the changing types of domestic bonds issued by the various countries over the last century. Nonetheless, maturities do change at several points for some countries. A few exceptions, such as the British consol, have a continuous time series. In measuring long-term real interest rates, we would naturally like to proxy long-

---

[11] These preconditions promote long-run purchasing power parity as well as the equalization of returns measured in the same numeraire. (See Obstfeld and Rogoff 1996, chap. 4.) The result is the long-run equalization of returns measured in national consumption-index baskets.

[12] In recent data there is evidence that international real interest differentials for short-term bonds are statistically stationary, that is, $I(0)$; see, for example, Meese and Rogoff (1988) and Edison and Melick (1999). As we discuss below, however, the corresponding results for long-term rates have heretofore been less clear-cut.

term inflation expectations, but that cannot be done reliably. Thus, we follow earlier empirical studies in utilizing a relatively short-horizon inflation measure (the 12-month forward inflation rate), notwithstanding the longer term of the corresponding nominal interest rates.we also note that, prior to 1914, most countries have only annual price indices meaning that our derived inflation series will also consist of annual observations, the exceptions being the United States and Britain. For the other two countries, we construct monthly series of ex post real interest rates by matching monthly nominal interest rates within a year t with the realized inflation rate π_{t+1} between years $t + 1$ and t.

A simple decomposition of a country's domestic real interest differential versus the United States throws light on its underlying determinants. Let e_t denote the logarithm of the nominal exchange rate (domestic-currency price of foreign currency), f_t a (perhaps hypothetical) forward price of foreign currency applicable to the maturity date $t + n$ of the bonds in question, and $i_t^\$$ the (again, perhaps hypothetical) domestic long-term interest rate on U.S. dollar loans. Then we can express the ex ante n-period real interest differential vis-à-vis the United States as

$$
\begin{aligned}
\tilde{r}_t &= r_t - r_{\text{US},t} \\
&= \left(i_t^\$ - i_{\text{US},t}\right) + (f_t - \mathrm{E}_t e_{t+n}) \\
&\quad + \left(\mathrm{E}_t e_{t+n} - e_t + \mathrm{E}_t \pi_{\text{US},t+n} - \mathrm{E}_t \pi_{t+n}\right),
\end{aligned}
\tag{3.3}
$$

where the operator $\mathrm{E}_t\{\cdot\}$ maps variables to their date-t conditional expectations. (The ex post real interest differential is derived from this equation by subtracting the ex post forecast error for differential inflation.)

The first term in equation 3.3 is the offshore-onshore difference analyzed earlier in this chapter, a clear indicator of capital mobility. The second term is the currency risk premium, the discrepancy between the forward and expected future spot exchange rates. Although currency risk premia could, in principle, be quite large, their determinants remain controversial and our discussion will assume that at very long horizons, those premia are approximately zero. The last term above is the expected real depreciation rate of the domestic currency, defined as the expected deviation from (relative) purchasing power parity (PPP).[13] While PPP is, on its face, a concept about goods-market integration, its relevance for capital-market integration is defensible on theoretical grounds. Long-run PPP will hold if capital is mobile internationally and if there is a

---

[13] *Relative* PPP asserts that exchange rate changes exactly offset inflation differentials, whereas *absolute* PPP asserts that exchange-rate adjusted price levels are the same internationally. Use of relative PPP avoids the need for internationally comparable national price indices, a difficult challenge in long-run historical data. See Krugman and Obstfeld (2000, chap. 15).

tendency for technological convergence across countries, perhaps as a result of knowledge diffusion through international trade and investment. In addition, goods-market barriers can simultaneously promote financial insularity on several dimensions.[14]

The PPP term in equation 3.3 need not be near zero, of course; its presence indicates that it is not straightforward in general to map changes in goods-market integration into the behavior of real interest differentials. For example, a low degree of goods-market integration might be characterized by very slow mean reversion in real exchange rates, and thus small expected changes even over long horizons. Other things equal, ex ante real interest differentials will be smaller as a result. In contrast, more rapid mean reversion (a result, perhaps, of more effective international commodity arbitrage) could widen real interest differentials by augmenting the predictable component of the real exchange-rate movement. But this is not the end of the story. The size of real interest differentials also will depend on those of the initial shocks to the real exchange rate, which determine expected rates of real currency depreciation back toward long-run trend levels. Those shocks will tend to be larger when markets are less integrated, creating, ceteris paribus, larger international real interest differentials. It is nonetheless suggestive to examine the comovements in international real interest rates over different historical epochs. Even though the mapping from goods-market integration to real interest-rate differences is not necessarily monotonic, the real interest discrepancy does depend on capital-market barriers, and real interest-rate equality remains a useful benchmark for describing the polar case of perfect market integration.

The ex post real interest-rate differential $\tilde{r}_t = r_t - r_{\text{US},t}$ for each of our three countries is shown in Figure 3.3. This is the first time real interest rates over more than a century have been analyzed for this set of countries at such high frequency, so it is of interest to start by evaluating some general features of the data. The most striking impression conveyed by the figure is that differentials have varied widely over time but have stayed relatively close to a zero mean. That is, the series appear to the naked eye to have been statistically stationary over the very long run, and even in shorter subperiods.

Figure 3.3 also reveals some of the changing coherence of real interest rates in the subperiods. To avoid noisy data from nonmarket periods, the wartime years (1914–18, 1939–45) have been omitted, as has the German hyperinflation period (1919–23). Again we can focus on the four different subperiods that correspond to four different monetary regimes: the gold standard (1890–1914),

---

[14] Obstfeld and Rogoff (1996, chap. 4; 2000).

Fig. 3.3. Long-term real interest differentials

Britain–U.S.

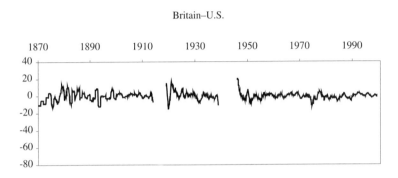

France–U.S.

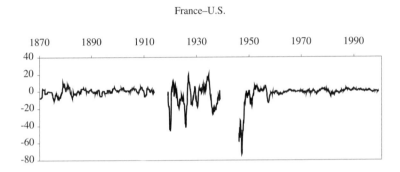

Germany–U.S

Notes: See text. The differential is in percent per annum relative to the U.S., $\tilde{r}_t = r_t - r_{US,t}$.

the interwar period (1921–38), Bretton Woods and the brief transitional period prior to generalized floating (1950–73), and the float (1974–2000).[15]

Allowing for the imperfect annual inflation data used before 1914, we can see that real interest differentials became somewhat more volatile in the interwar period, with a slightly higher variance (this is less obvious in the German case because the hyperinflation period has been omitted). There is a decline in this volatility after 1950, and perhaps very little change between the pre-1974 period and the float. The latter observation may seem surprising, but it is consistent with observations that, aside from nominal and real exchange-rate volatility, there is little difference in the behavior of macro fundamentals between the postwar fixed- and floating-rate regimes, at least for developed countries (Baxter and Stockman 1989). Overall, the evolution of variability in Figure 3.3 shows an understated version of the ∪-shape displayed by the indicators of capital mobility examined earlier.

With no real interest rate divergence apparent, these figures provide prima facie evidence that real interest rates in developed countries have been cointegrated over time, and specifically that the differentials between countries are stationary. A formal test of this hypothesis appears in Table 3.1, where we apply two stationarity tests to the data for the period as a whole, as well as in various subperiods. The first test is the traditional augmented Dickey-Fuller (ADF) unit root test, and the second is a Dickey-Fuller Generalized Least Squares (DF-GLS) test, one of a family of enhanced point-optimal and asymptotically efficient unit root tests recently proposed.[16] This table also reports a broader set of tests over the recent float, applied to an expanded sample including the G7 plus the Netherlands, for comparison with the contemporary literature.

Where the null of nonstationarity is rejected at the 1 percent level, the results show conclusively that the real interest differential has no unit root over the long run. Changes in the variances of series over time, of the kind evident in the preceding charts, may distort unit root tests (Hamori and Tokihisa 1997). However, the hypothesis of a unit root can be rejected in almost all cases at the 1 percent level in all periods except for the recent float. With respect to the recent float, the evidence against a unit root is stronger over the second subperiod (1986–2000) than over the first (1974–86). Over the entire floating-rate period, we always reject nonstationarity at the 10 percent level or better. These findings

---

[15] For the purpose of the present empirical analysis, we begin our floating rate period in early 1974 to be consistent with other empirical literature on the real interest rate-real exchange rate nexus. However, most historians would place the end of the Bretton Woods system in August 1971, the month President Richard Nixon shut the U.S. official gold window.

[16] See Elliott, Rothenberg, and Stock (1996) and Elliott (1999). We use the latter's DF-GLS test, to allow the initial observation to be drawn from the unconditional mean of the series.

Table 3.1. *Stationarity tests: Long-term real interest differentials*

		ADF	DF-GLS
(a) Historical Epochs			
GBR	1890:1 2000:7	−4.30***	−5.54***
FRA	1890:1 2000:7	−6.05***	−6.36***
DEU	1890:1 2000:7	−4.64***	−5.14***
GBR	1890:1 1913:12	−1.38	−3.44***
FRA	1890:1 1913:12	−3.18**	−4.36***
DEU	1890:1 1913:12	−3.86***	−3.70***
GBR	1921:1 1938:12	−3.59***	−4.01***
FRA	1921:1 1938:12	−2.39	−4.31***
DEU	1921:1 1938:12	−2.42	−2.84**
GBR	1951:1 1973:2	−5.09***	−5.37***
FRA	1951:1 1973:2	−3.81***	−3.34***
DEU	1951:1 1973:2	−3.32**	−3.51***
(b) Recent Float			
GBR	1974:2 2000:8	−2.42	−3.75***
NLD	1974:2 2000:8	−2.75*	−2.57*
FRA	1974:2 2000:8	−2.70*	−2.52*
DEU	1974:2 2000:8	−2.82*	−2.73*
ITA	1974:2 2000:8	−2.52	−2.87**
JPN	1974:2 2000:8	−2.20	−2.52*
CAN	1974:2 2000:8	−3.71***	−3.15**
(c) Recent Float – Early			
GBR	1974:2 1986:3	−2.61*	−2.82**
NLD	1974:2 1986:3	−1.28	−1.19
FRA	1974:2 1986:3	−2.21	−1.77
DEU	1974:2 1986:3	−1.77	−1.64
ITA	1974:2 1986:3	−2.56	−2.89**
JPN	1974:2 1986:3	−1.50	−1.72
CAN	1974:2 1986:3	−1.92	−1.93
(d) Recent Float – Late			
GBR	1986:4 2000:7	−2.01	−2.62*
NLD	1986:4 2000:7	−2.61*	−2.37
FRA	1986:4 2000:7	−2.25	−2.50*
DEU	1986:4 2000:7	−3.34**	−2.83**
ITA	1986:4 2000:7	−2.54	−2.55*
JPN	1986:4 2000:7	−2.43	−2.55*
CAN	1986:4 2000:7	−0.86	−2.28

Notes: See text. ADF is the Augmented Dickey Fuller *t*-statistic. DF-GLS is the test of Elliott (1999). *** denotes significance at the 1 % level; ** at the 5 % level; * at the 10 % level. The critical values are, respectively, $(-3.43, -2.86, -2.57)$ for the ADF test and $(-3.28, -2.73, -2.46)$ for the DF-GLSu test. Lag selection was via the LM criterion with a maximum of 12 lags.

refer to the more powerful DF-GLS test, which rejects the null more frequently than the standard ADF test. It is noteworthy that British, French, and German real-interest differentials against the United States appear stationary even for the interwar sample. We found above that for short-term securities, exchange-risk-free arbitrage between national capital markets broke down dramatically in that period.

The finding of a stationary long-term real interest differential, especially insofar as it applies to the recent period of floating industrial-country exchange rates, contradicts much of the empirical literature produced through the mid-1990s. Why do we find more evidence of stationarity than earlier researchers, such as Meese and Rogoff (1988) and Edison and Pauls (1993)? We note that previous authors had shorter samples and used tests of relatively low power, such as the ADF test.

Indeed, our data and methods are consistent with earlier findings. If we switch to the Meese-Rogoff sample of February 1974 to March 1986 and use the ADF test as they did, then we replicate their conclusions exactly (as shown in the penultimate panel of the table). Even if we switch to the DF-GLS test on the same data, we can reject the null in only 2 out of 7 cases. The results for the post-1986 sample show similar problems, even though for the post-1974 period as a whole we can reject the null, as we have observed.[17] These findings, which are supportive of stationarity in recent long-term real interest differentials, are consistent with another strand in the literature that finds support for international real interest-rate equalization at longer horizons (Fujii and Chinn 2000). We conclude that earlier analyses of recent data were hampered by the low power of standard unit root tests on samples of small span.[18]

---

[17] Edison and Melick (1999, 97) find mixed results on the stationarity of Canadian, German, and Japanese long-term real interest differentials against the United States but, nonetheless, base their econometric analysis of real interest parity on the assumption that all real interest differentials are stationary.

[18] A related literature examines directly the validity of long-term real interest parity – in essence, equation 3.3 with the risk-premium term set to zero. A focus on long-term real rather than nominal interest rate parity seems is of considerable interest because with mean reverting real exchange rates, it is easier to proxy long-run expected real exchange rates than the corresponding nominal exchange rates. Meese and Rogoff (1988) rejected a version of real interest parity based on the maintained assumption of an underlying sticky-price exchange rate model. More supportive is the recent long-run panel cointegration study by MacDonald and Nagayasu (2000) of 14 OECD countries relative to the United States. The statistical methodology of that work, however, assumes that long-term real interest differentials are nonstationary. Chortareas and Driver (2001) implement a similar approach using a 17-country panel of OECD countries versus the United States; their conclusions are similar to those of MacDonald and Nagayasu. Chortareas and Driver report mixed results for tests on the stationarity of long-term real interest differentials. One issue pervading all of the work in this area is the effect of alternative proxies for long-term inflation expectations. The proxies that are chosen often differ across authors, affecting some results. A systematic discussion of these differences lies beyond the scope of this chapter.

That international real-interest differentials appear consistently stationary, even over the turbulent interwar period, calls for further reflection given other indications of capital-market disintegration after World War One. Certainly, for a fixed set of impediments to international capital movement, long-term interest rates will display greater coherence than short-term rates such as were analyzed in this chapter's first section. A large part of the action, however, probably resides in the last term of equation 3.3, the expected departure from relative PPP. Motivated by the temporal behavior of real interest-rate differences, but also by the intrinsic interest of the subject, the next section studies the historical behavior of real exchange rates.

3.3 Purchasing power parity

As we have noted, purchasing power parity (PPP) remains a problematic concept for studies of capital-market integration. At first sight, it appears as essentially a reflection of goods-market arbitrage.[19] Though critics have worried about this problem, the concern may be misplaced, especially in the longer run. The important distinction here is between the general *absolute* price level and the structure of *relative* prices: aggregate PPP is a concept based on *absolute* prices. PPP is therefore distinct from the Law of One Price (LOOP) concept applied to individual commodities, and, more properly in the domain of monetary economics and the macroeconomic theory of price-level inflation.

On historical grounds, we would rapidly arrive the same conclusion. Advancing the idea of PPP in 1922, Cassel was motivated by a desire to understand the dynamics and behavior of exchange rates and prices following the vast dispersion in national price levels driven by wartime inflations in the various belligerent countries. Adjusting exchange rates to be consistent with PPP, so as to reinstate the gold standard credibly, was seen as a macroeconomic problem requiring monetary adjustments, notably stringent deflations in countries that had monetized fiscal gaps extensively in order to finance the war. In the interim, convertibility and disequilibrium exchange rates were sustainable only with strict exchange and capital controls that appeared in the war. These controls subsequently subsided through the 1920s but rose to unprecedented heights in the 1930s and persisted into the 1960s and beyond under the Bretton Woods system. Viewed in such terms, the historical success or failure of PPP can be seen as intimately tied to the mobility of global financial capital in the

his section draws heavily on Taylor (2002b).

course of the twentieth century.[20] And, as we have also noted, there are solid theoretical underpinnings linking PPP to aspects of capital-market integration.

From an historical standpoint, numerous studies of (relative) PPP exist for various countries over the period in question, some covering a particular era or monetary regime. McCloskey and Zecher (1984) argued that PPP worked very well under the Anglo-American gold standard before 1914. Diebold, Husted, and Rush (1991) explored a very long run of nineteenth-century data for six countries and found support for PPP based on the low-frequency information lacking in short-sample studies. Abuaf and Jorion (1990) found that a century of dollar-franc-sterling exchange rate data upheld PPP; Lothian and Taylor (1996) found the same for *two* centuries of dollar-franc-sterling data. Lothian (1990) also found evidence that real exchange rates were stationary for Japan, the United States, the United Kingdom, and France for the period 1875–1986, although yen exchange rates exhibited only trend-stationarity – an oft-repeated finding that the real yen exchange rate has appreciated over the long run against all currencies. In full-length monographs, both Lee (1978) and Officer (1982) found strong evidence in favor of PPP based on analysis of long time-series running from the pre-1914 gold standard period to the managed floating regime of the 1970s.[21]

Of late, new studies have appeared in abundance. In their comprehensive review of the PPP literature, Froot and Rogoff (1995) could declare that what was a "fairly dull research topic" only a decade ago has recently been the focus of substantial controversy and the subject of a growing body of literature. Recent empirical research, mostly based on the time-series analysis of short spans of data for the floating-rate (post–Bretton Woods) era, led many to conclude that relative PPP failed to hold, and that the real exchange rate followed a random walk with no mean reversion. However, a newly emerging literature exploits more data and higher-powered techniques and claims that, in the long run, PPP does indeed hold: it appears from these studies that real exchange rates exhibit mean reversion with a half-life of deviations of three to five years (M. P. Taylor 1995; Froot and Rogoff 1995; Obstfeld and Rogoff 2000).

Some of the newer findings have taken various steps to expand the size of samples used to test PPP and hence increase the power of the statistical tests used. As noted, it has been possible to use much longer-run time series for

[20] For the original work, see Cassel (1922). On adjustments in the 1920s, see Kindleberger (1986) and Eichengreen (1992). We discussed the long-run evolution of capital controls in Obstfeld and Taylor (1998), and we cover this subject in Chapter 4.

[21] Obviously, this section builds on a very strong foundation of historical work by a number of scholars, covering various countries in different time periods. Other studies of long-run data are numerous (Frankel 1986; Edison 1987; Johnson 1990; Kim 1990; Glen 1992).

certain individual countries, spanning a century or more; typically such exercises have concentrated on more-developed countries with good historical data availability (e.g., the United States, the United Kingdom, France). Alternatively, researchers have expanded the data for the recent float or postwar periods cross-sectionally to exploit the additional information in panel data (Pedroni 1995; Wei and Parsley 1995; Frankel and Rose 1996; Higgins and Zakrajšek 1999).

It is still too early to say whether the revisionist PPP findings will prove robust, and already challenges to this interpretation have emerged. One may find fault with the ways in which cross-sectional information and panel methodologies have been applied (O'Connell 1996; 1998). Some have noted that the inferences based on panel methods are sensitive to sample selection, and many results appear sensitive to the choice of base country, for example, the United States versus Germany (Edison, Gagnon, and Melick 1994; Wei and Parsley 1995; Papell 1997). Others caution that detecting a unit root in time series may be complicated by the fact that price indices can be viewed as the sum of a stationary tradable relative-price component and a nonstationary nontradable relative-price component (Ng and Perron 1999; Engel 2000). This finding echoes the classic Balassa-Samuelson amendment to pure PPP based on differential rates of productivity growth in traded and nontraded goods sectors (Balassa 1964; Samuelson 1964). Of course, such long-run trends may be purely deterministic (Obstfeld 1993a).

We should note that, given the differences in the definitions of national price indexes, the persistence of PPP deviations will reflect not only adjustment in goods markets, but also, the nature and mix of the stochastic shocks to the economy. Given the imperfect data available, the speed at which PPP is restored is itself an imperfect indicator of goods-market integration.

Below we model the dynamics of real exchange rates at different times in the twentieth century. Four epochs are investigated, the gold standard (1870–1914), the interwar period (1914–45), the Bretton-Woods period (now taken to be 1946–71), and the recent float (1972–96). The most important quantitative differences found are in residual variance. The floating regimes exhibit much larger shocks to real exchange rates, which, in turn, account for the much larger deviations from PPP during those eras. However, the history of PPP in the twentieth century reveals a surprisingly small trend decrease in the estimated half-lives of (log) real exchange rate shocks.

We argue that these findings have a natural interpretation and that the changes over time in shock variances reveal a great deal about the differing degrees to which monetary policy was kept in check by commitment mechanisms (under fixed rates) or their absence (under floating rates). We relate these findings to our previous results on international real-interest differentials, and revisit implications of exchange-rate regime choice under the constraints imposed by the macroeconomic policy trilemma.

3.3.1 Data and preliminary analysis

The data consist of annual exchange rates E_{it}, measured as domestic currency units per U.S. dollar, and domestic-currency price indices P_{it}^*, measured as consumer price deflators – or, when they are not available, GDP deflators. We will refer to the log levels of these variables, denoted $e_{it} = \log E_{it}$ and $p_{it}^* = \log P_{it}^*$. The index $i = 1, \ldots, 20$ covers the set of countries Argentina, Australia, Belgium, Brazil, Canada, Denmark, Finland, France, Germany, Italy, Japan, Mexico, the Netherlands, Norway, Portugal, Spain, Sweden, Switzerland, the United Kingdom, and the United States. The index t runs over the set of years from 1850 to 1996, but a complete cross section of 20 exchange rates does not exist before 1892, the starting date of the Swiss series.[22]

Given these data, some preliminary transformations and tests were performed. Let the U.S. dollar-denominated price level of country i at time t be denoted by $P_{it} = P_{it}^*/E_{it}$, with $p_{it} = \log P_{it} = p_{it}^* - e_{it}$. As an initial step, missing data were filled in for each series. In all cases, this amounted to imputing a value to a few wartime years for certain countries, using linear interpolation on p_{it}. This process yielded a balanced panel of data for 20 countries and 105 years from 1892 to 1996.

Such an interpolation procedure is certainly ad hoc, but it was deemed necessary to give any stationarity test a fair chance on these data, since, in several cases, the missing data appear after explosive inflations during which the real exchange rate often depreciated. Without interpolation in these periods, any subsequent reversion back toward the mean (or trend) in this variable would be missed by any estimation procedure, and a bias against stationarity would result. An important example would be the wide divergence in real exchange rates in the 1930s following the collapse of the gold standard; this episode was followed by war, leading to many missing observations in the data. Thus, much of the reversion of these divergent real exchange rates toward PPP during and

[22] In constructing the data set we have relied on standard sources. After 1948, the series are taken from the IMF's *International Financial Statistics* on CD-ROM. The principal pre-1948 price sources are the statistical volumes of Brian Mitchell. For providing us with electronically compiled price and exchange rate data from these and other sources, we are grateful to Michael Bordo. An appendix containing the data and full documentation is available from the authors upon request.

after the war would be omitted from the sample if we just used the raw data without any interpolation.

With interpolations complete, the real exchange rate series was generated two ways: first, relative to the U.S. dollar, as $q_{it} = p_{it} - p_{US,t}$; and second, relative to the "rest of world" ($N - 1 = 19$) basket of currencies, as $q_{it}^W = p_{it} - p_{it}^W$, where $p_{it}^W = \frac{1}{N-1} \sum_{j \neq i} p_{jt}$.[23] The second definition follows O'Connell (1996) and may help us avoid problems associated with the choice of the United States as a base country.[24]

The complete series q_{it} and q_{it}^W for all 20 countries are shown in Figure 3.4, where the scale differs by country. One way to test whether the real exchange rates display a tendency toward PPP over time is to ask: are these real exchange rates stationary, that is, mean-reverting? A cursory inspection suggests that for many countries real exchange rates have been fairly stable over the long run, and we might expect to support the hypothesis of stationarity easily. Nonetheless, our eyes are drawn to certain cases where there appears to be a long-run trend or random walk. Here, the most obvious and well-known problem would be the case of Japan, but similar symptoms of drift or nonstationarity might also be perceived for Switzerland, Brazil, and in some other countries' experience in specific periods, such as interwar Germany and Italy.

The most powerful univariate unit root tests available at present are the DF-GLS tests that we applied earlier in this chapter. The tests are of broad applicability because they apply to cases where the series have (i) no trend, (ii) a deterministic constant term $d_t = (1)$, and (iii) a deterministic constant term and drift $d_t = (1, t)$. We are, as always, working with index numbers in PPP tests, and we also might want to allow for possible deterministic trends in the spirit of Balassa-Samuelson. Thus, the DF-GLS test is very relevant to the problem at hand.

In the DF-GLS test, the series z_t to be tested is replaced in the ADF regression by $\tilde{z}_t = z_t - \hat{\beta}' d_t$, where $\hat{\beta}'$ is a GLS estimate of the coefficients on the deterministic trends d_t. That the DF-GLS test dominates others is shown via a local-to-unity asymptotic approach, and the power envelope is close to the frontier. The unit-root PPP controversy hangs on being able to pin down an autoregressive parameter ρ that is less than, but often very close to, unity. Hence, the DF-GLS test is an ideal tool for PPP testing.[25]

---

[23] Ideally, one might prefer to use trade-weighted real exchange rates, but such data do not exist in the form of annual time series for the entire twentieth century for a wide sample of countries. Future research would need to be directed to original sources to collate the necessary bilateral trade volumes, and this would be a significant undertaking.

[24] This discussion was omitted in O'Connell (1998).

[25] The DF-GLS test gives support for PPP in the post–Bretton Woods era (Cheung and Lai 1998).

Globalization in capital markets: Price evidence

Fig. 3.4. A century of real exchange rates

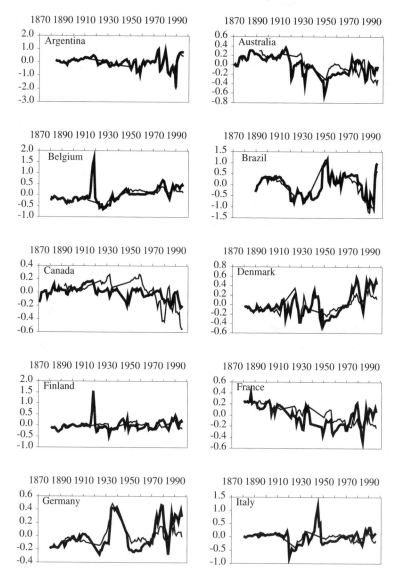

Figure 3.4 (continued)

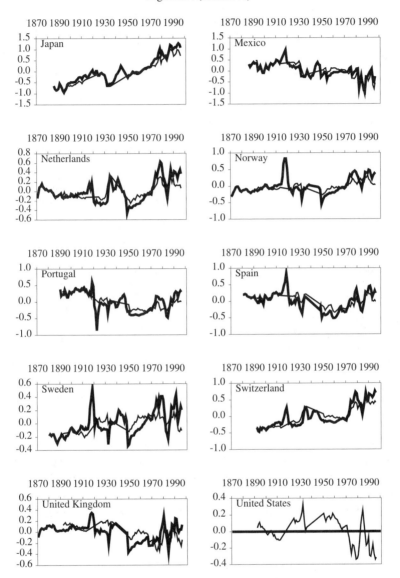

Notes and Sources: See text, appendix, and Taylor (2002b). The thicker line shows q_{it}, the real exchange rate relative to the U.S. dollar. The thinner line shows q_{it}^{W}, the real exchange rate relative to the "rest of world" ($N - 1 = 19$) basket of currencies. Note that the scale differs across countries.

Table 3.2. *Stationarity tests: Real exchange rates*

	Base: United States		Base: "Rest of world" basket	
	Demeaned	Detrended	Demeaned	Detrended
Argentina	−4.58***	−4.79***	−5.22***	−5.20***
Australia	−2.44**	−2.69**	−1.17	−3.49***
Belgium	−2.80***	−3.88***	−3.06***	−4.09***
Brazil	−2.46**	−2.73**	−2.35**	−2.35*
Canada	−1.61*	−1.93	−1.10	−2.13
Denmark	−2.13**	−2.69*	−2.84***	−3.23**
Finland	−4.42***	−4.67***	−4.71***	−4.72***
France	−2.25**	−4.06***	−1.58*	−3.98***
Germany	−2.59***	−3.31***	−1.75*	−1.83
Italy	−3.28***	−3.29***	−3.01***	−3.18**
Japan	0.66	−1.86	0.37	−2.37*
Mexico	−2.48**	−3.92***	−1.91**	−4.29***
Netherlands	−1.70*	−2.32	−1.98**	−2.51*
Norway	−1.43	−2.52*	−2.16**	−2.50*
Portugal	−1.85*	−2.41*	−2.05**	−3.74***
Spain	−2.07**	−2.28	−1.95**	−2.28
Sweden	−2.18**	−3.47***	−1.81*	−2.49*
Switzerland	−1.24	−3.44***	−0.27	−2.66**
United Kingdom	−2.82***	−2.99**	−1.70*	−2.81**
United States	—	—	−2.29**	−2.60*

Notes and Sources: See Taylor (2002b). The lag length is selected by the LM criterion. Demeaned is the case where each series is replaced by the residuals from a regression on a constant. Detrended is the case where the regression is on a constant and a linear time trend. Finite-sample critical values are shown based on 4, 000 simulations of the null. * denotes significance at the 10% level; ** denotes significance at the 5% level; *** denotes significance at the 1% level. The critical values corresponding to these significance levels are (−1.62, −1.95, −2.58) for the demeaned series and (−2.57, −2.89, −3.48) for the detrended series, respectively. See Elliott et al. (1996).

Table 3.2 shows the results of applying the DF-GLS tests to our real exchange-rate data. Four cases are considered: using the United States and the "rest of world" basket as a base; and using the series demeaned and detrended. These results offer quite powerful support for the long-run PPP hypothesis in the twentieth century. In all but a few cases, without detrending the null of a unit root is rejected; in those cases, inclusion of a trend is enough to find support for mean reversion (except for Japan with a U.S. base). Hence, with some allowance for the possibility of slowly evolving trends, we conclude that relative PPP has held in the long run for our sample of 20 countries.[26]

---

[26] It would be desirable to follow up this study with tests based on higher-frequency data. Still, that we can find evidence in favor of PPP with annual series is very encouraging, given the biases introduced by temporal averaging in historical data (Taylor 2001). For additional evidence on the stationarity of the long-run series see the discussion in Taylor (2002b) of the conventional ADF test and the multivariate Johansen test proposed by Taylor and Sarno (1998).

If PPP holds in the long run, it may not be productive to devote further attention to the stationarity question. Perhaps a more important and interesting problem is to explain what drives the short-run dynamics of real exchange rates.[27] That is, how do we account for the amplitude and persistence of PPP deviations, in different time periods and in different countries in the last century?

3.3.2 An overview of PPP in the twentieth century

In this section, given the earlier findings, deviations from PPP will be measured relative to the equilibrium real exchange rate. As we have seen, it is often necessary to allow for deterministic trends. As an empirical matter, they are usually found to be "small." However, their omission would undoubtedly upset any study of the deviations of real exchange rates over the very long run.[28] Accordingly, we will, for the remainder of this section, consider the dynamics of detrended real exchange rates in an attempt to measure the reversion speed toward equilibrium.

The first question to ask is: what has been the extent of deviations from PPP over the long run? One way to answer this question is to examine volatility via the size of changes in the real exchange rate Δq_{it}, since, according to a mean-reversion theory, this change would be proportional to the deviation from equilibrium plus some error. Another approach would be to detrend the series q_{it} and examine the deviations of the resulting detrended level q_{it}, that is, the error-correction term. For a cross section of countries, the extent of these deviations at a given time t can be measured by the corresponding standard deviations $\sigma(\Delta q_{it})$ and $\sigma(q_{it})$.

Figure 3.5 shows these two measures for our entire sample and both exhibit similar behavior over time. Real exchange-rate deviations and volatility were relatively small prior to 1914 under the classical gold-standard regime, as expected. The interwar period was a major turning point; deviations became much larger as many exchange rates began to float or stay fixed for only a few years. There was some reduction in deviations after 1945, notably during the heyday of Bretton Woods during the 1960s. Once the floating-rate era began in the 1970s, deviations and volatility once again rose. This chronology offers some prima facie reasons to view changes in the exchange-rate regime as a major determinant of real exchange-rate behavior.

[27] The same conclusion was reached by Higgins and Zakrajšek (1999).
[28] A trend of, say, 0.5% per annum might make little difference over a 1- to 10-year horizon, but over 100 years, if such a correction were left out, then log deviations from equilibrium could be mismeasured by an additive shift of 0.5, or in levels by a multiplicative shift of 65%.

Fig. 3.5. Real exchange-rate volatility and deviations from trend

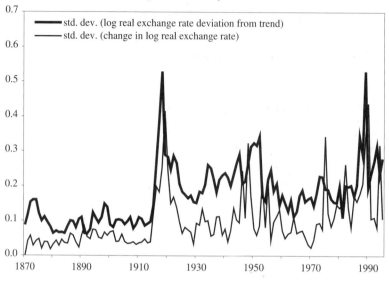

Notes and Sources: See text, appendix, and Taylor (2002b).

Although we can now see from the data where and when deviations have been large or small, we would like to know why they were large or small at particular times. In an autoregressive model, any changes in the properties of the deviations can only be attributed to two essential causes: either the dynamic process is subject to (stochastic) shocks of different amplitude; or else the process itself exhibits different patterns of (deterministic) persistence. To investigate this more fully, then, we need to apply and estimate a model. Given that we are taking trend stationarity as given, based on earlier findings, Table 3.3 reports the results of fitting an error-correction model to the detrended U.S.-based real exchange rate q_{it}, with a specification

$$\Delta q_{it} = \beta_0 q_{it} + \beta_1 \Delta q_{i,t-1} + \beta_2 \Delta q_{i,t-2} + \epsilon_t. \tag{3.4}$$

The coefficients β_1 and β_2 are not reported; columns labeled i and t indicate the samples, including pooled samples (P) across both countries and time periods; periods correspond to the exchange rate regimes, Gold Standard (G), Interwar (I), Bretton Woods (B), and Float (F); half-lives in years are reported (H); and

Table 3.3. *A model of real exchange rates*

i	t	β_0	s.e.	R^2	T	H	p_1	p_2
P	P	−0.21	(0.01)	.11	2,293	3.4	.00	.00
P	G	−0.21	(0.03)	.13	633	3.1		.01
P	I	−0.24	(0.03)	.20	640	3.1		.88
P	B	−0.43	(0.03)	.28	520	1.5		.63
P	F	−0.41	(0.04)	.19	500	2.1		.99
ARG	P	−0.47	(0.10)	.20	110	1.5	.96	
ARG	G	−0.09	(0.12)	.09	27	6.0		
ARG	I	−0.18	(0.10)	.14	32	4.1		
ARG	B	−0.47	(0.20)	.22	26	1.4		
ARG	F	−0.59	(0.24)	.24	25	1.2		
AUS	P	−0.18	(0.05)	.11	124	4.7	.15	
AUS	G	−0.19	(0.07)	.30	41	5.2		
AUS	I	−0.34	(0.13)	.20	32	2.3		
AUS	B	−0.23	(0.13)	.14	26	4.0		
AUS	F	−0.53	(0.18)	.32	25	1.6		
BEL	P	−0.30	(0.07)	.21	114	2.6	1.00	
BEL	G	−0.31	(0.14)	.16	31	2.3		
BEL	I	−0.31	(0.14)	.21	32	2.5		
BEL	B	−0.29	(0.10)	.39	26	2.1		
BEL	F	−0.34	(0.13)	.39	25	3.0		
BRA	P	−0.13	(0.06)	.07	105	4.8	.37	
BRA	G	−0.46	(0.14)	.38	22	2.0		
BRA	I	−0.27	(0.10)	.24	32	2.4		
BRA	B	−0.48	(0.18)	.28	26	1.2		
BRA	F	−0.22	(0.17)	.10	25	3.9		
CAN	P	−0.20	(0.06)	.10	124	3.4	.20	
CAN	G	−0.10	(0.10)	.05	41	3.2		
CAN	I	−0.19	(0.11)	.22	32	3.3		
CAN	B	−0.25	(0.15)	.19	26	2.2		
CAN	F	−0.35	(0.13)	.33	25	5.0		
DNK	P	−0.15	(0.05)	.10	114	4.9	.00	
DNK	G	−0.60	(0.19)	.38	31	1.5		
DNK	I	−0.36	(0.14)	.28	32	2.2		
DNK	B	−0.55	(0.18)	.35	26	0.8		
DNK	F	−0.38	(0.14)	.35	25	2.4		
FIN	P	−0.39	(0.08)	.28	113	1.8	.21	
FIN	G	−0.21	(0.11)	.25	30	4.3		
FIN	I	−0.40	(0.16)	.35	32	1.8		
FIN	B	−0.57	(0.22)	.51	26	0.5		
FIN	F	−0.41	(0.14)	.38	25	2.0		
FRA	P	−0.22	(0.06)	.17	114	3.3	.03	
FRA	G	−0.51	(0.23)	.27	31	0.9		
FRA	I	−0.44	(0.15)	.33	32	1.7		
FRA	B	−0.64	(0.20)	.34	26	1.3		
FRA	F	−0.36	(0.14)	.35	25	2.4		

Table 3.3 (continued)

i	t	β_0	s.e.	R^2	T	H	p_1	p_2
GER	P	−0.10	(0.04)	.23	114	6.8	.13	
GER	G	−0.19	(0.12)	.16	31	3.5		
GER	I	−0.06	(0.05)	.31	32	16.0		
GER	B	−0.23	(0.06)	.56	26	2.3		
GER	F	−0.36	(0.15)	.33	25	2.2		
ITA	P	−0.25	(0.06)	.15	114	3.6	.00	
ITA	G	−0.36	(0.15)	.28	31	1.9		
ITA	I	0.00	(0.14)	.09	32	−21.8		
ITA	B	−0.54	(0.06)	.81	26	1.0		
ITA	F	−0.32	(0.16)	.38	25	2.3		
JPN	P	−0.09	(0.04)	.15	109	9.3	.07	
JPN	G	−0.27	(0.14)	.26	26	2.9		
JPN	I	−0.08	(0.06)	.29	32	8.9		
JPN	B	−0.25	(0.11)	.69	26	1.6		
JPN	F	−0.35	(0.15)	.23	25	1.8		
MEX	P	−0.25	(0.07)	.15	108	2.4	.47	
MEX	G	−0.09	(0.14)	.31	25	3.6		
MEX	I	−0.15	(0.09)	.16	32	6.2		
MEX	B	−0.45	(0.17)	.25	26	1.6		
MEX	F	−0.45	(0.23)	.27	25	1.1		
NLD	P	−0.11	(0.04)	.13	124	7.8	.09	
NLD	G	−0.12	(0.06)	.13	41	6.8		
NLD	I	−0.23	(0.11)	.21	32	3.8		
NLD	B	−0.21	(0.13)	.13	26	3.2		
NLD	F	−0.37	(0.14)	.37	25	2.1		
NOR	P	−0.15	(0.04)	.20	124	6.2	.08	
NOR	G	−0.31	(0.09)	.39	41	2.7		
NOR	I	−0.20	(0.09)	.36	32	4.8		
NOR	B	−0.35	(0.16)	.18	26	2.0		
NOR	F	−0.42	(0.14)	.34	25	2.0		
PRT	P	−0.17	(0.06)	.10	104	5.2	.05	
PRT	G	−0.13	(0.14)	.11	21	3.0		
PRT	I	−0.48	(0.16)	.25	32	1.7		
PRT	B	−0.18	(0.07)	.50	26	3.3		
PRT	F	−0.17	(0.11)	.32	25	5.2		
SPA	P	−0.13	(0.04)	.15	114	7.1	.01	
SPA	G	−0.21	(0.14)	.10	31	3.0		
SPA	I	−0.27	(0.11)	.30	32	3.5		
SPA	B	−0.41	(0.15)	.29	26	1.3		
SPA	F	−0.22	(0.10)	.48	25	2.8		
SWE	P	−0.23	(0.06)	.19	114	3.3	.82	
SWE	G	−0.30	(0.12)	.31	31	2.9		
SWE	I	−0.28	(0.14)	.21	32	2.4		
SWE	B	−0.27	(0.15)	.21	26	2.3		
SWE	F	−0.37	(0.15)	.29	25	2.6		

Table 3.3 (continued)

i	*t*	β_0	s.e.	R^2	*T*	*H*	p_1	p_2
SWI	P	–0.13	(0.05)	.21	102	5.0	.04	
SWI	G	–0.38	(0.24)	.45	19	0.7		
SWI	I	–0.29	(0.12)	.37	32	3.1		
SWI	B	–0.28	(0.06)	.60	26	2.1		
SWI	F	–0.36	(0.14)	.34	25	1.7		
UKG	P	–0.20	(0.06)	.10	124	3.6	.10	
UKG	G	–0.22	(0.10)	.14	41	1.9		
UKG	I	–0.27	(0.14)	.21	32	2.6		
UKG	B	–0.42	(0.13)	.35	26	1.5		
UKG	F	–0.42	(0.19)	.20	25	1.7		

Notes and Sources: See text, appendix, and Taylor (2002b). The country abbreviations are: ARG Argentina; AUS Australia; BEL Belgium; BRA Brazil; CAN Canada; DNK Denmark; FIN Finland; FRA France; GER Germany; ITA Italy; JPN Japan; MEX Mexico; NLD the Netherlands; NOR Norway; PRT Portugal; SPA Spain; SWE Sweden; SWI Switzerland; UKG United Kingdom. Samples are P Pooled; G Gold Standard; I Interwar; B Bretton Woods; F Float.

significance levels are reported for tests of pooling across periods (p_1) and across countries (p_2).[29]

Note that these results are often for very short spans of data, so we are not using the coefficient β_0 as a basis for a stationarity test. Rather, we now have a maintained hypothesis of long-run trend stationarity based on the earlier tests. The pooling restrictions are not always rejected, but they are rejected sufficiently often that is seems safest to treat this as a heterogeneous panel and to examine the nature of the dynamics in different periods and countries. This is pursued in Table 3.4, by focusing on the two key features – one random, one not – that generate PPP deviations: the half-life of disturbances in years, which is calculated from the estimated model via (deterministic) forecast, and the variance of the (stochastic) error disturbances, $SEE = \sigma_\epsilon$.[30]

The striking aspect of these results is the relatively small variation in half-lives across the four exchange-rate regimes, especially for the median figures. There are notable exceptions. One is Italy in the interwar period, where the estimated root is explosive on this restricted sample; also, interwar Germany has slow reversion, which may not be surprising given the aftermath of hyperinflation in the 1920s and the extensive controls on the economy in the 1930s (see

[29] The lag choice $k = 2$ was sufficient based on LM tests in all cases except the cross-country pooled samples. A uniform lag structure was imposed to facilitate pooling tests.

[30] For a simple motivation of this rough division of sources of deviations, consider an AR(1) process for the real exchange rate, $q_t = \rho q_{t-1} + \epsilon_t$. The unconditional variance of q_t is $\text{Var}(q) = \sigma_\epsilon^2/(1 - \rho^2)$. The half-life is a simple function if the autoregressive parameter, $H = \log 0.5/ \log \rho$. Thus, the numerator of $\text{Var}(q)$ is a function of the size of the (stochastic) shocks, and the denominator a function of the (deterministic) half-life. With higher order processes, the separation is not so clean, but the intuition is the same.

Globalization in capital markets: Price evidence

Table 3.4. *Model half-lives and error disturbances*

	Half-life					SEE				
	P	G	I	B	F	P	G	I	B	F
Pooled	3.4	3.0	3.1	1.6	2.1	.14	.05	.15	.11	.20
Argentina	1.8	7.2	4.0	1.6	1.5	.33	.08	.12	.25	.64
Australia	4.3	3.0	2.6	4.1	2.1	.08	.04	.11	.08	.08
Belgium	2.6	2.5	2.5	2.6	3.1	.19	.07	.35	.04	.11
Brazil	4.9	0.8	2.6	1.5	3.3	.26	.07	.15	.30	.39
Canada	3.9	6.0	2.8	2.7	3.7	.04	.04	.04	.05	.04
Denmark	4.4	1.5	2.4	0.8	2.8	.10	.04	.11	.11	.11
Finland	1.9	3.9	2.0	0.6	2.5	.16	.04	.26	.12	.10
France	3.2	1.0	2.0	1.6	2.7	.08	.06	.08	.06	.10
Germany	7.2	2.7	11.7	4.5	2.5	.07	.03	.08	.04	.11
Italy	3.6	1.5	—	2.1	2.5	.14	.03	.20	.09	.10
Japan	8.4	3.2	8.8	3.9	2.2	.09	.07	.09	.04	.12
Mexico	2.1	6.2	5.3	2.2	1.3	.17	.10	.15	.13	.27
Netherlands	6.4	6.3	3.5	3.9	2.6	.08	.03	.10	.08	.11
Norway	5.3	3.4	4.2	2.4	2.7	.09	.03	.13	.09	.09
Portugal	4.7	4.2	2.2	4.1	4.2	.13	.06	.19	.05	.10
Spain	5.8	3.0	3.3	2.1	3.2	.11	.07	.13	.09	.10
Sweden	3.0	2.9	2.4	2.1	2.8	.09	.03	.11	.08	.12
Switzerland	5.2	0.7	3.0	1.8	2.1	.09	.03	.10	.03	.12
United Kingdom	3.7	3.1	2.5	2.3	2.1	.08	.02	.08	.07	.13
Mean	4.3	3.3	3.7	2.4	2.6	.13	.05	.14	.10	.16
Standard deviation	1.8	1.9	2.5	1.1	0.7	.07	.02	.07	.07	.14
Median	4.1	3.0	2.8	2.1	2.6	.10	.04	.12	.08	.11

Notes and Sources: See text, appendix, and Taylor (2002b). Samples are P Pooled; G Gold Standard; I Interwar; B Bretton Woods; F Float.

Figure 3.4).[31] Still, all the other half-lives in Table 3.4 are in the low single digits as measured in years. The mean and median half-lives hover around two to three years, a timeframe even more favorable to rapid PPP adjustment than most recent empirical studies. The variation in half-lives around the mean or median is small, around one or two years in most cases. There is evidence of only a modest decline in half-lives after World War Two, with a drop from 3.5 years to 2.5 on average, a decline of about one third. The results hint that floating-rate regimes increase persistence, an outcome consistent with the finding in Obstfeld and Taylor (1997) that exchange-rate variability may inhibit goods-market arbitrage, but the quantitative effect is small. In sum, we have found a new, quite provocative, result. Looking across the twentieth century, and despite

[31] Tests for PPP in the 1930s for Britain, the United States, France and Germany were undertaken by Broadberry and Taylor (1988). Consistent with the present interpretation, they found PPP held except for bilateral exchange rates involving the mark, a result attributed to the extensive controls in the German economy.

considerable differences in institutional arrangements and market integration across time and across countries, the *deterministic* aspect of the persistence of PPP deviations has been fairly uniform in the international economy, with persistence perhaps declining over time, but not dramatically so.[32]

What, then, accounts for the dramatic changes in deviations from PPP during the twentieth century seen in Figure 3.5? As one might guess, the *stochastic* components have to do most of the work to account for this given the fairly flat half-life measures. Under the gold standard, we find $SEE = .05$ on average, that is, a 5% standard deviation for the stochastic shocks. This rises by a factor of three to 14% on average in the interwar era, then falls by a third to 10% under Bretton Woods, before climbing by over half to 16% under the float. Of course, there are some notable outliers here, such as the Latin American economies that experience hyperinflation in the postwar period. We should also note that, due to lack of accurate, synchronized data, the German hyperinflation of the early 1920s is omitted from the data in this study, and is covered instead by interpolation (implying that German interwar volatility is understated).

To reinforce the point, Figure 3.6 shows a scatterplot of $\sigma(\Delta q_t)$ versus σ_ϵ for the complete set of AR models fitted to each country during each regime. Given that the model is linear, we may write $\sigma(\Delta q_t) = f(\rho_j)\sigma_\epsilon$ where the ratio f is a function of all the AR coefficients ρ_j. With no persistence $f = 1$ and more persistence causes an increase in $f > 1$. What is noteworthy here is how f has been uniform and almost constant over the twentieth century, and very close to one. The correlation of $\sigma(\Delta q_t)$ and σ_ϵ has been 0.99 across all regimes. From the regression, we see that a forecast of $\sigma(\Delta q_t)$ assuming $f = 1.1$ yields an R^2 of 0.9 and a tiny standard error of 0.01. As we have already surmised, the persistence of the processes has played little role here, and changes in the stochastic shocks explain virtually all changes in the volatility in the real exchange rate across space and time.

The error disturbances tell a rather consistent story, revealing much larger shocks to the real exchange rate process under floating-rate regimes than under fixed-rate regimes. This is a robust result in the literature and has been observed many times in contemporary data, but this study is the most comprehensive long-run analysis, based on more than a century of data for a broad sample of

---

[32] Another study that examines reversion to PPP across different monetary regimes is Parsley and Popper (2001). They focus only on postwar data for the period 1961–92 in 82 countries, but this encompasses a wide range of exchange-rate arrangements. They find only slightly faster reversion under the dollar peg, about 12% per year, versus pure floating, at 10% per year. This is consistent with the findings in this section. Interestingly in our table, the estimated half-lives for the pooled sample tend to be higher than for any of the subsamples, though again, some individual countries differ in this respect.

Fig. 3.6. A decomposition of real exchange-rate volatility
$\sigma(\Delta q_t)$ versus σ_ϵ

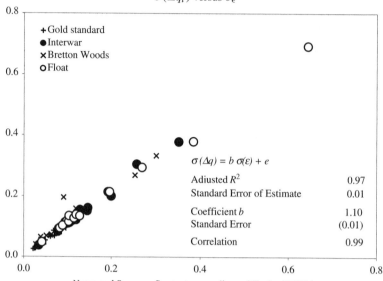

Notes and Sources: See text, appendix, and Taylor (2002b).
Vertical axis: $\sigma(\Delta q_t)$. Horizontal axis: σ_ϵ.

countries. Of particular historical note is the emergence of the interwar period
as a key turning point, an era when PPP deviations shifted to dramatically
higher levels.[33] Given the vast changes in institutions and market structure
over a hundred years or more, the relationship of real exchange-rate deviations
to the monetary regime now looks like a robust stylized *historical* fact.

A final piece of evidence reinforces this notion. One approach to explaining
real exchange-rate deviations in cross section has been to try to disengage the
effects of geography and currencies. Engel and Rogers (1998, 2001) have
shown that although "border effects" do matter, a very large share of deviations
from parity across countries is accounted for by the effect of currencies, that
is, by nominal exchange rate volatility.[34] We can follow a similar tack here,

---

[33] On the interwar period as a turning point, see Obstfeld and Taylor (1998; 2003). Various studies
of PPP in the interwar period have found results consistent with these findings (Eichengreen
1988; Taylor and McMahon 1988).

[34] An example of their approach would be to regress $\sigma(\Delta q_{it})$ on $\sigma(\Delta e_{it})$ and measures of distance
plus a "border" dummy (equal to one when the locations are in different countries). Within
Europe, for the 1980s and 1990s, they find there is an almost one-to-one pass through from
$\sigma(\Delta e_{it})$ to $\sigma(\Delta q_{it})$ (the coefficient is 0.92), and an inspection of the summary statistics for
each is sufficient to convey the message (Engel and Rogers 2001).

Table 3.5. *Real versus nominal exchange-rate volatility*

	G		I		B		F	
	$\sigma(\Delta q)$	$\sigma(\Delta e)$	$\sigma(\Delta q)$	$\sigma(\Delta e)$	$\sigma(\Delta q)$	$\sigma(\Delta e)$	$\sigma(\Delta q)$	$\sigma(\Delta e)$
Pooled	6	5	18	16	16	18	22	47
Argentina	8	13	12	10	27	25	69	112
Australia	4	1	13	10	8	8	10	10
Belgium	7	4	43	15	5	4	13	13
Brazil	9	15	16	15	33	39	38	101
Canada	4	2	4	4	5	4	5	4
Denmark	5	2	12	13	13	12	12	12
Finland	5	0	30	21	16	18	12	12
France	7	0	11	21	8	8	12	13
Germany	3	0	9	9	5	6	13	13
Italy	3	2	20	29	20	20	12	13
Japan	9	5	11	9	4	3	13	13
Mexico	11	7	15	8	14	13	29	35
Netherlands	4	2	11	10	8	8	13	12
Norway	4	1	17	15	10	8	10	10
Portugal	7	7	21	27	7	3	12	14
Spain	7	7	18	15	9	10	13	14
Sweden	3	0	12	10	9	8	13	13
Switzerland	5	4	11	10	4	2	14	14
United Kingdom	3	0	9	9	9	8	13	14
Corr($\sigma(\Delta q)$, $\sigma(\Delta e)$)								
By regime	0.74		0.52		0.99		0.94	
All regimes				0.87				

Notes and Sources: See text, appendix, and Taylor (2002b).

by looking at the sample variances for our four regimes and for each of the 20 countries. Of course, unlike Engel and Rogers, we cannot make within-country comparisons, but we do have a somewhat more controlled experiment: using an historical sample, as opposed to the post–Bretton Woods era, we do obtain much greater sample variation in exchange-rate volatility, even as geography – needless to say – has remained constant.

Table 3.5 tabulates real and nominal exchange rate volatility in the various subsamples. Under the gold standard, we see low real and nominal volatility among those countries that clung hard to the rules of the game (those with zero nominal volatility); but for other countries, as the nominal volatility rose, so did the real volatility (examine, for example, Japan and Switzerland, then Mexico, Portugal and Spain, and finally Brazil and Argentina). Overall, the cross-country correlation is 0.74. Under the mostly floating interwar period, a similar story can be told, although many more real shocks were present in the form of terms-of-trade fluctuations and financial crises, so it is perhaps not surprising to see the correlation fall to 0.52. Another reason for the correlations to be somewhat below unity in the early twentieth would be a degree of price flexibility greater than after World War Two. There is some evidence that this is indeed the case, although the question remains controversial.[35] In the postwar period, the correlation is very strong, 0.99 under Bretton Woods and 0.94 under the float for our sample. In the float, Brazil and Argentina pose problems for the correlation because of their hyperinflation experiences – episodes when, again, large price adjustments went in tandem with nominal exchange-rate movements. The correlation for the 20 countries over all regimes is 0.87, and the message we take from these results is that the dominant source of PPP failure over the very long run has been nominal exchange rate volatility, that is, the nature of the monetary regime.[36]

Our results indicate why it is difficult to track changes in capital-market integration over time through the behavior of international real interest-rate differentials, as defined earlier in this chapter. During periods when countries have resolved the trilemma through nominal exchange-rate flexibility, shocks to real exchange rates, and hence, short-run deviations from PPP, have been much bigger than under fixed-rate periods such as the gold standard and Bretton Woods. Because the speed at which these deviations have been eliminated does not differ dramatically on average across eras, expected real exchange-rate changes have therefore been greater in floating-rate periods. These expectations have often driven larger wedges between national real interest rates even when capital mobility is high. Indeed, in choosing nominal exchange-rate flexibility in response to the trilemma, policymakers have relied on flexibility of the domestic real interest rate as a main transmission mechanisms for monetary policy. This is one reason why we can reject the nonstationarity of international real-interest differentials with relatively less confidence over the recent floating-rate period. What is perhaps remarkable about postwar data is that the increase in international real interest-rate dispersion among industrial countries after 1973 is not even larger.

---

[35] See Obstfeld (1993b, 242–6). For a related discussion of historical changes in international business cycles, see Basu and Taylor (1999).

[36] Do all international relative prices move up and down together, as per the aggregate real exchange-rate movement, or do they show different patterns that are less well correlated with nominal exchange-rate volatility? Absent detailed disaggregated data, we cannot show, as Engel and Rogers (1998, 2001) did, how much of these PPP deviations are common to all goods' relative prices as a source of deviations from LOOP. This is an excellent topic for future research. However, unless contradicted by an array of large and offsetting LOOP deviations for various goods that virtually cancel out – an unlikely outcome – the patterns thus far are entirely consistent with the view that deviations from LOOP are similarly traceable to deviations from aggregate PPP, which, in turn, are in large part determined by the nature of monetary shocks rather than barriers to trade or geography.

3.4 Caveats: Price criteria

This chapter has reviewed several kinds of price criteria that might be used to evaluate the integration of global capital markets over the long run. The data are scarce, and we cannot cover all countries at all times. However, we have found that an examination of exchange-risk-free interest parity indicates a sharp fall in capital mobility for the interwar period, and a gradual increase in more recent decades. This pattern would support the view that global capital markets have witnessed two great phases of integration, one before 1914, and one in the contemporary period, with both separated by a long phase of disintegration during the two wars and the Great Depression. Our examinations of real interest differentials and deviations from PPP are much less informative about financial integration, for reasons we have discussed, although for Britain, France, and Germany, even real interest discrepancies conform to an understated U-shaped pattern after the late nineteenth century.

Although price criteria based on interest differentials may appear more persuasive than the quantity criteria, we must again caution that their interpretation still rests on auxiliary assumptions about structural change in the world economy at different times. It is in theory possible that all the price movements we have described were caused by structural shifts at the level of national economies having nothing to do with capital mobility and obstacles to market integration. These would be the same kinds of shocks outlined in Chapter 2 in the section on caveats regarding quantity criteria. Essentially we have to worry that certain kinds of shocks might have caused price divergence in the interwar and mid-century epochs, absent any change in arbitrage opportunities. Given what we know from the quantity criteria, such an explanation is implausible.

For suppose that arbitrage possibilities were unchanged over time. Then historically, the maximal deviations from interest parity would have to be considered the eras of maximal profit opportunities. In that case, the very greatest arbitrage activity, movement of stocks, and increase in flows ought to have been seen at those times. Such was precisely not the case. The maximal flows and changes in stocks took place in the initial and final phases of our time frame, before 1914 and in the recent decades. These were also times of minimal deviations from interest parity relations. At the same time, the period of maximal interest-rate deviations at mid-century was also the era of minimal quantity activity. This pattern contradicts the idea that structural changes in nonarbitrage aspects of the global economy could simultaneously explain both the evolution of price and quantity behavior. Rather, this empirical evidence is entirely consistent instead with the idea that there have been large shifts in the extent of arbitrage possibilities over time.

3.5 Summary

Many studies of market integration focus on a single criterion. This approach seems unreasonably restrictive to us, since the interpretation of narrow criteria rests on untested auxiliary assumptions. By contrast, we see no reason to dismiss any useful information, in either price or quantity form, especially given the paucity of historical data of certain kinds. Thus, we have opted for a broad battery of tests to try to limit the set of explanations that could account for the empirical record, and so, by a process of elimination, work toward a set of consistent conjectures concerning the evolution of the global capital market.

The last two chapters succinctly convey the benefits we think this kind of approach can deliver. Our quantity-based tests delivered a certain set of stylized facts, and the price-based tests, another set of facts. Combining the two, there is strong support for the notion that the major long-run changes in our quantity and price indicators had their origins in changes in the impediments to capital flows, rather than structural shifts within the economies themselves. That is not to discount the fact that such shifts have occurred, and no doubt played a role, but it is an assertion that the virtual disappearance of foreign capital flows and stocks in mid-century, and the explosion in price differentials, can be explained only by an appeal to changes in arbitrage possibilities as permitted by two major constraining factors in capital market operations: technology and national economic policies.

From this point, it is a short step to the conclusion that a full accounting of the phenomena at hand must rest on a detailed political and institutional history. Clearly, technology is a poor candidate for the explanation of the twentieth-century collapse of capital mobility. In the 1920s and 1930s, the prevailing financial technologies were not suddenly forgotten by market participants: indeed some technologies, such as forward markets for foreign exchange, came to fruition in those decades. Technological evolution was not smooth and linear, but, as we have already noted, it was at least unidirectional, and, absent any other impediments, would have implied an uninterrupted progress toward an ever more tightly connected global marketplace. Such was not allowed to happen, of course. Rather, the shifting forces of national economic policies, as influenced by the prevailing economic theories of the day, loomed large during and after the watershed event of the twentieth century, the economic and political crisis of the Great Depression. Understanding the macroeconomic and international economic history of our present century in these terms, and the associated changes in the operation of the global capital market, is a long and complex story, a narrative that properly accompanies the empirical record presented in the last two chapters. We take it up in the chapter that follows.

Part three
The Political Economy of Capital Mobility

In this part of the book we will examine politico-economic forces that have shaped the evolution of international capital markets. Policymakers confront a major macroeconomic constraint upon opening the economy: losing control of interest rates. How does this constraint bind on a country and what determines its operation? After reviewing the historical background, we assess interest-rate determination empirically using historical data. We examine the pass-through of foreign interest-rate shocks to the domestic economy, and look for a relationship with the exchange-rate regime and the degree of capital mobility, as suggested by the open-economy trilemma. Theory maps into history to a considerable degree, but the deviations from the simplest model reveal the "room for maneuver" that policymakers so jealously guard in the short run, while exposing the danger that too great a tendency to maneuver might easily dissipate long-run credibility no matter what policies are announced. We next focus directly on the changing credibility of exchange-rate commitments. Country risk, the key determinant of real long-term borrowing costs, can be shown to depend not only on variables such as prior levels of borrowing but also on economic and political regimes. We consider two such regimes: the gold standard (which epitomizes the search for credibility via fixed exchange rates) and colonial relationships (here, the British empire). The changing relationship between regimes and the level of country risk is consistent with the changing political forces that induced different accommodations to the trilemma.

4
Globalization in Capital Markets: A Long-Run Narrative

In this chapter we complement the quantitative analysis of the previous chapters with an historical narrative that follows the evolution of the global capital market from its formative stages in the late nineteenth century. How did the market evolve to such levels of sophistication and geographical extent by the period 1870–1913? Why did it then decline so dramatically in the first half of the twentieth century, from 1914 to the 1940s? And why was the pace of rebuilding so slow in the postwar era? Where do we stand now, at the start of the twenty-first century? And how do the economic, historical, and political events of the twentieth century inform these questions?[1]

4.1 Capital without constraints: The gold standard, 1870–1931

4.1.1 The classical gold standard era

The story begins with the emergence of a global gold-standard monetary regime in the 1870s and 1880s and the rise of a world capital market centered on the key financial center of that era, London. The story of the convergence by many different nations on a single monetary standard is now well know, and it exhibits all of the "network externality" properties. Of course, those same increasing-returns aspects driving the adoption of this institutional device, the gold standard, made it also equally susceptible to extinction in the event of crisis and suspension, as we shall see. Nonetheless, with British leadership, the gold standard eventually became an almost universal regime by the 1890s and 1900s, especially in the principal trading nations of the world, replacing silver and bimetallic standards along the way.[2]

---

[1] This chapter draws heavily on Obstfeld and Taylor (1998).

[2] See, for example, Bordo and Schwartz (1984); Bordo and Eichengreen (2001); Eichengreen (1996, chap. 1); Eichengreen and Flandreau (1996); Meissner (2002).

For our purposes, however, the most important feature of this era was not the monetary standard per se but the intellectual, philosophical, and political climate in which it flourished. Since the late eighteenth century, an overarching liberal world order had emerged, with scant interference by the governments of the main economic powers of the time in private commercial and financial activities. This may be a gross oversimplification, for, of course, there were tariffs, restrictions on migration in certain times and places, an emerging workers' movement pressing for controls in the labor market, and embryonic forms of welfare-state policies in some countries. And certainly, political and distributional tensions fueled these policies, as, for example, when the ideas of List and Hamilton on free trade versus protectionism were hotly debated.[3] But in relative terms, and considering the degree and extent of these activities as compared with what was to follow in the twentieth century, this was indeed an era of comparative laissez faire in economic terms.[4]

A vast expansion in world trade had brought all manner of new goods into international commerce, and transportation costs had shrunk to all-time lows. The New World's abundant land, embodied in its agricultural exports, flooded into Europe, and European manufactures were traded back in exchange. As the Second Industrial Revolution progressed, demanding new and bulky raw-material imports, peripheral trading nations lined up to provide the necessary nitrates, bauxite, rubber, coal, and oil. Textile production expanded the trades in cotton, wool, and silk.[5]

In labor markets too, there was a freedom simply unimaginable today. About 50 million emigrants left Europe for the New World in the century before 1914, most going to the United States, but large numbers also headed for the British Dominions, Argentina, and other parts of South America. In most countries, this massive flux of people took place with absolutely no governmental interference. Labor, whether skilled or unskilled, could, in principle, wander around the

---

[3] For an excellent intellectual history of the ideas of free trade versus protectionism – and the economists behind the ideas – see Irwin (1996).

[4] A very large literature has focused on the expansion of state intervention since the late nineteenth century, both as a national and a global phenomenon. For example, see Hughes (1991) on the United States. The landmark work on a global scale was Polanyi (1944). Here, the question we might pose ourselves today is whether this trend is at last beginning to break, and whether we are returning to a more liberal world order again. Many countries, both core and periphery, are shaking off state-led development ideas, privatizing public assets, and rolling back the scope of the welfare state. On this history, and the intellectual shift behind it, see Yergin and Stanislaw (1998) and Lindsey (2002). For an economically-oriented survey of the long-run issues, see Sachs and Warner (1995).

[5] For a survey of trade expansion in this era, see Bairoch (1989). For an exploration of the impacts of this "globalization" on economic structure, see O'Rourke and Williamson (1994, 1999) and O'Rourke, Taylor, and Williamson (1996).

world seeking out the best returns or the most desirable location, unhindered by quotas, immigration inspectors, and the like.[6]

The capital market was perhaps the most unfettered market of all. There were almost no transaction fees or restrictions on the cross-border movement of assets. As a prerequisite for being on the gold standard and playing by the "rules of the game," countries had to permit the free movement of the basic monetary asset, gold bullion, and the conversion of notes and coins into specie and vice versa. Beyond the exchange markets, prices of securities from around the globe were routinely quoted in financial centers like London, Paris, Berlin, New York, and Amsterdam. Outside of Europe and the United States, equally active markets were developing in centers like Melbourne, Buenos Aires, Montreal, Rio de Janeiro, and Mexico City. The net result was the potential for a huge movement of capital from country to country, a trend we have documented. Thus did Britain, as the prime example of a capital exporter, come to place a fraction approaching half of total national savings overseas during the years just prior to 1914.[7]

The pervasive economic freedoms that were taken for granted in the late nineteenth century might seem quite remarkable from our modern standpoint, for despite the recent wave of liberalization that has swept across many economies, we are still in many respects far removed from the economic world of our great-grandparents. Within the space of barely one generation following the Great War, however, the prevailing views on the benefits of economic liberalism, views once thought as unsinkable as the *Titanic*, indeed sank. The melancholy and nostalgia over those bygone days were famously and eloquently evoked by Keynes as early as 1919 in a much-quoted passage from *The Economic Consequences of the Peace*:

What an extraordinary episode in the economic progress of man that age was which came to an end in August 1914! The inhabitant of London could order by telephone, sipping his morning tea in bed, the various products of the whole earth, in such quantity as he might see fit, and reasonably expect their early delivery upon his doorstep; he could at the same moment and by the same means adventure his wealth in the natural resources and

---

[6] There were registers of movements kept, but no formal exclusions in most receiving countries. Australia was an exception with its tacit "white Australia" policy and a potentially arbitrary language test. Some receiving countries, including Australia, Argentina, and Brazil, from time to time would even subsidize the passage of immigrants in an attempt to boost population inflows. On the sending side, emigration was not discouraged, except by certain laws in Germany in the early nineteenth century, and by vestiges of feudal duties in Russia which endured much longer. For a general survey of migration history in this era, consult Nugent (1992). For an economic approach to the integration of global labor markets in this era, see Hatton and Williamson (1994, 1998) and Williamson (1995).

[7] See, for example, Edelstein (1982), Davis and Huttenback (1986), and Davis and Gallman (2001).

new enterprises of any quarter of the world, and share, without exertion or even trouble, in their prospective fruits and advantages; or he could decide to couple the security of his fortunes with the good faith of the townspeople of any substantial municipality in any continent that fancy or information might recommend. He could secure forthwith, if he wished it, cheap and comfortable means of transit to any country or climate without passport or other formality, could despatch his servant to the neighboring office of a bank for such supply of the precious metals as might seem convenient, and could then proceed abroad to foreign quarters, without knowledge of their religion, language, or customs, bearing coined wealth upon his person, and would consider himself greatly aggrieved and much surprised at the least interference. But, most important of all, he regarded this state of affairs as normal, certain, and permanent, except in the direction of further improvement, and any deviation from it as aberrant, scandalous, and avoidable.[8]

This was no case of exaggeration in making the "good old days" out to be better than they actually were. In reality, as we have observed, those times were in fact much as Keynes remembered them. We must still remember the institutional fragility of this period. Operation of this first global bazaar was predicated on a certain set of assumptions about how the world would work. A consensus in support of economic liberalism was taken for granted, notwithstanding the mounting populist and democratic pressures for change. Freedom to contract internationally, the confidence of rights of person and property around the world, and the assumption of minimal government intervention in the world of affairs was presumed. Over the long run, all of these axioms were to face mounting pressure. But in the immediate future lay a dramatic shock to the system that would shake one of its cornerstones, the gold standard, and the convertibility and capital-mobility protections it enshrined. With the advent of the first globalized war, governments' peacetime objectives of trying to maintain a flourishing economy in a global market system gave way to more immediate strategic concerns that would ultimately tear that system to pieces.

4.1.2 Rebuilding the gold standard

World War One and the return to gold

World War One demonstrated the capacity of governments to alter exchange rates and price levels radically, often with the assistance of explicit controls beyond and above normal central bank operations. These newly found powers were not quickly forgotten. In the early 1920s, they were sometimes used to ease the deflationary adjustments of economies seeking to repeg to gold and were abused in the monetary mayhem surrounding the hyperinflations in several European states. When the fleeting interwar gold-exchange standard took

---

[8] Keynes (1971, 6–7).

form after 1925, the older laissez-faire approach to the exchanges was briefly reestablished as many countries eliminated or relaxed exchange controls, but the international financial crisis of 1931 dealt a final blow to the old orthodoxy. Sterling's departure from its gold peg in September 1931 heralded the demise of the gold-based system as well as the return of exchange controls, "in many ways to an even greater extent than during and after the war."[9] Out of the resulting economic and political turmoil would emerge the new consensus on international macroeconomic coexistence embodied in the Bretton Woods agreement of 1944.

The effectiveness of interwar exchange controls varied greatly. Naïve policies contained loopholes through which regulations on capital flows might be evaded. Certain controls proved hard or even impossible to implement, but others, when sufficiently refined by the increasingly sophisticated authorities, served their purpose. A measure of the impact of such policies was the common appearance of the "black bourse" in some of the most tightly controlled economies. Free-market rates often diverged widely from official rates. This added further uncertainty to foreign exchange markets, already subject to frequent, often violent, movements after floating rates appeared in the wake of gold-standard suspensions during and after World War One. With the world's nominal anchor removed, massive exchange risks reentered the calculation of every foreign investor. Controls, if they threatened to compromise the secure and full repatriation of profits or principal, heightened risk further and could prompt capital flight or the collapse of lending. Speculative activity and the emerging threat to central banks and treasuries posed by increasing volumes of highly liquid, "hot" money prompted even greater caution in the bureaucratic supervision of foreign-exchange transactions. Exchange controls thus compounded the problems in what was already a deteriorating framework for international capital flows.

Direct controls over private exchange transactions were rarely employed under the gold standard before 1914. Central banks occasionally used "normal" measures to support exchange rates, broadly defined to include moral suasion over banks, direct interventions to alter gold export and import points, and other formally noncoercive devices. But if a central bank could no longer defend the exchange rate through such measures, as often occurred in Latin America, the currency was generally set free to float with no controls employed. Within Europe, the credibility of exchange parities was bolstered by Britain's hegemony within the world financial system and its espousal of free trade, as

---

[9] Einzig (1934, 1–2).

well as by central-bank cooperation and the overriding and largely unquestioned commitment of central banks to the goal of gold convertibility at an unchanging par.[10] Credibility ensured that capital movements were usually stabilizing. A high degree of international capital mobility was promoted by the gold-standard regime; and by reducing actual gold movements, capital mobility in its turn helped the system to function smoothly.

The Great War destroyed this equilibrium, and the classical gold standard too. Initially, countries kept up the appearance of the gold standard, maintaining official gold coinage, pegging official exchange rates, and, on paper, permitting the movement of gold, but obstacles and regulations, as well as heightened susceptibility to patriotic appeals, prevented normal functioning according to the prewar rules of the game.[11] The belligerent countries were the first to enforce controls. Wartime needs drove their trade balances into deficit, and monetization of fiscal deficits drove inflation, though to widely differing degrees in the several countries. Although exchange control became an "obvious necessity" in these circumstances, countries did not produce a full-blown, cut-and-dried system of controls at the outbreak of war. A gradual implementation of ever-stricter controls ensued, although trading with the enemy was quickly terminated. In 1914 and early 1915, the belief that the war would be short and swift kept the exchanges fairly stable. It was not until later in 1915 that general foreign exchange transactions came under restriction when the exchanges started to become much more volatile.[12]

Allied experiences varied considerably. The British began in 1915 by pegging the dollar rate of sterling, with the British Treasury acting via J. P. Morgan in New York to support sterling at $4.7640 using gold and dollar reserves. In the early war years, the country often came near to exhausting its reserves, as recounted by Keynes.[13] After 1917, the U.S. Treasury supplied the required funds, and the peg continued. France employed similar methods to defend a franc-sterling peg, albeit with both "passive" and "active" intervention by the Bank of France. In the later stages of the war, exchange controls grew much stricter than in Britain. Whereas appeals to patriotism and other types of moral suasion had sufficed to discourage outbound capital transfers for a while, in the end tougher measures were needed. France's more severe inflation problems undermined the credibility of the peg and capital outflows were harder to tame. Italy likewise pursued a policy of pegging against sterling. Like these peggers,

---

[10] Kindleberger (1986); Eichengreen (1992).
[11] Eichengreen (1992, 67).
[12] Brown (1940, 59–63); Einzig (1934, 22–23); League of Nations (1938a, 9).
[13] Keynes (1978, 10–12).

Allied powers that did not peg their currencies nonetheless resorted to exchange controls toward the end of the war. Even the United States applied direct controls after entering the war in 1917, despite its strong trade balance, as a result of the dollar's appreciation against several neutral currencies.[14]

In Germany, the mark was never pegged to another currency during the war, and the Reichsbank spent a mere 450 million marks on intervention to defend the mark in times when depreciation threatened to become a burden – a tiny fraction of the inter-Allied resources devoted to currency support. However, Germany's trade was effectively blocked by the Allies, so her adverse net export balance was rather small. Exchange restrictions did not come into force until 1916 and were only mild until they were dramatically reinforced in 1917.[15] Still Germany employed strong forms of compulsion in order to mobilize residents' foreign securities.[16]

Interwar exchange control

The Armistice gave hope that wartime exchange controls would soon be removed and the prewar state of affairs would soon prevail. The removal of controls was one of the few things the Brussels Conference of the League of Nations in 1920 could agree on.[17] In the United States, exchange control was dismantled, and in Britain, controls had largely ended by the time sterling rejoined the gold standard in 1925. The dollar peg ended in March 1919, and sterling was cut loose to take care of itself. The authorities refrained from direct control measures; however, occasional weak embargoes on British foreign loans were enforced starting in 1924, to bolster the currency as it inched back toward gold parity, as well as later in the 1920s.[18] By floating in 1919, Britain was able to open its capital market relatively quickly after the war's end. Elsewhere, however, exchange controls had to be maintained or reinforced after the war as a number of countries descended into economic chaos.[19]

When inter-Allied support ended, a rapid flight from the franc ensued with rampant bear speculation, and the Bank of France remained neutral and impas-

---

[14] Einzig (1934, 28–9); Eichengreen (1992, 73).
[15] Einzig (1934, 29–30).
[16] Eichengreen (1992, 83).
[17] Eichengreen (1992, 154–5).
[18] See Atkin (1977). The British government, for revenue reasons, also levied a stamp tax on foreign bearer bonds. See Moggridge (1971), who concludes, however, that British government suasion over foreign lending was largely ineffective in keeping capital at home, and that the stamp tax could be evaded. His conclusion receives support from Figure 3.1, which shows that from 1924 through 1930, sterling interest rates in London frequently exceeded the covered sterling return on New York loans.
[19] Einzig (1934, chaps. 4–5).

sive, preferring to husband its gold stock rather than intervene in a probable losing cause. Harsh exchange controls were promulgated, but it was not until after the franc stabilized in 1926, and vast sums were repatriated, that all could see how ineffective the controls had been. Moreover, other factors impinged on capital flows, notably the fierce controversy over the capital levy. With a broader franchise, political groups representing labor now tried to force capital to shoulder a larger part of the fiscal burden. Deadlock persisted as governments came and fell. In 1925, a 10 percent tax on all wealth over ten years was nearly enacted by the government, and although the government fell, the capital levy was killed for good only by the Poincaré government's fiscal stabilization package in late 1926. In the interim, the lingering possibility of a wealth tax sent capital fleeing abroad.[20]

As inflation seized Germany's economy between 1919 and 1923, even tighter exchange restrictions were deployed to halt the slump in the mark. Exporters and importers had all exchange requests subjected to government approval, and indirect controls were used to restrict imports. Even so, capital flight from Germany continued. Exchange controls in the successor states of the Austro-Hungarian empire took even more esoteric forms.[21] In Italy, the postwar fascist regime enjoyed greater success in controlling the exchanges, largely as a result of its extraordinary powers of enforcement. Restrictions eventually eased in most countries following stabilization. Still, there were delays. And often, stabilization had been achieved only by dint of exchange controls in the interim. Nonetheless, by 1927, most of the world's market economies had returned to "normalcy" in the form of pegged exchange rates and some form of gold standard, the latter understood to comprise considerable freedom to transact in foreign exchange.

But the restored gold-standard system came apart after only a few years, as we have noted. As countries started to leave gold even before Britain's September 1931 departure brought the interwar gold standard to a close, controls began to proliferate. In sharp contrast with the laissez-faire philosophy that prevailed under the classical gold standard prior to 1914, this period saw a marked increase in the adoption of peacetime policies to control not only international capital flows but foreign exchange transactions in general.[22] Controls over foreign-currency transactions took several forms. In assessing how controls affect capital mobility, we are primarily concerned with measures that would have

[20] Einzig (1934, chaps. 4–5); Eichengreen (1992, 172–9).
[21] During a brief period in 1919, Joseph A. Schumpeter served as Austrian finance minister. He favored a capital levy.
[22] Einzig (1934); Gordon (1941).

been viewed as "abnormal" under the gold standard: steps taken to defend or change the course of the exchange, ranging from direct measures such as loan embargoes and foreign exchange rationing to indirect measures exerting more subtle influences on foreign trade or foreign loan markets. Such measures were attempted fitfully in the 1910s and 1920s, but their reappearance in "extreme forms" dated from the crisis of 1931.[23]

The interventions served a variety of purposes of concern to policymakers of the period: to offset day-to-day fluctuations, to stem persistent speculation or capital flight, to smooth predictable seasonal and other normal tendencies, or to attempt to reverse fundamental trends. In many cases, such attempts to manage capital-account transactions were also complemented by commercial policies (tariffs and quotas) aimed at inhibiting the volume of current-account transactions. In fact, policymakers viewed certain exchange control and tariff policies as pure substitutes.[24] Controls enabled a government to maintain (at least nominally) a pegged exchange rate, while simultaneously using interest-rate policies and other policies based on divergences between internal and external prices to attain domestic economic objectives.

Exchange controls became "among the best-hated" forms of government intervention in free markets in the eyes of observers and market participants.[25] Controls were criticized for causing exchanges to diverge from their fundamental level (though identifying fundamental levels proved elusive in the interwar chaos) and for their damaging effect on international trade and finance (though the effect of exchange controls here could not be easily differentiated from the corrosive effects of tariffs, quotas, and other commercial policy choices). Even if not convicted on these charges, exchange controls were subject to even more stinging criticism, facing ridicule for being "utterly inefficient and impossible to enforce."[26] The nettlesome interferences with the exchange were thus in vain, critics charged, on account of weak policing and enforcement, and the numerous loopholes, which savvy exchange dealers could easily exploit to circumvent the intent of the restriction. If the speculators proved strong enough

---

[23] Bratter (1939, 274): "Direct and indirect measures are somewhat interchangeable as policy instruments. A regime of multiple exchange rates on goods operates like a variegated tariff schedule. Barter trade resembles the outcome of bilateral exchange clearing arrangement. Thus, although direct measures impinge directly on foreign capital movements, so too do the indirect measures."

[24] Bratter (1939, 274) again: "In effect control of the volume of foreign exchange transactions with foreign countries amounts to determination of the value or volume of goods and services exchanged with foreign countries. Exchange control accomplishes the purpose of a protective tariff or an import embargo. And it has the further 'advantage' that it often operates secretly as to the details."

[25] Einzig (1934, 106).

[26] Einzig (1934, 107).

for the task, the authorities faced certain defeat, and the incentive to exploit loopholes only loomed larger as the exchanges moved further from fundamentals, inviting arbitrage. Such was undoubtedly a major weakness of the early and rudimentary controls seen in the 1920s, as in the French and Belgian cases. Embargoes on loan issues might fail if investors were willing and able to purchase issues in a third country, or if short-term trade credits could be disguised and employed to finance longer term capital flows. Partial controls could be futile, as transactions might be easily disguised in false categories, necessitating full-blown supervision of every transaction.[27]

Evasion could never be totally eliminated, but authorities learned the lessons of failed controls and became more ruthless in imposing and enforcing trading restrictions as the 1930s wore on. The more desperate measures included increasingly restrictive allocations of foreign exchange for imports, the compulsory surrender of export proceeds, and the complete suspension of free dealings (i.e., a crackdown on the black bourse).[28] By the 1930s, the criticism that the controls were ineffective could be said to have lost much of its force.[29] Capital controls were now binding on the global capital market to an unprecedented extent. Although devised primarily as a response to short-run problems with capital flight, even the prospect of modest barriers to outward flows undermined the efficient allocation of global capital. As Ellis succinctly summarized, capital controls "may interfere with the tendency of capital to bring its marginal employments to equality and thus maximize yields....in preventing capital repayments, exchange control effectively discourages the investment of new foreign capital. Since the 'natural' direction of capital-flow was toward the debtor (now exchange-control) countries, this is probably the more serious consequence."[30] In addition, distributional conflicts over the tax burden raged on between labor and capital, provoking capital flight and further impeding potentially productive capital flows. France in the mid-1930s provides the example par excellence of social disorder coupled with budgetary impasse. Those tensions led to the formation of the Popular Front, a coalition of left-wing parties that gained power and abandoned gold in 1936.[31]

---

[27] Nurkse (1944, 165).

[28] Kindleberger (1984, 392) notes the harsh measures favored in fascist Germany and Italy. Punishments were increased in severity until they included the death penalty in both countries.

[29] Einzig (1934, 112).

[30] Ellis (1941, 22).

[31] See Eichengreen (1992, chap. 12) and James (2001, chap. 2) for discussions of the French case. As Kindleberger (1986, 251–2) observes, "The Popular Front had no real economic program....There was no provision for coping with the balance of payments or the capital outflow stimulated by the sit-in strikes [that followed the Front's election]. It was as if the Popular Front had been dealing with a closed economy."

4.2 Crisis and compromise: Depression and war, 1931–1945

4.2.1 Capital markets and the Great Depression

The global Great Depression and the financial instability accompanying it were directly responsible for the sharp turn toward exchange control in much of the world. Stability on the exchanges came to an abrupt end in 1931, though trouble had been brewing longer in many countries, especially at the periphery.[32] Currency crises in 1931 led to flights from the Austrian schilling, the Hungarian pengö, and the German mark following the Creditanstalt collapse. It appeared that exchange control might be the only policy alternative, because when "flight psychology" prevailed, "no increase in the discount rate may be sufficient to deter it. Indeed an increase in the discount rate, by shaking confidence further, is apt to produce the opposite effect." Yet, confoundingly, "the introduction of control itself...tended to upset confidence further, increasing the urge to export capital" making the exercise "self-aggravating to some extent."[33] Policymakers groped for a solution.

In July 1931, a flight from sterling began, leading to gold-standard suspension in September. Facing high unemployment, the British government had no stomach for an aggressive defense of the pound through budgetary retrenchment, which would have required scaling back the dole. Nor did the Bank of England carry out an aggressive interest-rate defense. Instead Bank Rate was raised shortly before the announcement of the gold standard's suspension "as a measure of reassurance against inflation."[34] Soon the dollar and other currencies were exposed to runs. Not all currencies fell from gold immediately, but the fear grew. In such circumstances, exchange controls inevitably returned to prominence: governments fought off depreciation and convertibility crises with intervention, exchange restrictions, and other forms of exchange control.[35]

Simple intervention usually proved ineffective in the face of continued gold drain, as with Germany, Austria, and Hungary in the summer of 1931. Reserves were spent in a futile effort. Coffeehouse transactions on the black market soon undermined rationing through the banks. German restrictions were severe, foretelling the blocked balances and other obstructions to come. In July 1931, a partial transfer moratorium was announced, suspending principal payments, and later extended in a full standstill agreement with Germany's creditors. Only thus was a collapse of the mark prevented. Both Austria and Germany's banking

[32] Einzig (1934, chap. 6); League of Nations (1938a, 10–11); Ellis (1941, 7); Yeager (1976, chap. 17).
[33] Nurkse (1944, 162–3).
[34] Sayers (1976, 412).
[35] Nurkse (1944, chap. 7).

systems stood on the verge of collapse. Choosing to sacrifice gold convertibility for bank stability, their governments adopted exchange control.

In the fall of 1931 Britain promulgated several mild exchange restrictions following suspension and lasting for six months, primarily to prevent capital flight. In general during the 1930s, Britain employed relatively limited controls, ranging from persuasion, to an embargo on large foreign bond issues, to official restrictions applied by private banks. But these measures were far from comprehensive.[36] The United States, under the Hoover administration, had maintained dollar convertibility into gold at $20.67 per ounce. Following President Roosevelt's suspension of gold convertibility in 1933, however, the United States began to deploy informal pressures similar to those used in Britain, though occasionally enforcing official supervision of banks when an assumption of loyalty could not be taken for granted.

Japan, back on gold only since 1930 and suffering the fiscal strains of the Manchurian campaign, left gold at the end of 1931. Depreciation heralded the end of convertibility and the application of more restrictions on foreign exchange to prevent capital flight. France also generally avoided direct measures, relying on tariffs, quotas, and other commercial policies to keep the trade balance favorable and gold stocks plentiful – but the gold bloc could not hold on forever.[37] Italy's government made very effective use of unofficial restrictions by dint of the powerful command of the banking system at the central government level, and capital flight in 1935 forced Belgium into controls.[38]

The tendency toward the forcible confinement of foreign exchange within borders was perhaps most famously institutionalized in the widespread adoption of the system of "blocked balances" in Central European and Latin American countries, and notably in Germany under the Gold Discount Bank.[39] Simply put, "blocked currencies" enshrined the idea that debtors could make debt payments not with foreign exchange but with domestic currency placed in special, earmarked accounts, funds that the creditor might then use only in limited ways – e.g., for renewed direct investment in the debtor country, or to buy more of the debtors exports. Thus, the "blocked account" became a new payoff option

---

[36] Stewart (1938, 57) noted: "There is, first of all, complete freedom of transferring pounds sterling into foreign currencies and, secondly, there are ample facilities for the purchase in London of foreign securities. The inconsistency of keeping these channels open while maintaining a strict embargo on new foreign issues has been severely criticised."

[37] Yeager (1976, chap. 18); James (2001).

[38] Einzig (1934, chap. 6); Eichengreen (1992, chap. 9). Italy's controls were "so stringent as to render her gold bloc status meaningless" (Eichengreen 1992, 357). The Belgian controls admitted loopholes and were rendered immaterial within weeks as speculators, anticipating a devaluation, provoked one (Eichengreen 1992, 362–3).

[39] Einzig (1934, chap. 12); Ellis (1941, 13–17).

unilaterally imposed by debtors, and effectively defaulting on the terms of their original loan contract.[40] Moreover, the payment into a blocked account was often illusory as a financial transaction, entailing no shift in the structure of international indebtedness, affording no liquidity to the creditor, and usually enforcing no loss of liquidity on debtor banks which often maintained currency issue backed by "blocked accounts."[41] Owing to this vehicle for credit creation, the "blocked accounts" were easily manipulated "for disguising the insolvency of the debtors, and especially of one particular debtor – the Government of the debtor country."[42] Thus, an insolvent government might pay off debts into its "blocked account" and then relend to itself out of the same funds. Inevitably, claims on such "blocked accounts" soon began trading on the secondary market at a heavy discount. An international market soon developed in the 1930s for four types of German marks, six types of Hungarian pengöes, and many other "blocked currencies." Market rates diverged dramatically from the official par rates of the exchange-controlled domestic currency.[43]

Germany, Austria, and Hungary all developed complex systems of "blocked currencies" and bilateral clearings.[44] Many other countries in Central and Southern Europe followed suit, causing the return of virtual barter conditions in many goods markets and stifling foreign investment. However, the German case remains the example par excellence of this type of exchange control – and by the late 1930s it had persisted beyond the point where it was economically defensible, seeming more a tool of national and international political power via favorable allocations of trading activity to domestic agents and foreign trading partners. Thus, after the immediate 1931 crisis, the reasons for keeping exchange control mutated, and the control "introduced in the first instance mainly to prevent capital exports[,] soon shifted its emphasis to the control of commodity imports."[45] Political as well as economic concerns surfaced, with the parallel market or black bourse as the only recourse for all but a few restricted transactions. "*De facto* and *sub rosa* devaluation transformed the official rate of exchange to a mere face-saving fiction."[46]

---

[40] This payment was an option typically more injurious to the creditor than even a temporary moratorium – a suspension that might only for a time prevent the discharge of debts but that did not inflict any change in the final terms of settlement.

[41] Put another way, the banks treated the accounts as reserves rather than as earmarked funds not strictly available.

[42] Einzig (1934, 126–7).

[43] Discounts were low for countries whose exports were in demand but very high for currencies whose only use was for very unattractive foreign investment in the debtor country.

[44] Ellis (1941); League of Nations (1938a, 16); Yeager (1976, 368–71).

[45] Nurkse (1944, 166).

[46] Ellis (1941, 293).

In contrast to Germany, Austria, long before anschluss, was already relaxing controls, and comparable measures to ease exchange controls and bilateral constraints were to be seen in Romania, Yugoslavia, Hungary, Czechoslovakia, Bulgaria, and elsewhere in the exchange-control bloc.[47] Bilateral exchange clearing was beginning to be seen as a welfare-reducing, trade-diverting choice justified by "ulterior ends"; one such end was protection, which "appeared as a by-product of attempting to defend the currency, but it proved to be so welcome a by-product as certainly to become an end itself."[48] By obstructing trade along lines of comparative advantage, clearings frequently depressed domestic exports, exacerbating the shortage of foreign exchange that exchange controls were supposed to alleviate. More and more countries turned away from trading under such constraints with countries in the clearing bloc.[49]

In Latin America, countries both depreciated their currencies *and* joined the movement toward exchange control as depression deepened and after sterling left gold. Most also defaulted on their foreign debts, an event that had a profound negative impact on subsequent capital inflows to the region, as many defaults were not settled until well after World War Two. Controls were initially a response to balance-of-payments crises resulting from a collapse of primary product prices and quanta in export markets, the stickiness of import demands, and large fixed nominal debt obligations in foreign currency. However, controls were generally less rigid than in Europe, with a liberal attitude taken to foreign-exchange transactions outside normal channels.[50]

Thus, in Latin America, some capital-account transactions were permitted and black markets were tolerated, while in Europe such flows were strictly controlled; Latin American countries were generally less inclined to adopt bilateral clearing arrangements save under duress. The key instrument was the rationing of exchange for different uses according to government priorities, implying multiple exchange rates.[51] High priorities were usually debt service (unless in default) and essential imports.[52] The more "reactive" countries soon

---

[47] Ellis (1941, chap. 2); League of Nations (1938a, 40–5).

[48] Ellis (1941, 297).

[49] League of Nations (1938a, 24–37); Nurkse (1944, 177–83). Absurd examples of trade diversion included the import of raw materials in a bilateral clearing deal and subsequent reexport at a large loss to a free-currency country, undercutting the original producer, simply as a means for the reexporter to obtain foreign exchange (League of Nations 1938a, 35).

[50] Bratter (1939); Nurkse (1944, 162); Díaz Alejandro (1983, 27).

[51] League of Nations (1938a, 15, 17); Nurkse (1944, 170).

[52] The discovery that such policies could radically alter the shape of foreign trade and the level of domestic economic activity eventually allowed new and broader purposes of economic control to motivate the use of exchange control, beyond the presumably temporary intent to manage transitory payments crises. It was partly thus that "reactive" policies of the 1930s paved the way

adopted controls: Argentina, Bolivia, Brazil, Chile, and Colombia (in 1931); followed by Costa Rica, Nicaragua, Paraguay, and Uruguay (1932); Ecuador (1933); Honduras (1934); and Venezuela (1936).[53,54]

Argentina, Brazil, Chile, and Colombia were locked in clearing agreements with Germany, and these plus Costa Rica and Uruguay controlled trade along bilateral lines via exchange controls or clearing agreements. Such arrangements had marked consequences for regional trade, and a good deal of Latin American trade was canalized bilaterally not by choice, but by the actions of European trading partners, and to the detriment of rival markets. In many countries, trading with Nazi Germany under ASKI ("compensation") marks was seen to have dramatically altered the composition of trade.[55] Although the Pan American Union called for moves to abolish controls in 1936, the 1937 recession once again exposed the underlying weakness of the periphery's balance-of-payments position, and as a result no concrete action was taken to lift controls before the outbreak of war.[56]

Australia was another typical primary-producing country caught in a balance-of-payments crisis and facing unsustainable capital outflows as early as 1929. The terms of trade had dived from a peak in 1924, reflecting oversupply in the wool market. Mild controls appeared first in the form of foreign-exchange rationing, and soon the currency slipped outside the gold points. It was 8 percent off par by April 1930. A steady devaluation ensued, and a black market appeared, compromising the policy of rationing via the banks. Eventually the system broke down and the currency was devalued to 30 percent below par at the start of 1931. In much the same fashion Canada took steps to limit gold export and convertibility, inevitably leading to devaluation of her currency.[57]

for a transition to import substitution strategies in the 1940s and 1950s. See Fishlow (1971) and Díaz Alejandro (1984).

[53] Of these, only Venezuela permitted a completely "free" parallel market; other countries intervened to greater or lesser extents. More "passive" countries such as Cuba, the Dominican Republic, Ecuador, El Salvador, Guatemala, Haiti, Mexico, Panama, and Peru did not institute any controls in the 1930s (Bratter 1939, 280–81).

[54] The methods of exchange control varied. For example, in Argentina, the government still favored allocation of foreign exchange to balance bilateral trade, much to U.S. consternation, and largely a result of the 1933 Roca-Runciman treaty with Britain – a deal struck to offset British imperial trade preferences established in the Ottawa treaty (Bratter 1939, 279–81; Salera 1941). A much stricter regime of controls held sway in Uruguay – four varieties of exchange rate were subject to manipulation, bilateral clearing arrangements were more constraining, and attempts to favor particular products and trading partners were more pervasive (Bratter 1939, 281–2).

[55] Between 1929 and 1937, the British shares of imports fell in Brazil (19.2 to 12.1%), Chile (17.7 to 10.9%), and Peru (15.0 to 10.3%), while German import shares to all three rose (Brazil: 12.7 to 23.9%; Chile: 15.5 to 26.1%; Peru: 10.0 to 19.7%). All figures from Bratter (1939, 284). On ASKI marks, see also Yeager (1976, 370–1).

[56] Bratter (1939, 286).

[57] Eichengreen (1992, 232–6 and 240); Shearer and Clark (1984, 282 and 297).

4.2.2 Policy responses and the trilemma

After the initial crisis of 1931 passed, policymakers faced a choice. On the one hand, they could treat exchange controls as a temporary expedient for the duration of the crisis and thereafter work toward free exchanges, sacrificing policy autonomy. On the other hand, they could retain and enhance the security of their controls and thereby expand the range of policy options. Thus, by the mid-1930s, countries could be classified as "free-currency" countries – whether on or off the gold standard – or "exchange-control" countries.[58] (Of course, even countries in the former group could employ mild or informal measures of capital-account control, such as moral suasion, in the interest of pursuing macroeconomic targets.)

The data in Table 4.1 illustrate some of the contrasts between the exchange-rate experiences of the two groups. The free-currency group included much of Scandinavia and Western Europe. Among these countries, Belgium, the Netherlands, Switzerland, and France (along with the United States until 1933) were in the gold bloc and avoided devaluation only through strong "indirect"measures (e.g., tariffs and quotas) in the early 1930s. By contrast, exchange-control economies included Germany, Austria, Hungary, and neighboring countries to the east, plus Turkey, Italy, and the Baltic states – a largely Central and Southeastern European grouping. In the latter group, some generally very severe exchange controls allowed governments the freedom to maintain parities (or else tolerate only relatively mild devaluations) without fear of speculative attacks, as capital flight was severely contained.[59]

After 1935, the gold bloc collapsed. France, Switzerland, and the Netherlands departed from their earlier policies, but without control. Some exchange-control countries did choose to devalue (e.g., Italy, Czechoslovakia, Greece), and some no longer adhered to official rates of exchange. The conclusion of the Tripartite Agreement among Britain, France, and the United States in 1936 lent a modicum of stability and a veneer of cooperation to international monetary arrangements, and worldwide economic conditions generally improved until the recession of 1937.[60]

Recent academic writing has emphasized the role of the international gold standard in propagating the Great Depression, showing systematically how countries that maintained gold parities and continued approximately to fol-

---

[58] League of Nations (1938a); Eichengreen (1992, 339).

[59] Equivalently, Eichengreen (1992, 258) uses a three-category classification consisting of "exchange controlled," "sterling area," and "gold bloc" – in practice, those not on controls or pegged to gold chose a sterling peg, with a few exceptions such as Canada, which pegged to a sterling-dollar basket.

[60] League of Nations (1938a); Eichengreen (1992).

Table 4.1. *Currency depreciation in the 1930s*

Percentage depreciation relative to official gold parity

Exchange-control countries		1932	1935
Bulgaria	(a)	0.0	0.0
Germany	(a)	0.0	0.0
Hungary	(b)	0.0	0.0
Romania	(a)	0.0	0.0
Latvia	(a)	0.0	1.7
Turkey	(a)	1.7	1.9
Italy	(a)	1.5	6.3
Czechoslovakia	(a)	0.0	16.2
Austria	(a)	22.0	22.0
Yugoslavia	(b)	6.8	23.0
Estonia	(b)	0.0	39.9
Denmark	(b)	29.7	51.5
Uruguay	(b)	54.5	53.9
Argentina	(b)	39.4	54.3
Free-currency countries (gold bloc)			
France	(a)	0.0	0.0
Netherlands	(a)	0.0	0.0
Switzerland	(a)	0.0	0.0
Poland	(a)	0.0	0.0
Belgium	(a)	0.0	3.2
Free-currency countries (devaluers)			
Ireland	(b)	28.0	40.2
South Africa	(b)	2.1	40.8
United States	(a)	0.0	40.8
Canada	(b)	11.9	40.9
United Kingdom	(a)	25.2	41.9
Sweden	(a)	25.9	45.6
Norway	(a)	26.9	47.0
Finland	(a)	36.4	50.4
New Zealand	(b)	34.2	52.3
Australia	(b)	42.5	52.6

Notes and Sources: Countries shown in order of 1935 devaluation percentage. (a) denotes annual average; (b) monthly average for March of 1932 or 1935. League of Nations (1938a, 50–1).

low other gold-standard "rules of the game" through the mid-1930s suffered much sharper output declines and deflation.[61] Countries willing to devalue

[61] See, for example, Choudhri and Kochin (1980), Díaz Alejandro (1983), Eichengreen and Sachs (1985), Hamilton (1988), Temin (1989), Campa (1990), Eichengreen (1992), Bernanke (1995), and Bernanke and Carey (1996). These writers have followed upon a nonformal tradition that quite clearly appreciated the basic monetary forces at work in propagating and prolonging the Depression, but that lacked a rigorous analytical and statistical framework for representing their global scope. Thus, Edward M. Bernstein, Harry Dexter White's deputy at the U.S. Treasury during the Bretton Woods negotiations and the first research director of the IMF, recalled in 1984 that "[we at the Treasury] held that the Great Depression was caused by the interaction

could lower the relative price of national output and expand their money supplies, boosting effective demand and employment while retaining a relatively open capital market. Exchange control countries addressed the macro policy trilemma by eliminating capital movements. Even countries that officially maintained their 1931 gold parities effectively devalued their currencies through a maze of restrictions on foreign exchange acquisition. Elimination of dependence on international capital markets in some cases increased the scope for domestic fiscal expansion, as in Germany. But countries in the gold bloc, despite resort to conventional trade policies, felt the full force of the policy trilemma, maintaining initial gold parities and free foreign exchange markets only at the cost of a deep and protracted domestic slump.

Econometric evidence points to independent roles for controls and exchange depreciation in mitigating the effects of the Depression. To examine these hypotheses we performed a 26-country cross-sectional regression of the 1929 to 1935 cumulative rate of growth of industrial production, ΔIP, on a constant and two dummy variables. FIXED takes the value 1 for countries that held their official exchange rates fixed at 1929 levels longer than the United States (which severed the dollar's link to gold in April 1933) and takes the value 0 for others. CONTROLS equals 1 for countries classified by the League of Nations in the mid-1930s as exchange-control countries and is 0 for free-exchange countries. (The exchange-control group comprises a wide variety of control strategies, some much more stringent than others, and omits countries that applied controls only fleetingly.)

The result of estimation (with standard errors in parentheses) is

$$\Delta\text{IP} = \underset{(0.060)}{0.028} - \underset{(0.080)}{0.261}\ \text{FIXED} + \underset{(0.079)}{0.213}\ \text{CONTROLS}, \tag{4.1}$$

$$R^2 = 0.41$$

As is now well known, countries that retained fixed exchange rates suffered harsher real contractions. According to equation 4.1, they experienced (on average) over the years 1929 to 1935 a 26 percent output decline avoided by countries that devalued. However, controls (which usually implied de facto

of the wartime inflation and the traditional gold standard,...The Great Depression did not end until every country had abandoned the gold parity of its currency" (Black 1991, 98). See also Haberler's (1976) evaluation. Eichengreen (1992) cites Ralph Hawtrey and Lionel Robbins as early precursors. Unfortunately, the insular focus of much American macroeconomic thinking for at least 35 years after World War Two tended to blind many U.S. scholars to the powerful international monetary transmission mechanism at work in the Depression.

devaluation) had a significant mitigating effect on the extent of output decline resulting from fixed exchange rates.[62,63]

The output effects of controls are mirrored by the behavior of the price level, as shown in the following regression in which the dependent variable is the cumulative 1929 to 1935 rate of wholesale price index (WPI) inflation:[64]

$$\Delta \text{WPI} = \begin{array}{ccc} -0.157 & - \ 0.227 \ \text{FIXED} & + \ 0.082 \ \text{CONTROLS}, \\ (0.026) & (0.035) & (0.034) \end{array} \qquad (4.2)$$

$$R^2 = 0.66$$

Here we see again the familiar deflationary effect of fixed exchange rates, but also a significant counter-effect of controls on the price level. Though statistically significant, the effect is small because the "devaluation" implied by controls did not generally lead to significant monetary expansion relative to the world average.

Fundamentally, these diverse experiences underscored the unattainable nature of the economic "trinity"; of three desirable policy goals – exchange-rate stability, policies to support full employment, and free capital mobility – only two out of three are mutually compatible. The free-currency devaluers discarded exchange stability and gained the freedom to pursue expansionary fiscal and monetary policies. The exchange-control countries sought the same freedom by inhibiting capital mobility, and, further, manipulated the levers of thorough-going exchange control and discriminatory trading in pursuit of domestic goals. Notably, neither group considered a full return to gold-standard orthodoxy, requiring the neglect of the full-employment goal and commitment to the other two goals – exchange parity and free exchanges – a testament to the transformation in the political economy of macroeconomic management, the power of new interest groups and enfranchised voters, and the resulting unwillingness of

---

[62]   The exchange-control countries in the sample are Argentina, Austria, Czechoslovakia, Denmark, Estonia, Germany, Greece, Hungary, Italy, Japan, Latvia, and Romania. The free-exchange countries are Australia, Belgium, Canada, Finland, France, the Netherlands, New Zealand, Norway, Poland (which imposed controls only in 1936), Spain, Sweden, Switzerland, the United Kingdom, and the United States. (Some countries, such as Argentina, Austria, and Denmark, both devalued early *and* imposed controls.) Industrial production data come from League of Nations (1938b), except for Argentina, Australia, and Switzerland, the data for which are used in Bernanke and Carey (1996) and were generously provided by Ben Bernanke.

[63]   The coefficient on CONTROLS in the last regression implies that, on average in the sample, imposing exchange controls nearly offset the negative output effect of not devaluing. This result appears at odds with the conclusion in Table 12.1, column 4, of Eichengreen (1992, 350), that exchange-control countries did better than gold bloc countries but much worse than devaluers. However, the exchange control group underlying the last regression is larger than Eichengreen's, including, in addition to his observations, Argentina, Japan, Romania, Greece, Latvia, Estonia, and Denmark.

[64]   WPI data come from League of Nations (1938b).

governments to tolerate deflation and labor unrest in a distributional fight under conditions of downward wage inflexibility.[65]

Much of the motivation for maintaining pegged exchange rates, both in gold-bloc and exchange-control countries, was the fear of hyperinflation and the attendant social conflict, as witnessed all too recently in Central and Eastern Europe. That fear was present, though not dominant, even in countries that chose open devaluation.[66] Ironically, exchange control, itself so inimical to the liberal principles of orthodox finance, nonetheless facilitated the persistence of orthodox monetary policies in those countries least willing, given recent inflationary experience, to sacrifice the nominal anchor of their official gold parity. Even in peripheral Latin America, "memories of wild inflation under inconvertible paper during the late nineteenth century, memories still fresh during 1929–31, hampered and slowed down the adoption of more self-assured and expansionist policies."[67]

The exchange-control countries, burdened by foreign debts and precarious reserve levels when the 1931 crisis hit, could not maintain their exchange parities except by controls. Once in place, however, controls were in most cases difficult to contain and were found to have other uses (albeit at foreigners' expense). The gold-bloc countries, in contrast, had the financial resources to cling to gold parities without radical controls, but as a result were defenseless against the deflationary forces of the Depression. As much as anything, the experience of these countries discredited the remnants of the gold-standard orthodoxy and opened the way for a new and interventionist Keynesian approach to international monetary relations after World War Two.

4.2.3 World War Two and its aftermath

Wartime intensification of exchange control

Private international capital mobility reached a nadir during and after World War Two, with much of the world left in the grip of bilateral payments arrangements. The postwar international economic order agreed at Bretton Woods in 1944, and inaugurated with the declaration of currency par values in 1946, mandated convertibility for current-account, but not necessarily for capital-account transactions. Even current-account convertibility proved hard to attain, how-

---

[65] Eichengreen (1992).

[66] Eichengreen (1992, 292); Nurkse (1944, 166); Sayers (1976, 412).

[67] Díaz Alejandro (1983, 18). If a lingering fear of uncontrolled inflation seems improbable in the midst of the Great Depression, consider present-day Japan, where similar fears have blocked the sustained monetary expansion needed to combat the current deflation of yen prices.

ever, in the circumstances following the war. Only at the end of 1958 was external (i.e., nonresident) convertibility on current account restored for the main European currencies.[68] The following decade was characterized not only by increasing capital mobility but also by speculative tensions that prompted industrial countries to intensify capital controls in an attempt to shore up the system of fixed exchange rates. These measures proved insufficient, and the modern era of floating dollar exchange rates finally dawned in 1973. Since then, the international flow of capital has expanded dramatically.

The onset of renewed war in 1939 led to an intensification of exchange control. In a memorandum written for British Treasury officials in September 1939, Keynes recalled of the emergency measures taken during World War One, "[c]omplete control was so much against the spirit of the age, that I doubt it ever occurred to any of us that it was possible."[69] Countries drew heavily on their interwar experiences with controls to mobilize their foreign-exchange resources for all-out conflict. By March 1940, dealings in nearly all the world's major currencies, the two important exceptions being the U.S. dollar and the Swiss franc, were subject to some form of exchange control.[70] An additional advantage of restricting capital outflows in wartime was that governments might thereby borrow at artificially low rates of interest.

Britain imposed controls in August and September of 1939, initially regulating residents' purchases of foreign currencies but not blocking sterling balances held by nonenemy aliens nor preventing all sterling transactions between residents and nonresidents. In response to these rules an offshore market in "free" sterling soon developed. As Keynes forcefully pointed out, nonresidents could buy British exports with free sterling, depriving the country of badly needed hard currency – basically, U.S. dollars or Swiss francs. This loophole and others were closed in June 1940, the same month Keynes took up a formal advisory position at the U.K. Treasury.[71] The sterling bloc, which had previously been a loose association of countries pegging to the pound, narrowed its membership and transformed itself into the Sterling Area, where similar external

---

[68] A currency is *externally* convertible if foreigners who hold it (but not necessarily residents of the issuing country) may exchange it freely for other currencies or for domestic goods and assets. The currency is externally convertible *for current transactions* if foreigners who have acquired it through exports or receipts of asset income can convert it into other currencies or domestic goods. (In contrast, a currency is *internally* convertible when *domestic* residents may freely exchange it for other currencies.) For a discussion of various notions of convertibility, see McKinnon (1979, 3–7).

[69] Keynes (1978, 10).

[70] Mikesell (1954, 15).

[71] Keynes (1978, 158–71); Mikesell (1954, 16). In August, Keynes was placed on the Exchange Control Conference.

exchange controls were enforced but internal currency transactions, including capital movements, were left free.[72]

Capital mobility in the Bretton Woods blueprint

Well before the end of the World War Two, officials in the Allied treasuries were turning their minds toward the design of a postwar international economic order. In 1941 and 1942 respectively, John Maynard Keynes in Britain and Harry Dexter White in the United States circulated different draft plans for postwar institutions designed to aid in the maintenance of exchange stability, macroeconomic stability, and orderly, generally nondiscriminatory trading relations among nations.

White's plan would, in 1944, become the basis for the Bretton Woods agreement that led to the establishment of the International Monetary Fund, the World Bank, and the General Agreement on Tariffs and Trade (GATT). Both plans are instructive, however, for the light they throw on official and academic attitudes toward the role of capital movements.[73] In essence, the plans reflected a broad policy consensus, growing out of the experience of the Depression, that the global economy would not necessarily be smoothly self-regulating if the wartime controls were to be dismantled. Hence, the planners believed that exchange rates and international capital movements would both have to be closely controlled and could not be left to the market.[74]

Keynes's plan stepped back from the extreme economic nationalism he had flirted with in his famous 1933 article on "National Self-Sufficiency."[75] But the plan's basic premise was that heavy government management of macroeconomic policies and exchange rates should be deployed in the defense of internal macroeconomic stability, and that such a resolution of the policy trilemma presupposed extensive restrictions over, not only capital movements, but also foreign exchange transactions in general.

---

[72] The Sterling Area's holdings of hard currencies were centralized at the Bank of England, which also supplied these resources when needed by Area members. Both internally and outside of the Sterling Area, sterling was inconvertible into hard currencies or gold.

[73] Various drafts of the Keynes and White plans are reproduced in Horsefield (1969). The French and the Canadians also advanced proposals (where the latter was known colloquially as the "off-White" plan).

[74] There were, of course, numerous dissenters from various aspects of this consensus such as Friedman (1953), who argued for floating exchanges and freedom of short-term capital movements, and Viner (1943a), who espoused fixed rates but believed they might be consistent with a liberal capital transfer regime. Some still argued for the gold standard (see the *New York Times*, March 30, 1943).

[75] Keynes (1982, 233–46). Harrod (1951, 525–6) ascribes the shift to Keynes's perception by the 1940s that in a new postwar order Keynesian economics might be applied on a global scale, rather than the national scale he envisaged in the 1930s.

Keynes also proposed an International Clearing Union (ICU) that would facilitate multilateral trade among members and extend credit (within limits) to cover current-account deficits. To these ends, countries with external surpluses would accumulate claims on the ICU and countries with deficits, liabilities. These positive and negative balances were to be denominated in a new international currency called "bancor." Fixed in gold value and in terms of national currencies, bancor would be used to settle trade imbalances, much as gold had been used in an earlier era. The instability associated with fluctuating interwar exchange rates remained a powerful influence over attitudes toward postwar monetary relations. In Keynes's view, floating rates were to be rejected both for their disruptive effects and as a reversion to discredited laissez-faire economics.

Exchange values under the ICU were not to be "unalterably" fixed, however; far from it. Instead, Keynes's conception, as expressed several years later in defending the proposed International Monetary Fund in the House of Lords, was that

> We are determined that, in future, the external value of sterling shall conform to its internal value as set by our own domestic policies....[I]nstead of maintaining the principle that the internal value of a national currency should conform to a prescribed *de jure* external value, [the Bretton Woods plan] provides that its external value should be altered if necessary to conform to whatever *de facto* internal value results from domestic policies, which themselves shall be immune from criticism by the Fund.[76]

In other words, exchange realignments rather than domestic deflation, as under the gold standard, were the preferred tool for rectifying payments deficits and unemployment in Keynes's system. Domestic policies would be geared toward high employment, with short-term international deficits being met by overdrafts on the ICU.

Seen in historical perspective, it is clear that Keynes's view on exchange-rate adjustment represented a sea change compared to the attitudes that had prevailed in the gold-standard era. As Haberler puts it in an insightful discussion of the Great Depression's causes and legacy:

> The sanctity of fixed exchange rates was a casualty of the Great Depression. It is true that there had been many exchange-rate changes in the nineteenth century and earlier. But the devaluation of the leading currencies of the world...made the operation "salon fähig," that is, fit for gentlemen.[77]

Keynes appreciated clearly that by resolving the policy trilemma in favor of internal employment goals and exchange-rate management, he was ruling

---

[76] Keynes (1980b, 16–18).
[77] Haberler (1976, 17).

out open capital markets. Indeed, Keynes's plan embraced exchange control wholeheartedly and explicitly called for curbs on capital movements, with some provision for international long-term capital movements added in as an afterthought.[78] The attitude toward private capital movement was set out explicitly in all drafts of Keynes's plan, for example, the fourth:[79]

It is widely held that control of capital movements, both inward and outward, should be a permanent feature of the post-war system – at least so far as we are concerned. If control is to be effective, it probably involves the *machinery* of exchange control for *all* transactions, even though a general open licence is given to all remittances in respect of current trade. But such control will be more difficult to work, especially in the absence of postal censorship, by unilateral action than if movements of capital can be controlled *at both ends*. It would therefore be of great advantage if the United States and all other members of the Currency Union would adopt machinery similar to that which we have now gone a long way towards perfecting in this country; though this cannot be regarded as *essential to* the proposed Union.[80]

White's alternative plan placed less emphasis on periodic exchange-rate adjustment than did Keynes's and viewed capital movements in a somewhat more favorable light. Dam quotes a passage from the April 1942 version of the White plan to support the assertion that White took a creditor's view of the postwar order, favoring reduced capital controls in contrast with "Keynes's enthusiasm for capital controls."[81] In fact, White was referring to generalized exchange controls on the model of interwar Germany in the quoted passage, not specifically to capital controls, and later in the plan advocated a prohibition of Fund resources for funding "illegitimate" capital flows.[82] Such a provision would have been necessary in any event to assuage Congressional fears that the United States would end up funding unlimited foreign imbalances. White's plan also called for international cooperation to limit capital flows inspired by "speculation" or tax evasion:

It would be an important step in the direction of world stability if a member government could obtain the full cooperation of other member governments in the control of capital flows....The assumption that capital serves a country best by flowing to countries which offer most attractive terms is valid only under circumstances that are not always

---

[78] In Keynes's conception, central banks would be monopoly dealers in foreign exchange within each country; they in turn would sell foreign exchange to the ICU for bancor credits, or settle directly with foreign central banks. As monopoly dealers, the central banks were ideally placed to scrutinize all foreign exchange transactions and deny foreign exchange for purposes of capital transfer (Keynes 1980a, 216).

[79] The draft is dated February 11, 1942.

[80] Horsefield (1969, 13).

[81] Dam (1982, 83); Horsefield (1969, 47).

[82] Horsefield (1969, 49–50).

present....A good case could be made for the thesis that a government should have the power to control the influx and efflux of capital, just as it has the authority to control the inflow and outflow of goods and of gold.[83]

In reality, Keynes and White were not far apart on the *principle* that capital flows might need to be regulated, although Keynes's methods for accomplishing this task were more realistic and therefore much more dirigiste.

This shared tolerant attitude toward capital-account prohibitions was fully reflected in the eventual Articles of Agreement establishing the IMF. A major goal of the IMF system was nondiscriminatory multilateral convertibility on current account (as set out in Article VIII). But Article VI (3) stated that "[m]embers may exercise such controls as are necessary to regulate international capital movements." Article VI (1) prohibited members from using Fund resources "to meet a large or sustained outflow of capital," and even empowered the Fund to request imposition of capital controls in such cases.[84] Keynes's plan had also included the latter feature.[85]

The United States' agreement to such provisions in 1944 and 1945 may seem contrary to its natural interests as the premier creditor and financial power of the postwar period. As noted previously, however, Congress was concerned about the extent of America's financial commitment. Anyway, the allowed restrictions seemed unlikely ever to be needed by the United States, would likely apply to other countries' outflows rather than inflows, and could only ensure New York's position as the world's leading financial center. Business interests in the United States were in any case more concerned with current-account convertibility and expanded export opportunities than with capital flows.

Moreover, New Deal Washington viewed the financial world with considerable distrust. That distrust was inherent in the Democratic Party's Jacksonian tradition. But it was greatly heightened by the perceived role of banks and security markets in bringing on the Great Depression. Disillusion with banks and financial markets prevailed in many countries, in fact, and led to a general reduction during the 1930s of central-bank independence in favor of treasury dominance.[86] Hand in hand with this view went stricter regulations on financial markets. Populist backlash was also reflected in Treasury Secretary Henry Morgenthau's pronouncement at Bretton Woods that the new institutions would "drive...the usurious money lenders from the temple of international finance,"

[83] Horsefield (1969, 66–7).
[84] Horsefield (1969, 193–4).
[85] In 1956, the IMF's executive directors interpreted Article VI as allowing countries (subject to some mild restrictions) to impose capital controls "for any reason" and "without approval of the Fund" (Horsefield 1969, 246).
[86] See Dam (1982, 53). On the United States, see Calomiris and Wheelock (1998).

and in his successor, Fred Vinson's, unilateral shift of Fund and Bank head-quarters from New York to Washington on the purported grounds that "the institutions would be fatally prejudiced in American opinion if they were placed in New York, since they would then come under the taint of 'international finance.'"[87] White himself undoubtedly shared these views, arguing in his plan that capital controls "would constitute another restriction on the property rights of the 5 or 10 percent of persons in foreign countries who have enough wealth or income to keep or invest some of it abroad, but a restriction that presumably would be exercised in the interests of the people – at least so far as the government is competent to judge that interest."[88]

4.3 Containment then collapse: Bretton Woods, 1946–1972

4.3.1 Stability without integration

At the height of the world war in 1943, the governments-in-exile of the Belgium-Luxembourg union and the Netherlands entered into a bilateral financial agreement which was the first of about 200 that would be in effect in Europe by 1947 and nearly 400 that would be in effect worldwide shortly thereafter.[89] Under the agreement, the two countries promised to peg their mutual exchange rate by standing ready to purchase the other's currency. This type of agreement aimed at conserving reserves of hard currency and gold through mutual credit arrangements but in practice entailed controls over resident transactions so as to prevent the buildup of unbalanced positions in partner currencies. A corollary of hard-currency scarcity was a continuation of currency inconvertibility and of wartime prohibitions on private capital movements, which might quickly strip a government of reserves. Domestic financial controls further limited international intermediation, and, along with the economic and political instabilities implied by reconstruction, blocked the channels through which potential capital-receiving countries might have borrowed privately abroad. Private international capital movements had essentially dried up.

Currency inconvertibility seriously compromised even the gains from current international trade. If country *A* had a trade surplus with country *B*, it could not

---

[87] Gardner (1980, xix); Keynes (1980a, 211).

[88] Horsefield (1969, 67). The evolution of White's political views is discussed by Rees (1973). In 1948, White was accused of spying for the Soviet Union. He died of a heart attack three days after denying the charge before the House Un-American Activities Committee. KGB archives declassified during the 1990s furnish evidence, however, that White indeed passed intelligence to the Soviets, his direct contacts beginning around the time of the Bretton Woods negotiations. For a detailed discussion see Skidelsky (2001, chap. 7).

[89] Yeager (1976, 407).

use its surplus accumulation of *B*'s currency to finance a deficit with country *C*, as would have been possible under general external currency convertibility. Somehow, country *A*'s payments would have to be balanced vis-à-vis both *B* and *C* individually, not simply vis-à-vis the rest of the world taken in totality. Bilateral trading agreements may have been superior to blanket, indiscriminate limitations on foreign transactions in allowing for mutual credits (the trade creation aspect), but they had the drawback of shunting demand from the cheapest source of supply worldwide toward countries with extensive demands for domestic products (trade diversion). A system of multilateral clearing had the potential to ease such constraints and promote a more efficient global resource allocation, if only a true multilateral payments system could be attained.

Unfortunately, universal convertibility, even limited external convertibility, was difficult for individual countries to attain in the immediate postwar circumstances. Restoring convertibility required countries to solve a serious coordination problem. In a setting of general inconvertibility, a single country allowing foreigners to convert its currency freely would face an uncomfortable net drain of foreign-exchange reserves: foreign exporters would convert the bulk of their domestic currency earnings into central-bank foreign reserves, whereas most of the foreign currency earned by domestic exporters would be unusable. The latter could insist on being paid in their own currency, but this would seriously injure sales, because the home country would likely have its best potential export markets in countries from which it did not itself import much. Furthermore, foreign countries might deliberately restrict imports from the convertible-currency country so as to maximize their hard-currency inflow at its expense.[90] Of course, one solution to the problem would have been for monetary authorities simply to refrain from trading domestic currency for foreign currencies and let exchange rates float, as did several countries after World War One. Indeed, Friedman's celebrated polemic "The Case for Flexible Exchange Rates," drafted in 1950, explicitly promoted floating rates as a strategy for moving immediately to general currency convertibility.[91] This step governments were reluctant to take, out of fear of the currency instability and inflation that they associated with interwar floating exchange rates.

Article VIII of the IMF Articles of Agreement, as noted earlier, called for convertibility on current account and unrestricted freedom of current international payments. Article XIV, however, allowed countries to maintain restrictions contravening Article VIII during a transitional period, and even to introduce new

---

[90] See Yeager (1976, 409–10) for further discussion of this "contagion of bilateralism." See also Triffin (1957, 88–93). The basic mechanisms at work were emphasized by Viner (1943b).
[91] Friedman (1953, 158).

restrictions. Only five years after the start of IMF operations was any member not yet in compliance with Article VIII required to begin annual consultations on its progress with the Fund.

At the time the Articles were drafted, a five-year breathing space was regarded as allowing a reasonable period for the general return to (current-account) convertibility. Nothing of the sort happened. Instead, controls generally proliferated. By 1953, more countries were engaging in multiple currency practices than in 1946, leading Mikesell to the exasperated remark that "the system of fixed exchange parities combined with a complex of neo-Schachtian devices has provided far less exchange stability in the postwar period than did the fluctuating free exchange rates of the 1930s."[92]

By 1957, only eight countries apart from the United States and Canada – Mexico, Cuba, the Dominican Republic, Guatemala, El Salvador, Honduras, Haiti, and Panama – had formally accepted the Article VIII obligations.[93] The proliferation of controls reflected the same forces preventing unilateral movements toward convertibility by dollar-hungry countries. A classic example is that of Switzerland, which, to protect foreign exchange reserves, made its franc inconvertible for Europeans while leaving it convertible for residents of the dollar area.[94]

Some countries responded to the situation by adopting floating exchange rates, IMF norms notwithstanding. Canada dismantled its exchange controls under cover of a floating rate; Mexico, Peru, and Chile likewise floated their currencies; and Churchill's government in Britain seriously debated a scheme for freeing the pound in 1952.[95]

Triffin argued that the IMF might have been able to move the world more quickly to convertibility if its structure had facilitated multilateral clearing, for example through Keynes's conception of a synthetic international currency. Instead, the Fund blueprint "dealt with the setting up and revision of par values, the elimination of exchange controls, and the Fund's lending operations as if these problems could be handled with each country individually against a background of general convertibility and stability in world trade and currency arrangements."[96] The coordination problem involved in moving to the latter type of equilibrium from the one left by the war was not addressed.

The hazards of a unilateral return to convertibility by war-torn countries are

---

[92] Mikesell (1954, 25–7).
[93] Triffin (1957, 115).
[94] Kaplan and Schleiminger (1989, 57); Yeager (1976, 409).
[95] Triffin (1957, 123); Cairncross (1985, chap. 9); Kaplan and Schleiminger (1989, chap. 10).
[96] Triffin (1957, 137).

well illustrated by Britain's abortive attempt to restore multilateral current-account convertibility for sterling in July 1947 – an experiment that had to be abandoned after only five weeks. In September 1945, a British delegation led by Keynes arrived in Washington to negotiate a loan of dollar reserves. The United States insisted (among other conditions) that sterling's convertibility on current account be restored no later than one year after the funds, totalling $3.75 billion, became available. Congress and American business interests strongly supported the convertibility provision (as well as an associated trade nondiscrimination clause).[97] In particular, these groups felt that the IMF Articles' timetable for restoring convertibility was lax. Immediate convertibility of so widely held a currency as sterling, it was believed, would hasten worldwide freedom of current payments, at the same time easing discriminatory trade practices intended to maximize bilateral trade surpluses with the United States.

Britain had little choice but to put aside its misgivings and agree to these terms. July 15, 1947, emerged as sterling's convertibility date after Congressional approval of the loan midway through 1946.[98] Britain's current-account deficit increased sharply after the harsh winter of 1946–7. By the end of June more than half the U.S. loan had been used up.[99] Despite continuing gold and dollar outflows, however, Britain fulfilled its commitment and declared convertibility on July 15, hoping desperately that convertibility would raise global confidence in sterling. Instead, reserve outflows accelerated and a crisis ensued. With only $400 million of the American loan remaining, Britain suspended convertibility on August 20.

The sharp acceleration in dollar losses in July seems largely to have been the result of capital outflows. It was feared that convertibility would be fleeting and that sterling might be devalued once the experiment failed. Now was the time to get dollars, and at a relatively cheap sterling price. (Convertibility did turn out to be very temporary, but the feared devaluation did not come until 1949.) The result was a classic speculative attack. How was an attack on sterling carried out in a world of seemingly pervasive capital controls? Some countries converted preexisting sterling balances into dollars, representing them as current earnings. On the basis of revised balance of payments data, Cairncross argues that this channel was not very important, notwithstanding a long tradition placing much of the blame for the debacle on such conversions.[100] More significant were "leads and lags" in trade credits – the practice of accelerating sterling pay-

---

[97] Gardner (1980, 197–8).
[98] Canada added $1.25 billion to the loan.
[99] Cairncross (1985, 132).
[100] Cairncross (1985, 157); see also, for example, Gardner (1980, 317–18).

ments and delaying foreign-currency receipts in the expectation of a sterling depreciation.[101] Finally, some reserves leaked out through capital transfers to other Sterling Area countries. Sterling Area members such as South Africa and Australia borrowed large sums of sterling in London and rapidly used the proceeds for imports from the dollar area.[102]

The crisis carried two distinct lessons. First, in the circumstances of the immediate postwar years, a single country like Britain with a structural current-account deficit caused by wartime changes could not unilaterally return to convertibility. Any such return would need to be coordinated among many nations. As Gardner puts it:

The fact is that the negotiators [of the Anglo-American loan agreement] did not fully understand the economics of convertibility. They did not appreciate the difficulty in which Britain might find itself in the event that it went on accumulating inconvertible currencies while other countries, deliberately restricting imports from the United Kingdom, presented large sterling surpluses for conversion. Given this hazard of making one currency convertible in a generally inconvertible world, the use of a rigid time-table was certainly injudicious.[103]

A second lesson of the crisis, one less appreciated at the time, was that damaging speculative crises could occur even under exchange control. Capital controls were porous, certainly porous enough to devastate the slim liquidity bases upon which most countries were operating in the late 1940s. The channels of capital flight revealed in the U.K. convertibility crisis, especially leads and lags, would remain widely operative through the end of the Bretton Woods system, coming strongly into play whenever the prospect of devaluation offered a large speculative gain over a short period. Indeed, the scope for such phenomena only increased as trade expanded in the 1960s.

Even before Britain suspended sterling's short-lived convertibility, the United States proposed the Marshall Plan with its accompanying call for economic cooperation within Europe. The Plan reflected a change in the U.S. "universalist" approach to postwar economic problems, motivated by the perception of a dire political threat to a region of unique strategic importance. American policymakers hoped that Marshall aid would promote intra-European trade, strengthening Europe's economies and creating a shared interest in political stability. However, the absence of any multilateral clearing system for intra-European payments frustrated this hope. Under prodding from the U.S. European Cooperation Administration, which administered the Marshall funds, the nations of

[101] Einzig (1968).
[102] See Wyplosz (1986) for a formal analysis of speculative attacks under capital controls.
[103] Gardner (1980, 218).

Western Europe in September 1950 created the European Payments Union. The EPU was a major success in facilitating trade liberalization within Europe (and indirectly with territories on other continents that belonged to some European country's currency area). The EPU worked by every month consolidating each member's bilateral payments deficits into a net debt to the Union, extending some credit but eventually requiring settlement in dollars or gold. This allowed European country A to use its surplus with European country B to finance its deficit with European country C, despite the inconvertibility of B's currency.[104]

The initial success of the EPU allowed some privatization of foreign exchange transactions, which had been concentrated in the hands of central banks. This liberalization allowed private banks to take over some of the EPU's clearing functions. Over the course of the 1950s, several EPU members, notably the United Kingdom and Germany, liberalized foreign exchange transactions further, with Germany going the furthest in allowing residents to retain foreign-exchange earnings and to hold foreign assets. (In the United Kingdom, residents could deal among themselves in a managed pool of foreign "investment currency" but otherwise were barred from acquiring foreign assets, while non-residents until 1967 had to trade sterling securities in a separate market for "security sterling.") During 1957–8, Europe's hard-currency reserves rose sharply, the counterpart of a huge U.S. payments deficit. On December 27, 1958, the EPU was terminated by mutual consent, with most members, including France, Germany, Italy, and the United Kingdom, declaring their currencies externally convertible on current account. (The former EPU countries formally accepted their Article VIII convertibility obligations in February 1961. Japan followed in April 1964.) Germany also moved to full convertibility on capital account, so that, as of January 1959, the Bundesbank could declare that

only the payment of interest on foreigners' balances, the sale of domestic money-market paper to foreigners and the taking of foreign loans running less than five years remain forbidden, the object being to check the inflow of "hot money" into the Federal Republic.[105]

Germany's motives for such wide-ranging liberalization were two. One was the free-market ideology characteristic of Economics Minister Ludwig Erhard's policies. Equally important, however, was the pressure on Germany's internal liquidity and prices due to the chronic balance of payments surplus that had developed after the early 1950s. By liberalizing capital outflows, the authorities hoped to reduce the payments surplus, whereas the remaining capital controls

---

[104] The IMF, in contrast, could perform no comparable clearinghouse function. On the EPU, see Triffin (1957), Kaplan and Schleiminger (1989), and Eichengreen (1993).
[105] Deutsche Bundesbank (1959, 52).

listed in the preceding quotation were intended to discourage capital inflows and provide scope for sterilization operations.[106]

In 1957, Belgium, France, Germany, Italy, Luxembourg, and the Netherlands signed the Treaty of Rome creating the European Economic Community (EEC). The Treaty called on signatories to undertake the progressive abolition "between themselves of all restrictions on the movement of capital belonging to persons resident in Member States."[107] This provision was viewed as fundamental to the long-term goal of a single European market. The first directive of the EEC's council of economics and finance ministers (the ECOFIN council) in May 1960 required member countries to free short- to medium-term trade credits, direct investments, and cross-border trades of listed shares.

Germany had pushed for full liberalization of capital movements in the negotiations leading to the directive, including movements between EEC members and nonmember states.[108] In May 1959, seeing a welcome fall in its official reserves and assuming that the policy of encouraging capital exports was working, Germany unilaterally abolished its remaining restrictions on capital import.[109] Despite policymakers' optimism, however, Germany was very shortly to experience the type of policy conflict that ultimately brought the Bretton Woods system down amid escalating capital controls.

4.3.2 Leakage, then deluge

Only the month after the EEC ECOFIN Council's directive on liberalization of capital movements, Germany reimposed some of the controls it had abolished a year earlier. Attempting to restrain a domestic boom through higher interest rates, the Bundesbank found itself frustrated by the large volume of reserves purchases it was obliged to make to maintain the Deutsche mark's exchange parity. Controls were brought back in the hope of discouraging renewed capital inflows, but they provided only a temporary breathing space. In March 1961,

---

[106] On Germany's attempts to counteract the inflationary potential of its balance-of-payments surpluses, see Boarman (1964) and Emminger (1977). Germany's relatively fast productivity growth in the 1950s and 1960s mandated a secular real appreciation of the Deutsche mark against the dollar, that is, a rise in Germany's price level measured in dollars against that of the United States. Given a fixed nominal exchange rate, however, this equilibrating real currency appreciation could occur only through higher inflation in Germany than in America – something German policymakers were largely unwilling to accept. The resulting tension made revaluation inevitable once German capital markets were fully open. In contrast, Japan did accept a higher inflation rate than that of the United States (Obstfeld 1993b).

[107] Article 67 (1), quoted in Bakker (1996, 279).

[108] Bakker (1996, 81).

[109] Yeager (1976, 496).

Germany, soon followed by the Netherlands, reluctantly revalued its currency by 5 percent against the dollar.

These events heralded a new era in which speculative capital flows regularly bedeviled policymakers in Europe and elsewhere. Concerted EEC progress on further capital-account liberalization bogged down, and fear of speculation made any open discussion of exchange parity changes impossible. Italy suffered a balance-of-payments crises in 1964, which it beat back with the help of loans from the United States and the IMF. Britain entered a prolonged period of crisis in the same year, giving in finally and devaluing sterling in November 1967. Nonetheless, individual European countries did take some liberalizing steps in the early and mid-1960s. Italy allowed its residents more freedom to invest abroad. France, enjoying a strong balance of payments during the mid-1960s, unilaterally eased its controls in 1967, motivated in part by a desire to promote the role of Paris as a global financial center.[110] However, the May 1968 disturbances sparked capital flight and a reimposition of French controls; at the same time, Germany, the recipient of much of the flight capital, tightened its own barriers to capital inflows. Speculation continued into 1969: France resisted until the speculation temporarily subsided and then surprised markets by devaluing in August. Speculation on a German revaluation reemerged in the same year in advance of parliamentary elections. Just prior to the election, the government closed the official foreign-exchange market and then allowed the Deutsche mark to float. The new government of Chancellor Willy Brandt revalued the currency by just over 9 percent at the end of October.

How could capital flows continue to undermine authorities' efforts to defend exchange parities even in the face of tightened capital controls? Leads and lags in trade credits again provided an important conduit for speculative capital flows; indeed, Einzig characterized leads and lags as "the main cause of devaluation" in his book on the subject, although his broad definition of the phenomenon included changes in the timing of goods orders (not just payments) as well as forward currency trades.[111] Ironically, the growth of international trade after the early 1950s – in itself a prime desideratum of the Bretton Woods architects – expanded the opportunities for disguised capital flows. The reopening of private foreign exchange markets and the emergence of the Eurocurrency markets in London in the 1960s further widened the scope for leakages from protected domestic financial systems. The growing tendency to delay realignments until the market forced the authorities' hand, itself a result of increasing possibilities for speculation, ensured that a speculative attack might produce

---

[110] Bakker (1996, 101).
[111] Einzig (1968).

large profits over a very brief period. Thus, even modest elasticities of trade credits, say, with respect to normal interest differentials could translate into large flows of reserves in crisis episodes.

The United States, meanwhile, had been facing its own problems since the end of the period of "dollar shortage" in the late 1950s. Growing U.S. balance-of-payments deficits were causing alarm. The counterpart of these deficits was a growing stock of short-term official dollar claims on the United States. Some of these claims were converted into gold, putting pressure on the American gold stock, but the bulk were held despite mounting anxiety that the dollar's gold content might suddenly be reduced. In response, the United States took a number of measures to counter private capital outflows. Starting in 1961, an escalating sequence of dividend and interest taxes, voluntary guidelines, and mandatory limits were imposed on American capital outflows abroad.[112] The ultimate effectiveness of these measures remains debatable even today. For example, New York banks, restricted from lending directly to foreigners, could legally set up London subsidiaries capable of taking dollar deposits and making the forbidden loans. Non-U.S. banks also competed for this business. Regulations meant to retain dollar inflows within U.S. borders therefore shunted these dollars into the London Eurodollar market, promoting that market's spectacular growth at the expense of onshore U.S. banks.[113]

The dollar itself came under concerted attack in the early 1970s, a development caused in part by President Lyndon Johnson's escalation of military and domestic spending and in part by divergent productivity trends. Increasingly volatile capital flows set the stage for the ultimate collapse of fixed exchange rates in early 1973.[114] Several industrialized countries temporarily floated their currencies prior to the Smithsonian dollar devaluation of December 1971, and several, including Germany, imposed restrictions on capital inflows.[115] When the new Smithsonian parities were attacked in 1972 and 1973, Japan, Switzerland, Germany, France, and the Netherlands all raised barriers to capital inflows, including quantitative borrowing restrictions, interest taxes, and supplemental reserve requirements. Concerned by the disruptive effect of floating intra-European exchange rates on its common agricultural policy and the ongoing drive for further economic integration, the European Community issued a

[112] Bordo (1993, 58); Solomon (1982, chaps. 3 and 6).
[113] On the origins of the Eurodollar market, see Schenk (1998). Concern about the U.S. balance-of-payments deficit was not universal. Kindleberger (1965) offers a cogent contrary position. For skeptical remarks on the "confidence problem" posed by an increasing ratio of official dollar liabilities to U.S. gold, see Obstfeld (1993b, 211).
[114] Solomon (1982, chaps. 11–13); Yeager (1976, chap. 28).
[115] Bakker (1996, 122).

general derogation from its May 1960 first directive on capital-account liberalization, and went further in directing members to develop or reinstate effective mechanisms for controlling capital flows and their effects on domestic money supplies.[116] The lira and sterling, like the dollar, were under selling pressure; Italy and Britain raised barriers to stem outflows as a result. In June 1972, the United Kingdom extended its exchange control system to apply to transactions within the Sterling Area, and let the pound float downward. The pressure of speculation remained unbearable, however. By March 1973, industrialized country currencies were floating against the U.S. dollar, with six EC currencies floating jointly within a "snake," while Italy and the Anglo-Irish currency union floated independently.

4.4 Crisis and compromise II: Floating rates since 1973

4.4.1 Integration without stability?

Bretton Woods proved untenable in the end because its rules could not reconcile independent national policy goals, pegged exchange rates, and even the limited degree of capital mobility implied by an open world trading system. After industrial countries had been forced to accept floating dollar exchange rates as an open-ended interim regime, however, at least some governments felt free to liberalize capital movements without sacrificing either their domestic policy priorities or an external currency commitment.

Over the years 1974 to 1975, the United States dropped its restrictions on capital outflows while Germany liberalized inflows. Germany would again deploy controls over inflows in the late 1970s when dollar weakness threatened to enhance the reserve-currency status of the Deutsche mark, a development the Bundesbank resisted.

France and Italy retained and even tightened some controls in order to loosen the link between monetary and exchange-rate policy. A strong motivation for these actions was the desire to limit intra-EC exchange-rate fluctuations, first within the informal EC currency snake and later within the European Monetary System (EMS).[117] The United Kingdom also tightened and retained controls until, in 1979, Thatcherite free-market ideology, allied with a fear that North Sea oil would bring the "Dutch disease" of sterling appreciation, led to suspension of the 1947 Exchange Control Act and full capital-account liberalization.

Japan largely opened its capital account in December 1980, the culmination of a series of steps beginning in 1974. Liberalization was typically undertaken

---

[116] Bakker (1996, 116–18).
[117] Giavazzi and Giovannini (1989); Bakker (1996).

to promote inflows or outflows that would counter yen depreciation or appreciation; only rarely were controls tightened. The liberalizing trend seems to have reflected pressures from the domestic business and financial community.[118] Further measures to ease foreign asset exchanges were taken in 1984, partly as a result of pressure from the United States.[119]

Developing countries generally retained or tightened capital-account controls throughout the Bretton Woods period, the most important sources of capital inflow being official loans and foreign direct investment. The two oil-price shocks of the 1970s produced large and persistent surpluses for oil producers but only transitory deficits for the industrialized world. The oil surpluses were "recycled" to developing countries through industrialized-country banks, so that by the early 1980s, developing market borrowers owed a substantial debt to the banks, most of it government or government-guaranteed. Most developing countries exercised strict control over *private* exchange transactions. As of April 30, 1980, only 50 of 140 IMF members had formally ceased operating under the "temporary" Article XIV derogation from Article VIII, although these countries accounted for most of world trade.[120]

The developing-country debt buildup turned into a crisis in August 1982 under the pressure of a global economic downturn and sharply higher world interest rates. Bank lenders became unwilling to extend new loans or even roll over maturing debts, and generalized default loomed, as in 1931. Open default was avoided through concerted rescheduling orchestrated largely by the United States and the IMF. Only toward the end of the 1980s did U.S.-brokered debt workouts under the Brady plan begin to pave the way for renewed private lending to the developing world, which boomed in the early 1990s. Direct investment has grown significantly, but more strikingly, bank lending to governments has given way to portfolio investment in bond and equity markets. The shift in the composition of developing-country liabilities is in part a reflection of wide-ranging financial-sector restructuring in these countries.

In the mid-1970s, several Latin American countries, notably Argentina, Chile, and Uruguay, opened their capital accounts as part of exchange-rate-based stabilization programs. These programs, flawed by insufficient fiscal stringency, inadequate domestic financial supervision, and inconsistent wage indexation structures, all proved to be unsustainable and were followed by renewed capital-account restrictions. More recently, numerous developing countries in East Asia have instituted domestic financial deregulation and at least

---

[118] Ito (1992, 316–21).
[119] Frankel (1984); Ito (1992, 329).
[120] Dam (1982, 101).

partial capital-account opening, often in the face of large external surpluses. Similar developments followed in Latin America against a background of generally deeper fiscal reform than in the 1970s episodes, privatization, and inflation stabilization.[121] Notable among the stabilization efforts was Argentina's ambitious (but ultimately unsustainable) convertibility plan of 1991, which enshrined in the national constitution a 1 : 1 peso-dollar exchange rate backed up by a currency board. The reform efforts were in some cases only partial, but they were enough to encourage renewed capital inflows, at least for a time. The decline in U.S. interest rates in the early 1990s was an important additional causal factor behind these capital inflows.[122]

4.4.2 The new global capital market

Investor interest in emerging markets weakened when U.S. interest rates rose in 1994, and several developing economies faced pressure in the aftermath of the 1994–5 Mexican crisis. Markets displayed greater resilience than in 1982 and Mexico was soon able to borrow again, albeit after extraordinary financial backing from the U.S. Treasury and the IMF.

Then, in 1997–8, a series of financial crises erupted in Asia, starting in Thailand but spreading quickly to Indonesia, Malaysia, Korea, and even Hong Kong. Repercussions extended outside the region, as crises eventually hit Russia (1998) and Brazil (1998–9). After a painfully long skid, Argentina's convertibility regime crashed, partly as a result of fiscal irresponsibility and insufficient structural reform, partly under pressure from Brazil's 1999 devaluation, though the respective contributions are hotly disputed. The end result was an external default at the end of 2001 and a sharp currency depreciation starting in January 2002. Neighboring Uruguay was soon dragged under. Outside of Argentina, however, there was no general retreat from open capital markets. Even Malaysia, which had imposed outflow controls at the height of the Asian crisis, loosened them afterward.

Brazil operated a flexible exchange-rate regime fairly successfully in the wake of its 1999 crisis. Other Latin American countries that moved toward exchange-rate flexibility coupled with inflation targeting, such as Chile and Mexico, also avoided crisis. There continues to be substantial debate over the appropriate degree of exchange flexibility in developing countries, as well as over the appropriate degree, form, and preconditions for capital mobility. Critics of an open capital markets regime have pointed to prior financial liberaliza-

---

[121] Edwards (1995, chap. 3) analyzes the forces behind economic liberalization in Latin America.
[122] See Calvo et al. (1996) for an insightful overview.

tions in East Asia as a precipitating factor in a crisis that, while fairly short-lived outside of politically-troubled Indonesia, was devastating in its short-term negative output effect. These criticisms have not been translated into policy action since, as we have noted, the developing countries that have carried out capital-account liberalizations so far show no appetite for a long-term policy reversal.

What explains the trend of capital-account liberalization in the developing world? Clearly one element has been the widespread failure in the periphery of populist policies adopted in the 1980s and earlier. Reactions to those failures gave free-market ideologies a greater influence. On a larger scale, the collapse of the Soviet empire in the late 1980s also highlighted the advantages of the capitalist model. The resulting decline in Cold War tensions held out the promise of greater fluidity in private international capital. Whether exchange rates float or are fixed, there has been much greater openness to private financial flows on the periphery since the 1980s. In part a reflection of U.S. business inte American administrations have pushed developing economies to liberali capital account; in some cases, liberalization ran far ahead of domestic fi cial systems' capacities and clashed with national exchange-rate policies. The resulting contradictions helped spark developing-country currency crises in the latter 1990s. To attract capital from the industrial world remains a prime goal on the periphery, however, and that requires market-oriented reforms, stable macro policies, and higher levels of quality and transparency in governance and legal systems. We will return to the topic of emerging-market financial opening in Part Four of this book.

Another dramatic move toward full capital-account liberalization occurred among the continental members of the European Union. Starting in the 1980s, these countries began moving toward the goal of free intra-European capital mobility foreshadowed in the Treaty of Rome – which in practice implied unrestricted mobility vis-à-vis the outside world as well, given Germany's commitment to openness and the difficulty in any case of enforcing partial restrictions. France joined the trend after 1983, when President François Mitterand abandoned his socialist growth agenda in favor of the franc's continued participation in the EMS exchange-rate mechanism. Germany has consistently pushed its European partners toward capital-account freedom, except while Bretton Woods was unraveling in the early 1970s. An important motive for this advocacy has been the belief that an open capital account would impose discipline over monetary and fiscal policies. Germany's capital account was completely open by 1981; that of the Netherlands by 1986; Denmark's by 1989; Belgium-Luxembourg's and Italy's by 1990; Spain's, Portugal's, and Ireland's by 1992;

and Greece's by 1994.[123] Austria, Sweden, and Finland, which joined the EU in 1995, also had open capital accounts of fairly long standing by that time.

Driving this broad liberalization was an acceleration in both commodity-market integration within Europe and in plans for monetary union. The EMS currency crisis of the years 1992–3 illustrated once again the untenability of fixed exchange parities when capital is mobile and domestic economic conditions assume primacy over the exchange rate. However, calls to reinstate capital controls after the crises of the early 1990s were rejected, and 11 EU countries (followed two years later by a twelfth) achieved full monetary integration on January 1, 1999. Thus, the once utopian goal of European economic union first espoused by the United States in the late 1940s is being substantially achieved a half century later. However, the operation of the euro zone in practice has led to several predictable tensions – in terms of inflation divergence, unsynchronized national economic growth rates, and disputes over the sizes of individual members' fiscal deficits. These problems illustrate again that the sacrifice of national economic priorities in favor of fixed exchange rates and financial integration is not easily made.

4.5 Measuring integration using data on legal restrictions

In Part Two of this book we focused on quantity and price indicators of international financial integration, assessing its degree in terms of economic outcomes. The evolution of those indicators corresponds broadly to the preceding narrative account of government policies toward international capital movements. Direct quantitative measurement of such legal restrictions on asset trade is difficult, since the restrictions imposed can be quite heterogeneous, their enforcement can be more or less strenuous, and they may be porous to differing degrees for different economies and time periods. Furthermore, any quantitative index of administrative restrictions must be based on a somewhat arbitrary coding, and at best must be viewed as a rough ordinal measure. Nonetheless, it is useful to examine some of the measures that have been devised. To start, we wish to know if existing indexes of financial openness confirm or contradict the statistical and narrative picture we have already assembled. Even in the case of confirmation, the indexes may reveal new subtleties. Subject to the preceding caveats, we therefore examine three sets of measures.

Figure 4.1 reports measures of the restrictiveness of capital-account policies as devised by the International Monetary Fund. In these figures, financial

---

[123] Bakker (1996, 220).

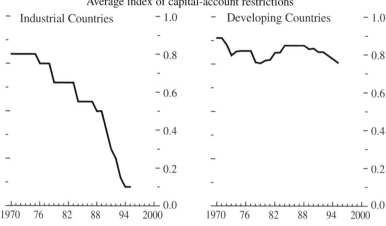

Fig. 4.1. Financial restrictiveness since 1970
Average index of capital-account restrictions

Source: International Monetary Fund, *World Economic Outlook*, September 2002, 110.

restrictiveness is measured by an index of capital account restrictions, a zero-one indicator, following Grilli and Milesi-Ferretti (1995). Since 1970, when these indicators begin, the financial restrictions of the industrial countries have plummeted more or less continuously. The picture for the developing world is more nuanced. For those countries, the 1980s debt crisis coincided with setbacks in financial opening, lasting until sometime around the end of that troubled decade. Subsequently, a trend of financial opening has reappeared.

Kaminsky and Schmukler (2003) develop a more refined index of capital-account restrictions based on a detailed chronology of 28 countries' experiences between 1973 and 1999. Averages for developed and developing countries are shown in Figure 4.2. In their coding, a value of 3 indicates complete repression, 2 indicates partial liberalization, and 1 indicates full liberalization. The data in Figure 4.2 are fully consistent with the dichotomous IMF measure shown in Figure 4.1.

So far, these data match our earlier conclusions. But it would be useful to have an even more finely graded measure of the restrictiveness of controls, going back further in time. A pioneering effort to construct more detailed liberalization measures by country can be found in the work of Quinn (1997) and subsequent papers from this still ongoing project.[124] This painstaking work relies on appraisals of regulatory measures in every country and their evolution

---

[124] We thank Dennis Quinn for permission to use unpublished data from this project.

Fig. 4.2. Capital-account restrictiveness, 1973–99
Average index of capital-account restrictions

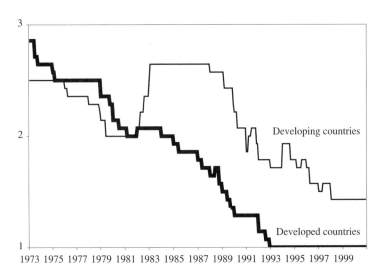

Source: Kaminsky and Schmukler (2003).

over time based on legislation, jurisprudence, and bureaucratic change. From
these verbal descriptions, a subjective index is built up for various forms of
financial restrictions, and an average is computed for two kinds of convertibility:
current account and capital account.

Figure 4.3 shows how this index behaves in the postwar period, with a plot
of the median index for various regional groupings of countries. According to
Quinn's measure of policy change, some major trends and turning points stand
out. First, over half a century there has been a marked shift to more open markets
in the world as a whole. The sharpest trend upward has been in the OECD
countries, with some other regions, notably East Asia, following strongly. South
America has had a more up and down progression on these policy measures,
and the Middle East and North Africa region and Subsaharan Africa have seen
much less progress. We clearly see the advance of convertibility in the early
Bretton Woods years of the 1950s, and then the slowdown in the late 1960s
as the system matured and had increasingly to withstand speculative attacks
on exchange rates. But since the late 1980s, we see increasing current- and
capital-account openness everywhere.

Fig. 4.3. Financial liberalization by region since 1950
Quinn's median index

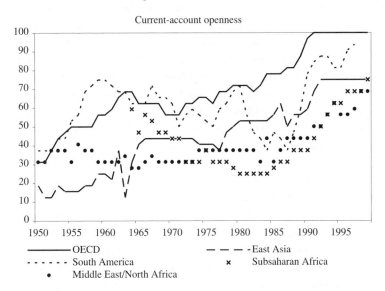

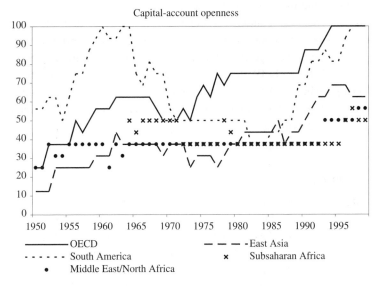

Source: Unpublished data based on Quinn (1997) and Quinn and Toyoda (n.d.).

The regional measures for the developing world deserve further discussion. As we noted earlier, all the countries that embraced Article VIII convertibility relatively early in the postwar period (other than Canada and the United States) were located in Central America and the Caribbean. The figure reflects this liberalization in the 1950s, but starting in the late 1960s, there appears to be considerable retrenchment for Latin America. That process accelerates sharply in the early 1970s as the Bretton Woods system breaks up and the OPEC oil price shock and other commodity shocks hit. The experience is an interesting one that once again illustrates the trilemma. Latin American countries wished to remain pegged to the dollar even as the Bretton Woods arrangements came apart. Economists such as Díaz Alejandro (1975) and Black (1976), in discussions quite similar to current ones, identified several reasons (immature financial markets, lack of facilities for hedging currency risks) why developing countries would find it hard to operate floating-rate systems as the industrial countries began to do in 1973. Given their retention of fixed dollar exchange rates, however, developing countries faced not only the obvious external shocks of the early 1970s but also shocks precipitated by changes in industrial countries' exchange rates against the dollar. Faced with these disturbances from abroad, countries in Latin America chose the only feasible means available for exercising some monetary control, restrictions on foreign transactions. The 1980s debt crisis led to another tightening of restrictions. Interestingly, while East Asia shows an almost monotonic upward trend in convertibility measures over the entire 50-year period, Quinn's measure shows a retrenchment in that region, too, in the early 1970s, though it is less pronounced than in Latin America. Once again, consistent with the logic of the trilemma, the recent upsurge of liberalization in developing countries has been accompanied by increased exchange-rate flexibility.

4.6 Summary

This chapter has chronicled both the decline of the international capital market after its gold-standard heyday and its gradual regeneration over the period following World War Two. A major unifying them has been the basic incompatibility of open capital markets with a policy regime that aims to attain both exchange-rate stability and domestic macroeconomic objectives.

Under the gold standard, exchange stability was the overriding goal of monetary policy and domestic objectives took a back seat. Thus, the monetary regime was consistent with considerable international capital mobility. The Great Depression discredited gold-standard orthodoxy, propelled Keynesian economics to intellectual ascendancy, and, worldwide, solidified the already vocal political constituencies favoring high employment and government intervention over laissez faire.

After the immediate post–World War Two dislocations, the world economy began to reconstitute its severed linkages, a process both promoting and promoted by the return of some degree of durable prosperity and peace. Postwar policymakers – through the establishment of the IMF, successive multilateral trade liberalization rounds, current-account currency convertibility, and other measures – successfully promoted growing world trade. By the late 1960s, the very success of these initiatives in expanding trading linkages among countries made capital flows across borders ever more difficult to contain. As a result, the trilemma reemerged with full force, and on a global scale, in the early 1970s. The Bretton Woods system, initially designed for a world of tightly controlled capital movements, blew apart. The major industrial countries retreated to floating exchange rates.

Although initially viewed as a temporary expedient, floating rates have become a durable feature of the international financial landscape. Floating rates helped reconcile the social demand for domestic macroeconomic stabilization with the interest of the business community for open markets in goods and assets. As a result, industrial countries' capital-account restrictions started to come down in the 1970s. Some episodes of exchange-rate misalignment have prompted calls for renewed protection and even capital-account restrictions. Some of these calls have been accommodated in rich countries, but not in the form of across-the-board restrictions on international transactions. Even in the developing world, forms of managed floating have spread, as has financial opening. Figure 4.4 documents the trend away from fixed and toward more flexible exchange rate regimes since the 1973 collapse of the Bretton Woods fixed exchange rate system.

As the data also show, however, the move to floating has been far from universal, and even in countries that shun flexible exchange rates, other forces have helped to promote liberalization. In Europe, the political and economic rationales for a large single market have prompted ongoing financial liberalization; at the same time, the political (and, some argue, economic) imperative of stable exchange rates has pushed toward the logical conclusion of a single currency, the euro. Other regions, likewise, have opted for fixed exchange rates, either by some form of ultra-hard peg or outright dollarization, in either case bending to the trilemma by giving up monetary policy autonomy. Fischer (2001) discusses the convergence of exchange-rate regimes toward the polar alternatives of free float and hard peg.

Fig. 4.4. Adherence to fixed exchange-rate regimes since 1973
Percentage of countries

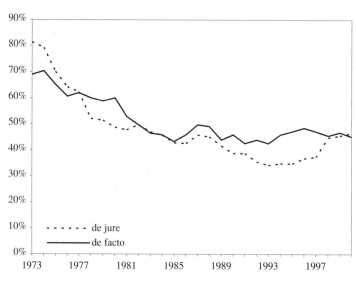

Source: Shambaugh (2004).

Domestic financial deregulation, like capital-account decontrol, also accelerated in the 1970s.[125] In part, that development flowed from the trend toward
freer international financial trade. After the 1950s, countries increasingly allowed homegrown financial institutions to compete for international business
within enclaves separated from domestic markets by a strict cordon sanitaire. As
resident capital controls were lifted, however, domestic deregulation became a
competitive necessity. Domestic deregulation and the consequent growth of the
financial sector, in turn, have made it much harder (technically and politically)
to reimpose capital-account restrictions effectively today.

Policymakers around the world continue to confront the trilemma and, subject
to the particular constellation of objectives and constraints in play, to find a
variety of solutions. The implication of a perspective based on the trilemma
is not that global capital leaves policymakers with no choices – only a more
limited set. However, a failure to understand those limits can be the undoing of
any plan for macroeconomic stability and growth. In the subsequent chapters of
this part, we document some of the policy constraints as they have impinged in

[125] Rajan and Zingales (2003) focus on the evolution of domestic deregulation.

history. We find evidence that the trilemma binds quite tightly – policymakers who imagine that a peg will still admit much room for maneuver in monetary policy are in for a rude shock. If policy autonomy is the goal, floating is the only way to go. We also find that shortcomings in policy credibility and fiscal prudence can have deleterious consequences even for ultra-hard pegs, meaning that policymakers should be careful about adopting such seemingly expedient tactics if markets will soon discover that they lack the will – or the political support – to remain committed.

5

Monetary Policy Interdependence
and Exchange-Rate Regimes:
Is the Trilemma Borne out by History?

Our account of the evolution of capital mobility centers on the open-economy trilemma as a fundamental organizing concept. The exchange-rate regime is often seen as tightly constrained by the trilemma, which imposes a stark tradeoff among exchange stability, monetary independence, and capital-market openness. Yet the trilemma has not gone without challenge. Some (such as Calvo and Reinhart 2001, 2002) argue that under the modern float, monetary autonomy often is limited. Others (such as Bordo and Flandreau 2003), that even under the classical gold standard, domestic monetary autonomy was considerable. How binding has the trilemma been in practice? In this chapter, we pursue one approach to answering the question, based on asking how the comovement of national interest rates varies with the exchange-rate regime and the presence of capital controls.[1]

There are few antecedents in the literature. The approach taken by Rose (1996) uses a classic monetary model of exchange rates to assess the trilemma. He noted that the quantity theory of money implies an exchange rate response to shocks to "fundamentals" such as money, output, and interest rates. He then tested how well the model fits the data (in the second moments) to see how exchange-rate flexibility is related to "monetary divergence" in two countries, with the optional addition of linear and interaction controls based on capital-mobility indices. His results were "somewhat favorable but surprisingly weak" (p. 926). Still, as many papers have pointed out, we are poorly equipped to identify monetary-policy shocks. Using monetary aggregates is dubious when one cannot easily distinguish between demand and supply shocks to money, and also when the stability of velocity has to be assumed.[2]

---

[1] This chapter summarizes joint work with Jay C. Shambaugh, whom we thank for allowing us to draw on our collaborative research (Obstfeld, Shambaugh, and Taylor 2003).

[2] An older approach to measuring the independence of monetary policy centers on the empirical

In this section, our measure of monetary independence is based, not on quantity aggregates, but on observed short-term money-market interest rates. This approach has intuitive appeal because interest-sensitive spending and the credit market are primary channels for monetary policy. Furthermore, modern monetary policy (a few experiments aside) has almost always taken the form of interest-rate targeting or manipulation, with reference to quantity targets generally being of little or no real consequence. The question we will pose is whether, over the long run, the exchange-rate regime has influenced the extent to which local interest rates diverge from the "world" interest rate (in some base market), and we will use the answer as a way to assess the potency of the trilemma as an overarching explanation of policy constraints in both the pre–World War One gold-standard period (1870–1913), the convertible Bretton Woods period (1959–73), and in the post–Bretton Woods era.[3]

An enlargement of the data universe is attractive on a number of grounds. First, we can see whether the trilemma has endured over a long period as a useful characterization of policy choice. The more durable it can be shown to have been over the long course of history, the more seriously its constraints should be taken by policymakers. Second, the larger historical sample adds useful variance to the data. That variance takes a number of forms. Adding the Bretton Woods convertible period allows us to study countries in an environment of widespread capital controls. Adding the gold-standard period introduces a different benchmark, an era with essentially no capital controls, but with a different dominant wisdom about the proper role for monetary policy. These two eras offer a useful and clean contrast with the recent era, when many countries have, to greater or lesser degree, dismantled their postwar systems of capital controls. Third, for all the talk of the recent revolutionary globalization, more nuanced scholarly work finds considerable evidence to suggest that the pre-1914 era was one of perhaps even greater market integration than today in certain key ways.

Thus, a study of history might reveal some meaningful benchmarks for exactly how tightly the straitjacket of globalization might eventually fit in different

---

offset coefficient, the fraction of an exogenous domestic credit expansion that leaks away through foreign reserve outflows under a pegged exchange rate. Unfortunately that approach is beset by identification problems caused by the endogeneity of central bank policy (Obstfeld 1982). For a recent contribution to this literature, see Brissimis, Gibson, and Tsakalotos (2002).

[3] As we will note later, our approach follows that of Shambaugh (2004) and is closely related to the work of Frankel (1999) and Frankel, Schmukler, and Servén (2000, 2002). A delicate question arises, of course, over whether an observed nondivergence of interest rates can be seen as evidence of a tight exchange-market constraint, rather than a conscious policy choice to follow the base country's monetary policy. The evidence we present below shows that this theoretical possibility does not prevent us from seeing in the data substantial differences across exchange-rate regimes.

times and places. In the last chapter, we reviewed narrative evidence of the different solutions to the trilemma adopted in earlier epochs, and the basic findings of this chapter offer additional confirmation. We have argued that the classical gold standard was a period of mostly fixed rates, unfettered capital mobility, and, hence, limited monetary independence. The interwar period was a time of divergent strategies, including floating and exchange controls, as monetary independence started to be asserted by domestic policymakers. The architecture of Bretton Woods was set up to preserve this autonomy, while preserving relatively stable fixed-but-adjustable exchange rates, necessitating strict limits on capital mobility. Finally, since the collapse of the Bretton Woods system, capital mobility has reasserted itself; some countries have adopted floating as a means to maintain independence, some have fixed and tied their hands, and others have endured crises and confusion while vacillating between the two "corner solutions."

The interest-rate data are quite supportive of this summary, as we shall see. We find pronounced and rapid transmission of interest-rate shocks during fixed-rate episodes under the classical gold-standard period, perhaps to an extent that has not yet been equaled even in the contemporary period. This once again confirms the classical gold standard regime as a useful benchmark for the study of globalization. In marked contrast, the Bretton Woods era reveals an episode where fixed exchange rates did not provide much of a constraint on domestic interest rates whatsoever, a clear by-product of capital controls. Now, in the contemporary post–Bretton Woods era, there are signs of reversion to the more globalized pattern, with increased interest-rate transmission among fixed-rate countries. Still, an alternative solution of the trilemma is also clearly present in our findings: floaters, both before 1914 and in the present, have enjoyed considerably more monetary independence than fixers.

Overall, given the systematic variation in policymakers' room for maneuver, we find strong evidence in support of the trilemma, which is shown to be a long-enduring and still very relevant constraint on the political policy equilibrium.

5.1 Measuring interest-rate interdependence

Alternative econometric specifications offer different measures of the degree to which a local country's interest rate follows that of a natural base country. The time-series properties of the data are quite important to the choices made. Nominal interest rates tend to behave in ways very close to unit roots, especially over finite samples. They are not literally unit roots; if they were, some series would wander into negative territory, and others would approach infinity. We do not observe this in practice, so clearly there are some bounds on the behavior of the data. Given the lack of power of most unit root tests, and the necessity of using relatively short time series in some cases to isolate individual peg or nonpeg episodes, we cannot posit unambiguously the time series properties of the data.[4] Thus, we pursue a variety of analyses under different assumptions.

In the case of nonstationary data, any simple regression of the levels of one series on another leaves open the possibility of spurious regression (Granger and Newbold 1974). Phillips (1988) demonstrates that analogous problems also arise with stationary but near-integrated data. If the data are truly nonstationary (or close) and are not cointegrated, an appropriate approach would be to difference the data and examine a simple equation such as

$$\Delta R_{it} = \alpha + \beta \Delta R_{bit} + u_{it}, \tag{5.1}$$

where R_{it} is the local interest rate and R_{bit} is the base interest rate for country i at time t. Because national interest rates typically trend together under conditions of international capital mobility, the levels regression may be misleading even when the rates are cointegrated. Under cointegration, a regression in levels will tend to force β toward 1, and this, too, will occur for stationary but highly persistent interest-rate data. A regression in differences is likely to be more informative about the scope for short-term interest-rate independence. One could simply assume the data are stationary and their persistence is not so dramatic as to require treating them as if they have unit roots. In that case, a levels analysis still requires a correction for the high levels of residual autocorrelation that are evident in practice. We found that the series are close enough to unit roots that uncorrected levels regressions seem problematic, but that any AR(1) correction comes close to a differences specification. Thus, our static analysis uses equation 5.1; we do not report static levels regressions below.

With perfect capital mobility and an exchange rate permanently and credibly pegged within a band that is literally of zero width, we would expect to find $\beta = 1$ above: home and base-country interest rates would always move one-for-one, and the pegging country's monetary independence would be nil. In practice, however, "fixed" exchange rates are fixed only up to a possibly narrow fluctuation band, and our methodology for selecting pegs (described later) must allow for this. As a result, even under a peg, β could conceivably be below or above 1. How far from 1 could it be? We have experimented with simulations of Krugman's (1991) target-zone model, using Svensson's (1991b) term-structure model to derive interest rates for noninfinitesimal maturities when the fluctu-

---

[4] Caner and Kilian (2001) show that tests with stationarity as the null are likely to entail spurious rejections when the data are stationary but highly persistent.

ation band is quite narrow ($\pm$ 1 percent). We find that for time-series data samples of realistic length, βs well below 1 are likely to arise even when domestic authorities mildly smooth short-term domestic interest rates in the face of foreign interest-rate shocks.[5] These simulations and others are discussed in detail in Obstfeld et al. (2003). Their results underscore the importance of having the classical gold standard (itself a target-zone system because of gold points) as a quantitative benchmark for results from later periods. Because the gold standard is widely acknowledged to be an era in which the exercise of monetary independence was strictly limited, results that look similar to those found in pre-1914 data, even if they entail a β below 1, can be construed as supporting the hypothesis that pegs greatly limit monetary autonomy.[6]

Despite the panel form of the data, fixed country effects are not needed because such an effect would assume a constant rate of change in the interest rate for an individual country, a highly unlikely scenario.[7] Given the fact that the response to a change in the base rate may not be immediate and may vary across countries, examining the differences with high-frequency data in pooled fashion generates unclear results. At an annual frequency, though, there appears to be sufficient similarity across the countries to allow for pooling the data.[8] Thus, in our basic static regressions, the data points are nonoverlapping differences of annually averaged monthly interest rates. While this basic specification cannot tell us much about the dynamics of the relationships nor about individual episodes, it can at least inform us about general patterns across the different eras and across exchange-rate regime types.[9]

---

[5] Of course, Krugman's (1991) model assumes effectively infinite foreign reserves, a factor that may exaggerate the ability of some countries to smooth the path of domestic interest rates.

[6] Thus, a β below 1 is not sufficient for monetary independence. We caution the reader that it is not strictly necessary either. An economy buffeted by permanent real shocks, for example, will be stabilized by a floating exchange rate even if its interest rate never deviates from the foreign rate. An important (and unanswered) question is whether independence at the short end of the term structure but not at the long end, as in a fairly narrow target zone, confers on a central bank much leverage over the economy. As we noted earlier, some scholars of the gold standard argue that the gold points allowed considerable monetary independence. If true, that contention would make the gold standard an unacceptable benchmark for judging the degree to which a pegged exchange rate hamstrings monetary policy. The dynamic cointegration results we report here throw doubt, however, on the hypothesis of substantial monetary independence under gold.

[7] Likewise one could question the need for a constant in equation 5.1. In practice, however, the estimated constant for this equation was very close to zero.

[8] This also means that if some of the series are cointegrated with the base rate, the differences specification is less problematic for annual data because the dynamic adjustments are likely to have settled down to a large extent after a year.

[9] There are, of course, many other factors one could expect to affect the degree to which a country follows the base country interest rate. Common shocks, world or regional trade shares, capital controls, level of industrialization, level of debt, and so on, could all have some impact. Shambaugh (2004) considers the impact of these factors in studying the post–Bretton Woods

Finally, we can try to examine the dynamics of individual country/exchange-rate regime episodes and test for the presence of significant levels relationships. Again, the technique depends on the properties of the data. If one is convinced that the data are nonstationary and that the individual local series are cointe-grated with the base interest rate, then one can use an error-correction (EC) form to analyze the dynamics. Given the uncertainty over the order of integration of the data, the technique developed by Pesaran, Shin, and Smith (2001) and also used in Frankel et al. (2002) is quite helpful. Rather than assume the order of integration, one can test a specification like the error correction form but exam-ine the critical values provided by Pesaran et al. (PSS) to test the significance of the levels relationship. Different critical values apply in the $I(0)$ versus the $I(1)$ case. Thus, if the test statistic either passes both critical values or fails to pass both critical values, we can either reject no long-run relationship or not without having to take a stand on the order of integration of the data. Only when the test statistic is in the middle are we thrust back into the position of having to ascertain the order of integration to make judgments about the data.[10]

To employ the PSS test, we adopt the specification

$$\Delta R_{it} = \alpha + \beta \Delta R_{bit} + \theta(c + R_{i,t-1} - \gamma R_{bi,t-1}) + u_{it}, \tag{5.2}$$

where we can include lags of ΔR_{bit} as necessary, and γ is a cointegrating coefficient. We can then test the significance of the adjustment speed θ to determine whether there is a significant long-run relationship. If the local interest rate adjusts to restore the equilibrium relationship after shocks to the base interest rate, we would find that $\theta < 0$. The size of the coefficient shows the speed of adjustment, with $\theta = -0.5$ implying a half-life of one month.[11]

5.2 Data sources

Prior to any statistical analysis, we must take a stand on the nature of a country's exchange-rate regime at any given time. This choice is far from straightforward, since officially declared regimes often fail accurately to reflect either exchange-

era. With the exception of capital controls, which are quite important, the exchange-rate regime tends to be the major determinant of how closely a country follows the base interest rate.

[10] It is difficult to try to analyze the pooled sample with PSS or EC techniques because the data are quite unbalanced with certain countries pegging at certain times and not others. Furthermore, the dynamics appear to differ widely across countries, making pooling questionable.

[11] In contrast to the PSS test, an error-correction form would involve testing for cointegration and then running equation 5.2, with γ set equal to the estimated slope coefficient from a cointegrating regression. If the data are nonstationary, we would expect that a long run relationship would be (roughly) one of equality. Any other would imply the possibility of an ever-widening spread in the levels of interest rates. Thus, one could also impose $\gamma = 1$ at the outset.

rate behavior or the external constraints monetary policymakers perceive. As a result, several different approaches have been used in the previous literature. In our analysis, exchange-rate regimes under the classical gold standard are determined based both on the legal commitment of countries to gold (the de jure status) as well as on the de facto behavior of the exchange rate. De jure coding is based on Meissner (2002), Eichengreen (1996), Global Financial Data, and Hawtrey (1947).[12] The de facto status follows the coding used for the post–Bretton Woods era developed in Shambaugh (2004). We test whether the end-of-month exchange rate stays within ±2 percent bands over the course of a year – that is, for at least the preceding 12 months.[13] In addition, single realignments are not considered breaks in the regime as long as the transition is immediate from one peg to another. Finally, single-year pegs are dropped because they possibly reflect a mere lack of volatility and it is unlikely that there exists either commitment on the government's part or confidence in the market that the rate will not change.[14] For the part of the Bretton Woods period that we analyze, all countries for which we have data with the exception of Canada in 1960–61 and 1970 and Brazil throughout the period are pegged both de jure and de facto. Finally, the post–Bretton Woods era coding comes from Shambaugh (2004) as described earlier.[15] While we will adopt the terms "peg" and "float" to describe countries' regimes, we do not suggest that the countries without pegged rates are pure floats or that they have no exchange rate management policy; they are best thought of as nonpegs.

For the PSS analysis below, individual country/regime episodes are examined using monthly data. Exchange rate regime coding follows much the same pattern as for annual data: we check that the end-of-month exchange rate has stayed within ± 2 percent bands over the preceding 12 months. The episodes for the gold standard and Bretton Woods eras are listed in the appendix to

[12] Bimetallic regimes are treated as fixed; we recognize that this choice is somewhat arbitrary, but it affects only a small number of observations.

[13] It can happen that a country goes on gold de jure but we do not consider it to be on gold de facto. For example, due to excessive movements in the exchange rate, Austria's de facto gold standard period begins only in 1894, even though that country adopted gold officially in 1892.

[14] When pursuing differences regressions, we also drop the first year of a peg to ensure that we are not differencing the interest-rate data across nonpegged and pegged observations.

[15] Because (as noted above) a country's actual exchange-rate regime choice often differs from its self-reported status, as published by the IMF, the preferred approach nowadays is to focus on what countries do, not what they say (Obstfeld and Rogoff 1995; Calvo and Reinhart 2001, 2002; Levy Yeyati and Sturzenegger 2000; Reinhart and Rogoff 2002). Shambaugh (2004) provides an extensive discussion of different options from IMF coding to other de facto classifications. Recent work by Reinhart and Rogoff (2002), which uses data on parallel market exchange rates, does not appear to be directly relevant for the present analysis. Because regimes with parallel rates rely on capital controls to enforce market separation, the behavior of the parallel rate is not a strong constraint on monetary policy.

Obstfeld et al. (2003). Short episodes of less than three years are excluded because of a lack of data. There are 13 defined peg episodes and seven nonpeg episodes based on de jure status under the gold standard, and 20 pegs and 5 nonpegs based on de facto status. Under Bretton Woods, there are 13 pegs and only one nonpeg (Brazil).[16] In addition, in the post–Bretton Woods era, there is a considerable amount of flipping back and forth from peg to nonpeg for many countries. For this era, a separate category of "occasional peg" is created. Occasional pegs have at least three short pegs lasting less than three years, and the episode is defined from the start of the pegging until the last peg period breaks. To prevent short nonpeg episodes that are really simply the middle of these occasional pegs from being counted as floats, floats must last at least ten years in this era. There are thus 70 pegs, 25 occasional pegs, and 32 nonpegs during this era.

In some regressions, we also want to code countries as either having or not having capital controls. As we indicated at the end of Chapter 4, this is not straightforward even for recent decades. De facto classifications are difficult to use for a number of reasons. Most are available for a limited number of countries and a limited amount of time. Some rely on interest-rate differentials (the phenomenon we study), and thus are inappropriate. While de jure codes are available for many countries courtesy of the International Monetary Fund (IMF), they are available only after 1973. And even these codings are quite crude, for reasons discussed in the last chapter. We proceed by assuming that all countries have open markets in the gold-standard era, that no countries are open during the Bretton Woods era, and that, for our purposes, the dichotomous IMF coding can be used as a reasonable approximation of capital controls for the post–Bretton Woods era.[17]

Finally, we describe our data on interest rates. The short-term interest-rate data for the gold-standard era reflect the arduous collection efforts of Neal and Weidenmier (2003), whom we thank for sharing the resource they have assembled. The Neal-Weidenmier data are available for 15 countries plus the United Kingdom. Before World War One, the U.K. interest rate is used as the base rate for comparison to the other countries. The data begin in 1870 for many countries and later for others, and all series end in 1914. The interest-rate data for

[16] While Canada was floating over 1959–61 and returned to a currency peg de jure in 1962, the extent of exchange-rate fluctuation over 1959 places Canada on a de facto peg for that year. Thus, this Canadian floating-rate episode is shorter than three years in duration and we exclude it from consideration here. Our estimates for Canada's Bretton Woods peg run from January 1963 through May 1970.

[17] A potential problem is the IMF switch after 1995 from a binary coding (line E2) to a disaggregated coding. Following Shambaugh (2004), we use changes in the disaggregated coding and descriptions in the yearbooks to determine changes in the binary codes.

the Bretton Woods era consist of both short-term money market rates (interbank and call money rates) and short-term treasury bill rates (generally three-month rates), all average monthly values taken from the IMF's *International Financial Statistics* (IFS) CD-ROM.[18] Availability determines which data we use. Even though the maturities of the two types of rate differ, they prove to be extremely highly correlated when both are available for the same country. The base interest rate under Bretton Woods is the U.S. interest rate that matches the interest rate used for each local country. Owing to a lack of monthly IFS data before 1957 and the expansion of convertibility that took place in 1959, the Bretton Woods data that we examine are limited to the years 1959–70. For the post–Bretton Woods era, which we take to be 1973–2000, the interest rate series used are once again month averages of short-term money market and short-term treasury bill rates from the IFS CD-ROM. Those data are augmented with information from Datastream and Global Financial Data.

The base rate chosen for the post–Bretton Woods period varies by country and is taken from Shambaugh (2004). For pegs, the interest rate is obviously the country to which the local country pegs. For nonpegged countries, the base country is the country that the local country would most likely follow if it were pegging. This choice is determined by previous pegging history, which is possible in almost all cases, but otherwise by the dominant currency in the region (the one to which neighboring countries peg).

Information from the IMF's *Annual Report on Exchange Arrangements and Exchange Restrictions* and from Global Financial Data (B. Taylor 2000) is used as well. Because almost all countries peg at some point in the sample, and those that switch bases usually switch from one peg to another, the assignment of a base currency is generally quite simple. Once again, the base interest rate used is always of the same type (money market or treasury bill) as the one for the local country.[19]

5.3 Persistence of nominal interest rates

While it is a fact of recent data that many countries' nominal interest-rate processes can be difficult to distinguish from unit roots, this is not necessarily true for the pre-1914 gold standard. Figure 5.1 shows the base interest rates

---

[18] The data series for the United States were extended back in time using information from FRED on the Federal Reserve Bank of St. Louis website.

[19] All interest rates are expressed in the form $\log(1 + R)$. While this transformation has a trivial impact on low to moderate interest rates, it does shrink the impact of outliers. In addition, hyperinflations are excluded from the post–Bretton Woods sample due to the excessive weight they take in the regressions.

during the three time periods that we consider. During the gold-standard, the U.K. interest rate appears to the eye to be far more stationary than U.S. post–World War Two rates. The post–Bretton Woods U.S. interest rate looks even less stationary than the Bretton Woods rate. This is to be expected given that expected inflation is the main component of the nominal interest rate responsible for nonstationarity. A credible commodity standard is more likely to produce stable inflation and a stationary nominal interest rate than is a discretionary fiat standard. Simple tests on monthly base and local interest rates back up the ocular evidence.

We employ unit root tests of the form suggested by Elliott, Rothenberg, and Stock (1996) and use the modified Akaike information criterion recommended by Ng and Perron (2001) to determine the appropriate number of lags to include. Over the entire gold-standard period, we reject a unit root in the U.K. interest rate (at the 5 percent level). Subsamples of the U.K. interest-rate data that start in 1890 or after often do not reject a unit root despite covering more than 20 years. After a look at Figure 5.1, this is not necessarily surprising: the U.K. rate shows somewhat less mean reversion starting in 1890. For the U.S. federal funds rate, one cannot reject a unit root over the full Bretton Woods period. For the U.S. treasury bill rate one can reject the unit root null using the full 1948–73 sample, but not based upon the 1959–70 sample that we analyze below. Over the full post–Bretton Woods era, one cannot reject a unit root in U.S. interest rates and in only 1.6 percent of the episodes can a unit root be rejected for the base interest rate.

Local rates follow a similar pattern. While one can reject a unit root in the local interest rate (including all of the long series) in eight out of 25 episodes during the gold standard, one can reject a unit root in only one of 14 Bretton Woods episodes and in only five of 127 episodes that fall within the post–Bretton Woods era.[20]

In the next section, the results from each of the tests are discussed for each era. Because of the high persistence displayed by nominal interest rates in the postwar eras, we conduct only the differences and PSS tests, as discussed above. At the same time, cointegration analysis on the gold-standard data may be inappropriate because interest rates appear to be much closer to stationarity in that period.

---

[20] If we were to use an augmented Dickey-Fuller unit root test we would generate a similar pattern to the previous tests with a slightly higher number of rejections. Likewise, using the optimal lag length of Ng and Perron (2001) allows a few more rejections for the gold-standard era. For the post–Bretton Woods period we find that the tests are generally so far from rejecting a unit root that lag length is irrelevant.

Fig. 5.1. The trilemma: Base interest rates

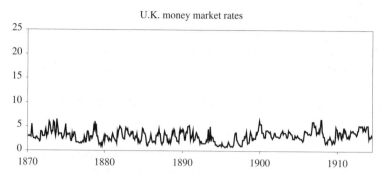

U.K. money market rates

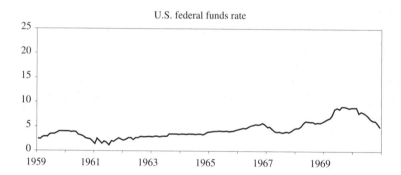

U.S. federal funds rate

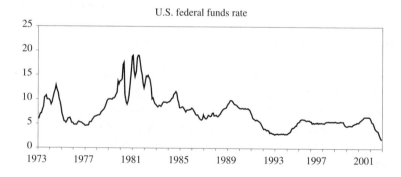

U.S. federal funds rate

Notes and Sources: See text. All rates are percent per annum. Not all countries' exchange rates were based to United States in the final period, but this rate is shown as an example.

5.4 Empirical findings: Pooled annual differences

The simplest first step is to examine comovements of annual interest-rate differences. This specification tests whether a change in the base interest rate is followed abroad. We pool annual data from different countries to examine the average response to changes in base interest rates. As we have argued, annual average data are preferred to higher frequencies for this purpose because, in monthly or quarterly data, differences in the dynamics across countries tend to wash out the results. After one year, however, it is plausible that the heterogeneous dynamics have settled down to a more uniform response, so that the differences in short-run adjustment patterns across countries are less salient.

The results of estimating equation 5.1 are shown in Table 5.1, which presents striking differences across the time periods. If we simply pool data within periods, with no distinction across exchange-rate regimes, we see that the gold-standard and post–Bretton Woods eras have fairly similar slope coefficients (0.42 and 0.36, respectively), especially when compared to the Bretton Woods era (-0.11).[21] The big difference between the gold standard and the current era appears in the R^2, where gold-standard base-rate changes can explain a large fraction of local-rate changes, but modern base-rate changes cannot ($R^2 = 0.26$ versus 0.03, respectively). For the Bretton Woods era, the R^2 is only 0.01, suggesting that the capital controls of the era seem to have essentially shut down the mechanism by which local countries are forced to follow the base country's interest rate.

While there are not enough floating episodes under Bretton Woods to examine floats separately, pegs and floats do appear to behave differently in both the gold-standard and modern eras. Intraregime differences, though, are more striking under the gold standard. The coefficients (and associated standard errors) on the base rate are similar for pegs in the two eras, but the R^2 is much higher under the gold standard (0.41 versus 0.19), implying fewer interest rate changes for reasons other than following the base rate. The lower R^2 that we find for modern pegs could reflect the relatively greater credibility of gold-standard exchange-rate commitments or the more frequent presence of capital controls in the modern era, although we can draw no firm conclusions without further investigation. In neither era do we see slope coefficients or R^2s close to 1, which a model with no exchange-rate bands, costless arbitrage, and perfect regime credibility would imply. One of the most useful roles of the gold-standard data is as a benchmark. Looking at the gold-standard results, we should not be surprised by the somewhat low slope coefficients and R^2s that we find for pegs

---

[21] We refer in the text to the de facto results, although de jure is always reasonably close.

Table 5.1. *The trilemma: Differences regressions on annual data*

Gold-standard de jure classification	Pool	Peg	Float	Pool
Observations	499	350	140	490
β	0.42	0.52	0.16	0.16
	(0.03)	(0.04)	(0.06)	(0.06)
β_2	—	—	—	0.36
				(0.07)
R^2	0.26	0.36	0.05	0.30
Gold-standard de facto classification	Pool	Peg	Float	Pool
Observations	499	399	85	484
β	0.42	0.52	0.05	0.05
	(0.03)	(0.04)	(0.09)	(0.10)
β_2	—	—	—	0.47
				(0.09)
R^2	0.26	0.41	0.00	0.33
Bretton Woods	Pool	Peg	Float	Pool
Observations	154	138	n.a.	n.a.
β	−0.11	−0.05	—	—
	(0.14)	(0.12)		
β_2	—	—	—	—
R^2	0.01	0.00		
Post–Bretton Woods	Pool	Peg	Float	Pool
Observations	1920	748	1103	1848
β	0.36	0.46	0.27	0.26
	(0.05)	(0.04)	(0.08)	(0.08)
β_2	—	—	—	0.19
				(0.09)
R^2	0.03	0.19	0.01	0.03

Notes and Sources: See text. Standard errors in parentheses. β is the coefficient on ΔR_{bit}; β_2 is the coefficient on $\text{Peg}_{it} \times \Delta R_{bit}$.

in the current era. As we have noted, even in the essentially capital-control-free era of the gold standard, pegs did not show a perfect correlation with the base interest rate because of exchange-rate movements within the gold points, which gives latitude for short-term interest-rate divergence (Svensson 1994). Now as then, most exchange rates that we consider to be pegged actually do move within specified narrow bands.

The more significant difference between the gold-standard and modern eras appears in examining the floats. The gold standard's (de facto) floats on average show almost no connection to the base rate ($\beta = 0.05$, standard error = 0.09, $R^2 = 0$), whereas the slope coefficient for the modern era is much closer to that for the pegs ($\beta = 0.27$). The modern-era R^2 is still quite low (0.01), implying considerable room for maneuver for reasons other than following the base rate, but the slope-coefficient gap is nowhere near as large for the modern era as it is for the gold standard.[22]

This point is seen more sharply when one pools the data and includes and interaction term for pegging times the base interest rate,

$$\Delta R_{it} = \alpha + \beta \Delta R_{bit} + \beta_2 \text{Peg}_{it} \Delta R_{bit} + u_{it}. \tag{5.3}$$

While under the gold standard, β is economically and statistically insignificant (coefficient of 0.05, standard error of 0.10), the coefficient β_2 is 0.47 (0.09). With current data, we estimate β to be 0.26 (0.08) and β_2 to be 0.19 (0.09).[23]

The general message from these tests is that the exchange rate regime does affect the extent to which a country follows the base, but that the capital controls of the Bretton Woods era seemed to stop or significantly slow these reactions. The results from the gold-standard era shed some light on the modern results, first by showing that the lack of a coefficient or R^2 close to 1 is not a surprise. Our comparison with the gold standard also shows, though, that the nonpegs of the modern era seem to follow changes in the base country's interest rate more closely than was true in the years before 1914.

Thus, the within-era information points to a significant role of the exchange-rate regime in the extent to which a country follows the base. Conversely, the across-era comparisons help show the role of capital controls. As a final check, we pool the eras and test the importance of the exchange-rate regime and capital control status. These results are reported in Table 5.2.

Panel (a) of Table 5.2 divides the sample two ways: pegs versus floats, then capital controls versus no controls. Looking first at the exchange-rate regime, we still see a stark difference between pegs and floats with coefficients of 0.44 versus 0.26 and R^2s of 0.19 versus 0.01, respectively. Similarly, we see the impact of capital controls, with countries that are free of controls showing a coefficient of 0.56 and R^2 of 0.11 and capital-control countries showing a coefficient of 0.27 and R^2 of 0.01. Thus, both legs of the trilemma appear to be validated.

Panels (b) and (c) of Table 5.2 test more carefully the interaction of these two sides. While, as expected, pegs with open capital markets have the highest

---

[22] It should be noted that some interest-rate series in the modern era are entirely flat (see Shambaugh 2004). When these are excluded, the results for pegs become $\beta = 0.59$ (standard error = 0.04, $R^2 = 0.26$) and for floats $\beta = 0.28$ (standard error = 0.08, $R^2 = 0.01$). Thus, removing these mostly small Caribbean countries increases the gap between the two and raises the R^2 on the pegs.

[23] Again, excluding the interest rates which are constant over the entire sample generates $\beta_1 = 0.31$ (0.08), $\beta_2 = 0.27$ (0.09).

Table 5.2. *The trilemma: Annual differences on pooled sample*

(a)	Pool	Peg	Float	No capital controls	Capital controls
Observations	2573	1285	1202	1076	1468
β	0.35	0.44	0.26	0.56	0.27
	(0.04)	(0.03)	(0.08)	(0.05)	(0.06)
R^2	0.03	0.19	0.01	0.11	0.01

(b)	Peg & no capital controls	Peg with capital controls	Float & no capital controls	Float with capital controls
Observations	613	669	423	753
β	0.61	0.38	0.53	0.15
	(0.05)	(0.04)	(0.07)	(0.11)
R^2	0.30	0.15	0.06	0.00

(c)	Pool	Pool	Pool & nonconstant R	Pool & nonconstant R
Observations	2456	2456	2235	2235
β	0.16	0.14	0.19	0.16
	(0.10)	(0.11)	(0.10)	(0.12)
β_2	0.19	0.24	0.26	0.34
	(0.09)	(0.12)	(0.09)	(0.12)
β_3	0.32	0.39	0.30	0.40
	(0.08)	(0.13)	(0.09)	(0.14)
β_4	—	−0.17	—	−0.25
		(0.15)		(0.16)
R^2	0.03	0.03	0.04	0.04

Notes and Sources: See text. Standard errors in parentheses. β is the coefficient on ΔR_{bit}; β_2 is the coefficient on Peg $\times \Delta R_{bit}$; β_3 is the coefficient on No Controls $\times \Delta R_{bit}$; β_4 is the coefficient on Peg $\times$ No Controls $\times \Delta R_{bit}$. "No constant R" signals that interest rates constant over the entire sample have been removed.

coefficient and R^2, there is some evidence of "fear of floating" (Calvo and Reinhart 2002). Open capital market floats have a β coefficient of 0.53 compared to the open capital market pegs' 0.61. On the other hand, the R^2 still shows a considerable gap, with open pegs having an $R^2 = 0.30$ versus only 0.06 for open floats. Thus, despite moving with the base country to some extent, only a small portion of the changes in the floats' interest rates can be explained by the base rate. In addition, we do not find that capital controls are completely isolating. Pegs with capital controls have higher β coefficients and R^2s as compared to floats with capital controls.

The pooled estimates in Panel (c) of Table 5.2 measure the interaction of the interest-rate linkage with both the exchange-rate regime and controls. These estimates are based on the specification

$$\Delta R_{it} = \alpha + \beta \Delta R_{bit} + \beta_2 \text{Peg}_{it} \Delta R_{bit} + \beta_3 (\text{No Controls})_{it} \Delta R_{bit}$$
$$+ \beta_4 \text{Peg}_{it} (\text{No Controls})_{it} \Delta R_{bit} + u_{it}.$$

Both the exchange-rate regime and capital controls matter, though in columns 1 and 2, capital controls appear to be substantially more important. Once again, removing the modern-era countries in which interest rates never change increases the importance of the peg variable (columns 3 and 4). We also see in columns 2 and 4 that the impact of capital controls and exchange-rate regimes is not purely additive because the interaction of the two has a negative coefficient. This finding matches the logic of the trilemma – either floating or controls will provide a good degree of independence; adding one to the other increases the independence, but not by as much as the policy on its own.

In total, the preceding evidence supports a modified view of the trilemma. While both the exchange-rate regime and capital controls clearly affect autonomy, the combination of floating with capital controls seems to provide unfettered autonomy and removing either side compromises some autonomy. Still, floats with open capital markets and pegs with closed capital markets seem to retain some autonomy, and, as expected, pegs with open markets have the least of all.

5.5 Empirical findings: Individual-country dynamics

We can learn considerably more about the relationships of local to base countries by using specific individual-country pairings to examine both the level relationships between interest rates and the dynamic adjustment patterns. Rather than assuming a levels relationship exists and estimating it, we test for the presence of a levels relationships and examine the dynamics of the system. Table 5.3, based on estimating equation 5.2, shows the results for individual-country regime episodes as well as averages across pegs and floats by era.

In the case of the gold standard, we see that in only two cases are we forced to assume the order of integration, as in all others the test statistic either passes both critical values or fails to do so. Looking at both the de jure and de facto gold-standard classifications, we see that there were floating-rate episodes that demonstrated considerable independence. Perhaps the clearest evidence comes from the fact that the levels coefficients γ have negative signs. For two of the seven gold-standard floats in the de jure panel and all five in the de facto panel, rates apparently moved away from one another over the long run. These perversely signed levels relationships obviously make mechanically calculated

Table 5.3. *The trilemma: PSS results*

	T	lag	θ	γ	t_θ	sig (0)	sig (1)	H	H <3	3–12	>12	EC_1
				Gold standard, de jure classification								
Pegs												
Austria	251	7	−0.10	0.27	−2.8	0	0	6.8	0	1	0	−0.04
Belgium	529	1	−0.22	0.60	−7.3	1	1	2.8	1	0	0	−0.14
Denmark	361	1	−0.09	0.57	−4.1	1	1	7.1	0	1	0	−0.08
France	520	0	−0.19	0.56	−7.4	1	1	3.3	0	1	0	−0.07
Germany	499	8	−0.20	0.59	−4.2	1	1	3.1	0	1	0	−0.19
India	198	8	−0.28	−0.13	−3.7	1	1	2.1	1	0	0	−0.21
Italy	107	0	−0.23	0.47	−3.5	1	1	2.7	1	0	0	−0.17
Netherlands	457	0	−0.18	0.63	−7.3	1	1	3.5	0	1	0	−0.13
Norway	245	0	−0.11	0.54	−4.4	1	1	5.8	0	1	0	−0.05
Portugal	77	0	−0.08	1.03	−1.7	0	0	8.0	0	1	0	−0.10
Sweden	258	2	−0.14	0.39	−3.9	1	1	4.7	0	1	0	−0.07
Switzerland	258	0	−0.22	0.43	−5.3	1	1	2.8	1	0	0	−0.04
U.S.	401	1	−0.66	0.41	−10.0	1	1	0.6	1	0	0	−0.35
Floats												
Austria	264	0	−0.19	0.50	−5.4	1	1	3.4	0	1	0	−0.10
India	163	1	−0.23	0.94	−5.1	1	1	2.6	1	0	0	−0.18
Italy	256	0	−0.21	0.49	−6.2	1	1	2.9	1	0	0	−0.11
Netherlands	60	0	−0.34	0.96	−4.2	1	1	1.7	1	0	0	−0.37
Portugal	276	6	−0.05	−0.10	−2.0	0	0	13.4	0	0	1	−0.01
Russia	309	0	−0.19	−0.06	−6.1	1	1	3.4	0	1	0	0.00
Spain	386	0	−0.09	0.06	−3.9	1	1	7.8	0	1	0	−0.02
Floats			−0.19	0.40	−4.7	86%	86%	5.0	43%	43%	14%	−0.11
Pegs			−0.21	0.49	−5.0	85%	85%	4.1	38%	62%	0%	−0.13

half-lives problematic as indicators of how closely countries followed the base interest rate. The floats of Portugal, Russia, and Spain (all de facto and de jure) show considerable independence from the U.K. interest rate.

At the same time, there certainly were some countries that exhibited fear of floating. Despite not being on the gold standard de jure, and thus officially floating, some countries followed the base interest rate quite closely. In the case of the Netherlands during the years 1870–75, the exchange rate was in fact pegged without official announcement, so it is unsurprising to see the interest rate move so tightly with the base. Austria de facto pegged on and off during its official float (during 1870–92, the complement of its de jure gold standard adherence). As a result, Austria's interest rate shows a reasonably tight relationship with the base rate.[24]

---

[24] Readers may notice a large difference between the estimates of γ for India's de facto and de jure floats despite a difference of only 18 observations. Early in India's de jure float, there were some large changes in the interest rate that affect the results. India was in a de facto peg at

Table 5.3 (continued)

	T	lag	θ	γ	t_θ	sig (0)	sig (1)	H	H <3	3–12	>12	EC_1
				Gold standard, de facto classification								
Pegs												
Austria 1	111	7	−0.70	0.27	−4.9	1	1	0.6	1	0	0	−0.13
Austria 2	242	7	−0.09	0.28	−2.6	0	0	7.4	0	1	0	−0.04
Belgium	499	4	−0.17	0.65	−5.2	1	1	3.6	0	1	0	−0.13
Denmark	361	1	−0.09	0.57	−4.1	1	1	7.1	0	1	0	−0.08
France	507	4	−0.13	0.45	−4.5	1	1	4.9	0	1	0	−0.07
Germany	504	8	−0.20	0.59	−4.2	1	1	3.1	0	1	0	−0.19
India 1	60	6	−0.32	−1.15	−2.4	0	0	1.8	1	0	0	−0.11
India 2	122	8	−0.49	0.25	−3.1	1	0	1.0	1	0	0	−0.39
Italy 1	95	0	−0.29	0.44	−4.2	1	1	2.0	1	0	0	−0.06
Italy 2	141	1	−0.19	0.38	−3.4	1	1	3.3	0	1	0	−0.14
Netherlands	529	0	−0.21	0.69	−8.9	1	1	3.0	1	0	0	−0.16
Norway	245	0	−0.11	0.54	−4.4	1	1	5.8	0	1	0	−0.05
Portugal 1	60	0	−0.06	1.14	−1.0	0	0	11.6	0	1	0	−0.10
Portugal 2	49	3	−0.64	0.01	−25.0	1	1	0.7	1	0	0	0.00
Russia	72	0	−0.26	0.29	−3.3	1	1	2.3	1	0	0	−0.05
Spain 1	93	0	−0.02	1.46	−1.0	0	0	29.0	0	0	1	−0.04
Spain 2	49	0	−0.32	0.31	−3.0	1	0	1.1	1	0	0	−0.06
Sweden	258	2	−0.14	0.39	−3.9	1	1	4.7	0	1	0	−0.07
Switzerland	258	0	−0.22	0.43	−5.3	1	1	2.8	1	0	0	−0.04
U.S.	377	1	−0.66	0.42	−9.6	1	1	0.6	1	0	0	−0.35
Floats												
India	145	6	−0.22	−0.16	−3.3	1	1	2.8	1	0	0	−0.18
Portugal	112	2	−0.15	−0.08	−2.5	0	0	4.3	0	1	0	−0.01
Russia 1	59	0	−0.18	−0.09	−2.0	0	0	3.4	0	1	0	0.02
Russia 2	71	2	−0.13	−0.41	−2.1	0	0	5.0	0	1	0	−0.03
Spain	112	0	−0.10	−0.14	−2.4	0	0	6.8	0	1	0	−0.02
Floats			−0.16	−0.18	−2.4	20%	20%	4.4	20%	80%	0%	−0.04
Pegs			−0.27	0.42	−5.3	80%	70%	4.8	50%	45%	5%	−0.12

In general, the pegs show little independence. All episodes for countries other than India show the expected positive sign for γ, and adjustment tends to be quick. The only peg episodes with very slow adjustment (Spain's and Portugal's early de facto pegs) are relatively short ones. Long-time members of the gold standard tend to show γ coefficients ranging from 0.4 to 0.6 and half-lives of adjustment from two to five months.

The fact that the levels coefficient γ is less than unity in nearly all cases seems odd until one considers the era. Because Britain's interest rate always resided within reasonably small bands, countries could partially adjust to the British rate change and use the margin afforded by the gold points and arbitrage

the time; thus, these observations are not in the de facto float. In addition, this episode is quite sensitive to the lag length chosen.

Table 5.3 (continued)

	T	lag	θ	γ	t_θ	sig (0)	sig (1)	H	H <3	H 3–12	H >12	EC_1
					Bretton Woods							
Belgium	144	1	−0.12	0.56	−3.2	1	0	5.3	0	1	0	−0.05
Brazil (float)	83	0	−0.04	0.07	−1.3	0	0	17.7	0	0	1	−0.05
Canada	89	2	−0.14	0.90	−2.6	0	0	4.6	0	1	0	−0.13
Germany	132	0	−0.10	1.10	−3.0	1	0	6.7	0	1	0	−0.10
France	83	0	−0.19	1.09	−3.4	1	1	3.4	0	1	0	−0.15
India	144	3	−0.40	0.17	−6.0	1	1	1.4	1	0	0	−0.11
Jamaica	115	1	−0.06	−0.14	−2.5	0	0	11.2	0	1	0	−0.01
Japan	144	2	−0.13	−0.29	−2.4	0	0	5.0	0	1	0	−0.04
Netherlands	131	0	−0.13	1.07	−3.3	1	1	5.1	0	1	0	−0.11
Pakistan	83	0	−0.05	−0.11	−1.6	0	0	12.5	0	1	0	−0.02
South Africa	144	4	−0.03	0.46	−2.2	0	0	25.5	0	0	1	−0.02
Sweden	96	0	−0.34	0.94	−4.6	1	1	1.7	1	0	0	−0.24
Trinidad & Tob.	72	0	−0.13	0.13	−2.2	0	0	5.2	0	1	0	−0.01
U.K.	83	1	−0.19	0.60	−3.5	1	1	3.4	0	1	0	−0.10
Floats			−0.04	0.07	−1.3	0%	0%	17.7	0%	0%	100%	−0.05
Pegs			−0.15	0.50	−3.1	54%	38%	7.0	15%	69%	15%	−0.08
					Post–Bretton Woods averages							
Floats			−0.06	−0.43	−2.2	31%	25%	35.2	3%	41%	56%	−0.04
Occasional pegs			−0.11	0.68	−2.4	24%	20%	10.6	16%	56%	28%	−0.08
Pegs			−0.19	0.93	−2.6	43%	27%	7.8	31%	50%	19%	−0.11

Notes and Sources: See text. T is the number of time-series observations; lag is optimal lag length choice based on Akaike information criterion; θ is the adjustment speed to shocks in the levels relationship; γ is the slope of the levels relationship; t_θ is the t-statistic for θ, which is used to determine the significance of the levels relationship; sig(0) signifies whether we can reject no levels relationship assuming the data are stationary; sig(1) signifies whether we can reject no levels relationship assuming the data are nonstationary; H is the half-life of a shock (in months) based on the adjustment speed θ; EC_1 is the adjustment speed when one runs the data in error-correction form after imposing $\gamma = 1$.

costs to cover the rest. If the U.K. rate continued long in one direction, a foreign country would eventually have to adjust fully, but because the U.K. rate reverted toward its mean, the estimated γ can be less than 1. This estimate reflects the constrained short-term interest-rate independence in exchange-rate target zones mentioned earlier. At the same time, though, countries had to move quite quickly to adjust to any change at all. Should one consider a levels coefficient of $\gamma = 0.6$ and a half-life to shocks of under three months to be evidence of monetary independence? Given the insignificant levels relationships and/or half-lives of over a year that are found in some floats, we would judge that pegs did not have extensive independence under the gold standard.

If one imposes a long-run levels coefficient of $\gamma = 1$, then the adjustment speeds appear to slow down because, in truth, the rates never did fully adjust.

Thus, Bordo and MacDonald's (1997) depiction of monetary independence under the gold standard as evidenced by slow adjustment speeds may require reexamination. (Their study covered only Britain, France, and Germany, with a data set starting in 1880.) By assuming nonstationarity in the gold-standard interest-rate data and imposing a unit cointegration coefficient between national rates (consistent with their estimates), the Bordo-MacDonald study may give an exaggerated impression of how slow adjustment speeds really were. In our data, most levels coefficients are significantly below 1, and allowing for this apparently raises estimated adjustment speeds. There was some room for independence under the gold standard, but it appears more obviously for countries that were floating. Some floats followed London anyway, but some did not, thereby exhibiting their potential for monetary independence.

The Bretton Woods era provides little room for comparison across regime types, since only Brazil is a nonpeg country. Brazil certainly shows independence with an insignificant levels relationship and a very slow adjustment speed (half-life of over 17 months). At the same time, capital controls appear to have isolated some of the pegs. Jamaica, Japan, and Pakistan all have levels relationships with a negative γ, and South Africa has an insignificant one with a very high half-life. Even for some countries where the levels relationship is close to 1 (such as Germany and Canada), adjustment is slow enough that the relationship is not clearly statistically significant. Sweden, France, and the Netherlands have levels relationships near one and half-lives from 2 to 5 months, implying a tighter relationship than even the gold-standard pegs.

On average, though, for only 38 to 54 percent of the pegs, the figure depending on interest rates being $I(1)$ or $I(0)$, can we reject the hypothesis that there is no levels relationship. The average adjustment speed for pegs is seven months, demonstrating far more flexibility than under the gold standard. Of course, it was the desire for such flexibility that had inspired the Bretton Woods design in the first place.

There are too many post–Bretton Woods episodes to consider individually, so we report only averages across three regimes. For pegs and occasional pegs, there are very few instances of negative levels relationships making the averages more reliable. Compared to the other eras, we see three striking features. The first is that far fewer of the episodes are statistically significant. Not only are fewer significant when assuming $I(0)$, but because the data are so close to being nonstationary, one should probably consider the $I(1)$ critical value as the more relevant one. This means that even fewer episodes are significant, especially compared to the gold standard. This finding, though, may result in part from the slightly shorter time spans of the modern episodes.

Second, the adjustment speeds are slower in the post–Bretton Woods era. This is especially true under the floats for which the average half-life is over 35 months. More than 50 percent of the floating-rate episodes show half-lives over a year, implying a considerable amount of autonomy. Like the low R^2s in the differences regressions, these results seem to point to a significant amount of autonomy for floating countries and a substantive difference between pegs and floats, in contrast to previous work on the subject arguing that only a few large countries can pursue independence regardless of the exchange-rate regime. The PSS results show even more independence for the floats, though, as the average nonpeg levels relationship γ is in fact estimated to be negative. This suggests that, on average, long episodes of nonpegs today show as much independence as those in the gold standard.[25] This result is directly opposite to the suggestions of Frankel et al. (2000, 2002) and the message of the fear-of-floating literature in general.[26] Pegs are also somewhat slower to adjust than during the gold standard, with an average adjustment coefficient θ of -0.19 compared to the de facto gold standard's average θ of -0.27. Still, the average θ for pegs in the current period is slightly greater in absolute value than under Bretton Woods.[27]

Even though the average adjustment speed of pegs is slower now than under the gold standard, the average γ estimate for the levels relationship is closer to 1. The average for modern pegs is 0.93, compared to between 0.4 and 0.5 for past eras. Once again, the explanation may lie in the rapidly moving and near unit root base interest rates characterizing the post-1973 period. Even if capital controls are present, the exchange rate may not last if a country fails to adjust fully over time.

Comparisons across different eras show that while the gold-standard era saw pegs with low levels relationships γ but fast adjustment, and the modern era has seen countries with slower adjustment but levels relationships closer to one, the Bretton Woods era had both slower adjustment speeds and lower levels relationships. Comparing the gold-standard and modern eras, we see that there appears to be room for floats to have independence especially when compared to the fixed-exchange-rate countries. The high levels relationships for pegs during the current era do represent a switch from the past. But the adjustment speeds

[25] While this result may appear to be inconsistent with the differences regressions (which show nonpegs having a tighter bond with the base today than in the past), the incongruity is understandable. The PSS results are only for long-standing nonpegs, while the pooled results include as nonpeg the nonpeg years of countries that flip back and forth.

[26] See Shambaugh (2004) for a more detailed discussion of these results. Borenzstein, Zettelmeyer, and Philippon (2001), using a different methodology and country sample, obtain results on monetary independence that are consistent with our conclusions.

[27] Observe that, owing to Jensen's inequality, the average half-life H generally exceeds the half-life for a country having the average value of θ.

seen today do not necessarily demonstrate the exigencies of today's capital markets: those speeds in fact seem to be below those that prevailed under the pre-1914 gold standard.

While useful for different types of data, the alternative tests all seem to lead to similar conclusions. Countries that peg do indeed have less monetary freedom than floaters, although the capital controls of Bretton Woods did succeed in weakening the linkages among national interest rates.[28] In addition, despite the gold points and less sophisticated communications technology, peggers under the gold standard arguably had even less freedom than do peggers today.

We must acknowledge that we cannot speak to ways in which the intent of the monetary authorities underlies the preceding evidence on interest-rate comovements. It is possible that common shocks, not constraints of the exchange-rate regime, make the interest rates of mutually pegged countries move together, and that fixed rates are adopted precisely when such common shocks prevail. Evidence in Shambaugh (2004) suggests that common shocks are not behind the correlation of pegs' interest rates after 1973, but without a fully specified model of monetary authorities' behavior – and data sufficient to test it – we can do little more than acknowledge the caveat and move on.

5.6 Summary

The overall lesson from our analysis is that the trilemma makes considerable sense as a guiding policy framework. Exchange rate pegs do result in a substantially closer connection to the base country interest rate than do floats. The interest rates of pegged countries react more strongly to changes in the base rate; the base rate can explain more of the changes in the local rate for pegs; and, the pegs react more quickly and have a stronger long-run relationship than do floats. Absent capital controls, countries choosing to peg lose considerable monetary independence. At the same time, floaters appear to have a reasonable amount of autonomy even without capital controls. Still, peggers are rarely completely handcuffed (in any era) because of exchange-rate bands and, possibly, arbitrage costs. Conversely, floats are never purely free and floaters often choose to follow the base-country interest rate to some degree.

The results also show some interesting perspectives across eras. Pegs in both eras of open markets show fairly similar relationships with the base interest rate. In particular, pooled regressions look somewhat similar, though the R^2 for the gold standard is always higher. In line with conventional wisdom, the gold

---

[28] Shambaugh (2004) finds that capital controls are quite important in distinguishing the degree to which a country follows the base in the modern era as well.

standard was not an era with extensive independence for the pegged countries: in that era the pooled slope coefficients on interest-rate differences are large and adjustment speeds are faster. The gold standard is a useful benchmark from which to judge the relationships between countries today. We see that slope coefficients and R^2 for pegs significantly below unity are not a surprise.

Based on the differences regressions, the floats of today do appear to have more of a connection to the base rate than in the past (especially absent capital controls). But many countries, not just a few large ones, consistently move their interest rates in ways that imply no long-run levels relationship with the base and show much slower adjustment to shocks. The longer run floats that are used as episodes show a very weak connection to the base interest rate with negative or insignificant relationships and slow adjustment. The fact that there are a few examples of countries exhibiting fear of floating under the gold standard strengthens the argument that although floaters can indeed exercise independence (for some certainly could in the gold-standard era), some may simply choose not to do so.

Finally, we can see that the architects of Bretton Woods achieved their goal of exchange-rate stability with more room for autonomy. Despite fairly rigid pegs, the Bretton Woods era shows both weaker levels relationships and slower adjustment speeds to the long run position. As capital controls became more porous in the 1960s, the combination of exchange-rate pegs and monetary independence became untenable. Looking at the interest-rate data, we can see the trilemma's lessons borne out over a very broad range of historical experience.

6

The Changing Nature of Government Credibility: A Tale of Two Gold Standards

It is widely believed that prior to 1914, gold-standard orthodoxy conferred credibility and was a sine qua non for access to global capital markets on favorable terms. A path-breaking study by Bordo and Rockoff (1996) found that adherence to gold-standard rules acted as a "seal of approval" for sovereign debt. Gold-standard countries had lower country risk, measured by their bond spreads in London relative to the British consol. This finding is consistent with the logic of the trilemma. Countries that embraced gold were viewed, by and large, as having forsworn activist macroeconomic policies, in favor of fixed exchange rates and a concomitant package of gold-standard rules guaranteeing freedom of international payments.

We have argued, however, that by the time the interwar gold standard was reconstituted starting in 1925, the underlying political equilibrium in most economies had changed. More political power had entered the hands of previously disadvantaged working class parties, and a greater awareness of government's role in steering economic outcomes prevailed. In the new political environment, the commitment to forgo policy activism implicit in pre-1914 gold-standard adoption was no longer necessarily credible. Indeed, divergent interest-group positions on macroeconomic policy were reflected in the high inflation rates rampant in the early 1920s and in the national debates over the appropriate exchange parity – devalued or not – at which to return to gold.

In this chapter, we seek hard evidence of a new political dynamic by asking if the relationship between country risk and gold changed after 1925. With the rules of the game in question after World War One, perhaps investors doubted that the mere adoption of a gold-standard regime would ensure the full repayment of public debts. Consistent with such imperfect credibility, other indicators that could reassure foreign investors about public solvency (such as the debt-GDP ratio) or protection of capital (such as membership in the British empire) might have had a bigger impact on international bond spreads under the reconstituted gold standard than under its prewar cousin. Do the data indeed support these conjectures?

There is no uniform and comprehensive study of bond spreads across the pre-1914 and interwar gold standards that would allow us definitively to answer such questions. A study of interwar spreads by Bordo, Edelstein, and Rockoff (1999), however, came to a conclusion that was surprising, even by the authors' own admission.[1] Looking solely at 1920s bond yields, they found continued evidence that the gold standard remained a seal of approval when a country returned to its prewar exchange parity with gold, lowering bond spreads significantly in that case. Devaluers were not so lucky with their bond spreads: for them, the effect of being on gold was found to be small and statistically insignificant. Such findings seem to challenge the conventional wisdom that the interwar gold standard was a pale and less credible shadow of its predecessor.

The papers by Bordo and Rockoff (1996) and by Bordo et al. (1999) are pioneering studies, but they are not ideal for comparative work across regimes because of differences in the type of data that each employs. The former study looked at long-term government bonds in the secondary market and examined their yield to maturity; the latter examined new issues and their yield at the moment of flotation only. The former study therefore had complete time series, whereas the latter had a small sample that was often interrupted by missing data in years when no issues took place – a not uncommon event in the 1920s, and one that raises a potential sample-selection issue (presumably, bonds tend not to be floated when conditions are unfavorable). Finally, the former study examined prices in London; the latter, prices in New York – a defensible switch as the hegemonic center of global capital markets shifted across the Atlantic around this time, and one that allowed the use of Cleona Lewis's (1938) figures on new issues during the 1920s.

To overcome the differences between these two earlier investigations, we compare the determinants of bond spreads in the pre-1914 and interwar years using a consistent set of data for a larger sample of countries from 1870 through 1939. We focus on a sample of more than 20 diverse countries – some within the British empire, some outside, some in the core and some in the periphery – to see how their country risk evolved. This allows us to focus on the same type of risk measure across both prewar and interwar eras. To isolate the effects of default (as opposed to exchange-rate) risk, spreads over London are

---

[1] See also Ferguson (2001, 333), who suggests that the surprising conclusion of the interwar study throws doubt on the findings in the original Bordo-Rockoff study of pre-1914 yields. However, the two studies use very different sources for their yield data, as we will explain.

exclusively for bonds denominated in gold or in sterling. Most of our yield-to-maturity data come from the Global Financial Data (GFD) source and pertain to bonds traded in London. When GFD did not report appropriate data for gold or sterling-indexed bonds, however, we collected it ourselves from contemporary journalistic sources, in a few cases resorting to yield quotations from the New York market.

Figure 6.1 offers an overview of our yield data over the full period 1870–1939. The mean bond spreads over London for two subsamples (the core and empire subset and the periphery nonempire subsets) are presented in the top and bottom charts, respectively, and each is surrounded by a measure of dispersion, a band equal to ±2 standard deviations.[2] The units are percentage points and the scales are deliberately the same on the two charts.

The differences between the two subsamples are very striking: the core had much smaller country risk than the periphery, as expected. Core and empire countries usually had interest rates within one or two percentage points of Britain's, at least from 1880 to 1930. The periphery could have spreads as large as 5, 10, or even 20 percentage points, the last spread usually tantamount to being in default.

The figures also show some similarities, once we normalize for this scale difference. Both core and periphery experienced a convergence in bond spreads up to 1914. For both country groupings, we observe a good deal of volatility in the interwar years, when spreads widened, but there appears to have been some convergence during Britain's brief interwar return to gold, 1925–31. We seek to understand the gold standard's role in these two convergence episodes.

Our empirical analysis allows public indebtedness to play a role in determining borrowing spreads. Macroeconomic variables correlated with gold-standard adherence, such as public debt, might be responsible for the apparent pre-1914 benefits of going on gold or might mask such benefits after World War One. Before the war, countries on gold may have had more disciplined fiscal policies, lower public debt, and hence more favorable treatment by the bond markets. On the other hand, countries that inflated away their public debts in the early or mid-1920s would have been unlikely to rejoin gold at prewar parity, making high public debts and a return to gold at par positively correlated variables. In these circumstances, one major concern is that failing to control for public debt

---

[2] In the figure, the core countries are Australia, Belgium, Canada, Denmark, France, Germany, New Zealand, Norway, Sweden, and the United States. The somewhat overlapping set of empire countries is defined to include Australia, Canada, India, New Zealand, and South Africa. The periphery nonempire countries are Argentina, Austria (or Austria-Hungary), Brazil, Chile, Finland, Greece, Hungary, Italy, Japan, Mexico, Portugal, Spain, Turkey (or the Ottoman empire), and Uruguay.

The changing nature of government credibility

Fig. 6.1. London bond spreads, core and periphery, 1870–1939

External bond spread: Core and empire bonds

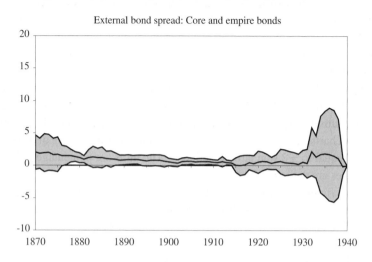

External bond spread: Periphery nonempire bonds

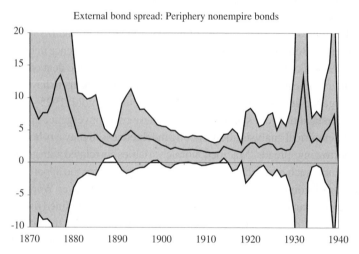

Notes: See text and appendix. *Source*: Global Financial Data and other sources.

could lead us to overestimate the prewar benefit of gold-standard adherence and underestimate the postwar benefit of returning to gold at the prewar exchange rate. A contribution of our analysis is its collection and use of historical time series on the public debts of a large number of borrowing countries. We also consider the effects of the terms of trade between exports and imports, potentially a major determinant of creditworthiness for the borrowers in our sample that are primary commodity exporters.[3,4]

This chapter's findings reinstate conventional wisdom concerning the low credibility of the interwar gold standard. We largely confirm the Bordo-Rockoff (1996) findings on the prewar gold standard, notwithstanding a larger country sample and the inclusion of a wider set of macrofundamental determinants of the borrowing spread. Before the First World War, gold-standard adherence was an effective credibility signal that shaved up to 30 basis points from a country's external public borrowing cost. The interwar results presented here, however, suggest that in the 1920s, returning to gold at prewar parity no longer was enough to soothe international investors. After World War One, there was no significant "good housekeeping" effect of returning to gold at prewar parity. At best, it was the countries returning to gold at depreciated levels that gained. Moreover, public debt and empire membership were important determinants of borrowing spreads after World War One, though not before.

---

[3] Bordo and Rockoff (1996) examined the effect on borrowing spreads of the public deficit relative to GDP, a flow variable, but found it to be statistically insignificant. Our experiments with the deficit variable led to the same negative conclusion. If we wish to assess solvency, however, the stock variable, public debt, seems preferable. Based on a specification that includes public debt, Flandreau et al. (1998) find prewar spread effects of gold-standard adherence similar in size to those reported by Bordo and Rockoff (about 35–55 basis points). We discuss the relation between our results and those of Flandreau et al. later.

[4] The discussion of omitted fiscal variables points to a deeper identification problem in any attempt to pinpoint a "pure" yield effect of gold-standard adherence. Countries' decisions over the monetary regime are, in most cases, endogenously determined, and without controlling for a broad range of economic and political variables, one cannot know whether bond spreads are being driven by gold-standard adherence per se or by the domestic economic circumstances that facilitate adherence or force suspension. We therefore urge extreme caution in the interpretation of our estimated spread "effects" of the gold standard. We can legitimately infer from them, not a gold impact that is independent of other economic factors but merely a partially unconditional average benefit accruing to countries in a position to adopt the gold standard. During both of the eras we study, countries able to adopt gold by and large did so, and we believe that our results provide a valid approach to understanding how the credibility of gold commitments changed after the First World War. We hope to address explicitly the regime selection problem in future work, although analysis is complicated by the very diverse scenarios through which various countries have adopted or left the gold standard at different times. Meissner (2002) models empirically the spread of the prewar gold standard. He shows that countries with large borrowing spreads over London were more likely to join the gold standard quickly. That selection effect implies that ordinary least squares would tend to underestimate the impact on the spread of joining the gold standard.

6.1 Five suggestive cases

Case studies are suggestive but not definitive; we present five for purposes of illustration. Ultimately, careful examination of a broader range of cases would be a useful complement to the more aggregative econometric analysis that we carry out in the next section.

In the United States, the Resumption Act came into force in January 1875. The Act legislated a return to a unified gold-backed currency on January 1, 1879. To assess the effect of gold-standard adherence on U.S. government bond spreads, we must account for the fact that the return to gold was anticipated well in advance. One way to do so is to track simultaneously the exchange rate. In Figure 6.2, we show the paths over time of the price of gold in terms of the floating paper greenbacks issued to finance the Civil War, as well as of the relative yield on gold bonds – specifically, Macaulay's (1938, A218) gold railroad bonds – relative to the London consol yield. The announcement that greenbacks would be redeemed at par nearly four years later obviously was not credible early in 1875. Rather than falling, the greenback price of gold initially rose. Only later in that year did the greenback begin its appreciation toward par.[5] The concomitant decline in the bond spread is impressive – around 200 basis points.

Argentina returned to the gold standard on October 31, 1899, nearly a decade after abandoning gold in the Baring Crisis. Starting in 1891, the country embarked upon a deflationary policy so as to be able to resume gold convertibility at an unchanged parity, even though the currency ultimately was pegged at a devalued rate (see della Paolera and Taylor 2001). Figure 6.3 shows how both the exchange rate and the borrowing spread over London behaved: both moved strongly together over the 1890s, suggesting that expectations of resumption and borrowing costs were indeed strongly interrelated. When Julio Roca, a strong advocate of the gold standard, was reelected to the presidency in the fall of 1898, the currency appreciated sharply and the spread over British borrowing costs fell, eventually dropping further as the restored gold standard endured. Roca announced the return to gold before Congress on May 25, 1899, and resumption occurred six months later. By the end of 1902 Argentina's external borrowing spread was nearly 200 basis points lower than it had been when Roca came to power.

Argentina's brief interwar return to gold at the prewar parity, lasting from August 1927 to December 1929, had no such dramatic effect on its foreign borrowing costs. The external borrowing spread over U.K. consols changed

[5] For discussions of the period, see Mitchell (1908) and Barrett (1931). Smith and Smith (1997) formally analyze exchange-rate dynamics prior to resumption.

Fig. 6.2. U.S. resumption in the 1870s

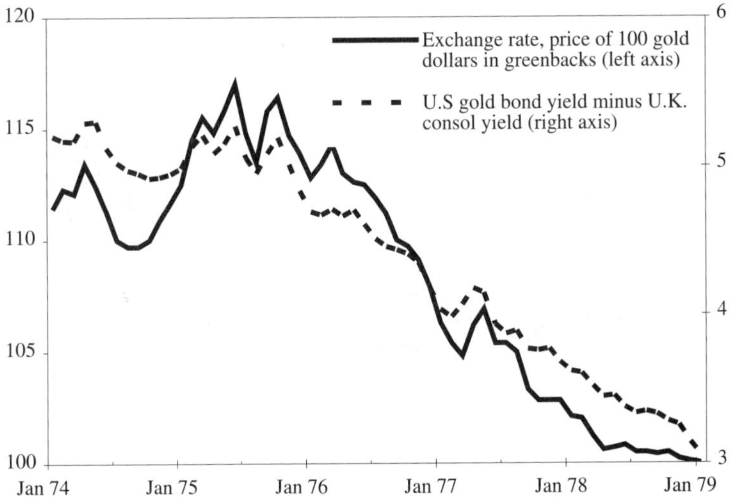

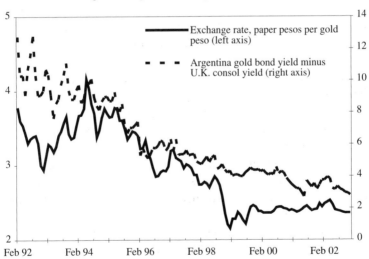

Notes: See text and appendix. *Source*: Global Financial Data and other sources.

Fig. 6.3. Argentine resumption in the 1890s

Notes: See text and appendix. *Source*: Global Financial Data and other sources.

Fig. 6.4. Australian resumption in the 1920s

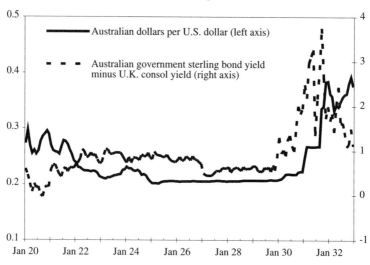

Notes: See text and appendix. *Source*: Global Financial Data and other sources.

hardly at all over the period 1926–28. The striking contrast with the previous resumption episode is consistent with the view that Argentina's brief interwar gold standard had a much smaller beneficial effect on the public finances than its prewar counterpart.

Australia's experience in the 1920s resembles that of Argentina, as shown in Figure 6.4. Australia returned to gold at the same time as Britain (April 1925); like Britain, it returned at the prewar parity. The decline in the government's borrowing cost (relative to London), however, was delayed and rather small. Australia effectively left gold at the start of 1930, well before Britain's departure on September 19, 1931, ended the interwar gold standard. Australia's abandonment of gold was forced by severe economic problems originating in sharp falls in the prices of its commodity exports (Eichengreen 1992, 232–6). The borrowing spread over London rose sharply after Australia went off gold, but it had already begun to rise in December 1929, the month before the country effectively left the gold standard. The spread increase clearly was driven by fears of default that quickly forced the country to curtail gold convertibility, not by a progressive abandonment of gold per se. Thus, for Australia also, the interwar gold standard was less successful than its prewar predecessor in instilling confidence in foreign investors.

Fig. 6.5. French resumption in the 1920s

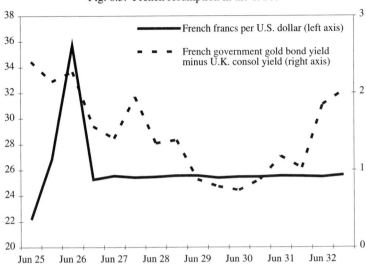

Notes: See text and appendix. *Source*: Global Financial Data and other sources.

France's interwar return to gold offers a contrast to the two preceding cases; however, France returned to gold at a sharply devalued parity. The return occurred in stages, and Figure 6.5 shows how the exchange rate (franc price of dollars) and the external borrowing spread over London covaried. Raymond Poincaré formed a government in July 1926 as the franc reached a low point, driven by a crisis of public deficits and inflation. As a result of the fiscal consolidation measures that the Poincaré government immediately introduced, the franc appreciated sharply and finally was pegged in December 1926. In the period leading to this de facto embrace of gold – by then, sterling along with the dollar was linked to the metal – the external gold borrowing spread over London dropped sharply. This response lends support to Sargent's (1993) thesis that Poincaré's consistent fiscal and monetary reform package enjoyed great credibility in the eyes of the financial markets. That is not the end of the story, though. As Figure 6.5 shows, France's de jure adoption of the gold standard on June 25, 1928, was followed by a further large decline in the borrowing spread. France remained on gold long after Britain departed, and one sees that in 1932 its borrowing spread over London paper rocketed upward as the worldwide depression progressed. But for this important case of a country returning to gold at a devalued parity, adherence coincided with a large decline in the cost of foreign borrowing through September 1931.

Obviously such evidence can be illustrative only, as it fails to control for several potential determinants of spreads, so we now turn to a more formal statistical analysis of a broader sample of countries.

6.2 Econometric analysis

We now proceed with a formal comparative analysis of sovereign borrowing risk in the prewar and interwar periods. Following Bordo and Rockoff (1996), we investigate the relationship between the dependent variable country risk, measured by the bond spread over London (expressed in percentage points per annum), $\mathrm{SPREAD}_{it} = \mathrm{YIELD}_{it} - \mathrm{YIELD}_{UK,t}$, and selected macroeconomic policy variables that could play a role for country i and time t. One such variable is gold-standard adherence, measured by dummy variables: GS_{it}, which equals 1 if on date t country i is on gold at any parity, GSPAR_{it}, which equals 1 if on date t country i is on gold after 1914 at its prewar parity, and GSDEV_{it}, which equals 1 if the country is on gold at a devalued parity after 1914.

Some countries in our sample were at times in full or partial default pre-1914, or in full default at some point during the interwar gold standard. Obviously this status would raise borrowing spreads, so we introduce the dummy variables $\mathrm{DFLT1}_{it}$ for countries in full default and $\mathrm{DFLT2}_{it}$ for countries in partial default. More subtly, we would expect the market's view of the value of gold-standard adherence to depend on whether a country is in full compliance with its debt contracts. Thus, all gold-standard-adherence dummies enter our regressions in the form $\mathrm{GS}_{it} \times \mathrm{NODFLT}_{it}$ and $\mathrm{GS}_{it} \times \mathrm{DFLT}_{it}$ (where, for this purpose, we do not distinguish between full or partial default). We look to the coefficient of $\mathrm{GS}_{it} \times \mathrm{NODFLT}_{it}$ for gold-standard credibility effects. Our prior is that such effects would show up less strongly, if at all, in the cases represented by $\mathrm{GS}_{it} \times \mathrm{DFLT}_{it}$; that is, countries already in default should not reap a reward for remaining on gold (and indeed may be punished).[6]

The appendix gives details of our coding procedure, which of necessity involves somewhat subjective judgments even for such an apparently clear-cut variable as gold-standard adherence. Several countries (notably Spain and Italy before 1914) spent many years posturing as "shadow" members of the gold standard – fixing and defending their exchange rates, yet not fully embracing gold convertibility or other "rules of the game." In the classifications of many

---

[6] A number of countries indeed remained on gold despite being in full or partial default. These include Brazil, Egypt, Turkey, and Uruguay, prewar, and Chile interwar.

scholars, this leads to a delicate decision as to whether such cases should be treated as on or off gold (see, e.g., Martín Aceña 2000; Fratianni and Spinelli 1984). The situation during the interwar period is murkier still. After World War One, many countries first stabilized their currencies de facto with respect to gold, moving only gradually toward the de jure embrace of gold-standard rules. Similarly, exits from the gold standard starting in 1929 sometimes were accomplished in piecemeal fashion, a first step often being some sort of formal or informal government control over gold outflows. Indeed, the tendency of governments to tinker with the interwar gold standard is a key reason scholars have viewed its credibility as being limited. Our classification corresponds largely to de jure gold-standard adherence, as we describe in the appendix.[7]

We also include the lagged inflation rate, $INFL_{i,t-1}$. Because many countries operated on fractional gold backing, this variable could be important as a way for markets to detect slippage in gold-standard commitments by governments, for example, at the start of episodes of overvaluation that might lead to reserve loss followed by eventual suspension and debt crisis. In addition, we examine the effects of lagged public debt levels, measured by the ratio of nominal debt to nominal output, $DEBT_{i,t-1}$. Typically the available data are for central government debt. Lagged debt is included to allow for the possibility that markets might impose more severe credit conditions on highly indebted governments, where, ceteris paribus, default risk is higher.[8] Country fixed effects are used to capture constant but unmeasured political, economic, institutional, or geographic features of individual countries (e.g., location on the "periphery").

We add several more economic variables often seen in country risk studies. The first is EXPGDP, a measure of the export-to-GDP ratio, which reveals the capacity of the country to earn the foreign exchange needed to service externally held debt. This indicator is commonly used as a risk measure today by emerging market credit analysts. LOGY, a measure of real income per capita

---

[7] Our interwar dates, although generally in agreement with those of Officer (2001), contradict in a number of cases the annual codings reproduced in Eichengreen (1992, 188–90).
A general problem with the type of coding we use is that reinstatement of gold was in some cases anticipated (recall the preceding section), with some fraction of the beneficial spread effects possibly front-loaded. In that case, our estimates of the benefit of gold adherence could be biased downward. One way to deal with the problem within this chapter's framework might be through anticipatory dummies. In our view, however, the diverse circumstances of countries' paths back to gold warrant a case-by-case analysis with more detailed macroeconomic and political control variables than are available for broad cross-sectional work. This we leave for future research. In cases such as that of interwar France, for example, one would ideally disentangle the benefits of gold from those of the Poincaré stabilization measures that made de jure resumption possible two years later.

[8] Bordo and Rockoff (1996) use the gap between money growth and real output as their measure of monetary laxity, but, even if we do not assume a stable velocity, the outcome variable INFL can serve as an adequate measure of excess money supply growth.

(relative to the sample mean), serves as a catch-all variable that proxies for all manner of social, political, institutional, and financial developments along the road to modernization that might make a country a better credit risk. In some of our specifications, we also control for the terms of trade (LTOT) and for international and civil wars (WARINT, WARCIV).[9]

Like Bordo and Rockoff, we find it necessary to account for global interest-rate shocks that affect spreads in all markets in a given year. To do this, following the logic of the "international CAPM" model, we include (with a country-specific slope, or "β") a measure of systematic "market risk" in the form $\text{SPREAD}_{W,t} = \text{YIELD}_{WORLD,t} - \text{YIELD}_{UK,t}$, where this term is the GDP-weighted average world spread over the "safe rate" (London) for the countries in the sample at time t.[10]

Using pooled annual data for a large sample of countries, the basic fixed-effects regression equation is then of the form

$$\text{SPREAD}_{it} = \alpha_i + \beta_i \text{SPREAD}_{W,t} + \gamma X_{it} + u_{it}, \qquad (6.1)$$

where typically the vector X includes gold-standard adherence, the lagged debt ratio, lagged inflation, and possibly other control variables.

Such a specification can be rationalized in a model where the government's bond rate reflects the central rate plus a default premium, and in which new government borrowing depends on the current interest rate. In that case, the regression coefficients are reduced-form coefficients incorporating the government's incentive to borrow less when the rate charged is high, but they nonetheless indicate whether the gold standard and macrofundamentals affected perceived risk. When we discuss "effects" of explanatory variables on the spread later, we refer to the reduced-form regression coefficients.[11]

---

[9] Real income per capita (at PPP prices) and the export ratio were included in the pre-1914 country risk analysis of Flandreau et al. (1998).

[10] We experimented with other ways to control for time-specific asset market shifts, such as simple time dummies, but the results appear robust.

[11] Suppose that

$$\text{SPREAD}_t = a + b\text{DEBT}_t + cZ_t + v_t,$$

where the variables Z_t are various solvency indicators. Furthermore, suppose that new government borrowing depends negatively on the spread,

$$\Delta\text{DEBT}_t = -d\text{SPREAD}_t + w_t.$$

Then the reduced-form equation for the spread is

$$\text{SPREAD}_t = \frac{a}{1+bd} + \frac{b}{1+bd}\text{DEBT}_{t-1} + \frac{c}{1+bd}Z_t + \frac{bw_t + v_t}{1+bd}.$$

For the dependent variable SPREAD, due care must be taken in constructing measures of country risk to ensure that the bonds in every case are properly comparable across countries. We want SPREAD to capture the effects of default risk only, and not the effects of the potential exchange-rate changes that are inherent in bonds' differing currency denominations. In this case, since we are using Britain as the base country, we elect to focus only on government bonds of long maturity (greater than 5 years, and usually at least 10 years) and payable in gold or sterling. It is, therefore, necessary to eliminate the polluting effects of Britain's departures from the gold standard – from August 1914 to April 1925 and from September 1931. Hence, we focus on only two periods: a prewar period based on annual December yields from 1870 to 1913, and an interwar period based on June yields from 1925 to 1931. This affords us up to 44 observations in the time dimension for the prewar sample and up to 7 for the interwar sample.

To construct SPREAD, we then need bond yields for each country, payable in gold or sterling, from which we can subtract the consol yield. Finding them is not always an easy task. Because, ideally, our test requires a gold or sterling bond as quoted in London, data construction requires considerable caution. It is a well-known problem that in standard secondary sources, the attributes of a particular bond issue are not always readily apparent.

Bordo and Rockoff (1996) split their samples into gold bonds and paper bonds, finding little effect of gold-standard adherence on the yields of bonds payable in domestic paper. Care is needed because many paper bonds in fact contained gold clauses or exchange clauses, which (if enforceable) would have allowed creditors to extract payment in specie or hard currency if the debtor devalued. This condition was frequently stipulated for borrowers with poor reputations for fiscal and monetary stability. Then as now, such borrowers suffered from "original sin" – that is, an inability to issue debt denominated in one's own currency. Only a handful of countries have been capable of own-currency borrowing in the last two centuries (Rousseau and Sylla, 2003). The history of nineteenth- and early twentieth-century bond issuance is only now being fully explored to give us some insight into the constraints that faced borrowers with respect to details of contracts, including denominations of debt issue (Bordo, Meissner, and Redish 2003; Flandreau and Sussman 2002).[12]

---

[12] If a government's gold-standard commitment had been permanent, noncontingent, and completely credible, then its paper bonds would have been "as good as gold," and any fall in external borrowing costs would have been inherited by the paper bonds. It therefore may seem puzzling that Bordo and Rockoff could not detect gold-standard effects on paper yields. If countries' exchange-rate commitments lacked credibility, why not their commitments to repay gold-denominated debt at par? Prewar gold-standard conventions, however, allowed for suspen-

A great many data on bond yields are contained in the reference Global Financial Data, of which we make extensive use. For our purposes, however, we sometimes found it necessary to corroborate the type of bond quoted in GFD using bond manuals such as *Kimber's Record* and other sources. In many cases, the bond yields quoted in GFD failed to satisfy our requirements, being only domestic rather than London quotations, or possibly yields denominated in domestic currency, and this eliminated several countries from our database (such as Denmark in the prewar years and Spain in the interwar years). We treated the United States during the 1870s just as Bordo and Rockoff (1996) did, using Charles Calomiris's series on gold equivalent yields, for a period in which the terms of payment were in doubt (Bordo et al. 2002). Countries like Belgium, France and Germany – which issued debt in domestic currency – had to be omitted in the prewar sample, but we were able to find interwar data on appropriately denominated Belgian and French bonds traded in New York and on the German Dawes Loan as quoted in London. Missing data were often a problem too. Some of the gaps in GFD, especially in the interwar years, could be filled by consulting newspapers such as the *Investor's Monthly Manual* (for a London quote) or, as a last resort, the *Wall Street Journal* (for New York quotes on gold-linked bonds). Full details of the construction of the yield data are in the appendix.

Other complications affect our use of historical bond yield data. The compiler of the GFD source, Bryan Taylor, warns in the documentation (September 2000) that "[f]or riskier issues, such as Latin American countries, not only was there a risk that coupons could be eliminated, but that the entire issue could go in default. At that point, the implied yield becomes meaningless, and any yield over 10% before World War Two should be treated as implying that the issue was in default on either coupon, on principal, or on both." Because our model is intended to capture country risk under conditions with a positive probability of full repayment, once an issue actually is in default, we might expect its yield to be volatile indeed, and perhaps far removed from any simple linear prediction given by a model of the form shown in equation 6.1. Such defaults were not uncommon in our data, and in some cases spreads grew to 20, 30, or even 60 percentage points on some issues, implying prices of less than 10 percent of

sion in the event of certain contingencies (notably, wars) provided resumption took place at the previous gold parity (Bordo and Kydland 1995). Thus, paper bonds might entail some shorter-term exchange risk even for countries following conventional gold-standard rules, whereas gold- or sterling-denominated bonds were supposedly payable in the currency of denomination re-gardless of the issuing government's circumstances. The different behavior of indexed and paper yields certainly warrants further investigation. Cook (2002) discusses the case of Russian bonds.

par value. Although such steep discounts on bonds affect only a small part of our sample, we will discuss the steps we can take to ensure that these types of observation do not bias the regression estimates.

The gradual convergence of bond spreads evident in Figure 6.1 warns us that the dynamics of evolving country risk might not be simple. In particular, the figure suggests high levels of persistence or serial correlation in bond spreads, and it is easy to imagine why. Bond spreads are a function of reputation, which in capital markets, as in any other repeated game, cannot be built overnight. Instead, one's reputation in the previous period is likely to have a substantial influence on one's reputation today. In our empirical results we present two alternative estimates based on different approaches to modeling of the persistence in spreads. One way is to impound all of the persistence in the error term, and we do so by using an AR(1) model. Another way is to use a lagged dependent variable model, so that spreads themselves follow a partial adjustment process toward long-run equilibrium.

6.2.1 Prewar findings, 1870–1913

As a cross check we begin our analysis with a simple attempt to replicate the findings of Bordo and Rockoff (1996), who used a sample of just seven countries in the prewar era – Argentina, Australia, Brazil, Canada, Chile, Italy, and the United States. Based on pooled data for gold bonds (267 observations), their headline number for the impact of the gold standard on country risk was presented as follows:

Indeed, if we were to single out one number to represent our findings with respect to the significance of the gold-adherence dummy it would be 40 basis points....In other words, all other things equal, the rate on a gold bond would be 40 basis points lower if the country were on the gold standard. Other factors, perhaps related to regional preferences, undoubtedly also played a role in determining country-risk premia. But our analysis suggests a willingness to commit to the gold standard was an important determinant of risk premia established in the London capital market.[13]

We are in broad agreement with this conclusion. Regression 1 of Table 6.1 shows that our data, some of it from different sources, enables us to duplicate the Bordo-Rockoff finding on their country sample. We have slightly longer time series that yield 308 observations for the Bordo-Rockoff countries, but we find, as they did, that adopting the gold standard was worth a statistically significant reduction in spread. At 30 rather than 40 basis points, our estimated effect is somewhat smaller than theirs, but it is still economically important.

[13] Bordo and Rockoff (1996, 413).

As Bordo and Rockoff noted, there is strong serial correlation in this context and this renders ordinary least squares (OLS) invalid. So, like them, we employ an AR(1) specification, allowing for possibly different autoregressive parameters in each member of the panel.[14] Our econometric approach is as follows. We estimate an equation of the form of 6.1 under the assumption that $u_{it} = \rho_i u_{i,t-1} + \epsilon_{it}$ and ϵ_{it} are white noise disturbances. We also find that the estimated ϵ_{it} appear highly heteroskedastic, so we also correct for country-specific values of the error variances $\sigma_{\epsilon_i}^2$.

Here, and throughout this rest of the chapter, the β_i coefficients are not shown to conserve space but they also accord with expectations and past results, being higher in "riskier" peripheral countries. The country fixed effects, which are reported, tend to be high for peripheral countries such as Brazil (235 basis points), Italy (144), Argentina (206), and Chile (169), but lower for the three core Western offshoots, Australia, Canada, and the United States (87, 23, and 1 basis point, respectively).

In Regression 2 we expand the analysis substantially by using our augmented data set covering more than 20 countries from 1870 to 1913. The sample size here increases by a factor of nearly 3, to 892 observations. We find that the estimated effect of the gold standard on borrowing spreads remains statistically significant but is now estimated to be about half the Bordo-Rockoff number, or 20 basis points.

In Regression 3 we add full and partial default to the model. Countries in full default had spreads 165 basis points higher, and the effect is highly significant although surprisingly small. Partial defaulters seem to have been penalized far less. Adding default variables brings the gold-standard effect down further, however, to a (still statistically significant) 14 basis points. This last result does not appear to be an artifact of a few badly behaved outliers in the data. Specifically, when we exclude observations with very high spreads (over 2,000 or 1,000 basis points) as in Regressions 4 and 5, we find that the effect of the gold standard remains statistically significant but it is still of approximately the same magnitude, 16 to 17 basis points.

Our broader aim is to consider the role of additional country characteristics in determining country risk. Because certain geopolitical features of countries remained fairly constant in this period, a natural place to start is by examining

---

[14] Unlike Bordo and Rockoff (1996), we do not employ seemingly unrelated regression (SUR) models, but we have explored SUR results for limited samples and find the results broadly similar. However, the larger cross-sectional size in our later regressions calls for a large parameter set in the unrestricted error covariance matrix under SUR, sometimes too large a set for the available degrees of freedom. In all our tables, the country coefficients identified vertically along the left are the country-specific intercepts.

Table 6.1. *Sovereign risk, 1870–1913*

Sample	(1) Bordo Rockoff	(2) All	(3) All	(4) SPREAD <20	(5) SPREAD <10
Observations	308	892	892	877	852
GS×NODFLT	−0.30(2.34)	−0.20(2.61)	−0.14(1.96)	−0.17(2.32)	−0.16(2.21)
GS×DFLT	−0.14(0.38)	1.06(3.49)	0.12(0.40)	0.02(0.08)	0.07(0.23)
DFLT1	—	—	1.65(6.72)	1.81(7.59)	1.21(5.72)
DFLT2	—	—	0.12(0.51)	0.14(0.60)	0.26(1.20)
ARG	2.06(4.44)	1.99(4.21)	1.83(4.41)	1.83(4.35)	1.89(4.63)
AUS	0.87(5.56)	0.76(6.60)	0.70(6.25)	0.74(6.44)	0.72(6.41)
AUT	—	0.49(1.87)	0.49(1.87)	0.49(1.87)	0.49(1.87)
BRZ	2.35(5.36)	1.99(3.20)	2.20(8.22)	2.20(8.56)	2.15(6.64)
CAN	0.23(1.42)	0.12(1.02)	0.06(0.54)	0.10(0.80)	0.08(0.70)
CHL	1.69(5.38)	1.68(5.40)	1.65(6.49)	1.65(6.01)	1.63(5.74)
EGY	—	−0.39(0.63)	−0.41(0.83)	−0.37(0.75)	0.26(0.54)
GRC	—	−6.40(3.17)	−6.10(3.28)	−0.66(0.38)	2.31(1.32)
IND	—	0.28(1.24)	0.30(2.00)	0.28(1.48)	0.27(1.44)
ITA	1.44(7.08)	1.42(7.49)	1.48(9.82)	1.46(8.91)	1.45(8.81)
JPN	—	2.08(7.34)	2.17(5.52)	2.12(6.28)	2.10(6.31)
MEX	—	−3.46(1.16)	−3.25(1.17)	−0.40(0.44)	−0.32(0.30)
NOR	—	0.44(3.91)	0.38(3.49)	0.41(3.72)	0.40(3.65)
NZL	—	0.54(2.89)	0.48(2.60)	0.51(2.76)	0.50(2.70)
PRT	—	1.45(1.05)	1.01(0.77)	0.96(0.73)	0.96(1.25)
RSA	—	1.03(4.56)	0.97(4.33)	1.00(4.45)	0.99(4.41)
SPA	—	−2.52(1.73)	−1.95(1.56)	−1.41(1.24)	−0.20(0.41)
SWE	—	0.56(4.09)	0.50(3.54)	0.53(3.82)	0.51(3.88)
TUR	—	0.28(0.60)	0.24(0.49)	0.28(0.56)	0.25(0.55)
USA	0.01(0.03)	−0.12(0.49)	−0.16(0.60)	−0.14(0.53)	−0.16(0.61)
URU	—	−1.63(1.03)	−1.88(1.26)	−1.84(1.23)	−1.17(0.98)
Empire	—	0.39(2.80)	0.35(2.91)	0.38(3.07)	0.47(3.93)
Nonempire	—	−0.12(0.38)	−0.09(0.33)	0.50(2.32)	0.82(4.43)
Difference	—	0.51(1.55)	0.44(1.49)	−0.12(0.52)	−0.35(1.69)

Notes: Dependent variable is SPREAD. Estimation is by panel Feasible Generalized Least Squares (FGLS) with heteroskedastic panels and country-specific AR(1) correction. Country-specific β_i and ρ_i are not reported; t-statistics are shown in parentheses. Empire and nonempire show average fixed effect for the group.
Sources: See text and appendix.

the country fixed effects for clues. And because Britain is being used as the reference country in the analysis, an important feature to examine would be any special country-specific links to Britain. An obvious criterion is membership in the British empire.

Ever since Marx and Hobson, students who view history through the lens of political economy – whether from left, right, or center – have regarded imperialism as a leading vehicle on the road to economic globalization. Its epitome, the British empire, is seen as, amongst other things, a privileged economic zone in both trade and capital markets. Empire connections among countries are believed to have conveyed some distinct advantages to would-be borrowers in London. Davis and Huttenback (1986) and Edelstein (1981) have suggested that empire membership meant a lower cost of capital to both public and private sectors in this era.

Taking the argument further, Ferguson (2002) places these ideas in the context of a broader political and financial history and claims support, on economic if not on other grounds, for his case that the British empire could be viewed as a global public good:

My hypothesis is that empire – and particularly the British Empire – encouraged investors to put their money in developing economies. The reasoning is straightforward. Investing in such economies is risky. They tend to be far away and more prone to economic, social and political crises. But the extension of empire into the less developed world had the effect of reducing such risks by imposing, directly or indirectly, some form of European rule. In practice, money invested in a *de jure* British colony such as India (or a colony in all but name like Egypt) was a great deal more secure than money invested in a *de facto* "colony" such as Argentina.

This effect should be – and is – quantifiable. There are two ways of posing the crucial question. First, did the existence of the British empire make investors more willing to put their money into poorer countries than they would otherwise have been? More precisely, did being a British colony reduce the cost of borrowing for a country? The hypothesis here is that it did, because being a colony implied a no-default guarantee. This was arguably a better "seal of good housekeeping" even than membership of the gold standard, though most British colonies had both.[15]

Here, one contrast to the Bordo and Rockoff (1996) claim is quite explicit. Empire, not the gold standard, was what really counted for attracting capital in large quantities at low cost, though the two forces need not have been mutually exclusive and, indeed, tended to be positively correlated. To settle the debate econometrically, however, requires careful controls for these and other possible risk determinants.

It is imperative, then, that we consider the empire effect in our analysis. The question is whether countries within the empire enjoyed preferential access to the market, and we interpret that to imply that, all else equal, empire countries should exhibit a smaller fixed effect than others. This can be studied by looking at each individual intercept in the regression. Or, for a summary comparison of the two groups, we can ask whether the mean fixed effect in the empire group was less than the mean in the nonempire group. The mean fixed effect for each

---

[15] Ferguson (2002, 12).

group is shown in the bottom panel of Table 6.1, together with the t-statistic for the estimated mean (where the null is a zero mean).[16]

Our results are not too favorable to the idea of an empire effect during the so-called Age of High Imperialism. In Regressions 2 and 3 even the sign is wrong. In the possibly more robust regressions (4 and 5), the sign is correct, and empire membership seems to be worth anywhere from 12 to 35 basis points as a point estimate. This was, however, possibly little more valuable than going on gold, and, unlike the effect of gold, this impact is not statistically significant.[17]

A detailed look at some of the fixed effects reveals some of the problem cases. Consider Regression 5. In the nonempire group, only some countries (once we include the effect of being on gold) paid a large risk penalty, namely Argentina (173 basis points), Brazil (199), Chile (147), Greece (215), Italy (129), Japan (194), and Portugal (80). Others appear to have paid no premium at all. Yet even the richest country in the world (by some measures) and empire member Australia had to pay a statistically significant risk premium of 56 basis points, while South Africa's burden was 83 basis points.[18]

The reasons for Australia's plight are easy to guess, given the severe and enduring consequences of the widespread defaults associated with the 1890 crash and subsequent depression, which crippled Australia's banks and dented the country's reputation in the London capital market (see Davis and Gallman 2001). Indeed, in the aftermath of the 1890 events, which originated in the Argentina-centered Baring crisis, Argentina was able to return to the London market earlier than Australia. The Australian results show that, even if empire borrowers were proof against outright sovereign default, they were not proof against a severe economic crisis. Some narrative evidence seems to back this up, as British and empire issues were not always viewed as pure substitutes by outside observers with a keen eye on the determinants of risk premia.[19]

Conversely, even some peripheral nonempire countries such as Uruguay (which was well within "contagion range" of Argentina and Brazil) seemed

---

[16] In this application, the set of empire observations is defined by countries that were formally part of the British empire, including dominions and those under de facto British rule, namely, Australia, Canada, Egypt (from 1882), India, New Zealand, and South Africa.

[17] A "strong" test of the empire hypothesis would also require the β coefficients to be zero for empire members, implying that their returns did not covary with changes in the global spread – in other words, that they were "safe" assets like the British consol itself, up to a white noise error. But this hypothesis is very decisively rejected. Although the β coefficients are not reported in the tables to conserve space, these results are available from the authors on request.

[18] These estimates are 16 basis points less than the reported intercepts because we also include the effect of going on gold.

[19] For example, during the Japanese government's internal debate over investing foreign reserves during the mid-1890s, the finance minister asked "Are the public bonds of the Indian Government as safe and reliable as those of England itself?" (Matsukata 1899, 221).

not to have been penalized in capital markets despite being outside the formal empire. Empire status was neither necessary nor sufficient for preferential access to the London market. Much seemed to depend on other aspects of the behavior of the borrower – in the specification of Table 6.1, an unobservable.

The preceding regressions do not yet add a number of plausibly important control variables. In Table 6.2, we use the full data set to check the robustness of the preceding results to additional controls for debt ratios, inflation, relative income per capita, the terms of trade, and other variables. Regression 1 in Table 6.2 adds DEBT and INFL to the spread equation. As we noted in the introduction, the omission of DEBT in particular could very plausibly lead to biases.[20] We are now restricted to a much smaller sample than in Table 6.1, since our new variables DEBT and INFL are not available for all countries in all years. From a maximum of 892 observations, we are now down to 563. For this pre-1914 sample, the gold-standard seal of approval is highly significant (conditional on no default) in all regressions (and estimated to be between 26 and 28 basis points).

Perhaps surprisingly, DEBT is not significant in Regression 1, neither economically nor statistically, although INFL is, and both variables are correctly signed. The gold-standard commitment appeared strong enough that markets could rely on debt repayment. Inflation, however, was viewed with alarm. In an interesting twist, we also find that the empire thesis is again rejected, but for an easily understood reason. In this smaller subsample, all countries could expect, once on gold, to converge to the British bond yield. Full default draws a smaller penalty than in Table 6.1, and partial default, a larger one, with both effects now statistically significant.

Regressions 2 through 4 successively add real GDP per capita, the export ratio, the terms of trade, and war dummies to the specification. None of these changes affects the conclusions about public debt, inflation, or default status. But we see that richer countries enjoyed significantly lower spreads. The export

---

[20] Flandreau et al. (1998) argue that a major force driving the evident convergence of bond spreads after the early 1890s and through 1914 is worldwide inflation resulting from gold discoveries, a factor that caused both an unexpected reduction in countries' ratios of public debt to nominal GDP and a more widespread adherence to the gold standard. For the pre-1914 period, Flandreau et al. investigate borrowing spreads over London using a country sample different from that of Bordo and Rockoff (1996) and an econometric specification encompassing the public debt ratio to GDP as well as gold-standard adherence. Unlike us, they find a strong positive effect of public debt on borrowing spreads even under the classical gold standard (and even in a linear model of spread determination). Unfortunately, we have not been able to obtain their complete data set, which includes some "European peripheral" countries with highly indebted governments, so we cannot say for sure whether differences in the country sample drive the discrepancy in results. The Flandreau et al. estimates of the value of gold-standard adherence before 1914 are, as we noted earlier, similar to those that Bordo and Rockoff find.

Table 6.2. *Sovereign risk, 1870–1913: Additional controls*

	(1)	(2)	(3)	(4)
Observations	563	563	563	563
GS×NODFLT	−0.26(3.71)	−0.28(4.15)	−0.27(4.05)	−0.27(3.98)
GS×DFLT	−0.18(0.50)	−0.24(0.68)	−0.25(0.71)	−0.28(0.82)
DFLT1	0.89(3.96)	0.95(4.31)	0.94(4.28)	1.03(4.67)
DFLT2	0.44(2.09)	0.41(1.99)	0.41(1.95)	0.41(1.97)
DEBT	0.13(1.60)	0.09(1.18)	0.09(1.10)	0.08(1.06)
INFL	0.35(2.42)	0.35(2.44)	0.36(2.45)	0.36(2.48)
LOGY	—	−0.46(4.34)	−0.45(4.32)	−0.46(4.34)
EXPGDP	—	—	−0.11(0.24)	−0.08(0.17)
LOGTOT	—	—	−0.11(1.03)	−0.11(1.03)
WARINTL	—	—	—	0.01(0.22)
WARCIV	—	—	—	0.28(1.03)
ARG	0.35(0.60)	0.75(1.29)	0.77(1.31)	0.78(1.33)
AUS	0.69(4.88)	1.11(5.92)	1.12(5.59)	1.11(5.53)
AUT	−0.27(0.72)	−0.20(0.59)	−0.18(0.51)	−0.19(0.53)
BRZ	1.13(1.59)	0.81(1.23)	0.81(1.22)	0.87(1.37)
CAN	0.02(0.16)	0.41(2.51)	0.43(2.35)	0.42(2.30)
CHL	1.49(5.70)	1.55(5.81)	1.59(5.88)	1.58(5.92)
EGY	0.37(1.47)	−0.05(0.22)	0.01(0.03)	−0.01(0.04)
IND	0.42(3.30)	−0.13(0.71)	−0.12(0.64)	−0.13(0.68)
ITA	1.42(5.67)	1.40(6.61)	1.41(6.68)	1.40(6.64)
JPN	0.04(0.10)	−0.23(0.72)	−0.26(0.81)	−0.27(0.82)
NOR	0.33(1.88)	0.40(2.61)	0.43(2.39)	0.42(2.34)
NZL	−0.11(0.49)	0.38(1.42)	0.43(1.41)	0.42(1.38)
PRT	1.33(0.99)	1.14(0.86)	1.16(0.87)	1.14(0.86)
SPA	−1.33(2.04)	−1.23(1.84)	−1.23(1.86)	−1.21(1.84)
SWE	0.35(1.63)	0.66(2.72)	0.70(2.83)	0.69(2.78)
USA	0.27(2.27)	0.64(4.13)	0.64(4.02)	0.64(3.96)
URU	−1.83(1.14)	−1.69(1.09)	−1.69(1.09)	−1.69(1.10)
Empire	0.28(2.63)	0.34(3.38)	0.37(2.69)	0.36(2.62)
Nonempire	0.27(1.26)	0.33(1.58)	0.35(1.59)	0.35(1.60)
Difference	0.00(0.02)	0.01(0.05)	0.03(0.12)	0.02(0.07)

Notes and Sources: See Table 6.1.

ratio is correctly signed, as are the terms of trade (which are defined so that an increase in LOGTOT is an improvement, a rise in the country's price of exports relative to imports). Perhaps surprisingly, neither variable is significant. Likewise, indicators of war are correctly signed, but their coefficients are small and insignificant. In all specifications in Table 6.2, the empire effect is found to be statistically indistinguishable from zero based on the difference between the mean fixed effects.

For a final sensitivity check, we augment the model in 6.1 to include a lagged dependent variable so that we estimate

$$\text{SPREAD}_{it} = \alpha_i + \phi(L)\text{SPREAD}_{it} + \beta_i \text{SPREAD}_{W,t} + \gamma X_{it} + u_{it}, \qquad (6.2)$$

where $\phi(L)$ is a polynomial in positive powers of the lag operator L. We retain fixed effects and possible serial correlation. This choice of model could be justified on a number of grounds. Lagged-dependent-variable models can be hard to distinguish from the previous AR(1) models we have used, but they might better approximate bond market behavior if agents employ Bayesian updating of country risk. In that setting, today's predicted risk is a linear combination of lagged risk and today's new information. Thus, deviations from steady-state risk may persist for a long time, whereas in the simple AR(1) model the fitted value adjusts immediately, and only the error term has persistence.

Naturally, such a flexible form calls for a different estimation strategy. Panel fixed effects with lagged dependent variables induce bias in OLS estimates. One solution is to use the generalized method of moments (GMM). We employ the Arellano and Bond (1991) one-step dynamic panel estimator, treating world risk and gold-standard variables as exogenous and lagged debt and inflation terms as endogenous but predetermined. We estimated the model in differences using at least twice-lagged levels of the endogenous variables as instruments. Selected results are shown in Table 6.3, and despite the very different estimation strategy, they show a basic consistency with the message from Tables 6.1 and 6.2.[21]

Like Bordo and Rockoff (1996), we conclude overall that a main significant policy determinant of country risk in the prewar period was gold-standard adherence. Gold was apparently a good enough seal of approval by itself, and risk was priced without much reference to public debt levels, the terms of trade, or whether the country was part of the British empire.

---

[21] As discussed by Sussman and Yafeh (2000, 457), the Japanese bond yield data are distorted by a debt conversion at precisely the time the gold standard is adopted. The conversion causes an artifically big drop in the conventional measure of long-term borrowing cost (the coupon-price ratio) in 1897 (see their Figure 1). We checked to see whether our findings are robust to the inclusion of the problematic data. Dropping the years 1891–99 from the Japanese sample did not affect the results reported in Tables 6.1 and 6.2 materially. All coefficients remained of a similar magnitude and significance, and the inference on empire effects was unchanged. For example, in our preferred GLS specification (Table 6.2, Regression 2) the gold standard impact, with no default, was a fall of 20 basis points (t-statistic 3.04). However, the GMM results of Table 6.3 were weakened once the off-on event of Japan in 1896–97 was removed from the sample. For example, in a typical GMM specification (Table 6.3, Regression 1) the gold standard impact, with no default, was a fall of 32 basis points (t-statistic 1.38). Although the point estimates are still signed correctly, imprecision may result from the small number of regime transitions in the sample, from which the effect is identified in this regression in differences. Overall, we think there are compelling econometric reasons to prefer levels-based estimation as in Tables 6.1 and 6.2. The GMM difference estimator is best suited for small-T, large-N situations, such as the interwar analysis that follows. It is included here for comparability with those later results (Table 6.6), but in the prewar data T is larger than N and the asymptotics favor levels regressions. In the GMM regressions, preliminary analysis indicated the need for two lags to ensure no second-order residual autocorrelation.

Table 6.3. *Sovereign risk, 1870–1913: GMM estimates*

	(1)	(2)	(3)	(4)
Observations	641	546	546	546
Sargan	438.7(0.00)	467.3(0.00)	549.2(0.00)	542.8(0.00)
m_2	−0.16(0.88)	1.34(0.18)	1.03(0.30)	1.08(0.28)
SPREAD(t−1)	0.72(20.30)	0.70(20.80)	0.72(21.78)	0.73(21.79)
SPREAD(t−2)	−0.31(9.61)	−0.35(11.17)	−0.31(10.19)	−0.31(10.19)
GS×NODFLT	−0.55(2.44)	−0.31(1.80)	−0.18(1.15)	−0.16(1.03)
GS×DFLT	0.52(1.15)	0.55(1.65)	0.74(2.25)	0.75(2.25)
DFLT1	1.02(3.74)	1.40(7.26)	1.41(7.63)	1.44(7.74)
DFLT2	0.18(0.56)	0.53(2.30)	0.39(1.88)	0.46(2.07)
LOGY	−1.48(1.83)	−0.96(1.71)	−0.31(0.60)	−0.24(0.47)
DEBT	—	0.10(0.70)	−0.06(0.52)	−0.03(0.23)
INFL	—	0.14(0.44)	0.11(0.36)	0.16(0.53)
EXPGDP	—	—	0.35(0.35)	0.46(0.45)
LOGTOT	—	—	−0.12(0.41)	−0.10(0.36)
WARINTL	—	—	—	−0.10(0.55)
WARCIV	—	—	—	0.62(2.00)
Long-run coefficients				
GS×NODFLT	−0.93	−0.47	−0.31	−0.28
GS×DFLT	0.88	0.85	1.26	1.28
DFLT1	1.72	2.16	2.39	2.46
DFLT2	0.30	0.81	0.65	0.78
LOGY	−2.50	−1.48	−0.52	−0.41
DEBT	—	0.15	−0.11	−0.05
INFL	—	0.22	0.19	0.28
EXPGDP	—	—	0.60	0.78
LTOT	—	—	−0.20	−0.18
WARINTL	—	—	—	−0.18
WARCIV	—	—	—	1.07

Notes: Dependent variable is SPREAD. Estimation is by GMM using the Arellano-Bond method. Country-specific β_i are not reported and t-statistics are shown in parentheses. "Sargan" is the Sargan test of overidentifying restrictions, distributed χ^2. m_2 is the Arellano-Bond test that average autocovariance in residuals of order 2 is 0, distributed asymptotically $N(0, 1)$. The one-step estimator is used; GS, DFLT1, DFLT2, LTOT, WARCIV, WARINTL, and the world spread are treated as exogenous; and DEBT, INFL, EXPGDP, and LOGY are treated as endogenous. See text for details.
Sources: See text and appendix.

6.2.2 Interwar findings, 1925–1931

Most narrative accounts of the transition from the classical gold standard to the interwar period stress one key difference: the rebuilt gold standard was a pale imitation of its predecessor. It did not long endure and seemed to lack both credibility and stability. As Temin (1989, 33) remarks, "The combination of changed conditions and some policy choices of the 1920s…created great strains in the operation of the interwar gold standard."

The key question is whether such a regime change can be detected in the data. To that end we repeat the previous country risk modeling exercise for the period 1925–31. One difficulty here is that, after 1914, many countries suspended and then resumed the gold standard at new, devalued parities that partially expropriated prior bondholders. In a conventional view of reputation (Bordo and Kydland 1995), devaluation would be viewed with suspicion by markets, and fear of such reactions prompted some governments to deflate in order to restore prewar parities – Churchill's pursuit of $4.86 is perhaps the most famous example. To account for differential market treatment of par maintainers and par adjusters, we use the policy dummy variables GSPAR and GSDEV described at the start of this section, as suggested Bordo, Edelstein, and Rockoff (1999). A second difficulty is that whereas previously we had up to 44 observations per country in the time dimension, we now have at most 7; it is therefore unwise to estimate country-specific autoregressive parameters ρ_i, so we adopt a specification with $\rho_i = \rho$ for all countries. For the same reason, we do not attempt attempt a heteroskedasticity correction.

Tables 6.4 and 6.5 can be directly compared with Tables 6.1 and 6.2. Table 6.4 shows the interwar analysis for the full sample, 167 observations, with no additional controls. Regression 1 in Table 6.4 suggests that unconditionally (that is, without reference to the restoration of the prewar parity), the gold standard had a statistically significant 45 basis point effect on spreads (for a nondefaulter). Regression 2 partitions the GS dummy to account for postwar devaluations. (No countries that returned to gold at par defaulted.) According to these estimates, countries returning to gold at the prewar parities gained in reduced spreads, but countries like France that returned after devaluing gained more – 62 basis points for devaluers versus 38 for parity keepers. Adding the full default dummy (there are no partial defaults in our interwar sample) changes nothing, and the variable itself is incorrectly signed and insignificant.

These findings run contrary to the Bordo-Edelstein-Rockoff results. Echoing the conventional wisdom of interwar policymakers, they found that sticking to the prewar parity was rewarded by markets with a continued (and large) discount on borrowing costs of over 100 basis points. But in their analysis, countries that resumed at a devalued parity gained nothing, as their credibility was damaged. What could possibly explain our result – a reversal of the classic ideology – according to which the market rewards devaluers better than parity keepers? The result is not so far-fetched when markets try to assess which promises actually can be kept. In this respect, our findings support the theoretical conclusion of Drazen and Masson (1994) that policymakers may hurt rather than enhance their credibility through policies that appear "tough" in the short term but are too

Table 6.4. *Sovereign risk, 1925–1931*

	(1)	(2)	(3)	(4)
Observations	167	167	167	167
GS×NODFLT	−0.45(4.90)	—	−0.45(4.91)	—
GS×DFLT	0.25(0.60)	—	0.49(0.97)	—
GSPAR×NODFLT	—	−0.38(3.53)	—	−0.38(3.54)
GSDEV×NODFLT	—	−0.62(3.72)	—	−0.62(3.73)
GSDEV×DFLT	—	0.02(0.04)	—	0.27(0.50)
DFLT1	—	—	−0.24(0.84)	−0.25(0.89)
ARG	0.31(1.01)	0.26(0.85)	0.31(1.01)	0.26(0.85)
AUS	1.05(3.48)	1.04(3.48)	1.05(3.49)	1.04(3.49)
AUT	1.47(4.67)	1.65(4.82)	1.47(4.68)	1.65(4.84)
BEL	1.66(4.96)	1.94(4.83)	1.66(4.97)	1.94(4.84)
BRZ	2.24(7.19)	2.39(7.23)	2.24(7.21)	2.39(7.25)
CAN	0.38(1.25)	0.36(1.19)	0.38(1.26)	0.36(1.19)
CHL	0.41(1.02)	0.70(1.52)	0.41(1.02)	0.70(1.53)
DNK	−0.66(1.99)	−0.77(2.22)	−0.66(1.99)	−0.77(2.22)
EGY	1.08(3.42)	1.02(3.21)	1.08(3.43)	1.02(3.21)
FIN	0.88(2.67)	1.15(2.94)	0.88(2.67)	1.15(2.95)
FRA	0.79(2.40)	1.05(2.70)	0.79(2.40)	1.05(2.71)
GER	2.44(7.74)	2.61(7.63)	2.44(7.76)	2.61(7.65)
HUN	3.26(10.34)	3.43(10.03)	3.26(10.37)	3.43(10.05)
IND	1.60(4.77)	1.50(4.35)	1.60(4.78)	1.50(4.36)
ITA	2.41(6.13)	2.68(6.03)	2.41(6.14)	2.68(6.04)
JPN	1.51(4.88)	1.46(4.73)	1.51(4.89)	1.46(4.75)
NZL	0.62(2.04)	0.61(2.02)	0.62(2.05)	0.61(2.03)
NOR	−0.42(1.27)	−0.51(1.50)	−0.42(1.27)	−0.51(1.51)
PRT	0.13(0.42)	0.11(0.36)	0.13(0.42)	0.11(0.36)
RSA	0.79(2.51)	0.73(2.31)	0.79(2.52)	0.73(2.32)
SWE	0.15(0.49)	0.09(0.28)	0.15(0.49)	0.09(0.28)
TUR	3.30(10.94)	3.30(11.06)	3.38(10.65)	3.38(10.81)
USA	−1.03(3.26)	−1.09(3.44)	−1.03(3.27)	−1.09(3.45)
URU	2.83(9.15)	2.77(8.96)	2.83(9.17)	2.77(8.98)
Empire	0.92(6.51)	0.88(5.97)	0.92(6.53)	0.88(5.99)
Nonempire	1.20(9.96)	1.29(9.36)	1.21(10.01)	1.30(9.41)
Difference	−0.29(1.96)	−0.41(2.27)	−0.29(1.99)	−0.42(2.31)

Notes: Dependent variable is SPREAD. Estimation is by panel OLS with homoskedastic panels and a common AR(1) correction. Country-specific β_i are not reported; t-statistics are shown in parentheses. Empire and nonempire show average fixed effect for the group.
Sources: See text and appendix.

draconian to be sustained for long. Our initial results are far from conclusive, but the question certainly warrants further research.

Our findings are so obviously at variance with the results of Bordo-Edelstein-Rockoff that some explanation is needed. The contrast could be ascribed to differences in concept (use of secondary-market bond yields, mostly in London,

Table 6.5. *Sovereign risk, 1925–1931: Additional controls*

	(1)	(2)	(3)	(4)
Observations	164	164	136	136
GSPAR×NODFLT	−0.34(3.61)	−0.26(2.79)	−0.14(1.36)	−0.09(0.80)
GSDEV×NODFLT	−0.60(4.18)	−0.56(4.00)	−0.34(2.08)	−0.33(2.03)
GSDEV×DFLT	0.74(1.21)	0.20(0.32)	0.09(0.14)	0.03(0.05)
DFLT1	−0.83(1.74)	−0.77(1.67)	−0.62(1.35)	−0.62(1.37)
DEBT	1.18(3.30)	1.08(3.12)	0.84(2.08)	0.95(2.34)
INFL	0.14(2.00)	0.15(2.18)	0.10(1.36)	0.10(1.32)
LOGY	—	−1.50(3.32)	−1.76(0.53)	−1.87(3.83)
EXPGDP	—	—	0.52(3.61)	0.32(0.32)
LOGTOT	—	—	−0.69(2.80)	−0.74(3.00)
WARINTL	—	—	—	−0.60(1.69)
ARG	−0.20(0.67)	0.65(1.67)	0.57(1.39)	0.59(1.45)
AUS	−0.83(1.33)	0.34(0.48)	0.59(0.77)	0.50(0.66)
AUT	1.47(4.92)	2.17(6.10)	—	—
BEL	1.00(2.22)	2.22(3.92)	1.59(2.32)	1.69(2.49)
BRZ	2.09(6.95)	1.04(2.43)	0.39(0.75)	0.29(0.57)
CAN	−0.06(0.22)	1.02(2.38)	1.08(2.42)	1.12(2.55)
CHL	0.40(1.00)	0.73(1.81)	0.36(0.82)	0.35(0.80)
DNK	−1.12(3.52)	0.09(0.19)	0.08(0.17)	0.12(0.24)
EGY	0.35(1.04)	−1.40(2.24)	−1.87(2.72)	−2.07(2.99)
FIN	0.99(2.91)	1.26(3.73)	0.96(2.37)	1.00(2.50)
FRA	−0.35(0.65)	0.76(1.22)	0.81(1.17)	0.76(1.12)
GER	2.91(7.40)	3.86(8.11)	3.68(7.20)	3.74(7.38)
HUN	3.33(10.17)	3.45(10.84)	—	—
IND	0.98(2.88)	−0.97(1.43)	−1.56(2.16)	−1.81(2.47)
ITA	2.06(4.79)	2.47(5.72)	—	—
JPN	0.92(2.94)	0.63(1.99)	0.44(1.31)	0.67(1.88)
NZL	−1.50(2.17)	−0.23(0.30)	0.11(0.13)	0.05(0.06)
NOR	−1.04(3.05)	−0.50(1.37)	−0.63(1.65)	−0.68(1.80)
PRT	−0.51(1.64)	−0.72(2.33)	−0.69(2.12)	−0.77(2.39)
RSA	0.21(0.65)	−0.15(0.45)	—	—
SWE	−0.17(0.59)	0.69(1.84)	0.67(1.72)	0.70(1.82)
TUR	1.08(1.83)	0.26(0.41)	0.34(0.53)	0.26(0.41)
USA	−1.32(4.71)	0.16(0.31)	0.35(0.63)	0.40(0.73)
URU	1.82(4.66)	2.89(5.82)	3.10(5.58)	3.05(5.50)
Empire	−0.14(0.42)	−0.23(0.70)	−0.33(0.87)	−0.44(1.15)
Nonempire	0.74(3.73)	1.23(5.09)	0.80(3.01)	0.81(3.08)
Difference	−0.89(3.91)	−1.46(5.22)	−1.13(3.78)	−1.26(4.09)

Notes and Sources: See Table 6.4.

versus new issue yields in New York) and differences in estimation method. Of these features in our empirical approach, the first, at least, seems necessary if we are to make comparisons on an equal footing with the prewar period and Bordo and Rockoff (1996). For the same reason, an autoregressive correction of some sort would seem essential, although Bordo, Rockoff, and Edelstein (1999) used simple OLS. One reason for their choice, we think, was an unfortunate feature of Cleona Lewis's interwar data on New York bond issues: these were primary issues, so not every country had a bond issue every year, leading to gaps in the time series, and hence the impossibility of an AR(1) correction. A more subtle difficulty, which our approach confronts, is an inherent problem of sample selection bias when using primary-issue data of Lewis's kind. Countries tend only to float bonds when they are creditworthy, so this yields a biased sample, as noted earlier. In contrast, by using secondary market data from London, we can track countries in all years, whatever their predicament.

But we cannot stop here, and Table 6.5 adds additional controls. In Regressions 1 and 2 the coefficients of GSDEV × NODFLT and GSPAR × NODFLT change relatively little compared to the previous table. In contrast to the pre-war results, public debt now has a statistically significant positive effect on borrowing costs. This is a second key contrast with the classical prewar gold standard. All four regressions in Table 6.5 indicate that the markets cared very much about public debt during the interwar period. For example, a coefficient of 1.18 on DEBT in our table (Regression 1) means that a 10 percentage point increase in a country's debt-to-GDP ratio would be expected to raise country risk by 11.8 basis points. Inflation, however, has a small effect and is of uneven statistical significance in the table. Regressions 2 adds a control for the level of development, which turns out to have a significant negative effect on spreads. Once again, we point out that the interpretation of the LOGY variable is unclear because it could be a proxy for various institutional, economic, or other factors affecting risk. In all regressions, the default variable is puzzlingly of the wrong sign, although the estimate is not very significantly different from zero.

Regression 3 adds exports (incorrectly signed and significant) and the terms of trade. The terms of trade have the right sign and are highly statistically significant. Adding them to the specification is quite important, as that change results in coefficients on GSDEV × NODFLT and GSPAR × NODFLT that are much closer to zero (but with GSDEV still more influential than GSPAR for the spread). Indeed, the benefit of returning to gold at par is now statistically insignificant. This effect of including the terms of trade is largely the result of the presence in our sample of several commodity exporters – including Australia, Argentina, and Uruguay – that departed from gold before Britain did so in September 1931. These countries were driven off gold in part by adverse export-price developments (Kindleberger 1986), and they experienced huge increases in their spreads over London as they freed their currencies. Regressions 1 and 2 in Table 6.5 implicitly give the gold standard "credit" for preventing those post-departure spread increases – which in reality were caused not by departure per se, but by the terms of trade and other shocks that made the gold standard unsustainable. Conversely, stronger terms of trade supported the gold standard in commodity-exporting countries. Thus, the terms-of-trade variable soaks up some of the apparent benefits of going on gold, which in reality derived from beneficial external conditions.[22] Regression 4, which adds a war dummy, leaves the main conclusions intact. There were some benefits from returning to gold at a devalued parity (slightly over 30 basis points) and essentially none from returning at par; public debt and the terms of trade mattered.

Given the apparent futility of returning to gold at par, the bottom line for the interwar period could be summed up as: the gold standard strikes out but the empire strikes back. Table 6.5 suggests that the value of being in the empire was higher than being on gold, and much higher than it had been prior to the war. Based on the mean fixed effects, an empire member might have expected a borrowing discount of anywhere between 89 and 146 basis points.

This finding makes intuitive sense. Prior to World War One, the long trend of globalization in the world economy and a convergence on a set of more or less liberal economic policy principles (a kind of "London consensus") had placed economic actions at center stage in the minds of market actors. The sudden specter of total war, the shock of political instability and revolution, the rise of belligerence in the core economies, and a general air of noncooperative policymaking could well have changed the weight given to various signals in the world bond market. Suddenly, the safe haven of empire investments might have looked more attractive, just as the gold standard began to lose its glitter. Consistent with our finding, Ferguson (2003a, 17), citing data from Cain and Hopkins (2001), observes that 39 percent of British foreign investment flowed to the empire between 1856 and 1914, whereas fully two thirds did so between 1919 and 1938. More generally, this interpretation sits comfortably with the conventional wisdom that the world economy as a whole was becoming increasingly organized along regional, bilateral, or imperial lines in the interwar years, due to preferential policies in both trade and finance. For example, after the onset of war, in the 1910s and 1920s, Britain began to curtail nonempire access to the London capital market and by the 1930s the British empire had become a heavily protected trading zone under the Ottawa accords.

---

[22] The results are fairly robust to leaving off the turbulent year 1931 and estimating only over 1925–30. The main differences are that the coefficient on public debt rises sharply to 2.14 (t-statistic of 6.46), whereas that on the terms of trade rises to -0.35 (t-statistic of -1.54). When we estimate regressions 1 and 2 over 1925–31 but restrict the sample to the 136 observations for which terms of trade data are available, the results are very similar to those for the full sample reported in Table 6.5. Thus, there is no prima facie reason for thinking that the subsample with terms of trade data is unrepresentative.

Table 6.6. Sovereign risk, 1925–1931: GMM estimates

	(1)	(2)	(3)	(4)
Observations	132	132	110	110
Sargan	29.15(1.00)	36.30(1.00)	31.28(1.00)	37.00(1.00)
m_2	0.01(0.99)	0.53(0.59)	0.49(0.63)	0.48(0.63)
SPREAD(t−1)	0.32(2.43)	0.10(0.70)	0.07(0.49)	0.13(0.96)
GSPAR×NODFLT	0.07(0.58)	0.02(0.17)	0.07(0.59)	0.10(0.80)
GSDEV×NODFLT	−0.19(1.00)	−0.28(1.46)	−0.07(0.33)	−0.06(0.30)
DFLT1	0.43(0.82)	−0.01(0.02)	−0.06(0.11)	−0.04(0.07)
LOGY	−1.25(1.54)	−1.22(1.66)	−1.70(2.25)	−1.78(2.37)
DEBT	—	2.03(2.30)	2.07(2.41)	1.68(2.03)
INFL	—	−0.36(0.47)	−0.10(0.15)	−0.26(0.39)
EXPGDP	—	—	0.37(0.26)	0.72(0.51)
LOGTOT	—	—	−0.61(1.98)	−0.71(2.33)
WARINTL	—	—	—	−0.75(1.87)
Long-run coefficients				
GSPAR×NODFLT	0.10	0.02	0.08	0.12
GSDEV×NODFLT	−0.28	−0.31	−0.07	−0.07
DFLT1	0.64	−0.01	−0.06	−0.05
LOGY	−1.85	−1.35	−1.83	−2.05
DEBT	—	2.25	2.22	1.94
INFL	—	−0.40	−0.11	−0.30
EXPGDP	—	—	0.40	0.84
LOGTOT	—	—	−0.65	−0.82
WARINTL	—	—	—	−0.86

Notes and Sources: See Table 6.3.

In a further sensitivity check, we turn to our alternative dynamic model once again, just as we did in Table 6.3. Table 6.6 reports GMM estimates for a lagged-dependent-variable model of spreads. (Now, GSDEV × DFLT and DFLT become identical.) Using the Arellano and Bond (1991) one-step dynamic panel estimator once again, we find results broadly consistent with the AR(1) estimates from Tables 6.4 and 6.5, although standard errors are much higher – which is perhaps no surprise given the shortness of the interwar panel and the loss of one cross section as a result of differencing. Here, returning to the gold standard at the prewar parity appears to have yielded no reduction in spreads, but parity devaluation yielded a long-run risk reduction somewhere around 10 to 30 basis points, an effect that is in some cases economically significant but never is statistically significant. Debt generally was punished by the markets, with the estimated effects in this table even higher than before. Inflation appears not to matter much, but the terms of trade remain correctly signed and significant. In the GMM interwar regressions in Table 6.6, we also find, as before, that higher income per capita reduced spreads.

What have we learned? By the late 1920s, the market's approach to risk pricing had changed dramatically. If markets rewarded gold adherence at all, they did so only when the adoption of gold was based upon a realistically competitive exchange rate. In addition, policymakers faced a world in which the mere word of their commitment to the gold standard was no longer good enough – now creditors also wanted to see the books. In a final contrast with the prewar era, interwar creditors looked at the terms of trade to judge how well a country could earn the export revenue needed to service foreign debt.

6.3 Summary

In the sovereign bond market before 1914, the gold standard did indeed confer a "seal of approval," whereas two key macrofundamentals, the public debt and terms of trade, seem to have mattered little, if at all. Apparently adherence to gold, in and of itself, was sufficient to enhance market credibility during that era. Membership in the British empire was neither a necessary nor sufficient condition for preferential access to London's capital market before 1914.

For the interwar period, a return to gold after devaluation seems to have been more credible, notwithstanding the arguments that led Britain and other countries to return to gold at par. Indeed, returning at par yielded essentially no benefit, and only a return after devaluation (as in the case of France) was beneficial. Moreover, high public debts were now punished, suggesting that policymakers' room for maneuver had been curtailed. In the troubled interwar environment, empire membership emerged as an important qualification for lower borrowing costs. Lenders now scrutinized a borrower's terms of trade in order to assess debt sustainability.

Our results suggest that the interwar gold standard was less credible than its pre-1914 predecessor. It remains to reconcile these results fully with findings such as those of Hallwood, MacDonald, and Marsh (1996) that indicate a credible gold standard during the late 1920s, at least in the short-term credit markets.[23] Perhaps the bond markets adopted a longer perspective under which protracted adherence to unchanging gold parities seemed less probable than short-term adherence.[24] The question certainly deserves further research, but our findings on bond markets serve to illuminate how different the interwar

[23] Using a more refined methodology, however, Eichengreen and Hsieh (1996) do find some evidence that sterling's gold parity lacked full credibility at times during the 1925–31 period.
[24] Collins (2003) proposes an empirical model that allows consistent estimation of crisis probabilities at different time horizons. Her approach is based on the first passage of a latent variable (e.g., a shadow floating exchange rate) across a fixed threshold (e.g., the current fixed exchange rate value). It would be illuminating to apply Collins's model to interwar data.

global capital market was from its antecedent, the classical gold-standard regime of 1870–1914. Evidently the global convergence in the bond market prior to 1914 was replaced by quite different, disintegrative forces afterwards.

Finally, if we seek lessons from the past, our results have some implications for today's attempts to gain capital market credibility through the use of pegged exchange rates. It is clear that the post–World War One political developments that rendered interwar exchange-rate commitments less credible have not receded in the meantime. Thus, policymakers should not expect to gain market credibility even through seemingly irrevocable exchange-rate commitments. Absent robust fundamentals and complementary economic and institutional reforms, efforts to forswear discretionary exchange-rate changes are of questionable value.

Part four

Lessons for Today

The previous chapters of this book have traced the very long-run evolution of global financial markets over several hundred years, with a strong emphasis on events since the latter nineteenth century. We have shown that the present globalization in financial markets is nothing new; indeed, by some measures, the first era of international financial integration from 1870 to 1913 went further and deeper than today's. Yet, if the important and relevant lessons from history are to be drawn, we must be careful to distinguish the features that past and present have in common, and the areas where they diverge. In this final part of the book we employ the historical perspectives developed so far to assess what we see as some of the major questions raised by financial integration today. First, after studying the forms and directions that capital flows take today, we contrast the involvement of rich and poor countries in the global capital market. Second, we review evidence on the benefits of financial integration and on the costs of financial crises – effects that are unevenly spread between rich and poor countries. We conclude by weighing up the risks of crises against the benefits of access to global financial markets, and set out some of the challenges faced by policymakers today, particularly in developing countries.

7

Uneven Integration

The principal goal of earlier chapters was to document the ebb and flow of aggregate capital flows in the world economy over the long run. But these fluctuations have hardly been uniform in character, whether in the types of capital or in the types of countries involved. This unevenness is useful for deeper empirical analysis because it may help to throw statistical light on the factors that have driven the broader dynamics of global financial integration.

Throughout this book we have concentrated on aggregate data and on the global view. One drawback of the global view is that it can mask important differences between countries. If today one listened only to news reports, one might be forgiven for thinking that financial globalization, as well as being a powerful force, is also ubiquitous.

Yet this is far from true in reality. Indeed, the unevenness of different country groups' integration into the global economy is, potentially, a cause for concern. The new financial globalization is for the most part confined to rich countries. A handful of developing countries ("emerging markets") also participate to some degree, but most other developing countries are left out, and to the extent that they receive foreign funds at all, they rely on occasional public debt offerings and official development assistance. If capital market participation includes some countries but not others, then a key question is: why, and with what effects? Exclusion may be the result of market failure, or it could be accounted for by institutions and policies. Inclusion may bring benefits, as well as costs, and the tradeoff can tell us whether policies to promote further integration are advisable, and for whom.

One way to see who's in and who's out is just to look at the places foreign investment tends to go and those that it tends to avoid. Here, history supplies some interesting perspectives once again.

7.1 Foreign capital stocks: Net versus gross

There is at least one critical dimension in which pre-1914 international capital flows differ sharply in nature from what we see today, with important implications for the periphery. To see this difference we distinguish between net and gross international asset stocks. A cursory glance at the data reveals that the net versus gross distinction is particularly important in recent decades but relatively unimportant in the pre-1914 era of globalization. The reason is simple. In the late nineteenth century, the principal flows were long-term investment capital, and virtually unidirectional at that. There was one notable exception, the United States, where both inflows and outflows were large. But in most cases, key creditor nations, principally Britain, but also France and Germany, engaged in the financing of other countries' capital accumulation. In doing so, they developed enormous one-way positions in their portfolios.

For example, circa 1914, the scale of Argentine assets in Britain's portfolio was very large, but the reverse holding of British assets by Argentines was trivial by comparison. Thus, the nineteenth century saw substantial international asset diversification by the principal creditor/outflow nations like Britain, but relatively little asset diversification by the debtor/inflow nations. To a first approximation, the gross asset and liability positions were very close to net in that distant era. The 1980s and 1990s are obviously very different. For example, the United States became in this period the world's largest net debtor nation. But while accounting for the biggest national stock of gross foreign liabilities, the United States *also* held the largest stock of gross foreign assets. In the postwar period until recently, net capital flows between countries have tended to be smaller (relative to national outputs) than before 1914, but there has been a much greater volume of asset swapping for the purpose of mutual diversification, that is, risk sharing. (Even these gross portfolio positions tend to be smaller, however, than those that simple models of optimal international diversification predict.)

We must modify our earlier discussion of the gross stock data, and our inferences concerning the post-1980 recovery of foreign assets and liabilities in the world economy, to take this difference into account. It is a significant issue for all the countries concerned: the rank of countries by foreign assets in the foreign position data reported by the International Monetary Fund (IMF) is very highly correlated with the rank by foreign liabilities. Countries such as Britain, Japan, Canada, Germany, and the Netherlands are all big holders of both foreign assets and liabilities. These asset and liability data are quite incomplete even today, as we have noted before, and the IMF's country coverage is uneven, but the numbers can still be useful as indicators of broad trends. Strikingly, when we net out these data, the result is that, since 1980, the net foreign asset position (or liability) positions in the world economy typically have remained rather low, as indicated by the GDP-weighted averages shown in Figure 7.1, even as gross stocks have boomed.

In the sample of OECD countries (which excludes Mexico, Korea, and the transition economies), gross assets and liabilities have expanded about four times relative to area GDP since 1980 (from about 0.25 to 1.0). But the *net* position of the industrial OECD as a whole, the region in the world from which one might expect net capital outflow, has changed little, remaining very small. This, of course, is another way of illustrating the Feldstein-Horioka (1980) phenomenon. If anything, the net external position of the OECD's pre-1994 membership has moved more from net credit toward net debit, reflecting the increasing external indebtedness of the United States in this period.

For countries outside the OECD, the lower panel of Figure 7.1 shows very little trend even in gross investment positions over the 1980s, though some increase follows during the 1990s. There is an upward bulge in the net foreign debt position of the nonOECD countries during the middle of the 1980s, followed by a retreat and a renewed, more rapid increase starting in the middle third of the 1990s. But the overall increase in the net debt position relative to GDP over the entire 1980–2000 period is a modest one, from about 15 to 30 percent of GDP. The developing-country averages should be approached with caution because the country sample is very small until the 1990s, but the findings are suggestive. The developing-country trends broadly echo the OECD's, where the sample sizes and the data themselves inspire more confidence. For poorer countries, however, the rise in gross positions is less dramatic and that in the net (debtor) position more noticeable. Overall, the difference between trends in the net and gross stocks of foreign capital in the rich and poor countries suggest that while the global capital market has grown rapidly in the 1980s and especially the 1990s, the bulk of this growth has taken the form of diversification investment between rich countries. Country-level data do reveal some important cases that depart from these crude averages (see Table 7.1), but in few cases do net positions reach very high levels for creditor or debtors, and rarely do we see very large changes over time in these ratios for any given country.

7.2 Foreign capital: Rich versus poor

The data on net capital stocks hint that most of the action in today's global capital market is "North-North" (that is, flows between rich countries) with comparatively little movement of capital (net or gross) in the "North-South"

Fig. 7.1. Postwar foreign capital stocks: Net versus gross

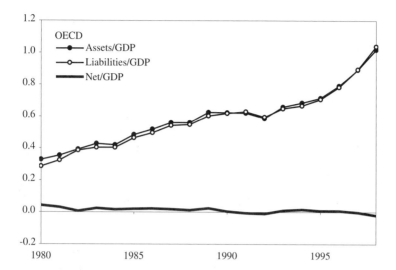

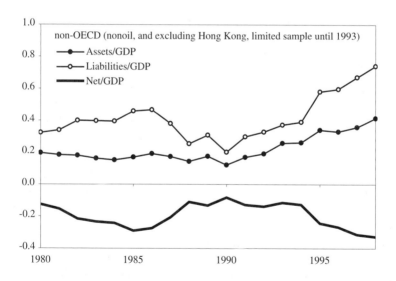

Notes and Source: Sample size ranges from 10 to 21 for the OECD sample, and from 4 to 41 for the non-OECD sample. Data are from IMF, *International Financial Statistics.*

Table 7.1. *Postwar foreign capital stocks: Net versus gross*

1980	Assets/GDP	Liabilities/GDP	Net/GDP
Austria	0.46	0.56	−0.09
Canada	0.35	0.70	−0.35
Colombia	0.18	0.24	−0.06
Finland	0.19	0.33	−0.14
Germany	0.32	0.28	0.04
Italy	0.30	0.22	0.08
Japan	0.15	0.14	0.01
Korea	0.14	0.15	−0.01
Malaysia	0.26	0.44	−0.18
Netherlands	0.33	0.16	0.17
Norway	0.25	0.53	−0.29
South Africa	0.23	0.46	−0.23
United Kingdom	1.03	0.95	0.08
United States	0.27	0.14	0.13

direction (from rich to poor countries). Can this inference be better substantiated? In order to confront that question, Figure 7.2 examines the same kind of flow data on the time series of CA/Y for the postwar period as did Figure 2.2, but it expands the sample to encompass all IMF member developed (labeled OECD) and developing (labeled non-OECD) countries.[1]

For the two country subsamples, we look at the sum of national current account flows as a share of total or aggregate output (equal to the GDP-weighted average of the subsample members' individual current account ratios to GDP). It is apparent that there was a surge in capital flows to developing countries in the late 1970s and again in the early 1990s; the resulting financial inflows far exceeded any flows in the preceding 50 years. Each lending boom was followed by a sharp reversal. Retrenchment occurred in the early 1980s following the developing-country debt crisis, and in the late 1990s following widespread currency and financial crises. The peak inflows have amounted to around 2 percent of developing-country GDP, but on average they have been much smaller, around 1 percent or less.[2]

Comparing postwar global averages with the size of flows seen in the late nineteenth century, one is struck by two features of the data. First, one notices how small even the large flows in the two booms were as a fraction of the re-

---

[1] The developing group excludes oil exporters. We draw on data from the IMF's *International Financial Statistics* here and in Figure 7.4. Note that because of errors and omissions, it appears that the world as a whole is usually running a current account deficit.

[2] For certain countries, this ratio would have been higher, but many of these are small countries, often in Africa, with larger official inflows.

Table 7.1 (continued)

1990	Assets/GDP	Liabilities/GDP	Net/GDP
Australia	0.27	0.73	−0.46
Austria	0.68	0.72	−0.04
Bahrain	14.40	13.55	0.85
Belgium	2.03	1.98	0.05
Canada	0.40	0.78	−0.38
Colombia	0.14	0.57	−0.43
Finland	0.33	0.62	−0.29
France	0.60	0.62	−0.02
Germany	0.72	0.50	0.22
Iceland	0.12	0.60	−0.48
Israel	0.32	0.64	−0.32
Italy	0.35	0.42	−0.08
Japan	0.61	0.50	0.11
Korea	0.11	0.08	0.03
Malaysia	0.32	0.57	−0.25
Namibia	0.86	1.17	−0.30
Netherlands	1.45	1.21	0.24
New Zealand	0.20	1.07	−0.87
Norway	0.43	0.58	−0.15
Peru	0.02	0.09	−0.07
Romania	0.15	0.09	0.07
South Africa	0.19	0.31	−0.12
Spain	0.27	0.40	−0.12
Swaziland	1.29	0.75	0.54
Sweden	0.61	0.88	−0.27
Switzerland	2.46	1.51	0.95
United Kingdom	1.75	1.77	−0.02
United States	0.39	0.42	−0.03
Venezuela	0.79	0.81	−0.03

ceiving region's output, as compared to similar receiving regions in the 1890s and 1900s. Second, one is surprised that this surge in inflows did not occur earlier in the postwar period. Instead, it took about 30 years for these flows to overcome whatever impediments to capital movement prevailed between core and periphery. Looking at the aggregate global picture, we argued above that, most likely, the ∪-shape in the long-run financial flow data reflects the considerable shifts in international transaction costs arising from policy environments that became more inimical to capital movements after 1914, and especially after 1929. Distinguishing flows between developed countries from flows to the developing world, we see that the phase of relative capital immobility between industrial center and developing periphery began to recede somewhat later than it did in the devloped world (though the bulk of developing-country borrowing was governmental or government-guraranteed until around 1990). Further-

Table 7.1 (continued)

2000	Assets/GDP	Liabilities/GDP	Net/GDP
Argentina	0.54	0.80	−0.26
Armenia	0.28	0.95	−0.68
Australia	0.61	1.12	−0.51
Austria	1.38	1.57	−0.19
Bahrain	12.21	11.56	0.65
Belarus	0.09	0.32	−0.22
Belgium	3.34	2.71	0.63
Benin	0.33	0.81	−0.49
Bolivia	0.32	1.24	−0.93
Bulgaria	0.83	1.14	−0.31
Canada	0.76	0.95	−0.19
Chile	0.70	1.07	−0.37
China, Hong Kong	6.91	5.58	1.33
Colombia	0.29	0.59	−0.29
Croatia	0.37	0.73	−0.36
Czech Republic	0.74	0.84	−0.10
Côte d'Ivoire	0.29	1.70	−1.41
Denmark	1.39	1.56	−0.17
Ecuador	0.14	1.58	−1.44
El Salvador	0.23	0.56	−0.33
Estonia	0.52	1.07	−0.55
Euro Area	1.07	1.12	−0.06
Finland	1.24	2.76	−1.52
France	1.87	1.81	0.06
Germany	1.40	1.36	0.04
Greece	0.50	0.92	−0.42
Hungary	0.46	1.07	−0.62
Iceland	0.44	1.06	−0.62
Israel	0.60	1.06	−0.46
Italy	1.05	1.00	0.05
Japan	0.62	0.38	0.24
Kazakhstan	0.24	0.82	−0.58
Kyrgyz Republic	0.20	0.89	−0.69

more, flows to the developing world remain quite limited by the standards of the pre-1914 economy, despite the recent upward creep in developing-country foreign liabilities measured as a share of borrower output.

To contrast further the situation now and a hundred years ago, it is worth examining how important capital flows are now, and were then, compared not just with GDP but also with total capital formation. How important were the inflows as a fraction of total capital formation in recipient countries, and how important were outflows as a fraction of total saving for source countries?

Consider first the data for the late nineteenth century. Figure 7.3 displays the ratio of average capital inflows to average investment for periphery countries

Table 7.1 (continued)

2000	Assets/GDP	Liabilities/GDP	Net/GDP
Latvia	0.55	0.85	−0.30
Lithuania	0.24	0.59	−0.35
Malta	3.00	2.97	0.03
Mauritius	0.37	0.35	0.02
Moldova	0.52	1.63	−1.11
Namibia	0.35	0.53	−0.17
Netherlands	3.09	3.19	−0.11
New Zealand	0.61	1.39	−0.78
Panama	2.40	3.21	−0.81
Paraguay	0.34	0.56	−0.23
Peru	0.27	0.77	−0.50
Poland	0.28	0.63	−0.35
Portugal	1.33	1.72	−0.39
Romania	0.29	0.52	−0.23
Russia	0.95	0.64	0.31
Rwanda	0.15	0.77	−0.61
Slovak Republic	0.51	0.73	−0.22
Slovenia	0.46	0.59	−0.13
South Africa	0.74	0.79	−0.05
Spain	1.01	1.20	−0.19
Swaziland	0.80	0.69	0.11
Sweden	1.59	1.84	−0.26
Switzerland	5.67	4.42	1.25
Tanzania	0.17	0.84	−0.68
Thailand	0.43	0.91	−0.48
Togo	0.27	1.42	−1.15
Tunisia	0.17	1.23	−1.06
Turkey	0.25	0.73	−0.47
United Kingdom	3.09	3.13	−0.03
United States	0.75	0.91	−0.16
Uruguay	0.69	0.78	−0.09

Source: IMF, *International Financial Statistics.*

in our 15-country sample, and the ratio of capital outflows to saving for core countries. We report data for the subperiods 1870–89 and 1890–1913. Of course, the pre-1890 Argentine figure must be taken with a pinch of salt, but in several cases, especially for the settler economies, we see the remarkable importance of capital inflows for capital formation. In several cases, foreign capital supplied up to half of investment demand. This squares with well-known data on the stocks of foreign capital in some of the settler economies: by 1914 about 50 percent of the Argentine capital stock was in the hands of foreigners; for Canada and Australia, the figure was in the range 20 to 30 percent.[3] Clearly these large flows cumulated over time into a very strong foreign (read: mostly

---

[3] See Taylor (1992) for more discussion of these comparative data and sources.

Fig. 7.2. Postwar foreign capital flows
CA/GDP, developed and developing country samples, annual data

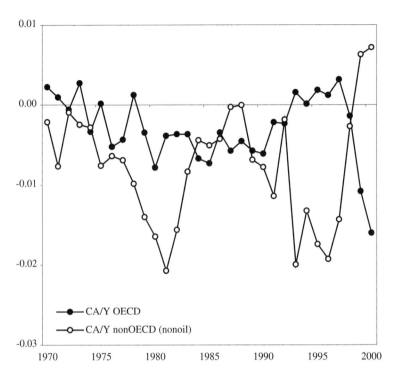

Source: IMF, *International Financial Statistics.*

British) interest in the total capital stock of many nations before 1914. On
the sending side, the British dominance is readily apparent in the figure: about
one-third of total British saving was devoted to overseas investment in the 1870–
1914 period. Moreover, in some periods, for example 1900–13, this fraction
crept as high as one half.[4] In contrast, few other capital exporters in the core
could register anything like so high a fraction of foreign investment relative
to total savings, with France, Germany, and the Netherlands each registering
less than 10 percent of domestic savings as destined for foreign countries in the
1890–1913 era.

   We again compare these numbers to modern data, examining the importance
of capital flows in relation to saving and investment in today's core and periph-

---

[4] On British foreign investment in this era, see Edelstein (1982).

Fig. 7.3. Capital flows in relation to saving and investment, 1870–1913
Fifteen countries, quinquennia, annual data

(a) Ratio of capital inflows to investment for periphery economies

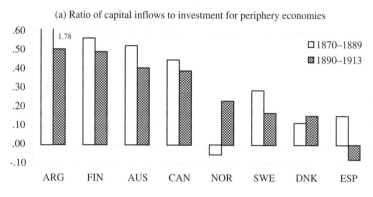

(b) Ratio of capital outflows to saving for core economies

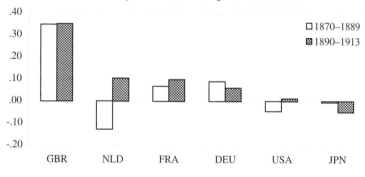

Source: See appendix.

ery. Using our long-run 15-country database, we would find postwar flows to be much lower relative to saving and investment as compared to the pre-1914 era, just as they are relative to output. But if we use only the limited long-run database to address this question, we open ourselves to the criticism that in focusing on so narrow a country sample, we miss much of the action in today's global capital market. Therefore, we examine a broader sample of post–World War Two data to see how important developed countries' outflows have been as a share of their total saving, and how important developing country inflows have been as a share of their total investment. These concepts match the pre-1914 data in Figure 7.3.

For the post-1970 period, Figure 7.4 supplies the details. As with the discussion of flows as a share of output in Figure 7.2, one is struck by the relatively

Fig. 7.4. Capital flows in relation to saving and investment, postwar
Developed and developing country samples, annual data

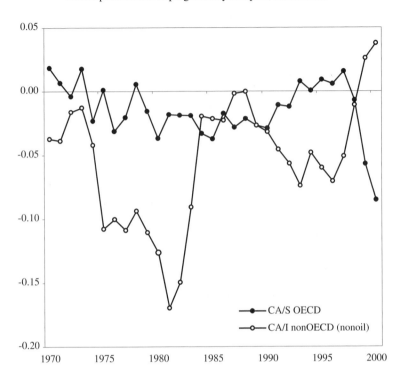

Source: IMF, *International Financial Statistics.*

small impact of net flows. Even at their peak, net inflows have never amounted to much more than about 10 to 15 percent of developing-country investment, and net outflows never approach 5 percent of developed-country saving (in large part because the 1980s and 1990s reflect very large U.S. current-account deficits). Even if we could adjust for the biases in the data that produce the statistical mirage of a global deficit, we would not dramatically alter this picture. Again, there are some recipients with exceptionally high ratios of external inflows to investment, but most of these are small countries with large development-assistance flows. This pattern contrasts with nineteenth-century experience, where a country like Britain exported as much as half its annual savings, and where countries such as Australia, Canada, and Argentina, imported up to half of their investment finance. Notwithstanding the usual measurement problems, corrections to the data probably would not affect the two key qualitative messages of this figure. First, flows into developing countries have grown large in the last 25 or so years, for the first time in the postwar era, but they have not yet regained their importance in the pre-1914 era either for receiving- or sending-region capital markets. The global capital market of the nineteenth century, centered in Europe and especially in London, extended relatively more credit to developing countries than does today's global capital market. Second, and as in the pre-1914 era, because the capital market of the core is so much bigger than those of the periphery, these flows nonetheless weigh as a much larger share of periphery investment than they do as a share of core saving.

Figure 7.5 illustrates both the periphery's need to draw on industrial country savings as well as another important dimension in which the globalization of capital markets remains behind the level attained under the classical gold standard. In the last great era of globalization, the most striking characteristic is that foreign capital was distributed bimodally; it moved to both rich and poor countries, with relatively little in the middle. Receiving regions included both colonies and independent regions. The rich countries were the settler economies, where capital was attracted (along with labor from abroad) by abundant land; the poor countries were places where capital was attracted by abundant labor.[5]

Thus, globalized capital markets are back, but with a difference. Capital transactions today seem to be mostly a rich-rich affair, consistent with the picture of modern capital flows as mostly "diversification finance" rather than "development finance." Because the international flows involved are more rich-rich than rich-poor, today's foreign investment in the poorest developing countries lags well behind the levels attained at the start of the last century. In other words, we see again the "paradox," noted by Lucas (1990), of capital failing to flow to capital-poor countries in which the marginal product of capital might be presumed to be very high.

Figure 7.5 indeed may understate the failure in some ways. A century ago world income and productivity levels were far less divergent than they are today, so it is all the more remarkable that so much capital was directed to countries at or below the 40 percent income level (relative to the United States). Today, a much larger fraction of the world's output and population is located in such low-productivity regions, but a much smaller share of global foreign investment reaches them. That is, the "Great Divergence" in per capita incomes (and real

---

[5] On the broad distribution of foreign capital then, see Twomey (2000). Note that the two panels of Figure 7.5 portray the distribution of foreign capital both as a percentage of the total world stock (upper panel) and relative to recipient-country GDP (lower panel).

Fig. 7.5. Did capital flow to poor countries? 1913 versus 1997

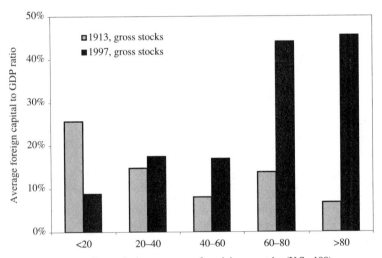

Per capita income range of receiving region (U.S.=100)

Per capita income range of receiving countries (U.S.=100)

Sources: The 1913 stock data are from Royal Institute for International Affairs (1937), for
investments in Europe, and Woodruff (1967), for all other regions; incomes are from Maddison
(1995). The 1997 data are from Lane and Milesi-Ferretti (2001a), based on the stocks of inward
direct investment and portfolio equity liabilities.

wages) over the last century has greatly reduced developing-country relative labor costs. If this were all, then capital should be even more eager to flow to poor countries today than a century ago. Yet, it is not. As Lucas puts it:

If it is profitable to move a textile mill from New England to South Carolina, why is it not more profitable still to move it to Mexico? The fact that we do see *some* capital movement toward low-income countries is not an adequate answer to this question, for the theory predicts that *all* new investment should be so located until such time as return and real wage differentials are erased. Indeed, why did these capital movements not take place during the colonial age, under political and military arrangements that eliminated (or long postponed) the "political risk" that is so frequently cited as a factor working against capital mobility? I do not have a satisfactory answer to this question, but it seems to me a major – perhaps *the* major – discrepancy between the predictions of neoclassical theory and the patterns of trade we observe.[6]

Figure 7.5 suggests that capital markets *were* more effective in directing global savings toward poorer countries before World War One, even if they fell short of achieving what a frictionless neoclassical model might predict.[7] The question why this was so seems intimately related to understanding why flows to poor countries are even more limited today, as we discuss in the next section.

7.3 Has foreign capital always been biased toward the rich?

Both because of the greater international divergence in wages nowadays and a lower degree of international labor mobility, one is at first surprised by Figure 7.5's long-run comparison of inflows to poorer countries, as we have noted. In addition, the configuration of 1913 asset holdings might seem a remarkable outcome given conventional wisdom: that so much of the capital outflow from the core countries in that era was destined to regions of recent settlement (Thomas 1954; Hall 1968; Edelstein 1982). These were New World regions with abundant land and scarce labor, countries such as the United States, Canada, Australia, and Argentina, all of which were then among the richest areas in the world. Thus, these were not poor labor-abundant countries at all in terms of income per capita; but their scarcity of capital and labor relative to *land* sucked in vast flows of both factors. The capital inflows account for the hump on the right-hand side of the distribution. Because no settler countries with such endowments exist today, the parallels of then versus now should not

---

[6] Lucas (1990, 16–17).

[7] Nonetheless, Davis and Huttenback (1986) demonstrate that from 1870 to 1914 the rate of return to foreign and empire investments did converge steadily downward to the same level as for domestic British investments, suggesting that over time the British investor was tending to allocate capital very much like an actor in a neoclassical model.

be exaggerated. But we should still recall that the bias goes the wrong way. Despite the absence of such relatively wealthy settler countries nowadays, capital tends to pile up even more in the rich countries.

There is perhaps one reason not to be so surprised by the 1913 findings that capital from rich core countries found its way into poor peripheral countries. Many of those core countries had empires; and many of those periphery countries were imperial outposts. If, as is common in some quantitative political science studies, one takes a strict view of polities and their boundaries, then such colonies were not really countries at all, and the investment flows to them from the core were not foreign investments as such, but intraempire (some might even say, domestic) investments. Not only did this factor mitigate the expropriation and default risks intrinsic to capital flows between fully sovereign states. Also, institutional, cultural, and personal links facilitated financial contracting. Did empire (and empire alone) bring poor countries into the global capital market then? (And, as a corollary, is the absence of empire today the source of their virtual exclusion?)

This point is much debated and remains an important avenue for further research (Ferguson 2002, 2003a,b). Empirical treatments are still few, but in our discussion of sovereign risk in Chapter 6, we found little evidence that empire membership conferred significantly lower borrowing costs on Britain's colonies before 1914, although it appears to have done so in the 1920s. Thus, it was not particularly favorable terms that gave colonies access to capital. Even so, we can ask if capital flowed to such colonies in larger volumes than is adequately explained by economic fundamentals, which is the approach of Clemens and Williamson (2002) in studying British capital export over the 1870–1913 period using the annual data on gross capital outflows by recipient country collected by Stone (1999).

Longer time series allow a more careful dissection of where capital went and, with suitable control variables, some explanation for why. The first question we want to ask is, did capital chase profits or follow the flag? In addition to the usual gunboat, cultural, and institutional explanations, Clemens and Williamson (2002) remind us of some of the plausible legal origins of an empire bias in capital flows, for example the Colonial Stock Act of 1900 that permitted institutional investors to buy colonial securities. Yet, at the same time, it is clear that great volumes of capital also flowed to independent countries, especially in the Americas (notably the United States and Argentina). Because much else might have mattered for attracting capital flows, only econometric analysis can resolve the point. Clemens and Williamson (2002) report a set of cross-sectional regressions of the share of British capital going to a particular destination against economic, political, policy, and geographic attributes (e.g., endowments, colonial status, distance from London). For the 1870–1913 period, their regressions show little evidence of empire bias (the British colony coefficient is small and statistically insignificant). This finding is consistent with ours in Chapter 6, that empire membership did not result in lower borrowing spreads before 1914. Rather, powerful economic fundamentals accounted for the vast inflows of pre-1914 capital flows to the rich, land-abundant, but capital- and labor-scarce countries of that era. Market forces mattered a lot and other attributes, such as colonial status and gold standard adherence, were distinctly second order. In a striking conclusion, Clemens and Williamson also find that a poor-country dummy indicator has a significantly positive effect on capital inflows from Britain:

[A]fter accounting for the effects of other variables, poor countries received more than twice the share of British capital than did rich countries in the years leading up to World War One. Natural resource endowment, education, and demography dominate all other variables in terms of elasticities and statistical significance. Capital flows are more than six times as sensitive to variation in natural resources endowment and more than twice as sensitive to variation in education levels than they are to any competing determinant. Minor, statistically significant determinants include participation in the gold standard, effective distance from London, lagged net immigration, and the yield spread between sovereign bonds and the riskless British Consol.[8]

These results reinforce the impression we have gained already – that the pre-1914 global capital market was relatively unimpeded by barriers and that market forces were left free to operate. Furthermore, this environment did not keep poorer countries from participation in financial globalization. Despite strong forces encouraging investment in rich, settler economies, poorer regions of the world, whether colonial outposts or not, also had substantial access to foreign finance. The factors behind the significance of the Clemens-Williamson poor-country dummy remain mysterious, however.

Clemens and Williamson (2002) also find a raw *positive* relationship between income per capita and capital imports from Britain. (They find that the same correlation also holds in today's data, because there is even less capital flow to poor regions today.) Figure 7.6 illustrates the correlation for the 1870–1913 period. The positive slope reflects the influential data points that are the rich, settler countries in the upper-right portion of the scatter plot, as well as the fact that a linear regression cannot capture a nonlinear bimodal relationship. Clearly some poorer countries, such as India, attracted substantial capital inflows from

---

[8] Clemens and Williamson (2002, 17).

Fig. 7.6. Raw wealth bias of British capital outflows, 1870–1913

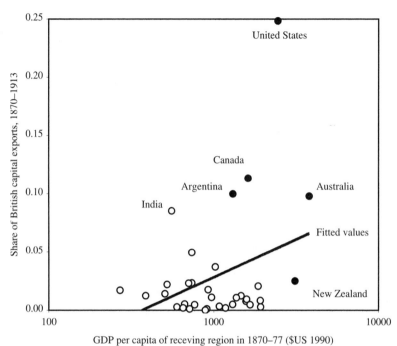

GDP per capita of receiving region in 1870–77 ($US 1990)

Note: The figure is based upon cumulated annual flow data measured in nominal terms.
Sources: Stone (1999), Clemens and Williamson (2002).

Britain, and overall the data are not inconsistent with the view that the wealth
bias in capital flows was lower before World War One than it is today.

The Clemens-Williamson (2002) results complement earlier descriptive accounts of the economic determinants of capital flows before 1914. In a celebrated paper, Nurkse (1954) pointed out that the conditions under which large-
scale net capital flows occurred before 1914 – involving concomitant large-scale
labor flows of European settlers to land-abundant regions – were unlikely to be
replicated in the postwar era. Before World War One, a substantial minority of
British capital exports went to the poorer, often densely settled and less temper-
ate regions – much more, as a share of the total, than flows to those economies
today. But it financed mainly what Nurkse called a "colonial" or "extractive"
pattern of foreign investment based on raw material production. The relatively
rich regions of recent settlement, in contrast, received the majority of Britain's

foreign investment capital, and it was there that the greatest early development successes were achieved. As Nurkse put it:

It was in the newly settled regions, which received two-thirds of the capital exports and practically all the emigrants, that nineteenth-century international investment scored its greatest triumphs. The remaining third of British capital exported (or more accurately a quarter, since some went to Continental Europe) was employed in a different type of area, where its achievements were much more dubious: tropical or subtropical regions inhabited, often densely, by native populations endowed in some cases with ancient civilizations of their own. The areas that formed a minor field for overseas investment before 1914 are the major problem today: the truly backward economies, containing now about two-thirds of the world's population. The empty and newly settled regions, from which international investment derived its brilliant record and reputation, are today, in *per capita* income, among the most prosperous countries in the world.[9]

Nurkse's account says little about institutional determinants of capital flows, yet subsequent scholarship suggests that changes in such factors are central to understanding both the pre-1914 and the modern patterns of long-run capital flow to developing countries. Recent research by Acemoglu et al. (2002) sheds light on three questions that turn out to be closely intertwined: the relative economic success of the former settler economies, their attractiveness to pre-1914 investors, and the inability of poor countries to attract substantial foreign investment today. Acemoglu et al. point to a striking fact. European colonies that were relatively rich and densely settled around 1500 later became relatively poor, whereas sparsely settled, low-income areas as of 1500 (such as North America, Australia, and Argentina) later became relatively rich. There was a "reversal of fortune," and the present income divergence begins to emerge around the time of the Industrial Revolution. How do Acemoglu et al. explain the reversal? They argue that Europeans tended to settle in the rich, empty largely lands of the regions of recent settlement, introducing institutions of governance that protected property rights and, thus, promoted the enterprise and investment at the heart of modern capitalistic growth. Where conditions were not friendly to European immigration, however – due to dense native populations or tropical diseases, for example – colonial administrators introduced "extractive" institutions, the aim of which was to mobilize the existing labor force to serve the economic interests of the colonizers. The resulting governance system did not protect property rights, but tended to persist, even after independence, because of the power it bestowed on the entrenched elites. The

---

[9] Nurkse (1954, 745).

latter set of economies accordingly has remained in poverty, unlike the former settler economies.[10]

The dual classification of economies stressed by Acemoglu et al. (2002) matches neatly the dichotomy at the heart of Nurkse's (1954) description of pre-1914 international investment. Moreover, the phenomena the two papers explain are mutually consistent. Poor protection of property rights can explain both poverty and a failure to attract private investment from abroad. As Nurkse (1954, 746) expressed the point, today's poor-country borrowers "have not grown up in a capital-minded milieu, and may not be culturally prepared for the use of western equipment, methods, and techniques." In addition, the superior institutional framework of the settler economies certainly enhanced the environment for foreign investment there, complementing the more conventional economic determinants of capital flows stressed by Nurkse and by Clemens and Williamson (2002).

But why was the flow of capital into the poorest pre-1914 economies noticeably greater than what we see today? The answers vary depending on the region. In areas that remained under colonial administration, such as India, investors could count on the mother country for property protection. While this effect is hard to discern empirically in cross-country data, we suspect that it nonetheless played a role in some cases. Latin America became independent early in the nineteenth-century, so it does not fit into the category of colonial borrower, although a number of countries in the region drew on foreign capital to some degree (Taylor 2003). Nonetheless, a number of factors promoted foreign investment before 1914. Source-country governments (notably Britain) were more willing and able to use diplomatic and even military pressure to compel repayment. In developing borrowers, the predatory power of the state was nowhere near as centralized as it would become after the interwar period. Administrative controls on capital flows were largely absent. Finally, the economic *zeitgeist*, emanating from Britain's industrial and financial leadership, was one of global economic interdependence, in which a number of developing borrowers indeed saw incentives to maintain reputation over the long run.

These reflections raise the interesting question of the "divergence of fortune" among the former settler economies. The most glaring case is that of Argentina, which was one of the world's richest economies before 1914, but since then has diverged sharply from the Anglo-Saxon settler economies in terms of both per capita income and attractiveness to international capital. We suspect that part of the answer rests on the different legal traditions transplanted by European

---

[10] For further evidence on the linkage between property-rights protection and income, see Hall and Jones (1999) and Parente and Prescott (2000).

settlers, with the more successful economies building on English common law, but others building on the French civil law, which can be less protective of property rights (Glaeser and Shleifer 2002). Thus, the former British colonies – the United States, Canada, Australia, New Zealand, even Singapore and Hong Kong – are endowed with legal systems that have protected property and promoted growth, whereas Argentina's system has proven much less successful over time. Clearly, this hypothesis calls out for further research, although it is generally consistent with the results on foreign investment, corruption, and transparency reported by Prasad et al. (2003).[11]

To summarize: for all the suggestion that we have returned to the pre-1914 type of global capital market, there is at least one major qualitative difference between then and now. Today's foreign asset distribution is much more about asset "swapping" by rich countries – mutual diversification – than it is about the accumulation of large one-way positions, which is the key component of the development process in poorer countries according to standard textbook treatments. Modern capital flows therefore are more about hedging and risk sharing than about long-term finance and the mediation of saving supply and investment demand between countries. This is true notwithstanding the persistent home bias in equity holdings, which suggests that asset swapping, though substantial compared to the pre-1914 era, may still fall short of levels that simple models of full diversification would suggest are optimal.

In today's world of generally limited net foreign asset positions, we have rarely come close to recapturing the heady times of the pre-1914 era, when a creditor like Great Britain could persist for years in devoting half of its asset accumulation to foreign capital, or a debtor like Argentina could similarly go on for years generating liabilities of which half were taken up by foreigners. Instead, to a very great extent today, a country's net capital accumulation still seems to depend on the provision of financing from domestic rather than foreign sources of savings (Feldstein-Horioka again). Poor countries have less access to international capital than they had before 1914. This phenomenon is related to their poor protection of property rights, an institutional feature with deep historical roots, as well as to general changes since World War One in the global political and economic environment.

---

[11] As Ferguson (2003b, 361–62) notes, the British empire was in most cases the conduit for disseminating the British legal system. We suspect it would be hard to find strong positive (lagged) empire effects on income per capita today, because of the much more limited impact of British legal traditions in extractive settings. Alfaro et al. (2003) document a positive effect of institutional quality on capital inflows over the period 1970–2000. In some of their regressions they use legal origins as instrument variables for institutional quality regressors, but the direct role of the legal system is not the focus of their study.

7.4 How much have poor countries liberalized their markets?

We have discussed the gradual integration of international capital markets in the post–Bretton Woods period. The first countries to liberalize were those in the rich, industrial core. But what about the developing countries? When did financial globalization spread to these, creating so-called emerging markets? And to what extent? We touched on these questions both in Chapter 4 and earlier in this chapter, but we now revisit them in greater detail.

At the most aggregated level, data from a variety of sources support our contention that the involvement of developing countries in the new global capital market has been quite limited. Data collected by the International Monetary Fund and shown in Figure 7.7 documents once again the relatively low ratio of foreign investment to GDP in developing versus industrial countries. And, as we have already seen in the companion figure from the IMF, Figure 4.1, there is reason to suspect that one cause for the limited flow of capital flow to the developing counties in recent decades has been the slow and limited progress they have made in removing the legal and administrative obstacles to the free flow of private finance.

Other data on capital flows and policy change in emerging markets offer corroborating evidence. It was in the late 1980s and early 1990s, for example, that net flows of U.S. capital exploded after long decades of quiescence dating back to the 1930s. According to the International Finance Corporation (IFC), this period also coincides with the official liberalization of many key emerging equity markets; see the first column of dates reported in Table 7.2.

Particularly in emerging markets, the officially reported dates of policy change should not automatically be accepted as accurate. They often fail truly to capture the extent to which markets are open at a given time. Because of lags in implementation, uneven enforcement, or more obscure regulations that have escaped inclusion in the coding, de jure reforms may not coincide with actual practice. One possible alternative approach is to scrutinize carefully the political and institutional history of each emerging market country, looking for significant policy changes and market reactions (Henry 2000a,b). Another is to watch for other signs, such as the establishment of the first country fund for overseas mutual-fund investors or the first American Depository Receipt (ADR) listings on the New York Stock Exchange (Bekaert et al. 1998). As Table 7.2 illustrates, such methods need not replicate the official dating, or even come particularly close.

Yet another approach is to ask whether any model-based measures of integration can confirm that emerging markets also became more integrated in the 1980s and 1990.The study of emerging equity markets by Bekaert et al.

Fig. 7.7. Assets owned by foreigners
Developed versus developing countries

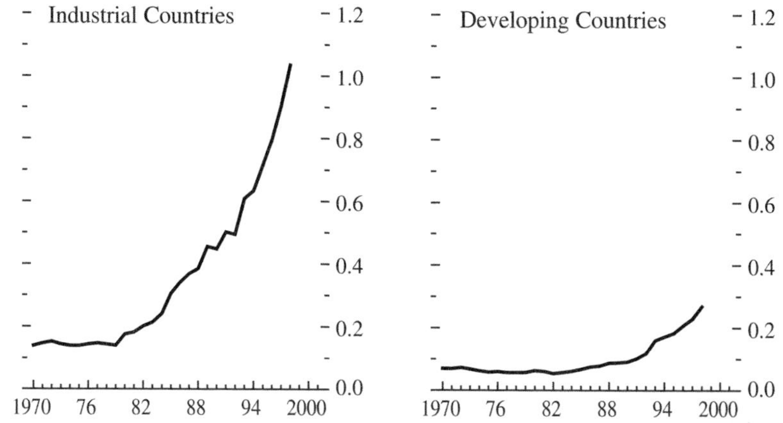

Industrial Countries

1970   76   82   88   94   2000

Developing Countries

1970   76   82   88   94   2000

Notes: The figure shows financial openness measured as the sum of the stocks of external assets and liabilities of foreign direct investment and portfolio investment, divided by GDP.
Source: IMF, *World Economic Outlook*, September 2002, 110.

(1998) offers insights into the gradual spread of financial globalization to the periphery in the late twentieth century. Without being tied to a specific asset-pricing model, the authors use a reduced-form vector autoregression (VAR) econometric model to study the correlations of high-frequency financial and macroeconomic time series in the 20 emerging markets listed in Table 7.2. Their criterion for market integration is simple: look for a date on which there is a significant and simultaneous change in all the data-generating processes for a country.[12] This estimation approach identifies breaks that often differ from the dates of reforms claimed in official reports. But the breaks do tend to lie within two years of at least one of the other events listed in Table 7.2, or of a large surge in capital inflows.

Conventional hypotheses about the effects of equity-market liberalization can be tested, given an estimated date for the change. (These tests give an indication of whether the observed statistical break indeed corresponds to market liberalization.) Consider an initially segmented local equity market. Policy-makers announce a future liberalization that will promote risk pooling between the local and the world market. The local market may begin to react, and reaction will be full when reforms are actually enacted in a credible and permanent

---

[12] A multivariate approach may outperform the analysis of a single time series because more information is being used (Bai et al. 1998). One caveat: given its circulation date, Bekaert et al. (1998) clearly could not analyze data on possible post-Asian-crisis breaks.

Table 7.2. *Dates of equity-market liberalizations*

Country	Official liberalization date	ADR introduction	Country fund introduction	Statistical break in returns and dividend yield
Argentina	Nov. 89	Aug. 91	Oct. 91	Feb. 89
Brazil	May 91	Jan. 92	Oct. 87	Apr. 90
Chile	Jan. 90	Mar. 90	Sep. 89	Feb. 83
Colombia	Feb. 91	Dec. 92	May 92	Oct. 91
Greece	Dec. 87	Aug. 88	Sep. 88	Jun. 86
India	Nov. 92	Feb. 92	Jun. 86	Nov. 87
Indonesia	Sep. 89	Apr. 91	Jan. 89	Aug. 92
Jordan	Dec. 95	—	—	Apr. 92
Korea	Jan. 92	Nov. 90	Aug. 84	Feb. 80
Malaysia	Dec. 88	Aug. 92	Dec. 87	Jan. 93
Mexico	May 89	Jan. 89	Jun. 81	Feb. 83
Nigeria	Aug. 95	—	—	Jun. 89
Pakistan	Feb. 91	—	Jul. 91	Dec. 90
Philippines	Jun. 91	Mar. 91	May 87	Oct. 87
Portugal	Jul. 86	Jun. 90	Aug. 87	Aug. 88
Taiwan	Jan. 91	Dec. 91	May 86	Aug. 88
Thailand	Sep. 87	Jan. 91	Jul. 85	Jan. 90
Turkey	Aug. 89	Jul. 90	Dec. 89	Jun. 89
Venezuela	Jan. 90	Aug. 91	—	Jan. 94
Zimbabwe	Jun. 93	—	—	Mar. 83

Source: Bekaert et al. (1998).

fashion. Local prices and market capitalization should increase permanently (and, given cash flow, dividend yields and the cost of capital should therefore fall). Equity returns should also be temporarily high during this transition. The correlation of local and world markets should rise. In addition, new capital inflows might be detected in other variables. Turnover may increase and a lower cost of capital may encourage initial public offerings, decreasing concentration in the local market. Reforms might also enhance the government's credibility leading to lower sovereign credit risk ratings, and macroeconomic policies may improve. (Of course, anticipations of future reforms, and their piecemeal or hesitant introduction, contribute to the difficulty of cleanly establishing dates for the regime change.)

The Bekaert et al. (1998) study found broad support for the preceding hypotheses, although a minority of their 20 countries yielded exceptions. For example, in a fixed-effects bivariate model of returns and dividend yields, yields failed to decline in accord with theory in 5 countries (Argentina, Chile, Indonesia, Nigeria, and Zimbabwe). In the other 15 cases, however, the predictions of theory were supported: after the break, dividend yields fell by 2 percentage points, and market capitalization divided by GDP increased by 18 percentage points (with both changes statistically significant). Other changes in financial variables were quantitatively minor, but there were strong positive impacts on macroeconomic variables such as growth and trade. It was also found that correlations of emerging market portfolios with the world market increased from about 0.17 for portfolios of prebreak ("segmented") countries to 0.43 in portfolios of postbreak ("integrated") countries. Looking at a broad array of country risk indicators, Bekaert and Harvey (1998) also found a marked improvement in credit ratings after liberalization.[13]

These findings suggest that the statistical-break method for detecting the date of market integration can perform a useful check on the "official" dates often used by applied economists. From the viewpoint of long-run economic history, however, they do not change our story very much at all – whether one uses official dates or the dates "revealed" by the data, the key message is that, judged by these 20 major players, most emerging equity markets were segmented until the late 1980s or early 1990s, but by the late 1990s, most had integrated with world markets to a greater or lesser degree. The official dates and the econometric evidence both confirm the claim that emerging equity markets became much more integrated into the global financial system in the late 1980s and early 1990s.

It is interesting to ask whether any model-based measures of capital mobility move over this period in accord with the policy index measures – such as the IMF indicators or the more refined Kaminsky-Schmukler (2003) and Quinn (1997) indicators discussed earlier (see Figures 4.1, 4.2, and 4.3). One indicator for which we have a high enough frequency of data (annual) and a broad enough sample of countries (developed and developing) is the simple annual cross-sectional investment-saving regression coefficient, following Feldstein and Horioka (recall Chapter 2). Regional averages for different time spans are shown in Figure 7.8, which is based upon IFS data for the post-1975 period, when coverage first becomes reasonably complete.

The results are suggestive. As noted earlier, this coefficient may be expected to range between unity and perhaps a lower bound of 0.5, given the nature of the long-run budget constraint. Indeed, this is more or less the case in our figure (the EU in the latter 1990s being the biggest exception). We also find that the developed countries, according to this measure, experienced capital mobility

---

[13] In a similar spirit, though using official dates, Voth (2001) studies the effects of limited currency convertibility and capital controls in postwar Europe. He finds that inconvertibility on current and capital account raised the cost of capital, as did capital-account restrictions introduced later in the Bretton Woods period in order to ward off speculation.

Fig. 7.8. Savings-retention coefficients by region, 1975–99

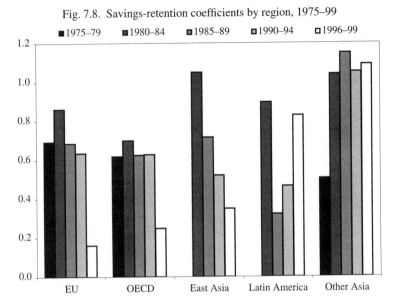

Source: IMF, *International Financial Statistics.*

much earlier than the developing countries: the OECD and EU coefficients lie well below those of the other regions on the whole and, if anything, trend downward over time.

The developing countries with the sharpest change in the coefficient over time are those in the East Asia region, where the coefficient falls from near unity circa 1980 to around 0.4 in the late 1990s – again, almost monotonically. The other Asian economies have not followed this path: in the 1980s they seem to have become more autarkic, with no evident reversal of that trend in the 1990s. Latin American countries have had an experience that is more up and down, and that by the late 1990s had come closer to the patterns seen in the Other Asia group, where the saving-investment correlation is strongest of all and near 1.0, suggesting relatively little capital mobility.

Though the samples do differ between the various official measures of policies on the one hand and the saving-investment regressions on the other, these alternative measures are basically all in agreement. The common message seems to be that the developed countries led the way in postwar financial liberalization, though even then it all happened quite late and had to wait for the demise of Bretton Woods.

Developing countries followed later, but with far from uniform experiences.

In the East Asian economies, liberalization typically proceeded rather steadily and faster than the developing-world average. The rest of Asia did not follow suit, and liberalization was slow or nonexistent. Latin America followed a more schizophrenic path, with some periods of openness and other times of closure, the end result being that liberalization moved forward slowly if at all. The time profiles suggested by Figure 7.8 mesh well with the Latin America versus overall Asia comparison of openness (foreign capital to GDP) and restrictiveness (of capital account policies) provided by the IMF and shown in shown in Figure 7.9.

As a final contrast with the experience of developed countries, we examine interest-rate differentials on dollar-denominated loans between a sample of developing countries and the United States. The data shown in Figure 7.10 are calculated as differences between domestic firms' borrowing rates and the U.S. commercial and industrial loan rate, as measured by the Federal Reserve. (The sole exception is Singapore, where we plot the difference between the domestic interbank dollar interest rate and the comparable U.S. three-month certificate of deposit rate.)

For Singapore, integration with the U.S. money market appears complete. The Latin American countries, however, display a broad range of interest-rate spreads. Chile, Argentina, and Uruguay all liberalized in the early 1990s, and their spreads are usually among the lowest. Upward spikes in Argentina's spread in connection with the Mexican crisis (1995), the Brazilian crisis (1999), and its own crisis (2001) coincided with widening spreads for its Southern Cone neighbors. Costa Rica suffered a similar spillover in the latest Argentine crisis, though it never achieved the convergence on U.S. interest rates seen in Uruguay and Chile. Bolivia and Peru, both less stable than Costa Rica politically, have had very large, often double-digit spreads in the 1990s, but even these have tended to decline over time, on average.

Overall, the figure depicts a fitful process of integration. The degree of interest rate convergence differs widely across developing countries, however, and can be sharply punctuated by crises, even for the relatively more open and politically stable economies. On this measure and on the others we have examined, the pace of financial integration of developing economies has lagged substantially behind that in the developed world. The adoption of flexible exchange rates has been less problematic for developed than for developing countries, as we observed in Chapter 4, and the latter group has been able to move only gradually toward exchange-rate arrangements consistent with free capital mobility. The pattern of delayed integration of the developing world therefore is quite consistent with the trilemma.

Fig. 7.9. Capital account openness and restrictions
Asia versus Western Hemisphere

(a) Openness (Foreign capital/GDP, right scale)

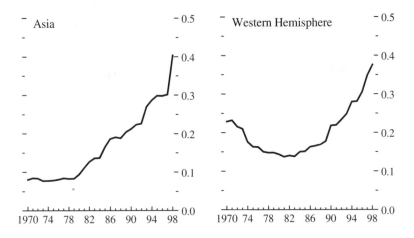

(b) Restrictions (Index of capital account restrictions, left scale)

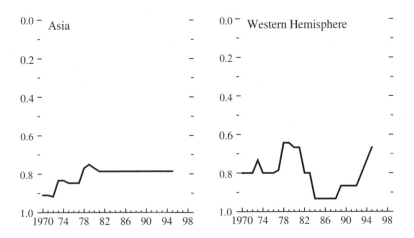

Source: IMF, *World Economic Outlook*, September 2002, 110.

Fig. 7.10. Dollar borrowing spreads in developing countries

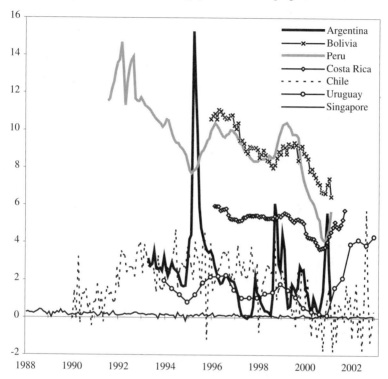

Notes and Sources: Chile: Central Bank of Chile; Singapore: Monetary Authority of Singapore; all other countries: Barajas and Morales (2002). All data are percent per annum.

7.5 Summary

Our examination of some regionally disaggregated flows does not, then, un-dermine the general narrative concerning the rise and fall, and rise, of capital mobility. We see, however, that the evolution of global financial integration has been different for the developing world, and indeed, across different parts of the developing world. On the eve of World War One, a number of developing regions enjoyed fair access to capital flows from the core countries, especially from Great Britain, the nerve center of the world financial system at that time. It seems plausible that European imperialism played some role in supporting this system, although hard econometric evidence of this has proven elusive.

The recovery of global capital markets after the Great Depression and World War Two was slow, but relatively slower in the poorer countries; indeed, many of these still remain isolated outside the global financial network. To a greater extent than was true before 1914, international capital flows move in a fairly balanced reciprocal pattern between richer countries and finance mutual diversification. One-way, net development flows from rich to poor countries have not yet recovered to the levels they reached at the start of the twentieth century.

As we have noted, capital is discouraged from entering poorer countries by a host of factors, and some of these were less relevant a century ago. Capital controls persist in many regions. In many developing countries the protection of property rights is much weaker than in the industrial economies, and the risks of investment may be perceived differently after a century of exchange risks, expropriations, and defaults. Domestic policies that distort prices, especially of investment goods, may result in returns too low to attract any capital. Foreign investment is further discouraged by the uncertainty of legal recourse in the borrowing country, by lax regulation, and by opaque modes of accounting and governance. Indeed, these types of factors have led to a series of emerging market currency crises since the early 1990s, crises that have plunged entire regions into deep recessions.

Almost none of the developing countries that had previously embraced financial opening retreated permanently behind capital controls after the recent crises (Fischer 2003). Poorer countries evidently believe they must draw on foreign capital to a greater extent than they do at present if they are to achieve an acceptable growth in living standards. That is a fundamental reason why reform and liberalization in the developing world, despite the setbacks of the late 1990s, seem likely to continue (albeit hopefully with due regard to the painful lessons learned in the recent past). But are such beliefs justified? What benefit can poorer countries gain from the kind of unfettered access to global capital markets that richer countries enjoy, and do such benefits indeed exceed the potential costs of capital flight and crises? These difficult and contentious questions lie at the heart of current debates about financial globalization. Without pretending to reach a definitive conclusion, the next chapter surveys what we have learned in recent years about the costs and benefits of financial integration.

8

Uneven Rewards and Risks

As we noted in the introductory part of the book, open capital markets allow countries to exploit the opportunities for risk-sharing and intertemporal smoothing that would be closed off under autarky. Yet we also noted that open markets impose additional constraints (including the trilemma) on the feasible choice sets of national policymakers. To the extent that these constraints discourage bad policy choices, they impose useful discipline on national authorities. But effective discipline must rely on a credible threat of punishment. Critics of financial globalization argue that market punishments often come too late to discipline policies effectively, that the incidence of punishment is capricious, and that in many cases the punishment – in the form of crisis-induced unemployment, forgone growth, and social instability – is excessive. The potential benefits of capital-market integration therefore have to be weighed against the potential costs, with due regard for the possibility that the benefit-cost calculus differs between countries at different stages of economic development.

Of course, if all governments and policymakers consciously restricted their actions to lie within the feasible set, the turbulence in international capital markets would be much reduced. And if all markets were perfect, complete, and efficient, then current global economic affairs would be less fractious – and financial history so much duller. In a distortion-free world of optimizing agents and policymakers, there would be no need to describe the trilemma, no policy debates about globalization, no trouble for governments to get into, and no International Monetary Fund (IMF) or other agencies required to manage disasters. In particular, in an ideal world, there would be no crises.

In the real world, we do not escape trouble so lightly. Crises broke out over the last decade in all corners of the developing world (emerging markets in Asia and Latin America), in transition economies (notably Russia), and also in developed countries. Often these have been so-called "twin crises," combining the collapse of an exchange rate peg with widespread domestic financial collapse (Kaminsky and Reinhart 1999), although accompanying fears about government solvency often arise, completing the set of crisis triplets mentioned in Chapter 1. To what extent did the progressive globalization of financial markets contribute to the proliferation of crises?

On the one hand, open markets mean that inconsistent policy choices by governments invite disaster. This is the case of government failure. On the other hand, if there are multiple policy equilibria, or if capital markets are subject to "contagion" or "herd" behavior by market actors, self-fulfilling crises can arise unnecessarily and proliferate. This is the case of market failure. We should not overdraw this distinction, for in reality, at least some degree of vulnerability in economic fundamentals must exist before expectational shifts can generate a crisis, so there is a broad middle ground in which government and market failure can reinforce each other, with significant multiplier effects.

Are periodic crises just the price to be paid for open markets, and, if so, is the price too high? The first step in answering this question is to assess the benefits countries derive in practice from open capital markets. There has been substantial research on this topic in recent years, and there is no scientific consensus yet – nor can we pretend to propose one here. This chapter does, however, offer a brief review of recent findings, including discussion of some of the orders of magnitude of the welfare gains that have been proposed.[1]

The second step in evaluating whether open capital markets are worth the accompanying risks is to consider crises. In this chapter, we also review the longer run history and show that global capital markets have always operated under the risk of crisis. Crises appear to do the most damage in developing countries, and because financial opening exposes a country to crisis, it is no accident that the estimated net benefits from financial opening appear, on at least some measures, to be smaller for poorer countries. Given the severity of the crisis problem, assessing the likely causes and consequences remains a central challenge for the field of international finance, and one that can benefit from a longer run perspective.

8.1 Borrowing to finance capital accumulation

One obvious benefit to countries from open capital markets is the ability to converge more quickly to desired capital-stock levels by borrowing foreign savings. At first glance, the opportunity would seem to be most valuable to developing countries, which often have low capital-labor ratios and limited

---

[1] Prasad et al. (2003) provide a complementary recent survey.

national savings to draw upon. In comparison to autarky, open capital markets imply a lower opportunity cost of capital at the margin. As the economy borrows investible resources from abroad and moves along its factor-price frontier, the rewards to other factors of production, notably labor, rise. Increased real wages and incomes result, and these more than pay for the servicing of the foreign capital inflow. Does this sound too good to be true?

As far as developing countries are concerned, even unrestricted capital inflows would effect only a limited reduction in the Great Divergence in per capita incomes. Consider a basic growth model in which output is given by the Cobb-Douglas production function $Y = K^\alpha (AL)^{1-\alpha}$, with K denoting the capital stock, L the labor force, α the factor-income share of capital, and A a labor-augmenting productivity factor. In terms of per worker (or per efficiency-worker) magnitudes, the relationship is $y = A^{1-\alpha} k^\alpha$ (or $y = A\tilde{k}^\alpha$), where $y = Y/L$, $k = K/L$, and $\tilde{k} = K/AL$. In the so-called "A versus k" debate, we have learned that most of the differences in per capita incomes between countries are not attributable to differences in k (and in human capital), but rather, in A (Klenow and Rodríguez-Clare 1997; Hall and Jones 1999; Easterly and Levine 2001).

This is not to say, however, that k doesn't matter. But suppose that A accounts for two-thirds of the variation in y and k for as much as one-third. Does this imply that, by opening the capital account, policymakers could raise k sufficiently to erase one-third of the gap in incomes or welfare between poor and rich countries?

It is not so simple. Because domestic saving should eventually drive the capital stock to steady state, such a rule of thumb could seriously overestimate the welfare gains from immediate convergence of the capital stock. In addition, external borrowings must be serviced. Moreover, the steady-state capital stock itself depends on A. Given full capital mobility, a capital depreciation rate δ, and a world real interest rate r^*, the steady-state capital stock k^* is given implicitly by

$$r^* = A^{1-\alpha} \alpha k^{*\alpha-1} - \delta. \tag{8.1}$$

In our assessment of the role of A in determining the return to capital, A must be construed, of course, as including the protection of investors' property rights through the rule of law, the control of corruption, and other institutional factors that are important in understanding both capital flows and per capita incomes (recall the last chapter). Conventional estimates of α and A imply that poor countries have levels of k far below the rich world's steady-state k^*, but perhaps not so very far below their own level of k^*. Thus, even instantaneous convergence to steady state might deliver relatively little welfare gain, if the steady state reflects heavy domestic distortions or institutional failures that deter capital accumulation even by domestic residents.

Gourinchas and Jeanne (2003) have carried out the most thorough study of the welfare gains countries may reap by drawing upon foreign capital as a means to speed convergence. They use a Ramsey growth model based on the "representative dynasty" welfare criterion

$$U_0 = \sum_{t=0}^{\infty} \beta^t N_t \left(\frac{c_t^{1-\gamma} - 1}{1 - \gamma} \right), \tag{8.2}$$

where $t = 0$ is the date of capital-account liberalization, $\beta < 1$ is the subjective discount factor, N is population, c is consumption per capita, and $1/\gamma > 0$ is the intertemporal substitution elasticity (with the flow utility function equal to $\log c$ when $\gamma = 1$). They estimate that for $\gamma = 1$ and $\beta = 0.96$, capital inflows that speed convergence are worth about 1 to 1.25 percent of GDP per year to a typical developing country.[2] This is a large number compared to the usual Harberger triangles of welfare analysis, yet it is hardly the sort of difference that would revolutionize standards of living. In contrast, increases in the productivity coefficient A (to close the productivity gap vis-à-vis the developed countries) could lead to welfare gains an order of magnitude higher than those due to financial opening. Financial opening could yield more substantial benefits if it induces an increase in A, for example, by deterring government incursions on private property rights. Indeed, Gourinchas and Jeanne briefly consider the political economy of domestic distortions and their removal. Their discussion brings to mind an older literature on investment distortions which themselves can be endogenously created by financial and commercial autarky.

Why do Gourinchas and Jeanne find such small welfare benefits from finan-cial liberalization? First and foremost, for a country very near its steady state, the gain from opening the capital account is of the second order, because the cost of foreign borrowing is very close to the return. For $\gamma = 1$ and $\beta = 0.96$, the convex function describing the net return to borrowing actually is quite flat for a large range of initial capital-labor ratios around the steady state, imply-ing that countries must start out with very low (or high) capital-labor ratios k relative to the domestic steady-state k^* in order to to reap big gains.

---

[2] In one version of the Gourinchas-Jeanne model, capital and labor are the only production factors and capital-account opening leads to an immediate jump to the steady state. In a second version, human capital is a third factor of production and because it must be accumulated domestically, the economy need not jump to the steady state immediately upon the opening of the capital account. Even in a two-factor model, investment adjustment costs could likewise induce gradual convergence.

Despite the starkness of these results, we think some care in interpretation is needed. Gourinchas and Jeanne emphasize that the gains from financial liberalization pale in comparison to the benefits that would accrue to a developing country, open or closed, if it could somehow undo the Great Divergence – that is, quickly close the productivity gap and raise A to a level closer to that of the developed countries. While this puts the different gains in perspective, the findings offer neither a great surprise nor a great deal of help. Given what we know about the magnitude of the Great Divergence in the twentieth century, and the fact that some developing countries labor with productivity levels perhaps one tenth or one twentieth of what the advanced countries enjoy, the biggest gains in almost any model would have to come from eliminating that overwhelming source of backwardness. As far as policy recommendations go, while it is easy to conceive of designs for open or closed capital markets, to advise policy makers to focus on closing the productivity gap is seemingly to replace elusive gains with an elusive goal.

There are also a number of other dimensions to the Gourinchas and Jeanne framework which tilt the results towards a finding of low welfare gains from financial opening. First, as is well known, the Ramsey growth model entails implausibly high convergence speeds towards the steady state. In the $\gamma = 1$ benchmark case noted above, the speed is 11 percent, whereas most econometric estimates of convergence speeds (via capital accumulation) tend to be in the single digits.[3] Fast convergence means that a closed economy spends very little time away from its steady state. Because the main benefit of external financing is an immediate jump to the steady state, the faster is convergence under autarky the less there is to gain from opening. Thus, if the convergence speed is too high in the model, the gains from financial opening are being understated.

Second, the benchmark case studied has a relatively low discount rate ($\beta = 0.96$), and most developing countries have population N_t growing at a gross rate n that is of the order of 1.02. Thus, the flow utility for the dynasty of equation 8.2 is being discounted by a factor βn which is typically around 0.98. This is very close to one and hence puts a large weight on the distant future (when the closed economy has neared the steady state) and relatively little weight on the present (when the capital gap really matters to flow utility in autarky). Thus, the costly period spent well below steady state is not only made quite brief, it is also given little weight. As Gourinchas and Jeanne recognize, if consumers are really more myopic, or if the short-run gains matter more for political economy reasons, then the calculations could change dramatically. In

---

[3] See, for example, Barro and Sala-i-Martin (1992) and Mankiw, Romer, and Weil (1992). Higher speeds have been estimated, however, by Caselli et al. (1996).

this model, the big gains accrue in early periods, and agents with short time horizons could be persuaded to liberalize by the fast growth that will result in the near term, setting aside the not inconsiderable debt servicing costs that will stretch out to infinity. We also note that the structure of the Gourinchas-Jeanne model imposes a common rate of subjective time preference in poor and rich countries, but intuition suggests that time horizons should be considerably shorter in conditions of relative poverty. In that case, the immediate period in which foreign savings speed the transition would be of much greater importance, and the welfare benefits of an open capital account correspondingly greater. A model with more complex demographics could capture these effects.

The results are sensitive, as well, to the choice of γ. Many empirical studies suggest that intertemporal substitutability is not so high as in the case $\gamma = 1$. Consumers with a higher value of γ (and therefore with a lower intertemporal substitution elasticity $1/\gamma$) find it relatively more difficult to cut consumption now in order to invest and enjoy greater consumption later. This aspect of dynamic preferences makes foreign financing of capital accumulation more valuable. Gourinchas and Jeanne find that when $\gamma = 3$, and the world steady-state capital stock is adjusted downward to reflect this higher value of γ, the welfare gain from capital-market opening roughly doubles for developing economies.

Third, just as myopia could matter on the consumption side, it also might be an issue for the supply side. The Ramsey model is solved by backward iteration from the steady state; thus, in simulations where the productivity gap is closed, forward-looking investors (whether domestic or foreign) install capital "today" secure in the knowledge that such capital will become magically more productive "tomorrow" when A begins to rise. Are such dynamics likely to obtain in developing countries? The issue is credibility. If the government were to announce a process of institutional reform that would eliminate the productivity gap versus the United States within 35 years, would investors act on that promise? Or would they wait and see? Expectations of future A drive some of the gains in this setting, and the perfect-foresight results might overstate gains from productivity advance in a world where policies are not always credible.

We also emphasize an important corollary to these results. There is a vital positive interaction between economic reforms that raise the productivity factor A and financial opening. Suppose that a country can find ways (such as credible, permanent institutional reform) to raise A in the future. Because such changes will increase the steady-state capital stock k^* without changing the initial capital stock k_0, the welfare gain from reform will be higher, perhaps much higher, when the capital account is open – and as we have noted, an open capital account may itself enhance credibility.

A simplified version of the Gourinchas-Jeanne model shows that over some range, the welfare gap between increasing A with an open capital account and increasing it with a closed capital account grows with the size of the increase in A. Thus, while financial opening may yield a comparatively slight gain on its own, it is potentially a very valuable component of a broader reform package. Illustrative results appear in Table 8.1 for a range of developing countries (low-income, lower-middle-income, and upper-middle-income) and parameters γ (equal to 1 or 2). In the actual data, average productivity levels in the three groups of countries are 10 percent, 14 percent, and 29 percent of the U.S. level, respectively. When $\gamma = 2$, the gains from financial liberalization, denoted μ, range from 3.2 to 0.4 percent of income per year (for the poorest and richest country groups, respectively), similar to the Gourinchas-Jeanne estimates.

Now suppose the authorities in these countries simultaneously engaged in economic reforms to close (say) half the productivity gap *and* initiated financial liberalization. Would the gains from liberalization be magnified? They would, and row 1 of the table, for example, shows how. This poor country begins with A at 10 percent of the U.S. productivity level, and is far (but not exceedingly far) from its steady state, with $k_0/k^* = 0.3$. Thus, as noted, the gains from liberalization are relatively modest. Once reforms have increased A to 0.55, however, the country finds itself much farther from its steady state, with $k_0/k^* = 0.05$. The country is now very scarce in capital (has a high rate of return to investment) and it therefore can gain enormously from financial integration: the incremental welfare gain owing to liberalization is now more than 11 percent of income per year, or 3.5 times the size of the gain without reforms. A similar result holds throughout the table for all the developing country groups: if countries can engage in productivity-enhancing reforms at the same time as financial liberalization, then the benefits that flow from the latter will be much greater.[4]

8.2 The role of cost distortions

We should note that the above argument has some more general implications. The previous discussion of the benefits of financial opening was based on a simple growth model with basic assumptions about the on and off nature of

---

[4] Obviously, these gains are still smaller than the direct gains from the productivity improvements themselves (compare the utility levels in rows 1 and 2, for example), but we do not dispute that escaping from the Great Divergence is the prime challenge for developing countries.

Table 8.1. *Economic reforms and the gains from financial liberalization*

Reform	β	γ	A_0	k_0	k^*	U_{aut}	U_{int}	$\mu(\%)$
				Low-income countries				
Before	0.97	2	0.10	0.11	0.37	−302.21	−290.67	3.21
After	0.97	2	0.55	0.11	2.04	−7.51	0.18	11.18
Before	0.95	1	0.10	0.11	0.37	−70.13	−68.59	4.12
After	0.95	1	0.55	0.11	2.04	−7.99	−5.32	7.26
				Lower-middle-income countries				
Before	0.97	2	0.14	0.24	0.52	−190.29	−184.52	2.28
After	0.97	2	0.57	0.24	2.11	−4.10	2.95	10.68
Before	0.95	1	0.14	0.24	0.52	−55.74	−55.31	1.12
After	0.95	1	0.57	0.24	2.11	−5.66	−3.75	5.11
				Upper-middle-income countries				
Before	0.97	2	0.29	0.73	1.07	−52.90	−52.40	0.41
After	0.97	2	0.65	0.73	2.39	9.59	11.25	2.88
Before	0.95	1	0.29	0.73	1.07	−27.52	−27.19	0.88
After	0.95	1	0.65	0.73	2.39	0.76	1.58	2.19

Notes and Sources: Based on simulations of the Ramsey growth model, following Gourinchas and Jeanne (2003). In all simulations, the production function is $y = A^{1-\alpha}k^{\alpha}$ with $\alpha = 0.3$; the utility function is as in equation 8.2 with annual population growth given by $N_t = N_0 n^t$ and assuming $n = 1.02$ for a representative developing country; the capital stock is assumed to depreciate at an annual rate of $\delta = 0.06$; the gross annual productivity growth rate in all countries (the trend rate of increase in A) is assumed to be $g = 1.012$. The productivity level A_0, initial capital stock k_0, and steady-state $k*$ before reforms ("Before") are given by the estimates in Gourinchas and Jeanne (2003) for low-, lower-middle-, and upper-middle-income developing countries. In these simulations we hold fixed the world interest rate $r^* = 0.06$ per annum, and this implies that for a given γ equal to 1 or 2, the value of the subjective discount factor β in equation 8.2 must be chosen such that $1 + r^* = g^{\gamma}/\beta$. The post-reform ("After") case refers to a counterfactual where half the gap between A_0 and A_{US} is eliminated at $t = 0$. U_{aut} is the implied utility level in autarky, U_{int} is the implied utility level with financial integration, and μ, expressed in percent, is the implied welfare gain (Hicksian equivalent variation), expressed as a percentage of income per year, where

$$\mu = \left(\frac{U_{\text{int}}}{U_{\text{aut}}}\right)^{\frac{1}{1-\gamma}} - 1.$$

international capital mobility. In the real world, however, there is no such a simple dichotomy. For example, developing countries' access to imported financial capital may be inhibited by a variety of frictions such as country risk premia, debt ceilings, or intermediation costs. Their access to imported physical capital – often an important component of domestic accumulation – may be affected by tariffs, quotas, commercial policies, exchange controls, and the like. All these barriers could be classified as either transaction costs or distortions, and many of them might be amenable to amelioration through more enlightened policy choice. But why should that matter? Because any or all of these factors can drive a wedge between the domestic and world costs of capital, thereby diminishing the equilibrium steady-state k^* for the domestic economy. Thus, like a shortfall in productivity A, cost distortions can repress long-run growth and, through exactly the kind of interaction effect described in the last section, reduce the gains from financial opening. Financial opening is not only complementary to policies, such as the enhancement of property rights through institutional reform, that raise investor perceptions of the productivity factor A. It is complementary to a whole raft of other policies, in macroeconomics, trade, finance, and elsewhere, that raise the effective cost of capital.

One very important source of such distortions, and one that directly affects the cost of installing capital, is any policy change that raises the relative price of capital goods themselves.[5] A common example would be heavy tariffs imposed on imported capital goods, such as the distortions noted by Díaz Alejandro (1970, chap. 6) that applied to Argentine machinery imports in the 1950s and 1960s, and forced the prices of many of these goods to twice or even three times the U.S. level. Such observations could no doubt be confirmed in many developing countries and might also apply not just a brake to growth, but also to the gains from financial openness.[6]

The variation in developing-country postwar economic performance offers a testing ground for the theory that capital market distortions dissuade growth, investment (and hence, on the margin, foreign investment) in developing countries. The raw data provide prima facie evidence that some such mechanism is at work: as income per capita rises, so does the investment share of GDP, just as the relative price of capital falls (De Long and Summers 1991; Jones 1994; Taylor 1994). The correlations in the raw data taken from the Penn World Table illustrate the point well, as shown in Figure 8.1.

Taylor (1998b) replicates the familiar growth empirics of the 1990s literature. In a robust finding isolated long ago by Levine and Renelt (1992), only one factor strongly and consistently predicts growth: physical investment. Yet, the obvious objection to focusing on flows of investment (i.e., the k term) is that it is endogenous – and, indeed, could be fully explained by A if we lived in a world of completely mobile capital (Clark and Feenstra 2003).

Accordingly, a simultaneous-equation structural model must be explored to explain not growth itself, but the underlying cross-country differences in investment levels. Performing this analysis, Taylor (1998b) found that certain policy choices did discourage investment and capital flows by raising the real

---

[5] The effects are clearly present in theory, as demonstrated by Jones (1994) for the Ramsey model, and recapitulated by Gourinchas and Jeanne (2003). See also Baldwin (1992) and Mazumdar (1996) for a discussion of similar impacts in the simpler Solow model.

[6] Taylor (1994) explores the Argentine case in more detail.

Fig. 8.1. Investment, development, and the relative price of capital

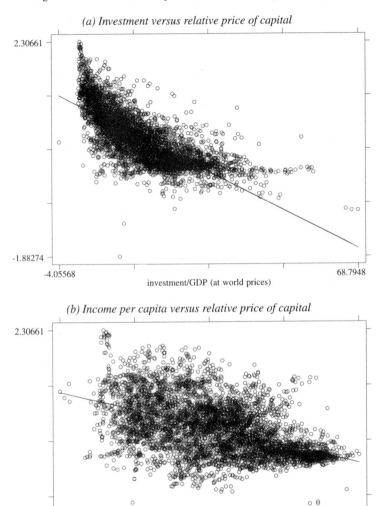

Source: Penn World Table 6.0. The data points plotted are for all countries, all years. The relative price of capital is the Penn World Table (PWT) variable $\log(pi/p)$. The investment share of GDP (measured at world prices) is PWT variable ci. Income per capita is PWT variable $\log(rgdpch)$.

relative price of capital and discouraging investment demand. When proxied by tariffs, distortions in the goods market, widely prevalent in postwar developing countries, tended to raise the relative price of imported investment goods and the cost of capital. Capital-market distortions, proxied by the black-market currency premium, likewise raised the cost of capital. These distortions are now widely accepted as having an impact in any reduced-form model of growth, although Hsieh and Klenow (2003) argue that the primary source of cross-country variation in the price ratio P_I/P_Y works through the denominator. Clearly, more structural analysis is needed before we understand the main transmission mechanisms.[7]

The economic laboratories that best expose the impact of policies on the cost of capital, investment, and growth are in Latin America and East Asia. As we have noted, these two emerging-market regions have exhibited quite different policy responses in the postwar period as regards openness to foreign capital and the extent of reforms. East Asia has liberalized more, invested more, and grown faster compared to Latin America, and the empirical results suggest that much of the gap in investment, and hence, growth can be attributed to the underlying policy differences. Moreover, if policies were even partially reformed in Latin America (say, cutting the investment relative-price distortions in half relative to world levels), foreign investment to the region could surge to unprecedented levels, as a counterfactual analysis by A. M. Taylor (1995) shows.

Both financial and trade openness appear to be important ingredients in achieving this goal of lowering the user cost of capital in developing countries. The major lesson here is that financial openness, though it might speed convergence in a neoclassical world, may not deliver most of its welfare gains to poor countries through that channel. But it will make a real difference if it can take these countries to a much higher level of steady-state income. One very effective way to raise steady-state income would be to remove investment-inhibiting distortions.[8]

The other way to raise living standards in the long run, of course, is to raise the net productivity of investment. An important issue is the extent to which capital-account liberalization indeed might lead to higher productivity – a better realization of the productivity indicator A, which was defined earlier. In this

---

[7] In the presence of domestic goods-market distortions, of course, capital inflows could have an overall negative welfare effect even on a capital-poor recipient, as argued by Brecher and Díaz Alejandro (1977).

[8] An implication is that such distortions can help account for Lucas's (1990) puzzle that capital does not flow to poor countries. Indeed, correcting for price distortions, the marginal product of capital is brought much closer to uniformity across developed and developing countries (Higgins 1993; Taylor 1998a).

setting, the welfare effects of opening the capital account can be enormous. Obstfeld (1994a) presents a stochastic model in which international diversification allows greater specialization on production activities with high expected values of A but relatively high output variability.[9] A very different mechanism is at work when an open capital account inhibits the funneling of public subsidies to politically favored sectors.[10] On this topic, much more research is needed before any sort of causality can be claimed: as we have seen, financial opening typically is not imposed exogenously. Instead, it emerges out of a particular political equilibrium in which the institutional and social infrastructures play key roles.

To summarize: when taken literally, the workhorse neoclassical growth model predicts rather modest gains from financial liberalization. Poor countries will gain relatively little, perhaps on the order of 1 to 3 percent of income per year, if they liberalize financially. Against such small putative gains have to be weighed potential costs such as those imposed by crises, a feature absent from this kind of long-run growth model but a big danger in reality, as we see later in this chapter. For a poor country, the decision to liberalize could be very finely balanced indeed, and might even favor financial autarky. A poor country with failing institutions, inadequate rule of law, and rampant corruption will have a productivity level so low that foreign capital can do little to change the country's prospects. Moreover, were such a country to open its capital market, the risk of a crisis would be high, given the likelihood of ineffective prudential safeguards in the financial sector and short-sighted macroeconomic management. But the calculus could be quite different for a developing country that is serious about improving its institutional structure and has taken steps to improve property rights, diminish corruption, and make government more responsible and efficient. For such a country, the steady-state levels of capital and income can be greatly amplified, raising the benefits to financial integration, just as the costs of crises are minimized through the development of a more mature fiscal, monetary, and financial environment. In other words, institutional reform and financial integration are complementary development strategies.

Must such cost-benefit calculations be based largely on abstract models, or is there some direct empirical evidence to back them up? The progress of research has been rather slow in this area, but we next discuss some of the conclusions that can be gleaned from the econometric literature on the economic effects of financial opening.

---

[9] Kalemli-Ozcan et al. (2003) present empirical evidence that enhanced risk sharing promotes industrial specialization. Their data cover OECD countries and subnational regions.

[10] For some fascinating recent evidence from Malaysia, see Johnson and Mitton (2001).

8.3 Financial opening and economic performance

Policies that induce some measure of financial autarky can inhibit international risk sharing and intertemporal smoothing and could cause a damaging increase in welfare-relevant forms of macroeconomic volatility. Another downside may be the discouragement of financial development, investment, and trade (activities closely linked to financial openness), and, through such channels, a reduction in efficiency and growth. There is a potential opposing effect of capital controls on economic outcomes, however. If controls help countries to avoid disruptive financial crises, for example, they may, in fact, contribute positively to some policy desiderata, such as economic growth or stability.

What is the statistical evidence on these hypotheses? The large empirical literature on economic growth has found that the reduced-form connection between deep policy changes and ultimate outcomes can be very difficult indeed to uncover. Postwar cross-sectional data has been mined to exhaustion, but controversy continues over how to measure policies (fuzzy) and institutions (fuzzier still), what econometric specifications to use, and how to interpret the results, given problems of endogeneity.

In one strand of the literature, empirical researchers have tried to ascertain the underlying linkages from financial openness to important channels of economic growth – endogenous variables such as financial development, investment, and trade. Here the results suggest that financial openness has beneficial effects on several determinants of economic performance. Other empirical studies have, however, estimated reduced-form equations that attempt to measure the direct linkage from financial openness to growth. Here, as one might expect, the waters are muddier. Because the debate over trade openness and growth continues (Sachs and Warner 1995; Rodriguez and Rodrik 2001), it is unsurprising that the even more recent debate over financial openness and growth is still far from settled. On the whole, however, the conclusions of empirical studies on financial openness and growth seem more ambiguous than those reached in studies of trade-account openness and growth (as Prasad et al. 2003 stress). Most contemporary empirical studies of trade openness agree in finding a positive effect on growth – the debate mainly concerns the statistical and economic significance of that effect – but the estimated effects of financial openness are far less uniform across the literature.

Bekaert et al. (1998), based on data that did not include the late-1990s Asian crisis, is one of the earlier studies to document positive effects of financial-market opening. In Chapter 7 we discussed that paper's method of dating equity-market integration, which relies on a search for statistical breaks in multivariate time series. The authors found some significant changes after the occurrence of international integration. Trade ratios (imports plus exports divided by GDP) rose by 11 percentage points on average after their statistically determined date of liberalization. Domestic financial development was also seen to advance upon opening (a result of broader capital-account liberalizations as well, according to Klein and Olivei 2000). Bekaert et al. (2001) is a broader study based on data through 1997. The paper finds that equity-market liberalization was associated with a roughly 25–45 percent increase in financial development as measured by the ratio of private credit to GDP; a 50 percent increase in the number of stocks listed on the domestic bourse; a large decrease in the cost of capital; and an increase of at least 1 percentage point in the investment to GDP ratio. The regressions pool rich and poor countries, however, and the authors do not ask if the effects of liberalization differ between developed and developing countries. Henry (2000a) and Stulz (1999) discuss evidence on declines in the cost of capital for emerging markets. Given the robustness of the investment-growth correlation (Levine and Renelt 1992), an important result in the literature is contained in the event study of 11 emerging markets by Henry (2000b), who finds that equity-market liberalizations have been associated with investment booms, as shown in Figure 8.2.

Space prevents us from exploring in further detail the econometric evidence associated with these and related studies, but the raw data are suggestive concerning some of the linkages we have just described. Using a quantity-based measure of openness proposed by Lane and Milesi-Ferretti (2001a) – the gross stock of foreign assets plus the gross stock of foreign liabilities relative to GDP – Figure 8.3 shows that, even within the group of developing countries, more financially open economies have generated larger values of private investment and (more strikingly) of foreign direct investment. Figure 8.4 shows that on average over the 1980–99 period, financially more open economies have tended to have higher measures of domestic financial development in terms of both credit to the private sector and equity-market turnover (both expressed relative to gross domestic product).

The preceding results are merely suggestive, but they have been confirmed in formal statistical analysis, and they indicate that financial openness seems to be associated with a number of correlates of economic growth. There are strong a priori reasons to expect such linkages: foreign capital inflows should broaden the financial market, open up a larger pool of foreign savings to fund domestic investment, and ease provision of the trade credit needed to grease the wheels of commerce. In turn, many studies have shown that incomes and growth rates are improved by higher levels of financial development, higher

Fig. 8.2. Investment booms after liberalizations

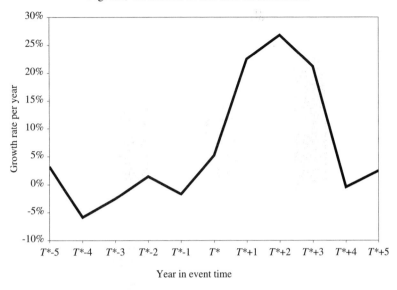

Year in event time

Notes: This figure shows the response of private investment to stock market liberalization, with the average growth rate of private investment in real local currency terms across all 11 countries plotted against stock market liberalization time. For example, the value on the y-axis corresponding to the x-axis value of T^* is the average growth rate of private investment across all 11 countries in the year the stock market was liberalized.
Source: Henry (2000b, Figure 1).

levels of investment, and higher levels of trade.[11] Does this mean that the direct connection running from financial-account liberalization to growth (or income) should be easy to detect? The answer is no, because the reduced-form effect is difficult to identify statistically. Although many have tried, the empirical work to date remains inconclusive and beset with apparent contradictions.

A pioneering work in this respect was that of Quinn (1997), who initiated the mammoth task of coding policy change on an annual basis for all countries in the postwar period (a project that is now being extended back to the nineteenth century). His work, as described earlier in Chapter 4, improves on earlier approaches by coding capital-market openness, not as a binary variable (the approach used in the well-known IMF coding), but on a much finer scale, in

---

[11] All of these literatures are enormous. We cite only a subset of major contributions. On financial development see King and Levine (1993), De Gregorio and Guidotti (1995), and Rousseau and Sylla (2003). On trade see Sachs and Warner (1995), Frankel and Romer (1999), and (for a skeptical view) Rodriguez and Rodrik (2001). On investment see Dowrick and Nguyen (1989), Levine and Renelt (1992), and Mankiw, Romer, and Weil (1992).

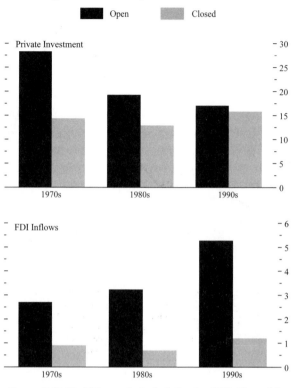

Fig. 8.3. Financial openness and investment

Source: IMF, *World Economic Outlook*, October 2001, Figure 4.5.

order to capture more subtle shifts in the policy environment. Using pure cross-sectional analysis over the 1960–89 period for up to 64 countries, Quinn found that financial liberalization was associated with economically meaningful and statistically significant increases in the rate of economic growth. Not all prior or subsequent research, however (including the early Grilli and Milesi-Ferretti 1995 study that uses the IMF coding method to gauge openness), reaches the same conclusion as does Quinn (1997).

Differences in sample, data, definition of liberalization, and methodology could be responsible for the variation in findings. A convenient summary of much of the work that has been done is given in Prasad et al. (2003, table 3), who interpret the very mixed findings concerning the association between liberalization and growth as indicating that "if financial integration has a positive effect on growth, it is probably not strong or robust" (p. 33). A further issue is to

Fig. 8.4. Financial openness and financial development

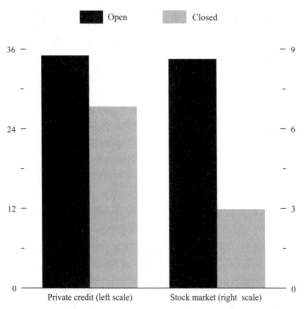

Source: IMF, *World Economic Outlook*, October 2001, Figure 4.6.

sort out causality, as it might very well be that whatever positive association can be found in the data results from common factors that drive both liberalization and economic growth.

It would lengthen this book inordinately to survey all these contributions, but we can examine some of the most salient differences in approach. Much of the current debate now centers on higher frequency studies using panel data, where the time variation offers a better chance of identifying causal effects, but much more refined econometric techniques are required. One such study is that of Bekaert et al. (2001), and Table 8.2 summarizes some representative results. These authors find a positive one-percentage-point effect of equity-market liberalization on annual economic growth over the five subsequent years, controlling for the usual growth determinants, policies, and world economic conditions. They also find, however, that this growth effect declines sharply over time; and, as Gourinchas and Jeanne (2003) stress, a growth effect of this magnitude is consistent with rather small welfare gains. The results of Bekaert et al. (2001) also indicate, consistent with our conjecture in Chapter 7, that legal

Table 8.2. *Liberalization effect on growth*

Sample	I	II	III	IV
Constant	−0.2241	−0.2371	−0.1536	−0.224
	(0.0185)	(0.0220)	(0.0309)	(0.0670)
Log(GDP/capita)	−0.0093	−0.0087	−0.0115	−0.0161
	(0.0007)	(0.0007)	(0.0008)	(0.0011)
Government/GDP	−0.0084	−0.0203	−0.0233	−0.0307
	(0.0087)	(0.0098)	(0.0107)	(0.0165)
Enrollment	0.0367	0.0174	0.0302	0.0634
	(0.0076)	(0.0098)	(0.0115)	(0.0164)
Population growth	−0.5574	−0.5619	−0.7824	−1.0136
	(0.0623)	(0.0699)	(0.0855)	(0.1240)
Log(life expectancy)	0.0744	0.0778	0.0631	0.0883
	(0.0050)	(0.0057)	(0.0081)	(0.0168)
OECD GDP growth	0.1469	0.1177	0.1435	0.1695
	(0.0301)	(0.0328)	(0.0315)	(0.0394)
World real interest rate	−0.0625	−0.0484	−0.0132	−0.0182
	(0.0282)	(0.0309)	(0.0300)	(0.0372)
Official liberalization indicator	0.0097	0.0085	0.0124	0.0141
	(0.0016)	(0.0017)	(0.0020)	(0.0036)

Notes: I, II, III, and IV refer to samples of 95, 75, 50 and 28 countries, respectively. The dependent variable is the 5-year average growth rate of real per capita gross domestic product. Log(GDP/capita) is the log real per capita GDP level in 1980. Government/GDP is the ratio of government consumption to GDP; Enrollment is the secondary school enrollment ratio; Population growth is the growth rate of total population; Log(life expectancy) is the log life expectancy of the total population; and the official liberalization variable takes a value of one when the equity market is liberalized, and zero otherwise. GMM estimation provides a correction for cross-sectional heteroskedasticity. Standard errors in parentheses account for the overlapping nature of the data.
Source: Bekaert et al. (2001, table 3).

systems seem to matter a great deal in determining the impact of liberalization on economic growth.

Bekaert et al. (2001) maximize their utilization of information by taking overlapping annual observations on five-year growth rates as the data to be explained. The estimation method is the generalized method of moments (GMM). Use of Arellano-Bond (1991) and related panel GMM techniques was avoided by two choices: first, the use of a time-invariant catch-up term equal to per capita income in some base year, avoiding the problem of a continuously updating lagged dependent variable; and second, by the omission of fixed effects, which enables the authors to keep cross-sectional identification of the liberalization effect in play. Using the same methodology, Bekaert et al. (2002) find comparable growth effects of equity-market liberalization taking local less world consumption growth as the dependent variable. For the 1980–97 period (excluding the Asian crisis), their point estimates of the growth effect are not appreciably different as between their full sample of 95 industrial and developing countries, a sample of 50 industrial and developing countries for which detailed data on equity-market trading are available, and a sample of 30 developing countries with emerging equity markets. Once the estimation period is extended through 2000, however, the positive growth effect becomes relatively smaller for all country samples, most dramatically for the emerging-market sample (though it is still positive and statistically significant).

The potential impact of the omission of country fixed effects is illustrated by the study of Edison, Levine, Ricci, and Sløk (2002). Those authors employ a dynamic panel model with fixed effects, examine alternative measures of international financial integration (including one based on actual capital flow volumes), and use instrumental variables in the hope of reducing biases caused by the potential endogeneity of some liberalization measures.[12] They find no association between the various measures of financial integration and growth.[13]

Additional differences in method, however, cloud a direct comparison with the results of Bekaert et al. (2001, 2002). To take one, Edison, Levine, Ricci, and Sløk (2002) look at measures of *overall* financial openness whereas Bekaert et al. (2001, 2002) look at equity-market liberalization only. There are a number of reasons why a narrow liberalization of the equity market might have positive growth effects where a broader financial opening would not. Equity claims are contingent liabilities whereas noncontingent liabilities such as bank loans and bonds can be written down only as the result of costly renegotiation or outright default. The suspicion that a renegotiation initiative or default is imminent, however, can give rise to an external debt crisis and the accompanying disruption of real activity. Equity-market liberalization has a direct, targeted effect on the cost of capital and domestic investment, in contrast to a wider opening that exposes the economy to the social risks of overborrowing by poorly regulated intermediaries. Finally, there is some evidence that economies with higher corruption levels rely relatively heavily on bank loans as opposed to FDI for

---

[12] This study uses the Arellano and Bond (1991) GMM estimator, as extended by Arellano and Bover (1995) and Blundell and Bond (1998). Eichengreen and Leblang (2002), in a study we discuss later in this section, also use these techniques.

[13] Their purely cross-sectional results lead to a similar conclusion. A defense of omitting fixed effects, as do Bekaert et al. (2001, 2002), might run as follows. First, lagged income is highly volatile across time periods, and the catch-up term should capture the long-run growth tendency of poorer countries to converge on rich countries. Use of a fixed base year to filter out business-cycle deviations in income levels therefore is preferable. Second, fixed effects represent a step too far because they deny any cross-sectional identification of the effects of policies on performance (which was the original point of Quinn and others). Furthermore, time-series identification alone does not add much information because most countries go through one (or zero) liberalizations in this period. The liberalization effect is then being identified based on a number of observations roughly equal to the cross section.

external finance (Prasad et al. 2003, figure 13). If countries that have allowed borrowing from foreign banks tend to be more corrupt on average than those that liberalize equity markets only, then it is not surprising that positive growth effects of general capital-account liberalization will be harder to detect. Thus, it is not clear if the differing findings of these dynamic studies reflect differences in econometric methodology or true differences in the economic impacts of the distinct liberalization experiments considered.[14] Another potential difference is that the timing of a broad capital-account liberalization may be harder to ascertain precisely than that of an equity-market initiative. The issue deserves more detailed study than it has so far received, including attention to the interest-group pressures and institutional environments that generate alternative patterns of financial-account liberalization.

Another econometric feature of the Edison, Levine, Ricci, and Sløk (2002) study makes its interpretation difficult. Rather than using overlapping five-year growth periods with a GMM correction for the resulting moving average structure of the equation disturbance, the authors divide their sample (1976–2000) into five nonoverlapping five-year periods. Their econometric specification then links growth over a period to a measure of international financial integration averaged over the same period. Conceptually, it seems more natural to link growth to prior integration measures, as Bekaert et al. (2001, 2002) are able to do using their overlapping data on growth rates. It may be that use of lagged variables as instruments for international financial integration mitigates potential timing problems, but this is another issue that deserves further study.

Overall, then, the empirical literature is mixed, with some studies (preponderantly those that focus more narrowly on equity-market liberalization) pointing to positive impacts on presumed causes of economic growth or on growth itself. One serious objection to that interpretation of these positive findings is that correlation is not causation: not financial opening but accompanying macro stabilization, or market-friendly reforms such as trade liberalization, could be responsible for subsequent growth. We cannot argue that this omitted variable problem is not a potential problem, but the methodology of these studies and the nature of postwar policy changes minimizes this danger. Econometric analyses by Bekaert and coauthors, Henry, and others in this literature have been careful to document financial reforms to the year and even to the month. As we have suggested, the use of these data in event analysis can better link the timing of

---

[14] Consistent with the hypothesis that more general capital-account opening yields lower benefits on average, Bekaert et al. (2002) find that equity-market liberalization leads to greater reductions in consumption- and income-growth volatility than does capital-account liberalization (as measured by the IMF index).

policy changes to outcomes than a 20-year cross-sectional regression, or even the more dynamic approach of Edison, Levine, Ricci, and Sløk (2002), can. We should also note that trade reform and financial reform have proceeded at very different rates in developing countries in the postwar period, and this is reflected in the data. Many countries were experimenting with liberal trade policies as early as the 1970s, but the move toward financial openness, as we have seen, came later in the 1980s and, mostly, in the 1990s. If policies are accurately measured (admittedly, a big if), then statistical analysis at a high enough frequency should be able to distinguish between impacts of trade and financial liberalization episodes in a large enough sample. In that spirit, Bekaert et al. (2001, 2002) do control for other economic reforms, and find that their results are robust.

8.4 The role of institutions

A deeper objection to many studies in this literature is that, timing aside, any steps taken toward liberalization are endogenous and really reflect deeper parameters, that is, "institutions" however defined (Rodrik 1998; Rodrik, Subramanian, and Trebbi 2002). Countries with strong institutions will both liberalize and deploy complementary policy reforms, creating positive statistical correlations between financial integration and a variety of beneficial economic outcomes. That correlation need not imply, however, that countries can gain by liberalizing à la carte, without making the necessary complementary policy changes. For example, denial of the trilemma through a move to financial opening without exchange-rate flexibility (or without a financial system that can tolerate such flexibility) has often led to trouble.

Edison, Klein, Ricci, and Sløk (2002) find that Quinn's favorable cross-sectional results, as well as those in a number of other studies, disappear when a measure of "government reputation" is included as an explanatory variable in an ordinary least squares regression of economic growth on its theoretical determinants, following Rodrik (1998). The implication is that better governments both liberalize external payments and create environments favorable to faster growth, but any independent effect of financial liberalization on growth remains unidentified in much of the cross-sectional analysis of growth effects.

In addition, as our earlier simulations with the neoclassical growth model suggest, there could be an important nonlinear interaction between quality of governance (which improves the prospects for productivity growth, raises returns to investment, and hence the demand for capital) and the benefits of financial opening (which speeds convergence to the steady state by augmenting the supply of lower-cost capital). In a recent study that examines the interaction between governmental quality, financial liberalization, and growth, Klein (2003) finds that indeed the biggest gains in economic performance – and, hence, implicitly in welfare – accrue to developing countries that have reached some minimum level of institutional capability. Although any mapping from theory to empirics is problematic here (we cannot measure welfare directly and we have only proxies for institutional quality), the flavor of these results is suggestive.

To give an illustration, we follow Klein (2003) and implement a cross-country regression of the form

$$g = \beta_0 + \beta_1 X + + \beta_2 I + \beta_3 L + \beta_4 LI + \beta_5 LI^2, \tag{8.3}$$

where g is the measure of the growth of real income per capita during the sample years, X is a vector of conventional reduced-form (exogenous) growth determinants, I is a measure of the country's institutional quality, and L is a measure of the extent of financial liberalization over the period. The linear and quadratic interaction terms in this equation allow the marginal product of liberalization to depend on institutional quality.

More specifically, what might one expect to see in the data? Income is correlated with institutional quality. Rich countries have little to gain from financial liberalization because they are relatively capital abundant and are close to their steady state. Poor countries potentially have a great deal to gain from liberalization, but if they have institutions of low quality, they may be able to do little to make good use of capital inflows. In between, the countries of middling incomes and middling institutions may have the most to gain, because in addition to being somewhat capital scarce, they also have a good enough governance infrastructure that productivity catch up is somewhat likely to occur.[15] The functional form of equation 8.3 allows for such differential effects of liberalization along the institutional-quality spectrum.

In our analysis, we included in X initial income (to control for "catch-up" potential), an Africa dummy (always significant), population growth rates, and schooling measures (a proxy for human capital). We excluded investment levels, which we consider potentially endogenous and determined by liberalizations (Henry 2000b) – as well as by institutions and much else.[16] Table 8.3 shows some representative results, where we use an index of the control of corruption as the measure of institutional quality I, and we use two alternative

---

[15] An alternative specification, therefore, could be to use a quadratic in the initial income level, which Klein (2003) also implements with essentially similar results.

[16] Klein (2003) includes investment as a regressor, but obtains very similar results.

Table 8.3. *Growth, governance, and financial liberalization*

L indicator	(1) Quinn		(2) IMF	
N	55		85	
R^2	0.60		0.55	
Constant	1.87	(0.66)	1.27	(0.62)
Log(schooling)	0.01	(0.13)	0.02	(0.12)
Africa dummy	-1.12	(0.15)	-0.52	(0.21)
Population growth rate	-0.61	(0.42)	-0.42	(0.46)
I	0.45	(0.25)	0.42	(0.12)
L	0.03	(0.15)	-0.57	(0.57)
LI	0.26	(0.12)	1.28	(0.52)
LI^2	-0.09	(0.02)	-0.33	(0.11)

Notes and Sources: See text and Klein (2003). The dependent variable is the change in natural log of real per capita income in the period 1976–95. Log(schooling) is the logarithm of the secondary school enrollment rate. Population growth rate is for the 1976–95 period. I is the control of corruption according to Kaufmann et al. (2002). L is the measure of financial liberalization using either (1) the average of the Quinn (1997) index in the years 1973, 1982, and 1988, or (2) the average of the IMF zero-one indicator over the 1976–95 period. Standard errors in parentheses.

measures of financial openness L, the Quinn index for a small sample of countries and the IMF indicator for a larger sample.[17] The nonlinear interaction between institutional quality and financial liberalization is clearly seen, and, to give a better picture of the potential growth benefits of full liberalization, Figure 8.5 shows the fitted value of the liberalization effect $\beta_3 L + \beta_4 I L + \beta_5 I L^2$ as the index I varies, where we use regression 2 based on the larger sample (using IMF codings of liberalization) and we set $L = 1$. According to these results, over two decades the growth effects of financial liberalization could be large indeed, and statistically significant, for a wide range countries in the middle range of incomes and institutions. The cumulative effects add up to about 0.4 to 0.6 in log levels over 20 years, which translates into a nontrivial growth rate boost of up to 2.5 percent per annum.

To summarize, these results offer support for a view that financial liberalization is certainly no panacea for developing countries and – in isolation – may offer only small gains for some countries. On the other hand, there are important complementarities with productivity-enhancing reforms. Viewed as part of an overall package of reforms, an opening to world capital markets can greatly assist countries that are able to get their institutional houses in order.

[17] It may be asked if our results are sensitive to the definition of I. The control of corruption measure is taken from Kaufmann et al. (2002), who also report several other indices including rule of law and government efficiency. These latter two indices are also used by Klein (2003), who finds similar quadratic relationships in all cases, though with varying confidence intervals.

Fig. 8.5. Growth, governance, and financial liberalization
Growth effect of financial liberalization versus institutional quality

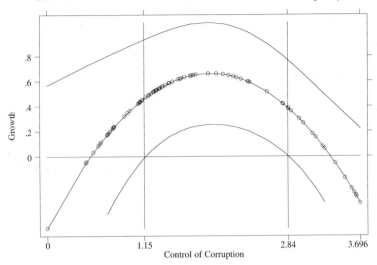

Note: 95 percent confidence intervals are shown.
Source: See Klein (2003) and Table 8.3, regression 2.

For example, a glance at the underlying data for the index of the control of corruption indicates a very large range of countries where the predicted impact of
financial liberalization is positive and significant, as shown in Table 8.4. Here
the 26 economies with the worst institutional scores – most of them in Africa
– appear to have little to gain from liberalization. According to these results,
countries such as Niger, Nicaragua, Pakistan, or Mali have too high a level
of corruption to gain a significant long-run benefit from opening their capital
market. But for a large share of the sample, the 43 countries with middling
institutional quality, the gains could be large and significant. Countries such
as India, Argentina, Thailand, or Côte d'Ivoire fall in to this group. At the top
of the institutional ladder sit most of the industrialized countries where, as we
have argued, we might expect the gains to be less dramatic.

Results like these, which spring from a particular dataset and empirical setup,
should not be taken literally for policy purposes: they cannot give failsafe predictions as to which countries should or should not pursue financial liberalization. However, the tenor of the results argues for a policymaking approach that
understands the delicate relationship between the potential gains from capital
market integration and the institutional maturity of the country in question.

Table 8.4. *Growth, governance, and financial liberalization: Fitted values*

Country	I = Control of corruption	Liberalization impact ($L = 1$)
(a) Insignificant effects (I low)		
Niger	0.00	−0.57
Cameroon	0.46	−0.05
Myanmar	0.47	−0.04
Sudan	0.55	0.03
Paraguay	0.61	0.08
Honduras	0.63	0.10
Tanzania	0.64	0.11
Papua New Guinea	0.71	0.17
Guinea	0.72	0.18
Nicaragua	0.73	0.18
Guatemala	0.75	0.20
Ecuador	0.75	0.20
Syria	0.78	0.22
Benin	0.79	0.23
Dominican Republic	0.79	0.23
Pakistan	0.80	0.24
Kenya	0.92	0.32
Zambia	0.95	0.34
Chad	0.98	0.36
Colombia	1.08	0.42
Mali	1.09	0.43
Madagascar	1.10	0.43
Uganda	1.10	0.43
Panama	1.11	0.44
Bolivia	1.13	0.45
Ethiopia	1.13	0.45
(b) Significant gains		
Lebanon	1.17	0.47*
Burkina Faso	1.20	0.48*
El Salvador	1.21	0.49*
Vietnam	1.24	0.50*
India	1.26	0.51*
Ghana	1.27	0.51*
Bangladesh	1.28	0.52*
Mexico	1.29	0.52*
Argentina	1.29	0.53*
Egypt	1.30	0.53*
Togo	1.33	0.54*
Senegal	1.33	0.54*
Philippines	1.34	0.54*
Peru	1.37	0.56*
Malawi	1.37	0.56*
Thailand	1.40	0.57*
Sri Lanka	1.44	0.58*

Table 8.4 (continued)

Country	I = Control of corruption	Liberalization impact ($L = 1$)
(b) Significant gains (continued)		
Jamaica	1.45	0.58*
Côte d'Ivoire	1.49	0.60*
Guyana	1.55	0.61*
Sierra Leone	1.55	0.61*
Gambia	1.55	0.61*
Swaziland	1.57	0.62*
Tunisia	1.59	0.62*
Brazil	1.63	0.63*
Morocco	1.69	0.64*
Jordan	1.71	0.64*
South Korea	1.73	0.65*
Lesotho	1.76	0.65*
Mauritius	1.90	0.66*
Uruguay	2.00	0.66*
Trinidad and Tobago	2.08	0.65*
Costa Rica	2.14	0.64*
Malaysia	2.20	0.64*
Belgium	2.24	0.63*
Japan	2.29	0.62*
Italy	2.37	0.60*
Fiji	2.37	0.59*
Greece	2.39	0.59*
Chile	2.60	0.51*
Spain	2.78	0.42*
Portugal	2.79	0.42*
Israel	2.84	0.38*
(c) Insignificant effects (I high)		
France	2.85	0.38
Hong Kong (China)	2.88	0.36
United States	2.97	0.30
Austria	3.02	0.26
Ireland	3.13	0.18
Australia	3.17	0.15
Norway	3.25	0.08
United Kingdom	3.27	0.06
Iceland	3.40	−0.05
Singapore	3.52	−0.17
Netherlands	3.59	−0.26
Canada	3.62	−0.29
New Zealand	3.64	−0.31
Sweden	3.65	−0.32
Finland	3.65	−0.32
Denmark	3.70	−0.37

Notes and Sources: See text and Table 8.3, regression 2. * denotes significant impact at the 95 percent level. Liberalization impact is change in log income level over 20 years.

8.5 Capital controls and growth

These ideas are now at the center of official discussions on the sequencing of capital-account liberalization and other economic reforms (see, for example, IMF, *World Economic Outlook*, October 2001, 167–69). Rightly so – as history can attest, absent the political will to undertake the steps that credibly sustain financial openness, reforms will have a low probability of success. To invoke the trilemma is to invoke a second-best world of policymaking. It would be a costly mistake to forgo the benefits of integrated capital markets in the long run; but it is also costly to risk crises by opening the capital accounts of countries that have neither the political nor the institutional capacity to cope with speculative capital flows.

One recent study examines this tradeoff in more detail. Revisiting the literature on the effects of capital controls on growth, Eichengreen and Leblang (2002) look at the interactions between controls, crises, and growth outcomes. They find that controls affect growth through two channels, as we have noted before, but they are able to measure each channel in turn: a direct negative effect on growth and an opposing indirect effect of limiting growth-reducing crises. Some of their results are shown in Table 8.5 for a historical sample of 21 countries from 1880 to 1997, and also for a broader cross section of 47 countries from 1975 to 1995. In both sample periods estimates are based on nonoverlapping 5-year averages and panel methods. In these regressions, the left-hand side variable is percentage growth over a five year period, measured as 100 times the change in the logarithm of real GDP per capita.

The basis for the empirical specification is the standard regression from the empirical growth literature, in which the growth rate of per capita income depends on initial per capita income (the "catching-up" term) and controls for the initial human capital endowment and distortions (the size of government and other proxies). Then controls are added for financial openness, and two types of crisis, called "domestic" and "international." Here, a domestic crisis is defined by a binary indicator that signals a *home-country* banking or currency crisis, as in the study by Bordo et al. (2001) that we discuss in more detail later. The international crisis variable is a count of the number of crises occurring in the rest of the world during the same quinquennium.

Eichengreen and Leblang hypothesize that in stable periods, when there is no domestic or international crisis, capital controls are a drag on growth performance. But in times of distress, controls can provide useful insulation from financial turbulence. The authors find this hypothesis to be consistent with the data. The coefficient on controls alone is negative, as is the coefficient on crises. But the coefficient on the interaction of these two variables is positive,

Table 8.5. *Capital controls, crises, and economic growth*

Sample of 21 countries, quinquennia, 1880–1997			
	(1)	(2)	(3)
Log (GDP per capita)	−14.63*	−14.28*	−14.59*
	(6.45)	(5.80)	(5.98)
Log (primary enrollment)	−3.77*	−2.91	−3.19
	(1.81)	(1.85)	(2.23)
Log (secondary enrollment)	3.23*	2.62*	2.93*
	(1.34)	(1.37)	(1.13)
Interwar period	4.24*	9.00*	8.82*
	(2.12)	(2.67)	(3.06)
Bretton Woods period	14.64*	19.15*	17.76*
	(5.42)	(5.57)	(5.98)
Post–Bretton Woods period	18.59*	23.28*	22.07*
	(9.57)	(9.15)	(10.00)
Capital controls	3.27	−3.43	−2.86
	(2.20)	(2.22)	(2.38)
Domestic crises – (controls × domestic crises)	−4.53*	—	−2.71*
	(1.16)		(1.24)
International crises – (controls × international Crises)	—	−0.700*	−0.60*
		(0.11)	(0.11)

Sample of 47 countries, quinquennia, 1975–95			
	(4)	(5)	(6)
Log (GDP per capita)	−4.94*	−5.80*	−5.59*
	(1.75)	(1.68)	(1.58)
Schooling	−1.43	−0.11	−0.54
	(2.69)	(2.53)	(2.61)
Government consumption	−2.89	−2.73	−4.14*
	(1.82)	(1.93)	(1.67)
Log(inflation)	−2.60*	−3.47*	−1.76
	(1.24)	(1.44)	(1.51)
Log(black-market premium)	−1.68*	−1.45*	−2.03*
	(0.51)	(0.49)	(0.65)
Trade openness	2.91*	2.56*	2.42*
	(1.19)	(1.17)	(1.08)
Capital controls	−0.3	−5.00*	−2.73
	(0.93)	(1.91)	(1.53)
Domestic crises – (controls × domestic crises)	−1.02*	—	−0.71
	(0.45)		(0.39)
International crises – (controls × international crises)	—	−0.16*	−0.09*
		(0.06)	(0.05)

Source: Eichengreen and Leblang (2002). Standard errors in parentheses. * denotes significance at the 5 percent level.

showing that activating controls in a time of crisis may provide some beneficial offset. (In the specifications we report in Table 8.5, the offset is restricted to be complete, that is, the interaction and crisis coefficients sum to zero.)

From a historical standpoint, these results make it easier to understand why the worldwide financial distress associated with the Great Depression led so many policymakers to reach for capital controls as a solution. For the contemporary period, the Eichengreen-Leblang results indicate how costly controls can be in tranquil times. The authors subtitle their work "Was Mr. Mahathir Right?" and in the midst of the Asian crisis, Malaysia's controls might have seemed like a useful short-run device. In the longer run, however, the costs of controls are likely to exceed their benefits, so when calmer times returned, Mahathir Mohamad's government was quick to remove them. Indeed, as we noted at the end of Chapter 7, the recent crises did not lead developing countries to retreat from earlier steps they had taken toward more open capital accounts. In a number of them, domestic reforms complementary to financial opening are being pursued.

A difficulty in interpreting these correlations is that they may offer little guidance as to the formulation of policy. In particular, the expectation that capital controls would be applied in a crisis could increase the frequency of crises. In a provocative finding, Glick and Hutchison (2004) analyzed 69 developing countries over the period 1975–97 and showed that the imposition of capital controls *increased*, rather than decreased, the likelihood of a currency crisis, even controlling for additional theoretical determinants of crises. They concluded that

in the context of the sequencing literature on economic reform, an environment where the capital account is liberalized does not appear to be more vulnerable to exchange rate instability. Surprisingly, the opposite appears to be the case. Countries without capital controls appear to have greater exchange rate stability and fewer speculative attacks. This result holds even when taking account of macroeconomic factors – inconsistent policy regimes – that lead to speculative attacks, as well as country-specific political and institutional factors that induce countries to maintain a system of capital controls.[18]

On reflection, this conclusion is perhaps not too surprising. Impositions of capital controls over the last three decades were often cases of "too little, too late," and could not prevent an incipient crisis from running its course. These results warn us that in practice, the use of controls on a contingent basis may be problematic.

[18] Glick and Hutchison (2004).

8.6 Open markets, volatility, and crises

Do open capital markets encourage crises and, hence, do they also increase economic volatility? Although the answer is usually assumed to be yes as far as developing economies are concerned, the empirical evidence is not so clear. First, we should note that there are really multiple chains of causation that cloud the issue. Open capital markets may encourage crises, but crises might also depend on other factors. Likewise, crises may increase volatility, but so might other economic characteristics. In other words, closed economies could, in principle, be as volatile (or even more volatile) than open economies if other features of those economies are systematically different. A definitive empirical analysis of volatility must control for those features, difficult as they may sometimes be to observe.

Some preliminary evidence from the present era is illustrative here, because there exist macroeconomic data on a wide variety of countries, some open and some closed, and there are long enough time series for us to begin to assess volatility differences between the two kinds of regime.[19] Using this partition of the data leads to a surprising result for developing countries: financially closed developing economies seem to be, on several real dimensions, *more* volatile than open developing economies. Defining output volatility as the unconditional standard deviation in the growth rate of real GDP per capita over 1975–99, the IMF summarizes the data as follows:

Developing countries that are relatively more integrated into global capital markets tend to have lower output volatility on average than financially closed countries....This is true for the period as a whole, but not in the early 1980s and late 1990s, when global financial shocks were especially large....Financial openness appears to be associated with lower output volatility through two channels: the magnitude of inflation and exchange rate shocks is lower, and the impact of all shocks on output is dampened. Financially open countries – which are also more open to trade and have slightly higher debt ratios – experience larger external shocks, as measured by the volatility of the terms of trade, trade flows, and financial flows....However, financially open countries have somewhat more stable real exchange rates (the volatility of fiscal balances is similar in financially open and closed economies).[20]

The IMF goes on to observe that these results could reflect a disciplining effect of financial integration, or the reverse causality from a sound domestic policymaking structure to a desire for greater integration. Notwithstanding the likelihood that the quality of a country's governing institutions determines both the quality of its policies and its willingness to pursue economic integration,

---

[19] Caution is nonetheless warranted as sample sizes still are not large.

[20] IMF, *World Economic Outlook*, September 2002, 135–6.

the preceding regularities suggest (yet again) that when a country can develop its institutional capabilities, gains from financial openness are available.

For an analysis of economic welfare, the variability of consumption growth is arguably of more direct relevance than that of output growth. Indeed, in models such as the one in Obstfeld (1994a), financial integration raises the volatility of each nation's GDP growth by promoting production specialization; nonetheless, welfare increases. Effects on consumption volatility are especially important in developing countries, because measured consumption volatility in the developing world tends to exceed measured output volatility, in contrast to the situation in most industrial countries.[21] However, in a model where global financial integration leads to specialization in risky but high-expected-return investment activities, it cannot be presumed in general that economic integration decreases the volatility in consumption growth either.

The study by Prasad et al. (2003, table 4) contains a comparison of annual consumption growth volatility between more and less financially integrated developing economies. The median standard deviation for the more financially integrated group is below that of the less financially integrated group for every decade of the period 1960–99. Between the 1980s and 1990s, however, consumption volatility rose for the more financially integrated group while dropping sharply for the less financially integrated group.

A number of authors have attempted to evaluate the potential welfare impact of increased international consumption risk sharing (see van Wincoop 1999 for a discussion). While there is disagreement about the precise gains that feasible risk sharing can bring, there is a rather broad consensus that the potential gains are much higher for developing countries, where consumption variability and its welfare cost tends to be much higher than in the developed world (Obstfeld 1995; Pallage and Robe 2003). In that connection, it is sobering that in their emerging-market sample, Bekaert et al. (2002) estimate much smaller volatility declines as a result of equity-market liberalization than for mixed samples that include industrial countries. For the latter samples, in contrast, they find that equity-market liberalization significantly reduces the volatility in consumption and output growth, even when the Asian crisis years are included and even after controlling for certain macroeconomic reforms and the level of financial development.[22] Apparently the risk sharing benefits that developing countries

[21] The industrial economies as a group have about half the output volatility of the developing economies and less than half the consumption volatility.

[22] These authors find much weaker results using the IMF's zero-one index of overall capital account openness, as we noted above. The shortcomings of that index were discussed earlier. Using a different methodology, Kaminsky and Schmukler (2003) find that, particularly in emerging markets, stock-market booms and busts intensify shortly after financial liberalization but are

have been able to derive from liberalization are smaller than for industrial economies (though such gains as can be reaped may be quite valuable, in welfare terms, at the margin).

Indeed, for developing countries, Bekaert et al. (2002) find significant volatility declines following liberalization only over the 1980–97 period. Once the sample is extended through 2000 so as to include the Asian crisis years, equity-market liberalization is estimated to have an insignificantly negative (and small) or even positive impact on the volatility of consumption and real GDP growth rates. The mean growth-rate effects discussed earlier in this chapter are also lower in a longer sample period that includes the Asian crisis. As we have noted, the greatest decline in the estimated growth effect can be seen in the emerging-market subsample of countries.

The data thus leave no doubt that for the developing countries, the crises of the 1990s exacted a high price in terms of reduced growth and volatility. Should we think of crises differently from other sources of macro volatility? A crisis is just one particular form of economic convulsion, where a fall in output is associated with other external or domestic financial indicators (such as devaluation or banking collapse). But there may be plenty of other economic cycles, of greater or lesser amplitude, that do not register as crises per se. So at some level, the distinction may be overdrawn.

There might still be reasons to worry specifically about crises if the kinds of downturns associated with them are systematically different or if we think they could be managed in a better way through possible changes in the international or domestic policy environment. One way to determine whether we can handle crises more effectively, or limit their occurrence, is to look back again at the long-run historical record.

The history of financial crashes extends into the distant past. The turbulence associated with the Great Depression still stands prominently in our collective memory; it wrought havoc on the currencies and banking systems of many countries, industrialized and developing.[23] But the nineteenth century also had its share of crises. A notable one, mentioned previously in Chapter 6, was the infamous Baring crash of 1890. That crisis originated in Argentina but threatened the solvency of a major London investment house, precipitated a bailout orchestrated by the Bank of England, and, as an early example of a generalized emerging-market crisis, caused repercussions worldwide (see della

---

dampened in the longer run. Based on empirical evidence, they conjecture that this pattern may be caused by a tendency for liberalization to spur institutional reforms.

[23] See Kindleberger (1986); Bernanke and James (1991); Feinstein (1995); Feinstein, Temin, and Toniolo (1997); James (2001).

Table 8.6. *Crisis frequency*

Unconditional probability of crisis in one country in any given year, percent

Year	Banking Crises	Currency Crises	Twin Crises	All Crises
1880–1913	2.30	1.23	1.38	4.90
1919–1939	4.84	4.30	4.03	13.17
1945–1971	0.00	6.85	0.19	7.04
1973–1997 (21 countries)	2.03	5.18	2.48	9.68
1973–1997 (56 countries)	2.29	7.48	2.38	12.15

Source: Eichengreen and Bordo (2002).

Paolera and Taylor 2001). And there are many earlier examples (Kindleberger 1978; Neal 1990).

Going beyond a mere cataloging of events, the study of the history of crises has progressed in recent years with the introduction of formal empirical methods. Eichengreen and Bordo (2002) apply to historical macro data the same kinds of classification criteria for banking crises, currency crises, and their joint occurrence ("twin crises") that researchers have applied to contemporary data (subject to the limitations of the historical record). This research allows us to assess quantitatively how the incidence and severity of various crisis types differ across historical epochs.

A summary of the frequency patterns in the Eichengreen-Bordo (2002) historical data for 21 countries is shown in Table 8.6. Evidently, crises are nothing new, as the final column indicates. For this sample of countries, the annual probability that a randomly selected country would experience some kind of crisis – banking, currency, or twin – was about 5 percent over the 1880–1913 period. For that same group of countries, the probability was as high as 13 percent in the interwar period, as low as 7 percent under the Bretton Woods period and around 10 percent in the years 1973–97. For comparison with a broader post-1973 sample, the last row shows that in a set of 56 countries (including more developing countries), the crisis probability has been about 12 percent in recent years.

Could the underlying real shocks to the world economy have moved in ways that account for these changes over time? This is possible to some extent, and the massive shocks to world trade and output in the 1920s and 1930s might explain the large interwar blip. Indeed, in some sense, the interwar period was almost one long international crisis, with at least a few countries somewhere in a crisis during almost every single year. But we think changes in the underlying economic shocks cannot account for all the variance here, and much is left to be explained by the regimes under which policymakers have acted in different eras. It is especially striking that at a time when the political economy of the trilemma was arguably simpler to resolve (under the classical gold standard, at least for the core countries), the incidence of all financial crises was about half that of today (and largely concentrated in countries of the periphery). We agree with the assessment of Eichengreen and Bordo that "evidently, the credibility of the commitment to peg the exchange rate under the gold standard was part of the explanation for the stability of the pre-1914 financial environment" (Eichengreen and Bordo 2002, 17).

Thus, the underlying policymaking environment certainly affects crisis frequencies – financial globalization, in itself, is not the entire story. As we have observed, industrial countries (outside the euro area) have established capital mobility on the basis of flexible exchange rates, but for emerging-market economies, exchange-rate flexibility is more problematic (Calvo and Reinhart 2001, 2002). For example, the economy may be obliged to denominate its debts in foreign currency, so that a home currency depreciation induces a sharp and contractionary negative wealth effect, as emphasized long ago by Díaz Alejandro (1965). Such factors are among those making financial globalization more perilous in the developing world. Conversely, as the Bretton Woods experience shows, there are limits to the ability of capital-account restrictions to contain crises when an exchange-rate peg loses credibility.

The results in Table 8.6 also break down the kinds of crises witnessed at different times, and the findings here suggest differences between the different major epochs. First, we can see that there were no banking crises and almost no twin crises during the Bretton Woods era; however, in a time of fixed exchange rates under pressure, there were plenty of currency crises, as many as at almost any other time (many of them concentrated in the system's final years). Thus, the ability of a fairly stringent capital controls regime – even one as institutionalized as Bretton Woods – to prevent currency crises remains in doubt. Cross-border capital controls combined with concomitant controls over domestic banking systems, also a legacy of the Great Depression, did, however, seem to limit banking-sector problems. Because these data largely omit the Asian crisis, there is little difference between the frequency of banking crises in the two globalization eras 1880–1913 and 1973–97, which are of roughly equal length. Thus the overall doubling in crisis frequency between these two periods is attributable almost entirely to the increase in currency crises (and to a lesser extent, twin crises). Does this imply that our search to understand the higher incidence of crises today should focus mostly on outside money (or external convertibility), rather than inside money (or internal convertibility)? Not at all.

The two are interdependent: bank balance-sheet effects have been central to the transformation of currency crises into twin crises, while conversely, runs sparked by devaluation fears have weakened banks.[24] In addition, the incidence of banking crises and twin crises rose after 1987, as noted by Bordo et al. (2001, 58). Pure currency crises were more prevalent in 1973–87 than afterward, which is consistent with the progressive deregulation of banking in many countries.

If crises have become more frequent in recent decades, have they also become more costly – and relative to what? The obvious benchmark for comparison is the typical non-crisis recession, at least if we wish to know if there is anything particularly harsh about the economic impact of a crisis that countries might wish to avoid. This comparison was undertaken by Bordo et al. (2001). Unavoidably, their results depend on arbitrary assumptions concerning the dating of recessions and the measurement of output losses, but the orders of magnitude nonetheless provide a useful starting point for discussion. We briefly summarize their analysis of all recessions over 1880–1997, for a historical sample of 21 countries before 1973, and for 56 countries after 1973.

A first pass at these data suggests that recessions with crises entailed a cumulative output loss 10 percent of GDP greater than those without crises both during the 1973–97 period and before 1914. Thus, crises nowadays are not obviously more costly than they were in the earlier era of globalization. The incremental cost of crises is, not surprisingly, much higher (roughly twice as high) during the interwar years 1919–39. It is lowest during the overlap with the Bretton Woods years, 1945–71, when the cumulative additional GDP loss during a recession-cum-crisis was around 8 percent.

In a further econometric analysis of their data, Bordo et al. (2001) find unexpectedly that crises have, on average, been associated with more severe GDP losses in industrial (*not* developing) economies. They also find that twin crises are about twice as costly as pure currency crises, which are, in turn, about twice as costly as pure banking crises. They express surprise at the latter result, though it may reflect governments' abilities to contain banking crises in various ways when the currency peg is not in question. Unfortunately, the costly twin crises have become much more prevalent since the Bretton Woods period, and would appear even more so with the addition of data covering the Asian crisis of the late 1990s. The results just summarized constrain crises to have identical output effects across different epochs, a strong assumption. Nonetheless, the

---

[24] For historical investigations of crises centered on the internal-external convertibility nexus see, for example, Díaz Alejandro (1985), Feinstein, Temin, and Toniolo (1997), James (2001), and della Paloera and Taylor (2002, 2003). For theoretical discussion of internal-external convertibility links see, for example, Velasco (1987), Marion (1999), and Chang and Velasco (2001).

apparent severity of twin crises warns of the dangers of financial opening when domestic financial intermediaries are unsound.

A problem in assessing these results (noted by the authors) is bidirectional causality: some crises are consequences of recessions, so it is not clear that the numbers reported above reflect a genuine causal influence of crises on recession severity. For example, it may be that only particularly harsh recessions result in currency devaluation, and that the devaluation itself, by enhancing the economy's competitiveness, sets the stage for recovery. In that case, a strong association between currency crises and the depth of recessions might actually reflect a not entirely malign economic outcome. Bordo et al. (2001) deploy an instrumental-variable procedure in an attempt to isolate the incremental causal impact of crises on the output cost of recessions, and estimate 14 percent of GDP for the cumulative extra output loss in their full sample.

There is reason to believe, however, that the impact of crises differs systematically across developed and developing countries. This difference has important implications for the questions of whether and for whom capital-account liberalization is worth the risks that may come with it.

Figure 8.6 uses the post-1973 currency crisis episodes (pure currency crises plus twin crises) described in Bordo et al. (2001) for their sample of 56 countries. The typical output paths around a year-T currency crisis are obtained through panel fixed-effects regressions of output per capita growth rates on dummy variables representing the years from $T-3$ through $T+3$, plus a time trend and a lagged output per capita level (interpreted as a "catch-up" term). We do not attempt to adjust these data by subtracting the output effect of noncrisis recessions. In the comparison, two differences stand out. First, in these unadjusted data, the output loss associated with a crisis appears to be more severe (and persistent) in the developing world. For a typical developing country, the output growth rate at the trough of a crisis is about 3 percent off the normal level. For a typical developed country, on the other hand, the shortfall is only about half as big – output growth at the trough of a crisis is about 1.5 percent per year below normal. The second major difference concerns timing. In industrial countries the recession trough (the year of weakest growth) typically occurs in the year before the crisis strikes. But in the developing world, it is the year of the crisis itself in which output falls most sharply. This regularity suggests that in a typical developed-country crisis, slow growth is the result of an overvalued currency; therefore, a currency realignment restores competitiveness and sets the stage for renewed growth (the United Kingdom in 1992 being an example). These factors may be at work in developing countries as well. But there, currency devaluation is associated with a "sudden stop" in capital inflows (Calvo

Fig. 8.6. Growth effects of currency crises

(a) Industrial countries

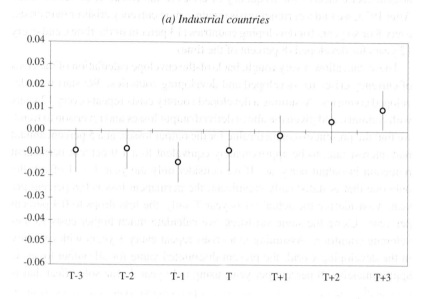

(b) Nonindustrial countries

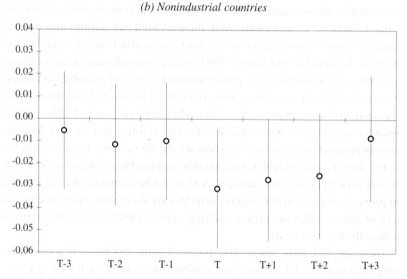

Notes: Coefficients on leads and lags of a currency-crisis dummy variable in a fixed (country) effects regression with real GDP per capita growth rate as the dependent variable, and crisis dummies, a time trend, and the lagged GDP per capita as independent variables.
Source: Authors' calculations, based on data from Bordo et al. (2001).

1998) that hits the economy with contractionary devaluation effects. Another notable fact concerns the frequency of crises in the Bordo et al. (2001) data. After 1973, we find a currency crisis (again, a pure currency crisis or twin crisis) every 8 or so years for developing countries (13 percent of the time), and every 12 years for developed (8 percent of the time).

These data allow a very rough, back-of-the envelope calculation of the costs of currency crises for developed and developing countries. We start with developed countries. Assuming a developed country crisis repeats every 12 years with certainty, and given the above derived output losses and reversion to trend, we find the present discounted value for the output losses, at a 5 percent annual real interest rate, to be approximately equivalent to a 1.9 percent permanent reduction in output per year. If we consider only the year $T - 1$ effect, the only one that is statistically significant, the permanent loss is 0.8 percent per year. Considering the actual crisis year T only, the loss drops to 0.4 percent per year. Using the same yardstick, we calculate much higher costs for developing countries. Assuming that crises repeat every 8 years with certainty in the developing world, the present discounted value for all output losses is approximately 4.8 percent per year; using only year T, the sole effect that is statistically significant, the costs are 1.3 percent per year. Admittedly, these costs may be an overstatement because we do not net out the costs of "normal" – that is, noncrisis – recessions. Still, these stylized calculations may be compared with our earlier analysis of the long-run growth benefits from financial opening. Gourinchas and Jeanne (2003) present a developing-country estimate of a flow 1.2 percent per year welfare gain due to a greater availability of investment capital, but we noted that this effect might be two to three times higher if consumers' intertemporal substitution elasticity is below 1. Furthermore, if financial opening can be combined with other reforms that increase long-run growth potential (by raising A or reducing the size of investment-cost distortions), then the gains might be multiplied by an even bigger factor, with benefits in excess of 10 percent not unlikely. And, as we have argued, any reforms that improve governance in developing countries may also reduce the frequency and cost of crises. Likewise, greater exchange-rate flexibility, if feasible, also can reduce the risk of a crisis.

There are, of course, many other potential gains and losses that our earlier rough calculations did not take into account: for example, risk-sharing effects on the plus side versus increased volatility, income-distribution fluctuations, and social unrest on the negative side. Nor have we accounted for a conceptual difficulty mentioned earlier, that there is two-way causality between output losses and crises, making any attempt to identify crisis "costs" problematic.

Even so, for many developing countries, the costs and benefits would appear to be delicately balanced. The situation could be rather more favorable to financial opening in some of the higher-income developing countries with better-quality institutions and, by the same token, more risky in the very poorest countries, where institutional failure is widespread. Of course, the net benefits are clearer for the developed countries with their superior institutional infrastructure, more sophisticated financial markets, and extensive social safety nets. In the industrial world, capital mobility is a clear winner, which is why its progress has been more uniform there but much more limited and uneven elsewhere. In developing countries, however, capital mobility becomes a clear winner only under domestic reforms that simultaneously limit the risk of crises and raise the productivity of investment.

To recapitulate: current thinking about crises suggests that they are not as arbitrary as might be thought, nor as novel. They have been a part of the international financial scene for well over a century. They can impose costs on the economy over and above those of "normal" business cycle downturns. But they are not unavoidable. Their prevalence has varied across different political economy regimes, and appears to depend systematically on the ways in which policymakers have either solved – or denied – the trilemma. Policymakers who can strongly commit not to intervene in an inconsistent way, as was mostly true for core countries under the gold standard, can enjoy a life relatively free from currency and twin crises (though pure banking crises can remain a problem). But an adequate degree of precommitment is difficult, if not impossible. If policymakers are truly unwilling to sacrifice their ability to intervene actively in the economy, then they cannot simultaneously enjoy exchange-rate stability and an open financial account. For developing countries, the expected benefits and risks due to financial integration seem finely balanced, and options for the exchange-rate regime look to be more limited. The development of adequate institutional capacity appears to be an important and necessary precondition for reaping net gains.

8.7 Summary

Can the benefits and costs of global capital markets be neatly summarized and quantified? The historical record indicates the very contingent nature of any attempt to do so. Some countries have flourished upon financial opening, others have suffered disaster. This book has surveyed the long and tumultuous history of international capital markets, not only to give an account of these important events in their own right, but also to inform the contentious debates that swirl around the question of financial globalization today. As we have shown, contemporary problems, questions, and arguments are in most respects nothing new. The ever-present trilemma of macroeconomic management, the daunting costs of recurrent crises, and the prospective benefits of a larger, deeper, more diverse, open capital market – all have been a feature of the international economy for well over a century.

The variety of historical experience with open capital markets lends encouragement to both sides in the debate – those who view the globalization of financial (and other) markets as a liberal, beneficial force, and those who believe that the risks outweigh the benefits. Motivating a more extreme negative reaction is the observation that the disasters more often than not occur in developing countries, which usually have little capacity to absorb negative economic shocks without severe strain on the social and political fabric.

Who wins as a result of financial globalization? Who loses? For true pessimists there may appear to be no winners, for the optimists, something for everyone. Even a glance at literature illustrates the coexistence of these opposing views over the long history of international capital markets. The longevity of the debate suggests that we will not arrive at definitive answers anytime soon, but also that the march of international capital-market integration will nonetheless continue.

Oscar Wilde's play *An Ideal Husband* was first staged in 1895, at the height of the first great era of financial globalization. In contrarian fashion, however, Wilde reminds his audience of the dark underside of global capital markets as revealed a few years earlier in the Baring crisis – those aspects associated with monitoring costs, moral hazards, and the like:

Mrs. Cheveley: Quite seriously. I want to talk to you about a great political and financial scheme, about this Argentine Canal Company....

Sir Robert Chiltern: Believe me, Mrs. Cheveley, it is a swindle....I sent out a special Commission to inquire into the matter privately, and they report that the works are hardly begun, and as for the money already subscribed, no one seems to know what has become of it....I hope you have not invested in it. I am sure you are far too clever to have done that.

Mrs. Cheveley: I have invested very largely in it.

Sir Robert Chiltern: Who could have advised you to do such a foolish thing?[25]

In contrast, a seemingly more positive view of global capital movement is expressed by King Magnus in George Bernard Shaw's *The Apple Cart*, first staged, ironically, in 1929:

[25] Wilde (1899).

We have not abolished poverty and hardship. Our big business men have abolished them. But how? By sending our capital abroad to places where poverty and hardship still exist: in other words, where labor is cheap. We live in comfort on the imported profits of that capital. We are all ladies and gentlemen now.[26]

Neither Shaw nor Wilde tells us what is happening at the other end of the financial transaction, but we can imagine some differences. With Shaw the capital appears stable, in for the long run and earning a solid return overseas. In other words, it is productive, meaning that some local labor is employed and the economic capacity of the recipient country is enlarged. If the capital suddenly left, locals would be out their jobs – but there is no hint of a crisis, and the capital has no urge to flee. Absent monopoly or other market failures, the capital inflow benefits both the poor borrower and the rich creditor: win-win.

With Wilde, however, things don't look so rosy down on the Pampas. The capital has been borrowed yet no canal has been built. The money has disappeared but the fraud will have consequences. Those with liability may still have to repay the debt and the country as a whole has been saddled a little more firmly with a bad reputation as a place to do business. A crisis could ensue. Perhaps capital flight will follow. The country will pay for that dearly and face a higher risk premium on future foreign funds – should any be available. Because the creditors have lost their money, it's lose-lose, except for the thieves. In this version, globalization gets a bad name.

The passages from Wilde and Shaw suggest that whether financial opening is a winning or losing proposition can depend greatly on the environment. These may be special examples, but they well illustrate the range of possible experience – and, in history, almost all of that range has been explored in various times and places. Because a great diversity in economic and institutional conditions still obtains today, a one-size-fits-all policy recommendation is inappropriate. Financial liberalization is not a universal panacea, a benefactor to all. Yet neither is it a menace to all, a risk that is never worth taking. Unfortunately, the questions are hardest to answer where the needs are most pressing – in the poorest countries.

That the tradeoff between costs and benefits is much more problematic in the developing world is what one would expect given the prevalence there of an interrelated nexus of disabilities: micro- and macroeconomic distortions, rudimentary financial markets, corruption, poverty, weaker enforcement of property rights, and dysfunctional politics. Much of the recent discussion of reforming the international financial "architecture" has suggested innovations in financial markets that might reduce the frequency and severity of crises, as well as

[26] Shaw (1930), cited in Nurkse (1954).

macroeconomic policy strategies (such as inflation targeting rather than rigid exchange-rate targeting) that could also help. To the extent that these reforms are implemented and actually work, the case for some form of capital-account opening is strengthened for developing countries. There is always the danger, however, as Tirole (2002), among others, has emphasized, of treating symptoms rather than causes, so that in a second-best or indeed n^{th}-best situation, correction of one apparent distortion makes matters worse. Fundamentally, the social and political "deep structure" of the economy can generate an Argentina or a Chile, and in the former case, absent truly fundamental change, no sequencing of the financial opening process, no resolution of the trilemma, will produce good economic outcomes for long. Indiscriminate financial opening among the poorer countries, absent adequate progress in achieving the right preconditions, is a bad idea and will not generally produce the benefits that the industrial countries have been able to reap from financial integration. Hopefully, the preconditions supportive of liberalization can eventually be achieved in developing countries. The entire world stands to benefit.

Data Appendix

Saving, investment and the current account

The basic data from Taylor (2002a) consist of annual saving and investment rates for each of the 15 countries in the sample. Data were collected for every available year between 1850 and 1992. For some purposes in this book the data were revised and extended up to year 2000, based on the IMF's *International Financial Statistics* for the entire 1975–2000 period.

1850–1945: The investment rate measure $(I/Y)_t$ is the ratio of gross investment I_t to national income Y_t at current local prices; the saving rate $(S/Y)_t$ was usually calculated implicitly, via the current account identity, as the investment rate $(I/Y)_t$ plus the ratio of the current account CA_t to national income: $(I/Y)_t = I_t/Y_t$, $(S/Y)t = (I_t/Y_t) + (CA_t/Y_t)$. Except as otherwise indicated, these data are taken from Jones and Obstfeld (2001), who revised the standard sources to correct for flows of gold and changes in stocks.

1946–1959: The investment and saving rates are defined as for 1850–1945: saving rates are still calculated residually from the current account. Except as otherwise indicated, these data are taken from Mitchell (1992; 1993; 1995) using his national income and overall current balance series at current prices. The overall current balance series are converted from U.S. dollars using his exchange-rate series as necessary.

1960–1992: Estimates of gross domestic saving, gross domestic investment, and gross domestic saving at current prices from World Bank (1994).

Exceptions are as follows:

Argentina: From the reconstruction of Argentina's historical balance of payments in Taylor (1998a).

Australia: 1946–88 from N. Butlin (1962), M. Butlin (1977), and McLean (1994), as described in Taylor and Williamson (1994).

Canada: 1946–84 from Urquhart (1988).

Germany: Before 1945, raw data are for net capital formation. This is inflated by adding 9 percentage points to give an approximation of gross capital formation, using an assumed capital-output ratio of 3 and an assumed annual depreciation rate of 3 percent.

The Netherlands: Before 1914, raw data are for net capital formation. This is inflated by adding 9 percentage points to give an approximation of gross capital formation, using an assumed capital-output ratio of 3 and an assumed annual depreciation rate of 3 percent.

Spain: Before 1965, based on revisions to Albert Carreras's macroeconomic statistics chapter in Barciela López and Carreras (1989); unpublished revisions of the investment figures, and unpublished saving estimates by Leandro Prados. For 1965–6 investment based on Carreras, with the current account from Mitchell, as noted previously.

Exchange-risk-free nominal interest parity
Exchange rates United States-United Kingdom

Before 1921 spot and 60-day sterling bill exchange rates (in U.S. dollars) are from the *Financial Review* or *Commercial and Financial Chronicle*; 1921–36 spot and 90-day forward rates are from Einzig (1937); 1937 to November 1946 spot and 90-day forward rates are from the *Economist,* December 1946 to May 1947 spot and 30-day forward rates are from the *Wall Street Journal*; June 1947 to 1965 spot and 90-day forward rates are from the *New York Times*; and thereafter from *OECD Historical Statistics* and (starting in January 1976) from Reuters (as reported by Datastream) until December 1980. Finally, from January 1981 to April 2003, spot and three-month forward dollar-sterling exchange rates come from Datastream. The foreign exchange data taken from Einzig are monthly averages, whereas all the other exchange rate data are taken at or near the end of the month.

Exchange rates United Kingdom-Germany

Data are monthly averages up until January 1981 and end-of-month thereafter, as follows. From October 1877 to July 1914 we used the month-average spot mark-sterling exchange rate from the National Bureau of Economic Research (NBER) macro-history database, series 14106. London sterling prices for three-month bills on Berlin are "money" rates taken from the "Course of Exchange" table in the *Economist.* From January 1921 to September 1931 we average the weekly spot and three-month forward exchange rates listed by Einzig (1937).

From May 1955 to December 1980, spot exchange rates are from the *Economist* through 1957 and thereafter from Datastream. Forward exchange rates are from the London *Times* (May 1955 to October 1958), from the *Economist* subsequently through 1964, from the London *Times* through 1975, and, finally, from January 1976 to April 2003, from Datastream.

Interest rates United States-United Kingdom

For the United States, from 1937 to April 1940, we used rates on banker's acceptances in New York from the *Economist* (at or near end-of-month). From May 1940 to May 1947, the same rates are monthly averages as reported by the Federal Reserve (at or near end of month). From June 1947 to 1965, 30- to 90-day banker's acceptance interest rates in New York come from the *New York Times*, observed (at or near end-of-month). Data for January through April 1966 are month averages of 90-day banker's acceptance rates reported by the Federal Reserve (at or near end-of-month). Starting in May 1966, the Fed reports month-end data, which we have used in the calculations up to December 1980. From January 1981 to April 2003, we use the discount rate on 90-day bankers' acceptances, from Datastream (end-of-month).

For the United Kingdom, from 1870 to 1920, we used three-month rates on London bank bills from Capie and Weber (1985), data taken at or near end of month. From 1921 to 1936, month average data on London and New York three-month market discount rates from Einzig (1937). United Kingdom interest-rate data for 1937 through April 1971 are three-month London bank bill rates from Capie and Weber (1985); from May 1971 through December 1974, three-month London bank bill rates from Datastream (all at or near end-of-month); and from January 1975 through April 2003, the three-month bank bill middle rate, from Datastream (end-of-month).

Interest rates United Kingdom-Germany

Data are monthly averages up until January 1981 and end of month thereafter, as follows. For the United Kingdom we use the open market three-month discount rate, NBER series 13016, through September 1931. Data for 1955 to 1974 came from the Federal Reserve banking database (and are similar to the well-known Capie-Webber series). Starting in January 1975, we used the U.K. interbank (money-market) three-month middle rate of interest.

For Germany, from October 1877 through September 1931, where observations are available, we use the Berlin private open-market discount rate for prime bankers' acceptances given as NBER series 13018. The German three-month money-market rate for 1955–9 is an average of monthly high and low rates taken from *Monthly Report of the Deutsche Bundesbank* and thereafter, through end-1980, comes from *International Financial Statistics*. Subsequently, the German data are taken from Datastream, using the three-month dead middle money-market rate. Starting in January 1999, we use the three-month European Interbank Offered Rate.

Purchasing power parity

All series 1948–96 are from the IMF, *International Financial Statistics*. The sources for other years are as follows:

Argentina: Bordo and Schwartz (1997).
Australia: Bordo and Rockoff (1996); Bordo and Schwartz (1997).
Belgium: Bordo and Jonung (1996); Maddison (1991).
Brazil: Bordo and Jonung (1996).
Canada: Bordo and Rockoff (1996); Bordo and Schwartz (1996).
Denmark: Bordo and Jonung (1996); Mitchell (1992).
Finland: Bordo and Jonung (1996); Bank of Finland (1942).
France: Bordo and Jonung (1996).
Germany: Bordo and Jonung (1996); Maddison (1991).
Italy: Bordo and Jonung (1996).
Japan: Bordo and Jonung (1996).
Mexico: INEGI (1994).
The Netherlands: Bordo and Jonung (1996); Maddison (1991); Altes (1996).
Norway: Bordo and Jonung (1996); Unpublished data from Jan Tore Klovland; Central Bureau of Statistics of Norway (1968).
Portugal: Bordo and Jonung (1996).
Spain: Bordo and Schwartz (1997).
Sweden: Bordo and Jonung (1996).
Switzerland: Bordo and Jonung (1996); Maddison (1991).
United Kingdom: Bordo and Rockoff (1996); Bordo and Jonung (1996).
United States: Bordo and Rockoff (1996); Bordo and Jonung (1996).

We define $p_{it} = \log P_{it}^* - \log E_{it}$ as the log dollar price level. Interpolation by linear trend was used to fill in missing data for the following observations in the series for p_{it}: Australia 1939–46; Belgium 1920, 1941–5; Canada 1940–5; France 1914–20, 1939–47; Germany 1915–23, 1940–7; Japan 1945–9; Mexico 1914–17; the Netherlands 1942–4; Norway 1940–5; Spain 1936–46; United Kingdom 1939–46.

With interpolations complete, the real exchange rate series was generated two ways: first, relative to the U.S. dollar, as $q_{it} = p_{it} - p_{US,t}$; and second, relative to the "rest of world" ($N - 1 = 19$) basket of currencies, as $q_{it}^W = p_{it} - p_t^W$, $p_{it}^W = \frac{1}{N-1} \sum_{j \neq i} p_{jt}$.

Sovereign risk, credibility, and the gold standard

The database covers the period 1870 to 1939 at an annual frequency. The core countries are defined as Australia, Belgium, Canada, Denmark, France, Germany, New Zealand, Norway, Sweden, and the United States. The empire countries are defined as Australia, Canada, India, New Zealand, and South Africa. The peripheral countries are defined as Argentina, Austria (and Austria-Hungary), Brazil, Chile, Egypt, Finland, Greece, Hungary, India, Italy, Japan, Mexico, Portugal, South Africa, Spain, Turkey, and Uruguay. The base country for yields is the United Kingdom. Before World War One, Turkey refers to the Ottoman empire, and Austria denotes Austria-Hungary (and there are no independent data for Hungary). There are missing data for most variables.

Exchange rate

The exchange rate versus the U.S. dollar is from Bordo and Schwartz (1997) and Global Financial Data (GFD), except as follows.

Argentina: from della Paolera and Taylor (2001).

Chile: 1870–79 annual average from Braun et al. (2000).

Gold standard

The gold standard dummy variable is equal to one when a country is on the gold standard, otherwise zero. The gold standard parity dummy (GSPAR) is equal to one when a country rejoins gold after 1914 at a parity that is the same as the previous one. The gold standard devalued dummy (GSDEV) is equal to one when a country rejoins gold at a parity after 1914 that is devalued relative to the previous one. (There are cases where countries rejoined gold at a *re*valued parity, such as India in the 1920s, but these are not coded in any special way.)

Prewar coding. Data are from Meissner (2002), available for all countries in all years, except as follows.

Argentina: On gold for 1899–1902 (see della Paolera and Taylor, 2001).

India: Off gold 1870–97 following Hawtrey (1947) and based on exchange-rate volatility.

Uruguay: On gold for 1885–99 (Luis Bértola, private communication); we have no exchange-rate data for Uruguay prior to 1885 to verify adherence.

Interwar coding. As discussed in the text, the interwar coding of gold standard adherence involves greater subjective judgment than for the prewar period. In addition, because we use June observations for the interwar period, annual summaries of adherence are patently insufficient; we must know the month, and in some cases the day, of entry to or exit from the gold standard. We do not attempt to distinguish among various degrees of adherence, that is, gold bullion standard, gold coin standard, or gold exchange standard. In most cases, however, we demand not only that a currency be stable de facto in terms of gold, but also that it be convertible de jure, with the free import and export of gold allowed by the issuing country. Countries on gold are considered to leave the gold standard if they prohibit cross-border gold flows or impose other exchange controls, even if they do not simultaneously devalue or float their currencies.

The dates that we use for the interwar transitions to and from the gold standard are as shown in Table A1. Our sources are as follows.

Argentina: Brown (1940, 401, 893).

Australia: Eichengreen (1992, 192, 235).

Austria: *Federal Reserve Bulletin* (August 1928, 562); Brown (1940, 926).

Belgium: Brown (1940, 426); Yeager (1976, 359).

Brazil: The on gold date is for de facto adoption of a gold peg through a currency reform law. See Fritsch (1988, 122). The departure date, from Fritsch (1988, 156), is the day on which the Banco do Brasil withdrew foreign exchange support. Fritsch (1988, 122–23) explains that the currency reform law provided for a phased transition from de facto to de jure convertibility, with the date of de jure convertibility left open and dependent on the level of government gold holdings. Brazil left gold, however, before the transition was completed. Because Brazil's adherence to gold was codified in legislation, we use the date of passage as our on gold date.

Canada: Shearer and Clark (1984, 282, 297); Brown (1940, 396, 906).

Chile: Brown (1940, 396, 912).

Denmark: Lester (1939, 200); Brown (1940, 1075).

Egypt: The on gold date is inferred from the exchange rate's behavior against sterling, as reported in GFD, and Britain's date of adherence to gold. See Rifaat (1935). The off gold date is from Brown (1940, 1075).

Finland: Brown (1940, 396, 1075).

France: Yeager (1976, 329, 362). We treat France as off gold in June 1928.

Germany: Brown (1940, 469); Yeager (1976, 340).

Hungary: Eichengreen (1992, 192); Brown (1940, 1198).

Table A1. *The interwar gold standard*

	On Gold	Off Gold
Argentina	Aug. 1927	Dec. 1929
Australia	April 1925	Jan. 1930
Austria	March 1925	Oct. 1931
Belgium	Oct. 24, 1926	March 1935
Brazil	Dec. 18, 1926	Dec. 7, 1929
Canada	July 1, 1926	Jan. 1929
Chile	Jan. 11, 1926	July 1931
Denmark	Jan. 1927	Sept. 1931
Egypt	April 1925	Sept. 1931
Finland	Dec. 31, 1925	Oct. 1931
France	June 25, 1928	Sept. 26, 1936
Germany	Oct. 1924	July 1931
Hungary	April 1925	Aug. 1931
India	March 1927	Sept. 1931
Italy	Feb. 26, 1928	Dec. 1934
Japan	Jan. 1930	Dec. 1931
New Zealand	April 1925	April 1930
Norway	May 1928	Sept. 1931
Portugal	July 1, 1931	Oct. 1931
South Africa	April 1925	Jan. 1933
Sweden	March 1924	Sept. 1931
Uruguay	Jan. 1928	Dec. 1929
United States	June 1919	April 1933

India: Brown (1940, 839, 1075).

Italy: Brown (1940, 951); Kindleberger (1986, 162); Yeager (1976, 360).

Japan: Yeager (1976, 330); Brown (1940, 1075).

New Zealand: Yeager (1976, 323, n. 30); Brown (1940, 1075).

Norway: Lester (1939, 213); Brown (1940, 1075).

Portugal: *Economist* (June 6, 1931); Brown (1940, 1075).

South Africa: Yeager (1976, 323, n. 30); Brown (1940, 1075).

Sweden: Yeager (1976, 323, n. 30); Lester (1939, 229).

Uruguay: De facto adoption inferred from Officer (2001) and the exchange rate's behavior, as reported in GFD. The December 1929 date for gold abandonment is from Brown (1940, 893) and Kindleberger (1986, 89), though the currency was allowed to depreciate below par in April 1929. According to a private communication from Luis Bértola, Uruguay never returned to gold after August 1914; instead, it simply pegged the exchange rate. Brown's account suggests, however, that contemporaries viewed Uruguay, like its neighbor Argentina, as being effectively on gold, and we code it as such.

United States: Brown (1940, 207–8, 1075).

Yield

See discussion in the text. Yield on long-term gold or sterling government bonds (usually at least 10 years) is measured typically by the coupon-price ratio, with definitions and sources as follows, based on London quotations where available.

Argentina: 1884–1913 from della Paolera (1988). 1914–34 from Nakamura and Zarazaga (2002).

Australia: From GFD. The sterling bonds quoted are the N.S.W. 5 percent Terminable 1874/1902 (1870–87); N.S.W. 4 percent funded Stock 1912 option (1887–1900); all N.S.W. and Commonwealth issues maturing in more than six months (1901–15); 5.25, 5.5 and 5 percent bonds (1920–40). Australian prices are used from 1875 to 1887 and from 1894 to 1915.

Austria: From GFD. For pre-WWI Austria-Hungary the bonds quoted are the Gold 5s (1879–1915); for interwar Austria, the bonds quoted are the 6s of 1923–43 (1923–32) quoted in London and payable in sterling.

Belgium: No prewar yields (except in domestic currency). 1925–33 from the *Wall Street Journal*. The bond is the 7 percent of 1955 quoted in New York and payable in U.S. gold.

Brazil: From GFD. The bonds quoted are the 5s (1870–86); the Gold 4.5s (1887–99); the 4.5s of 1883 (1900–13); the 5s of 1912 (1914); and the Funded 5s of 1914 (1915–37).

Canada: From GFD. The bonds quoted are the 5s (1860–73); 4s of 1910 and 1935 (1874–1924); and Gold 5s of 1952, quoted in New York (1925–40).

Chile: 1870–1918 from GFD. The bonds quoted are the 6s (1870–4); the 5s (1875–86); the 4.5s (1887–1918). 1919–33 from the *Investor's Monthly Manual*, the London *Times*, and the *Economist*. The 4.5 percent Bond of 1886 is used between 1919 and 1930; thereafter the 6 percent Loan of 1929–62. Both debt instruments were issued in London and were payable in sterling.

Denmark: 1919–33 from the *Investor's Monthly Manual*, the London *Times*, and the *Economist*. The bond quoted is the 3 percent Sterling Loan of 1897–1948. This bond was issued by the Danish government in London and was payable in sterling.

Egypt: From GFD. The bonds quoted are the Unified Stock (1870–1931), which had a variable coupon rate of 7 percent through March 1877, 6 percent through June 1882, and 4 percent from July 1883 until 1931.

Finland: 1891–1917 from GFD. 1919–33 from the *Investor's Monthly Manual*, the London *Times*, and the *Economist*. The bond quoted is the 6 percent Sterling Loan of 1923–63. This was issued in London and its associated payments were made in sterling.

France: No prewar yields (except in domestic currency). 1925–33 from the

Wall Street Journal. The bond is the 7 percent of 1949 quoted in New York and payable in U.S. gold.

Germany: No prewar yields (except in domestic currency). 1925–38 from GFD. The bond quoted is the 7 percent Dawes Loan of 1924.

Greece: From GFD. The bonds quoted are the 5s of 1824/1879 (1870–86) and the Monopoly 4s (1887–1924).

Hungary: Not included before WWI; see Austria. From GFD. The bond quoted is the 7.5 percent Dawes Loan of 1924 (1924–39).

India: From GFD. The bonds quoted are the 5s of 1880 (1870–3); 4s of 1888 (1874–80); 3.5s of 1931 (1881–1940).

Italy: 1919–30 from the *Investor's Monthly Manual* and the London *Times*. The bond quoted is the Maremmana Railway Bond issued in London and payable in sterling.

Japan: From GFD. The bonds quoted are the 9s (1870–2); 7s (1873–97) converted to 5s (1898–9); Sterling 4s (1900–23); and 6s of 1924 (1924–38).

Mexico: From GFD. The bonds quoted are the 3s (1870–88); the 6s (1889–99); and the External Gold 5s of 1899 (1900–32).

New Zealand: From GFD. The bonds quoted are the 5s (1870–80); 4s (1881–94); 3s of 1945 (1895–1914); no data 1914–24; 3.5s of 1940 (1925–27); 5s of 1946 (1928–32); 4s of 1952–5 (1933–6); and 3.5s of 1953–7 (1937–40).

Norway: 1870–1918 from GFD. The bonds quoted are the 4.5s, (1876–80); 4s (1881–6); 3.5s (1887–92); and 3s (1893–1918). 1921–31 from the *Investor's Monthly Manual*, the London *Times*, and the *Economist*. The bond quoted is the 6 percent Loan of 1921, issued in London and payable in sterling.

Portugal: From GFD. The bonds quoted are the consols, which had a variable coupon rate of 3 percent through October 1895, 1 percent from November 1895 through 1902, and 3 percent thereafter; no data for 1903, 1920–1, and 1928–30. Data are fourth quarter for 1931–2. June 1929 and 1930 observations from the *Investor's Monthly Manual* and the London *Times*, coupon-price ratio. In July 1924, the Portuguese government unilaterally decided to pay all its foreign currency debt in escudos except to foreign holders of its debt.

South Africa: From GFD. The bonds quoted are the Cape Colony 4.5s and 4s (1884–1913); Union of South Africa 4s and 4.5s (1914–21); and the Union 5 percent Inscribed Debt (1922–40).

Spain: From GFD. The bonds quoted are the 3s (1870–80) converted into 1s (1881), to 4s (1882–1913). Part of the 4 percent perpetual exterior debt of 1882 was payable in foreign currency but only at a fixed exchange rate as written in the bond. This deal was only available to non-Spaniards. After 1913, we have no data, because all bond quotes are in domestic currency.

Sweden: 1919–33 from the *Investor's Monthly Manual*, the London *Times*, and the *Economist*. The bond quoted is the 3.5 percent loan of 1908. This bond was issued by the Swedish government in London and was payable in sterling. The corresponding price is quoted in the *Investor's Monthly Manual* (1919–29) and the *Economist* (1930–33).

Turkey: 1870–1918 from GFD. The bonds quoted are the 6s of 1854 (1870–76); the 4.25 percent External Tribute Bonds (1877–1913); and the Unified 4 percent Bonds (1914–18). 1919–33 from the *Investor's Monthly Manual*, the London *Times*, and the *Economist*. The bond quoted is the Government 4 percent Unified Debt of 1903–62. This bond was issued in London, and its payments were payable in sterling.

United Kingdom: From GFD. The bond quoted is the consol.

United States: 1870–1914 the Calomiris gold rate from Bordo and Rockoff (1996). 1914–39 from GFD. The bonds quoted are the 4s of 1925 (1915–1916); the 4 percent Liberty Bonds (1917–18); and the Federal Reserve Board's 10 to 15 year Treasury Bond index (1919–39).

Uruguay: 1870–1918 from GFD. The bonds quoted yielded 6 percent through 1884, 5 percent from 1885 through February 1893, and 3.5 percent thereafter. 1919–33 from the *Investor's Monthly Manual*, the London *Times*, and the *Economist*. The bond quoted is the government 5 percent Gold Bond of 1914 until 1922 and then the 5 percent External Loan 1919. This debt instrument was issued in London and the associated payments were made in sterling.

Exports

Exports in U.S. dollars are from the collected volumes of Mitchell (1992, 1993, 1995) as collated by Estevadeordal, Frantz, and Taylor (2003), and converted to local currency using the exchange rate.

Public debt

Public debt is total central government debt, unless otherwise stated. From Bordo and Jonung (1996) for the years 1870–1913, and from United Nations (1948) for 1914–39, supplemented as follows.

Argentina: 1884–1913 from della Paolera (1988).

Australia: from Barnard (1987).

Austria: Austria-Hungary 1880–1912 from series provided by Niall Ferguson based on data collected by Marc Flandreau (unpublished).

Brazil: 1880–1910 consolidated (federal, state, and municipal) foreign debt in sterling from IBGE (1990), and domestic debt in contos from Levy (1995).
Chile: 1870–1913 from Mamalakis (1978–89, vol. 6, 493, Table 8.62); thence from U.N. data, with appropriate conversions of some series from (gold) pesos of 6 pence (the interwar parity) to current pesos via the exchange rate series as previously from Braun et al. (2000).
Egypt: 1876–1913 from data provided by Niall Ferguson based on Crouchley (1938). Interwar U.N. data are foreign debt only 1924–8, but the domestic debt (included after 1928) was negligible.
Hungary: Interwar U.N. data are foreign plus domestic long-term debt only 1924–8, but the domestic short-term debt was negligible.
India: From Reserve Bank of India (1954).
New Zealand: From Lloyd Prichard (1970).
Portugal: From Valério (2001, Table 9.7).
Spain: From Barciela López and Carreras (1989, Table 10.31).
Turkey: 1925–8 from Tezel (1986).
Uruguay: Unpublished data from Reto Bertoni, kindly provided by Luis Bértola, and based on the official data from *Anuarios estadísticos*.

Nominal GDP

From the collected volumes of Mitchell (1992, 1993, 1995), collated or augmented by Bordo and Schwartz (1997) and GFD, supplemented as follows.
Argentina: 1884–1939 from della Paolera and Ortiz (1995).
Austria: Austria-Hungary 1880–1913 data provided by Niall Ferguson based on data collected by Marc Flandreau (unpublished).
Belgium: Interpolations for missing data in 1925–6, 1928–9, and 1931–3.
Egypt: From Yousef (2002).
France: From Jones and Obstfeld (2001).
Greece: Missing data 1924–6 from backcast of 1927–9 trend.
Hungary: 1924 based on 1925–6 trends in real GDP per capita and inflation, as below.
India: From Goldsmith (1983).
New Zealand: From Hawke (1975), except 1934–9 from Lineham (1968).
Portugal: From Nunes et al. (1989).
Spain: From Prados de la Escosura (2002).
Uruguay: 1870–1936 real GDP from Bértola (1998) et al., inflated using a price deflator, rescaled, and linked to Bertino and Tajam (2002).

Real GDP per capita

From Maddison (1995), supplemented as follows, and interpolated as necessary.

Argentina: 1884–1939 GDP from della Paolera and Ortiz (1995) and population from Vázquez Présedo (1971–76) scaled to Maddison (1995) 1913 benchmark.

Austria: Austria-Hungary 1880–1913 from Schulze (2000) scaled to Maddison 1913 benchmark, using population weights for Austria and Hungary.

Belgium: 1870–1913 estimate constructed from real GDP index and consumer price index, scaled to Maddison (1995) 1913 benchmark.

Chile: From Braun et al. (2000), scaled to Maddison (1995) 1913 benchmark.

Egypt: From Yousef (2002), scaled to Maddison (2001) 1913 benchmark.

Portugal: From Nunes et al. (1989), scaled to Maddison (2001) 1913 benchmark.

Uruguay: Real GDP from same sources as nominal GDP; population from Maddison (2001) for 1870 and Mitchell (1993) for 1900–39; scaled to Maddison (2001) 1913 benchmark.

Government deficit as a fraction of GDP

From Bordo and Schwartz (1997), supplemented as follows.

Australia: 1871–9 deficit calculated as change in public debt as previously. Nominal GDP as previously.

Austria: Austria-Hungary 1881–1912 deficit data provided by Niall Ferguson based on data collected by Marc Flandreau (unpublished). Austrian interwar deficit calculated as change in public debt as previously. Nominal GDP as previously.

Belgium: Deficit calculated as change in public debt as previously. Nominal GDP as previously.

Chile: From Braun et al. (2000).

Egypt: Deficit calculated as change in public debt as previously. Nominal GDP as previously.

Hungary: Interwar deficit calculated as change in public debt as previously. Nominal GDP as previously.

India: Deficit from Reserve Bank of India (1954). Nominal GDP as previously.

New Zealand: 1890–1939 deficit from Lloyd Prichard (1970). Nominal GDP as previously.

Mexico: Deficit calculated as change in public debt as previously. Nominal GDP as previously.

Portugal: From Valério (2001, Table 9.3). Nominal GDP as previously.
South Africa: Deficit calculated as change in public debt as previously. Nominal GDP as previously.
Spain: From Barciela López and Carreras (1989, Table 10.25). Nominal GDP as previously.

Inflation

Calculated as the rate of change of the consumer price index. From Bordo and Schwartz (1997) and GFD, supplemented as follows.

Argentina: 1870–9 based on Irigoin (2000); 1879–84 based on Cortés Conde (1989); and 1884–1939 based on della Paolera and Ortiz (1995).

Austria: Austria-Hungary 1880–1913 an implicit GDP deflator, based on nominal GDP as previously and real GDP from Schulze (2000).

Brazil: implicit GDP deflator.

Chile: From Braun et al. (2000).

Egypt: an implicit GDP deflator, based on nominal GDP as previously, and real GDP from Yousef (2002).

India: From Goldsmith (1983).

New Zealand: 1870–1914 an implicit GDP deflator, based on nominal GDP as previously, and real GDP from Maddison (1995).

Portugal: From Nunes et al. (1989).

Uruguay: an implicit GDP deflator, from same sources as nominal GDP.

Terms of trade

Deviation of log terms of trade from the panel mean (LTOT). From unpublished data kindly provided by Jeffrey G. Williamson from his ongoing tariff project, supplemented as follows.

Belgium: 1880–1940 from Bordo and Schwartz (1997).

Chile: 1870–1939 from Braun et al. (2000).

Finland: 1870–1939 from Hjerppe (1989).

Default

Dummy variables equal to one when a country is in a state of full (DFLT1) or partial (DFLT2) default, or in either state (DFLT). From unpublished data in Tomz (2001) kindly provided by Michael Tomz.

War

Involvement in a major interstate war (WARINT) or intrastate war (WARCIV), where major means that the state suffers over 2,000 fatalities. From the Correlates of War 2 (COW2) database (http://cow2.la.psu.edu/). See Sarkees (2000).

Bibliography

Abuaf, Niso, and Philippe Jorion. 1990. Purchasing Power Parity in the Long Run. *Journal of Finance* 45 (March): 157–74.

Acemoglu, Daron, Simon Johnson, and James A. Robinson. 2002. Reversal of Fortune: Geography and Institutions in the Making of the Modern World Income Distribution. *Quarterly Journal of Economics* 117 (November): 1231–94.

Alesina, Alberto, Vittorio Grilli, and Gian Maria Milesi-Ferretti. 1994. The Political Economy of Capital Controls. In *Capital Mobility: The Impact on Consumption, Investment and Growth*, edited by Leonardo Leiderman and Assaf Razin. Cambridge: Cambridge University Press.

Alfaro, Laura, Sebnem Kalemli-Ozcan, and Vadym Volosovych. 2003. Why Doesn't Capital Flow from Rich Countries to Poor Countries? An Empirical Investigation. Harvard Business School and University of Houston (April). Photocopy.

Altes, W. L. Korthals. 1996. *Van £ Hollands tot Nederlandse f: De geschiedenis van de Nederlandse geldeenheid*. Amsterdam: NEHA.

Angeletos, George-Marios, Christian Hellwig, and Alessandro Pavan. 2003. Coordination and Policy Traps. Working Paper Series no. 9767, National Bureau of Economic Research (June).

Arellano, Manuel, and Stephen R. Bond. 1991. Some Tests of Specification for Panel Data: Monte Carlo Evidence and an Application to Employment Equations. *Review of Economic Studies* 58 (April): 277–97.

Arellano, Manuel, and Olympia Bover. 1995. Another Look at the Instrumental-Variable Estimation of Error-Components Models. *Journal of Econometrics* 68 (July): 29–52.

Arrow, Kenneth J. 1971. *Essays in the Theory of Risk Bearing*. Chicago: Markham.

Atkin, John Michael. 1977. *British Overseas Investment, 1918–1931.* New York: Arno Press.

Bai, Jushan, Robin L. Lumsdaine, and James H. Stock. 1998. Testing for and Dating Breaks in Stationary and Nonstationary Multivariate Time Series. *Review of Economic Studies* 65 (July): 395–432.

Bairoch, Paul. 1989. European Trade Policy, 1815–1914. In *The Cambridge Economic History of Europe,* vol. 8, edited by Peter Mathias and Sidney Pollard. Cambridge: Cambridge University Press.

Bakker, Age F. P. 1996. *The Liberalization of Capital Movements in Europe: The Monetary Committee and Financial Integration, 1958–1994.* Dordrecht: Kluwer.

Balassa, Bela. 1964. The Purchasing Power Parity Doctrine. *Journal of Political Economy* 72 (December): 584–96.

Baldwin, Richard E. 1992. Measurable Dynamic Gains from Trade. *Journal of Political Economy* 100 (April): 162–74.

Balke, Nathan S., and Mark E. Wohar. 1998. Nonlinear Dynamics and Covered Interest Rate Parity. *Empirical Economics* 23 (December): 535–59.

Banerjee, Anindya, Juan José Dolado, John W. Galbraith, and David F. Hendry. 1997. *Cointegration, Error-Correction, and the Econometric Analysis of Non-stationary Data.* Oxford: Oxford University Press.

Bank of Finland. 1942. *1941 Year Book.* Helsinki: Bank of Finland.

Barajas, Adolfo, and R. Armando Morales. 2002. Explaining Dollarization of Liabilities: Empirical Evidence from Latin America. IMF Working Paper (May).

Barciela López, Carlos, and Albert Carreras. 1989. *Estadísticas historicas de España: Siglos XIX–XX.* Madrid: Fundación Banco Exterior.

Barnard, Alan. 1987. Government Finance. In *Australians: Historical Statistics,* edited by Wray Vamplew. Broadway, New South Wales: Fairfax, Syme & Weldon.

Barrett, Don Carlos. 1931. *The Greenbacks and Resumption of Specie Payments, 1862–1879.* Cambridge, Mass.: Harvard University Press.

Barro, Robert J., and Xavier Sala-i-Martin. 1992. Convergence. *Journal of Political Economy* 100 (April): 223–52.

Basel Committee on Banking Supervision. 1997. *Core Principles for Effective Banking Supervision.* Basel: Bank for International Settlements (September). http:// www.bis.org/publ/bcbs30a.pdf.

Basu, Susanto, and Alan M. Taylor. 1999. International Business Cycles in Historical Perspective. *Journal of Economic Perspectives* 13 (Spring): 45–68.

Baxter, Marianne, and Alan C. Stockman. 1989. Business Cycles and the Exchange-Rate Regime: Some International Evidence. *Journal of Monetary Economics* 23 (May): 377–400.

Bayoumi, Tamim A. 1990. Saving-Investment Correlations: Immobile Capital, Government Policy or Endogenous Behavior? *IMF Staff Papers* 37 (June): 360–87.

Bayoumi, Tamim A. 1997. *Financial Integration and Real Activity*. Ann Arbor, Mich.: University of Michigan Press.

Bekaert, Geert, and Campbell R. Harvey. 1998. Capital Flows and the Behavior of Emerging Market Equity Returns. Working Paper Series no. 6669, National Bureau of Economic Research (July).

Bekaert, Geert, Campbell R. Harvey, and Robin L. Lumsdaine. 1998. Dating the Integration of World Equity Markets. Working Paper Series no. 6274, National Bureau of Economic Research (September).

Bekaert, Geert, Campbell R. Harvey, and Christian Lundblad. 2001. Does Financial Liberalization Spur Growth? Working Paper Series no. 8245, National Bureau of Economic Research (April).

Bekaert, Geert, Campbell R. Harvey, and Christian Lundblad. 2002. Growth Volatility and Equity Market Liberalization. Columbia University, Duke University, and Indiana University (August). Photocopy.

Bernanke, Ben S. 1995. The Macroeconomics of the Great Depression: A Comparative Approach. *Journal of Money, Credit, and Banking* 27 (February): 1–29

Bernanke, Ben S., and Kevin Carey. 1996. Nominal Wage Stickiness and Aggregate Supply in the Great Depression. *Quarterly Journal of Economics* 111 (August): 853–83.

Bernanke, Ben S., and Harold James. 1991. The Gold Standard, Deflation, and Financial Crisis in the Great Depression: An International Comparison. In *Financial Markets and Financial Crises*, edited by R. Glenn Hubbard. Chicago: University of Chicago Press.

Bertino, Magdalena, and Héctor Tajam. 2002. El PBI de Uruguay. Instituto de Economía, Universidad de la República, Montevideo, Uruguay. http://www.iecon.ccee.edu.uy/histo/PBIindice.htm.

Bértola, Luis, et al. 1998. El PBI de Uruguay 1870–1936 y otras estimaciones. CSIC-FCS, Montevideo. Photocopy.

Bhagwati, Jagdish N. 1998. The Capital Myth. *Foreign Affairs* 77 (May–June): 7–12.

Black, Stanley W. 1976. Exchange Policies for Less Developed Countries in a World of Floating Rates. *Princeton Essays in International Finance* 119.

Black, Stanley W. 1991. *A Levite among the Priests: Edward M. Bernstein and the Origins of the Bretton Woods System.* Boulder, Colo.: Westview Press.

Blanchard, Olivier J., and Francesco Giavazzi. 2002. Current Account Deficits in the Euro Area: The End of the Feldstein-Horioka Puzzle? *Brookings Papers on Economic Activity*, no. 2: 147–209.

Blundell, Richard, and Stephen R. Bond. 1998. Initial Conditions and Moment Restrictions in Dynamic Panel Data Models. *Journal of Econometrics* 87 (August): 115–43.

Boarman, Patrick M. 1964. *Germany's Economic Dilemma: Inflation and the Balance of Payments.* New Haven, Conn.: Yale University Press.

Bordo, Michael D. 1993. The Bretton Woods International Monetary System: A Historical Overview. In *A Retrospective on the Bretton Woods System: Lessons for International Monetary Reform*, edited by Michael D. Bordo and Barry J. Eichengreen. Chicago: University of Chicago Press.

Bordo, Michael D., Michael Edelstein, and Hugh Rockoff. 1999. Was Adherence to the Gold Standard a "Good Housekeeping Seal of Approval" During the Interwar Period? Working Paper Series no. 7186, National Bureau of Economic Research (June).

Bordo, Michael D., and Barry J. Eichengreen, eds. 1993. *A Retrospective on the Bretton Woods System: Lessons for International Monetary Reform.* Chicago: University of Chicago Press.

Bordo, Michael D., and Barry J. Eichengreen. 2001. The Rise and Fall of a Barbarous Relic: The Role of Gold in the International Monetary System. In *Money, Capital Mobility, and Trade: Essays in Honor of Robert Mundell*, edited by Guillermo A. Calvo, Rudiger Dornbusch, and Maurice Obstfeld. Cambridge, Mass.: MIT Press.

Bordo, Michael D., Barry J. Eichengreen, and Jongwoo Kim. 1999. Was There Really an Earlier Period of International Financial Integration Comparable to Today? In *The Implications of the Globalization of World Financial Markets*, edited by Allan H. Meltzer. Seoul: Bank of Korea.

Bordo, Michael D., Barry J. Eichengreen, Daniela Klingebiel, and María Soledad Martinez-Peria. 2001. Is the Crisis Problem Growing More Severe? *Economic Policy* 32 (April): 51–82.

Bordo, Michael D., and Marc Flandreau. 2003. Core, Periphery, Exchange Rate Regimes, and Globalization. In *Globalization in Historical Perspective*, edited by Michael D. Bordo, Alan M. Taylor, and Jeffrey G. Williamson. Chicago: University of Chicago Press.

Bordo, Michael D., and Lars Jonung. 1996. Monetary Regimes, Inflation, and Monetary Reform: An Essay in Honor of Axel Leijonhufvud. In *Inflation,*

Institutions, and Information: Essays in Honor of Axel Leijonhufvud, edited by Daniel E. Vaz and Kumaraswamy Velupillai. London: Macmillan.

Bordo, Michael D., and Finn E. Kydland. 1995. The Gold Standard as a Rule: An Essay in Exploration. *Explorations in Economic History* 32 (October): 423–64.

Bordo, Michael D., and Ronald MacDonald. 1997. Violations of the "Rules of the Game" and the Credibility of the Classical Gold Standard, 1880–1914. Working Paper Series no. 6115, National Bureau of Economic Research (July).

Bordo, Michael D., Christopher M. Meissner, and Angela Redish. 2003. How "Original Sin" Was Overcome: The Evolution of External Debt Denominated in Domestic Currencies in the United States and the British Dominions 1800–2000. Working Paper Series no. 9841, National Bureau of Economic Research (July).

Bordo, Michael D., and Hugh Rockoff. 1996. The Gold Standard as a "Good Housekeeping Seal of Approval." *Journal of Economic History* 56 (June): 389–428.

Bordo, Michael D., and Anna J. Schwartz, eds. 1984. *A Retrospective on the Classical Gold Standard, 1821–1931*. Chicago: University of Chicago Press.

Bordo, Michael D., and Anna J. Schwartz. 1997. Monetary Policy Regimes and Economic Performance: The Historical Record. Working Paper Series no. 6201, National Bureau of Economic Research (September).

Bordo, Michael D., Alan M. Taylor, and Jeffrey G. Williamson, eds. 2003. *Globalization in Historical Perspective*. Chicago: University of Chicago Press.

Borenzstein, Eduardo R., Jeromin Zettelmeyer, and Thomas Philippon. 2001. Monetary Independence in Emerging Markets: Does the Exchange Rate Regime Make a Difference? IMF Working Paper 01/1 (January).

Bratter, Herbert M. 1939. Foreign Exchange Control in Latin America. *Foreign Policy Reports* 14 (February): 274–88.

Braun, Juan, Matías Braun, Ignacio Briones, José Díaz, Rolf Lüders, and Gert Wagner. 2000. Economía chilena 1810–1995: Estadísticas históricas. Documento de Trabajo no. 187, Pontificia Universidad Católica de Chile, Instituto de Economía (Enero).

Brecher, Richard A., and Carlos F. Díaz Alejandro. 1977. Tariffs, Foreign Capital, and Immiserizing Growth. *Journal of International Economics* 7 (November): 317–22.

Brewer, John. 1989. *The Sinews of Power: War, Money, and the English State, 1688–1783*. New York: Knopf.

Brezis, Elise S. 1995. Foreign Capital Flows in the Century of Britain's Industrial Revolution: New Estimates, Controlled Conjectures. *Economic History Review* 48 (February): 46–67.

Brissimis, Sophocles N., Heather D. Gibson, and Euclid Tsakalotos. 2002. A Unifying Framework for Analysing Offsetting Capital Flows and Sterilization: Germany and the ERM. *International Journal of Finance and Economics* 7 (January): 63–78.

Broadberry, Steven N., and Mark P. Taylor. 1992. Purchasing Power Parity and Controls in the 1930s. In *Britain in the International Economy*, edited by Steven N. Broadberry and Nicholas F. R. Crafts. Cambridge: Cambridge University Press.

Brown, William Adams, Jr. 1940. *The International Gold Standard Reinterpreted, 1914–1934*. 2 vols. New York: National Bureau of Economic Research.

Bryant, Ralph C. 2003. *Turbulent Waters: Cross-Border Finance and International Governance*. Washington, D.C.: The Brookings Institution.

Butlin, Matthew W. 1977. A Preliminary Annual Database 1900/01 to 1973/74. Research Discussion Paper no. 7701, Reserve Bank of Australia, Canberra (May).

Butlin, Noel G. 1962. *Australian Domestic Product, Investment and Foreign Borrowing 1861–1938/39*. Cambridge: Cambridge University Press.

Cain, Peter J., and Anthony G. Hopkins. 2001. *British Imperialism, 1688–2000*. 2nd ed. Harlow, England: Longman.

Cairncross, Alec. 1985. *Years of Recovery: British Economic Policy 1945–51*. London: Methuen.

Calomiris, Charles W., and R. Glenn Hubbard. 1996. International Adjustment under the Classical Gold Standard: Evidence for the United States and Britain, 1879–1914. In *Modern Perspectives on the Gold Standard*, edited by Tamim Bayoumi, Barry J. Eichengreen, and Mark P. Taylor. Cambridge: Cambridge University Press.

Calomiris, Charles W., and David C. Wheelock. 1998. Was the Great Depression a Watershed for American Monetary Policy? In *The Defining Moment: The Great Depression and the American Economy in the Twentieth Century*, edited by Michael D. Bordo, Claudia D. Goldin, and Eugene N. White. Chicago: University of Chicago Press.

Calvo, Guillermo A. 1998. Capital Flows and Capital-Market Crises: The Simple Economics of Sudden Stops. *Journal of Applied Economics* 1 (November): 35–54.

Calvo, Guillermo A., Leonardo Leiderman, and Carmen M. Reinhart. 1996. Inflows of Capital to Developing Countries in the 1990s. *Journal of Economic Perspectives* 10 (Spring): 123–39.

Calvo, Guillermo A., and Frederic S. Mishkin. 2003. The Mirage of Exchange Rate Regimes for Emerging Market Countries. Working Paper Series no. 9808, National Bureau of Economic Research (June).

Calvo, Guillermo A., and Carmen M. Reinhart. 2001. Fixing for Your Life. In *Brookings Trade Forum 2000*, edited by Susan M. Collins and Dani Rodrik. Washington, D.C.: The Brookings Institution.

Calvo, Guillermo A., and Carmen M. Reinhart. 2002. Fear of Floating. *Quarterly Journal of Economics* 117 (May): 379–408.

Cameron, Rondo E. 1993. *A Concise Economic History of the World: From Paleolithic Times to the Present*. 2nd edition. New York: Oxford University Press.

Campa, José M. 1990. Exchange Rates and Economic Recovery in the 1930s: An Extension to Latin America. *Journal of Economic History* 50 (September): 677–82.

Campillo, Marta, and Jeffrey A. Miron. 1997. Why Does Inflation Differ across Countries? In *Reducing Inflation: Motivation and Strategy*, edited by Christina D. Romer and David H. Romer. Chicago: Unievrsity of Chicago Press.

Caner, Mehmet, and Lutz Kilian. 2001. Size Distortions of Tests of the Null Hypothesis of Stationarity: Evidence and Implications for the PPP Debate. *Journal of International Money and Finance* 20 (October): 639–57.

Capie, Forrest, and Alan Webber. 1985. *A Monetary History of the United Kingdom, 1870–1982*. London: George Allen & Unwin.

Caselli, Francesco, Gerardo Esquivel, and Fernando Lefort. 1996. Reopening the Convergence Debate: A New Look at Cross-Country Growth Empirics. *Journal of Economic Growth* 1 (September): 363–89.

Cassel, Gustav. 1922. *Money and Foreign Exchange after 1914*. New York: Macmillan.

Central Bureau of Statistics of Norway. 1968. *National Accounts 1865–1960*. Oslo: Central Bureau of Statistics of Norway.

Chamley, Christophe. 2003. Dynamic Speculative Attacks. *American Economic Review* 93 (June): 603–21.

Chang, Roberto, and Andrés Velasco. 2001. A Model of Financial Crises in Emerging Markets. *Quarterly Journal of Economics* 116 (May): 489–517.

Cheung, Yin-Wong, and Kon S. Lai. 1998. Parity Revision in Real Exchange Rates During the Post–Bretton Woods Period. *Journal of International Money and Finance* 17 (August): 597–614.

Chortareas, Georgios E., and Rebecca L. Driver. 2001. PPP and the Real Exchange Rate-Real Interest Rate Differential Puzzle Revisited: Evidence from Non-Stationary Panel Data. Working Paper no. 138, Bank of England (June).

Choudhri, Ehsan U., and Levis A. Kochin. 1980. The Exchange Rate and the International Transmission of Business Cycle Disturbances: Some Evidence from the Great Depression. *Journal of Money, Credit and Banking* 12 (November): 565–74.

Clark, Gregory, and Robert C. Feenstra. 2003. Technology in the Great Divergence. In *Globalization in Historical Perspective*, edited by Michael D. Bordo, Alan M. Taylor, and Jeffrey G. Williamson. Chicago: University of Chicago Press.

Clemens, Michael, and Jeffrey G. Williamson. 2002. Wealth Bias in the First Global Capital Market Boom, 1870–1913. Harvard University (May). Photocopy.

Clinton, Kevin J. 1988. Transactions Costs and Covered Interest Arbitrage: Theory and Evidence. *Journal of Political Economy* 96 (April): 358–70.

Cohen, Benjamin J. 1996. Phoenix Risen: The Resurrection of Global Finance. *World Politics* 48 (January): 268–96.

Collins, Susan M. 2003. Probabilities, Probits and the Timing of Currency Crises. Georgetown University (March). Photocopy.

Cook, Lisa D. 2002. Did the Classical Gold Standard Reduce the Price of Capital for Russia? Center for International Development, Harvard University (February). Photocopy.

Cooper, Richard N. 1974. *Economic Mobility and National Economic Policy.* Uppsala: Almqvist & Wiksell.

Corbin, Annie. 2001. Country Specific Effect in the Feldstein-Horioka Paradox: A Panel Data Analysis. *Economics Letters* 72 (September): 297–302.

Cortés Conde, Roberto. 1989. *Dinero, deuda y crisis: Evolución fiscal y monetaria en la Argentina, 1862–1890.* Buenos Aires: Editorial Sudamericana.

Crouchley, Arthur Edwin. 1938. *The Economic Development of Modern Egypt.* London: Longmans Green.

Dam, Kenneth W. 1982. *The Rules of the Game: Reform and Evolution in the International Monetary System.* Chicago: University of Chicago Press.

Davis, Lance E. 1965. The Investment Market, 1870–1914: The Evolution of a National Market. *Journal of Economic History* 25 (September): 355–99.

Davis, Lance E., and Jonathan R. T. Hughes. 1960. A Dollar-Sterling Exchange, 1803–1895. *Economic History Review* 13 (August): 52–78.

Davis, Lance E., and Robert A. Huttenback. 1986. *Mammon and the Pursuit of Empire: The Political Economy of British Imperialism.* Cambridge: Cambridge University Press.

Davis, Lance E., and Robert E. Gallman. 2001. *Evolving Financial Markets and International Capital Flows: Britain, the Americas, and Australia, 1865–1914.* Japan-U.S. Center Sanwa Monographs on International Financial Markets. Cambridge: Cambridge University Press.

De Gregorio, José, and Pablo E. Guidotti. 1995. Financial Development and Economic Growth. *World Development* 23 (March): 433–48.

della Paolera, Gerardo. 1988. How the Argentine Economy Performed during the International Gold Standard: A Reexamination. Ph.D. dissertation, University of Chicago.

della Paolera, Gerardo, and Javier Ortiz. 1995. Dinero, intermediación financiera y nivel de actividad en 110 años de historia económica argentina. Documentos de Trabajo no. 36, Universidad Torcuato Di Tella (December).

della Paolera, Gerardo, and Alan M. Taylor. 2001. *Straining at the Anchor: The Argentine Currency Board and the Search for Macroeconomic Stability, 1880–1935.* NBER Series on Long-Term Factors in Economic Growth. Chicago: University of Chicago Press.

della Paolera, Gerardo, and Alan M. Taylor. 2002. Internal Versus External Convertibility and Emerging-Market Crises: Lessons from Argentine History. *Explorations in Economic History* 39 (October): 357–89.

della Paolera, Gerardo, and Alan M. Taylor. 2003. Gaucho Banking Redux. *Economía* 3 (Spring): 1–42.

De Long, J. Bradford, and Lawrence H. Summers. 1991. Equipment Investment and Economic Growth. *Quarterly Journal of Economics* 106 (May): 445–502.

De Roover, Raymond. 1948. *Money, Banking and Credit in Mediaeval Bruges.* Cambridge, Mass.: The Mediaeval Academy of America.

Deutsche Bundesbank. 1959. Foreign Trade and the Balance of Payments. *Monthly Report of the Deutsche Bundesbank* 11 (January): 43–52.

Díaz Alejandro, Carlos F. 1965. *Exchange-Rate Devaluation in a Semi-Industrialized Country: The Experience of Argentina, 1955–1961.* Cambridge, Mass.: MIT Press.

Díaz Alejandro, Carlos F. 1970. *Essays on the Economic History of the Argentine Republic.* New Haven, Conn.: Yale University Press.

Díaz Alejandro, Carlos F. 1975. Less Developed Countries and the Post-1971

Internatonal Financial System. *Princeton Essays in International Finance* 108.

Díaz Alejandro, Carlos F. 1983. Stories of the 1930s for the 1980s. In *Financial Policies and the World Capital Market: The Problem of Latin American Countries*, edited by Pedro Aspe Armella, Rudiger Dornbusch, and Maurice Obstfeld. Chicago: University of Chicago Press.

Díaz Alejandro, Carlos F. 1984. Latin America in the 1930s. In *Latin America in the 1930s: The Role of the Periphery in World Crisis*, edited by Rosemary Thorp. New York: St. Martin's Press.

Díaz Alejandro, Carlos F. 1985. Good-Bye Financial Repression, Hello Financial Crash. *Journal of Development Economics* 19 (September/October): 1–24.

Dickson, P. G. M. 1967. *The Financial Revolution in England: A Study in the Development of Public Credit, 1688–1756*. London: Macmillan.

Diebold, Francis X., Steven Husted, and Mark Rush. 1991. Real Exchange Rates under the Gold Standard. *Journal of Political Economy* 99 (December): 1252–71.

Dillen, Johannes Gerard van. 1930. Isaac le Maire en de handel in actiën der Oost-Indische Compagnie. *Economisch-Historisch Jaarboek* 16: 1–165.

Dobson, Wendy, and Gary Clyde Hufbauer. 2001. *World Capital Markets: Challenge to the G–10*. Washington, D.C.: Institute for International Economics.

Dowrick, Steven, and Duc-Tho Nguyen. 1989. OECD Comparative Economic Growth 1950–85: Catch-Up and Convergence. *American Economic Review* 79 (December): 1010–30.

Drazen, Allan, and Paul R. Masson. 1994. Credibility of Policies versus Credibility of Policymakers. *Quarterly Journal of Economics* 109 (August): 735–54.

Easterly, William, and Ross Levine. 2001. It's Not Factor Accumulation: Stylized Facts and Growth Models. *World Bank Economic Review* 15 (August): 177–219.

Eatwell, John. 1997. *International Financial Liberalization: The Impact on World Development*. Discussion Paper Series 12. New York: United Nations Development Programme.

Edelstein, Michael. 1981. Foreign Investment and Empire 1860–1914. In *The Economic History of Britain Since 1700*, vol. 2, edited by Roderick Floud and Donald N. McCloskey. Cambridge: Cambridge University Press.

Edelstein, Michael, 1982. *Overseas Investment in the Age of High Imperialism*. New York: Columbia University Press.

Edison, Hali J. 1987. Purchasing Power Parity in the Long Run: A Test of the Dollar/Pound Exchange Rate, 1890–1978. *Journal of Money, Credit and Banking* 19 (August): 376–87.

Edison, Hali J., Joseph E. Gagnon, and William R. Melick. 1994. Understanding the Empirical Literature on Purchasing Power Parity in the Long Run: The Post–Bretton Woods Era. International Finance Discussion Papers no. 465, Board of Governors of the Federal Reserve System.

Edison, Hali J., Michael Klein, Luca Ricci, and Torsten Sløk. 2002. Capital Account Liberalization and Economic Performance: Survey and Synthesis. IMF Working Paper no. 02/120 (July).

Edison, Hali J., Ross Levine, Luca Ricci, and Torsten Sløk. 2002. International Financial Integration and Economic Growth. *Journal of International Money and Finance* 21 (November): 749–76.

Edison, Hali J., and William R. Melick. 1999. Alternative Approaches to Real Exchange Rates and Real Interest Rates: Three Up and Three Down. *International Journal of Finance and Economics* 4 (April): 93–111.

Edison, Hali J., and B. Dianne Pauls. 1993. A Re-Assessment of the Relationship between Real Exchange Rates and Real Interest Rates: 1974–1990. *Journal of Monetary Economics* 31 (April): 165–87.

Edwards, Sebastian. 1986. The Pricing of Bonds and Bank Loans in International Markets: An Empirical Analysis of Developing Countries' Foreign Borrowing. *European Economic Review* 30 (June): 565–89.

Edwards, Sebastian. 1995. *Crisis and Reform in Latin America: From Despair to Hope.* Oxford: Oxford University Press.

Eichengreen, Barry J. 1988. Real Exchange Rate Behavior under Alternative International Monetary Regimes: Interwar Evidence. *European Economic Review* 32 (March): 363–71.

Eichengreen, Barry J. 1990. Trends and Cycles in Foreign Lending. In *Capital Flows in the World Economy*, edited by Horst Siebert. Tübingen: Mohr.

Eichengreen, Barry J. 1991. The Comparative Performance of Fixed and Flexible Exchange Rate Regimes: Interwar Evidence. In *Business Cycles: Theory, Evidence and Analysis*, edited by Niels Thygesen, Kumaraswamy Velupillai, and Stefano Zambelli. New York: New York University Press.

Eichengreen, Barry J. 1992. *Golden Fetters: The Gold Standard and The Great Depression, 1919–1939.* Oxford: Oxford University Press.

Eichengreen, Barry J. 1993. *Reconstructing Europe's Trade and Payments: The European Payments Union.* Ann Arbor, Mich.: University of Michigan Press.

Eichengreen, Barry J. 1996. *Globalizing Capital: A History of the International Monetary System*. Princeton, N.J.: Princeton University Press.

Eichengreen, Barry J. 2001. International Financial Crises: Is the Problem Growing? University of California, Berkeley (August). Photocopy.

Eichengreen, Barry J., and Micahel D. Bordo. 2002. Crises Now and Then: What Lessons from the Last Era of Financial Globalization? Working Paper Series no. 8716, National Bureau of Economic Research.

Eichengreen, Barry J., and Marc Flandreau. 1996. The Geography of the Gold Standard. In *Currency Convertibility: The Gold Standard and Beyond*, edited by Jorge Braga de Macedo, Barry J. Eichengreen, and Jaime Reis. London: Routledge.

Eichengreen, Barry J., and Chang-Tai Hsieh. 1996. Sterling in Decline Again: The 1931 and 1992 Crises Compared. In *European Economic Integration as a Challenge to Industry and Government*, edited by Richard Tilly and Paul J. J. Welfens. Berlin: Springer.

Eichengreen, Barry J., and David Leblang. 2002. Capital Account Liberalization and Growth: Was Mr. Mahathir Right? Working Paper Series no. 9427, National Bureau of Economic Research (December).

Eichengreen, Barry J., and Jeffrey D. Sachs. 1985. Exchange Rates and Economic Recovery in the 1930s. *Journal of Economic History* 45 (December): 925–46.

Einzig, Paul. 1934. *Exchange Control*. London: Macmillan.

Einzig, Paul. 1937. *The Theory of Forward Exchange*. London: Macmillan.

Einzig, Paul. 1968. *Leads and Lags: The Main Cause of Devaluation*. London: Macmillan.

Elliott, Graham. 1999. Efficient Tests for a Unit Root When the Initial Observation Is Drawn from Its Unconditional Distribution. *International Economic Review* 40 (August): 767–83.

Elliott, Graham, Thomas J. Rothenberg, and James H. Stock. 1996. Efficient Tests for an Autoregressive Unit Root. *Econometrica* 64 (July): 813–836.

Ellis, Howard S. 1941. *Exchange Control in Central Europe*. Cambridge, Mass.: Harvard University Press.

Emminger, Otmar. 1977. The D-Mark in the Conflict between Internal and External Equilibrium, 1948–75. *Princeton Essays in International Finance* 122.

Engel, Charles. 2000. Long-Run PPP May Not Hold After All. *Journal of International Economics* 51 (August): 243–73.

Engel, Charles, and John H. Rogers. 1998. Regional Patterns in the Law of One Price: The Roles of Geography vs. Currencies. In *The Regionalization of the World Economy*, edited by Jeffrey A. Frankel. Chicago: University of Chicago Press.

Engel, Charles, and John H. Rogers. 2001. Deviations From Purchasing Power Parity: Causes and Welfare Costs. *Journal of International Economics* 55 (October): 29–57.

Epstein, Gerald A., and Juliet B. Schor. 1992. Structural Determinants and Economic Effects of Capital Controls in OECD Countries. In *Financial Openness and National Autonomy*, edited by Tariq Banuri and Juliet B. Schor. Oxford: Clarendon Press.

Escher, Franklin. 1918. *Elements of Foreign Exchange*. 8th edition. New York: The Bankers Publishing Company.

Estevadeordal, Antoni, Brian Frantz, and Alan M. Taylor. 2003. The Rise and Fall of World Trade, 1870–1939. *Quarterly Journal of Economics* 118 (May): 359–407.

Feenstra, Robert C. 1998. Integration of Trade and Disintegration of Production in the Global Economy. *Journal of Economic Perspectives* 12 (Fall): 31–50.

Feenstra, Robert C. 2004. *Advanced International Trade: Theory and Evidence*. Princeton, N.J.: Princeton University Press.

Feinstein, Charles H. 1990. Britain's Overseas Investments in 1913. *Economic History Review* 43 (May): 288–96.

Feinstein, Charles H., ed. 1995. *Banking, Currency, and Finance in Europe between the Wars*. Oxford: Clarendon Press.

Feinstein, Charles H., Peter Temin, and Gianni Toniolo. 1997. *The European Economy between the Wars*. Oxford: Oxford University Press.

Feis, Herbert. 1931. *Europe, The World's Banker, 1870–1914: An Account of European Foreign Investment and the Connection of World Finance with Diplomacy Before the War*. New Haven, Conn.: Yale University Press.

Feldstein, Martin S. 1983. Domestic Saving and International Capital Movements in the Long Run and the Short Run. *European Economic Review* 21 (March/April): 129–151.

Feldstein, Martin S., and Philippe Bacchetta. 1991. National Savings and International Investment. In *National Saving and Economic Performance*, edited by B. Douglas Bernheim and John B. Shoven. Chicago: University of Chicago Press.

Feldstein, Martin S., and Charles Y. Horioka. 1980. Domestic Saving and International Capital Flows. *Economic Journal* 90 (June): 314–29.

Ferejohn, John A., and Barry R. Weingast, eds. 1997. *The New Federalism: Can the States Be Trusted?* Stanford, Calif.: Hoover Institution Press.

Ferguson, Niall. 2001. *The Cash Nexus: Money and Power in the Modern World, 1700–2000*. New York: Basic Books.

Ferguson, Niall. 2002. Globalization with Gunboats: The Costs and Benefits of the British Empire Revisited. Jesus College, Oxford (April). Photocopy.

Ferguson, Niall. 2003a. British Imperialism Revisited: The Costs and Benefits of "Anglobalization." New York University (January). Photocopy.

Ferguson, Niall. 2003b. *Empire: The Rise and Demise of the British World Order and the Lessons for Global Power*. New York: Basic Books.

Fischer, Stanley. 1998. Capital-Account Liberalization and the Role of the IMF. In Should the IMF Pursue Capital-Account Convertibility? by Stanley Fischer et al. *Princeton Essays in International Finance* 207.

Fischer, Stanley. 2001. Distinguished Lecture on Economics and Government – Exchange Rate Regimes: Is the Bipolar View Correct? *Journal of Economic Perspectives* 15 (Spring): 3–24.

Fischer, Stanley. 2003. Globalization and Its Challenges. *American Economic Review* 93 (May): 1–30.

Fishlow, Albert. 1971. Origins and Consequences of Import Substitution in Brazil. In *International Economics and Development: Essays in Honor of Raúl Prebisch*, edited by Luis Eugenio Di Marco. New York: Academic Press.

Flandreau, Marc, Jacques Le Cacheux, and Frédéric Zumer. 1998. Stability Without a Pact? Lessons from the European Gold Standard, 1880–1914. *Economic Policy* 26 (April): 115–62.

Flandreau, Marc, and Marie-Chantale Rivière. 1999. La Grande "retransformation"? L'Intégration financière internationale et contrôles de capitaux, 1880–1996. *Économie Internationale* 78 (Deuxième trimestre): 11–58.

Flandreau, Marc, and Nathan Sussman. 2002. Old Sins: Exchange Clauses and European Foreign Lending in the 19th Century. Institut d'Études Politiques, Paris (July). Photocopy.

Frankel, Jeffrey A. 1984. *The Yen/Dollar Agreement: Liberalizing Japanese Capital Markets*. Washington, D.C.: Institute for International Economics.

Frankel, Jeffrey A. 1986. International Capital Mobility and Crowding Out in the U.S. Economy: Imperfect Integration of Financial Markets and Goods Markets? In *How Open Is the U.S. Economy?*, edited by R. W. Hafer. Lexington, Mass.: Lexington Books.

Frankel, Jeffrey A. 1991. Quantifying International Capital Mobility in the 1980s. In *National Saving and Economic Performance*, edited by B. Douglas Bernheim and John B. Shoven. Chicago: University of Chicago Press.

Frankel, Jeffrey A. 1999. No Single Currency Regime Is Right for All Countries or at All Times. *Princeton Essays in International Finance* 215.

Frankel, Jeffrey A., and David Romer. 1999. Does Trade Cause Growth? *American Economic Review* 89 (June): 379–99.

Frankel, Jeffrey A., and Andrew K. Rose. 1996. A Panel Project on Purchasing Power Parity: Mean Reversion Within and Between Countries. *Journal of International Economics* 40 (February): 209–24.

Frankel, Jeffrey A., Sergio L. Schmukler, and Luis Servén. 2000. Global Transmission of Interest Rates: Monetary Independence and Currency Regime. The World Bank (August). Photocopy.

Frankel, Jeffrey A., Sergio L. Schmukler, and Luis Servén. 2002. Global Transmission of Interest Rates: Monetary Independence and Currency Regime. Working Paper Series no. 8828, National Bureau of Economic Research (March).

Fratianni, Michele, and Franco Spinelli. 1984. Italy in the Gold Standard Period, 1861–1914. In *A Retrospective on the Classical Gold Standard, 1821–1931*, edited by Michael D. Bordo and Anna J. Schwartz. Chicago: University of Chicago Press.

Frenkel, Jacob. 1981. The Collapse of Purchasing Power Parities During the 1970s. *European Economic Review* 16 (May): 145–65.

Frieden, Jeffry A. 1997. Monetary Populism in Nineteenth-Century America: An Open Economy Interpretation. *Journal of Economic History* 57 (June): 367–95.

Friedman, Milton. 1953. The Case for Flexible Exchange Rates. In *Essays in Positive Economics*. Chicago: University of Chicago Press.

Fritsch, Winston. 1988. *External Constraints on Economic Policy in Brazil, 1889–1930*. Pittsburgh, Pa.: University of Pittsburgh Press.

Froot, Kenneth A., and Kenneth S. Rogoff. 1995. Perspectives on PPP and Long-Run Real Exchange Rates. In *Handbook of International Economics*, vol. 3, edited by Gene Grossman and Kenneth S. Rogoff. Amsterdam: North Holland.

Fujii, Eiji, and Menzie D. Chinn. 2000. Fin de Siècle Real Interest Parity. Working Paper Series no 7880, National Bureau of Economic Research (September).

Gallarotti, Giulio M. 1995. *The Anatomy of an International Monetary Regime: The Classical Gold Standard 1880–1914*. New York: Oxford University Press.

Gardner, Richard N. 1980. *Sterling-Dollar Diplomacy in Current Perspective*. New York: Columbia University Press.

Gerschenkron, Alexander. 1943. *Bread and Democracy in Germany*. Berkeley and Los Angeles: University of California Press.

Giavazzi, Francesco, and Alberto Giovannini. 1989. *Limiting Exchange Rate Flexibility: The European Monetary System*. Cambridge: MIT Press.

Giovannini, Alberto. 1993. Bretton Woods and Its Precursors: Rules versus Discretion in the History of International Monetary Regimes. In *A Retrospective on the Bretton Woods System: Lessons for International Monetary Reform*, edited by Michael D. Bordo and Barry J. Eichengreen. Chicago: University of Chicago Press.

Glaeser, Edward L., and Andrei Shleifer. 2002. Legal Origins. *Quarterly Journal of Economics* 117 (November): 1193–229.

Glen, Jack D. 1992. Real Exchange Rates in the Short, Medium, and Long Run. *Journal of International Economics* 33 (August): 147–66.

Glick, Reuven, and Michael M. Hutchison. 2004. Capital Controls and Exchange Rate Instability in Developing Economies. *Journal of International Money and Finance*. Forthcoming.

Goldsmith, Raymond W. 1983. *The Financial Development of India, 1860–1977*. New Haven, Conn.: Yale University Press.

Goldsmith, Raymond W. 1985. *Comparative National Balance Sheets: A Study of Twenty Countries, 1688–1978*. Chicago: University of Chicago Press.

Gordon, Margaret S. 1941. *Barriers to World Trade*. New York: Macmillan.

Goschen, George J. 1861. *The Theory of the Foreign Exchanges*. London: Effingham Wilson.

Gourinchas, Pierre-Olivier, and Olivier Jeanne. 2003. The Elusive Gains from International Financial Integration. Working Paper Series no. 9684, National Bureau of Economic Research (May).

Granger, Clive W. J., and Paul Newbold. 1974. Spurious Regressions in Econometrics. *Journal of Econometrics* 2 (1974): 111–20.

Green, Alan, and Malcolm C. Urquhart. 1976. Factor and Commodity Flows in the International Economy of 1870–1914: A Multi-Country View. *Journal of Economic History* 36 (March): 217–52.

Grilli, Vittorio, and Gian Maria Milesi-Ferretti. 1995. Economic Effects and Structural Determinants of Capital Controls. *IMF Staff Papers* 42 (September): 517–51.

Haberler, Gottfried. 1976. *The World Economy, Money, and the Great Depression 1919–1939*. Foreign Affairs Study 30. Washington, D.C.: American Enterprise Institute.

Hakkio, Craig S., and Mark Rush. 1991. Is the Budget Deficit "Too Large"? *Economic Inquiry* 29 (July): 429–45.

Hall, Alan R., ed. 1968. *The Export of Capital from Britain 1870–1914*. London: Methuen.

Hall, Robert E., and Charles I. Jones. 1999. Why Do Some Countries Produce So Much More Output per Worker than Others? *Quarterly Journal of Economics* 114 (February): 83–116.

Hallwood, C. Paul, Ronald MacDonald, and Ian W. Marsh. 1996. Credibility and Fundamentals: Were the Classical and Interwar Gold Standards Well-Behaved Target Zones? In *Modern Perspectives on the Gold Standard*, edited by Tamim Bayoumi, Barry J. Eichengreen and Mark P. Taylor. Cambridge: Cambridge University Press.

Hamilton, James D. 1988. The Role of the International Gold Standard in Propagating the Great Depression. *Contemporary Policy Issues* 6 (April): 67–89.

Hamori, Shigeyuki, and Akira Tokihisa. 1997. Testing for a Unit Root in the Presence of a Variance Shift. *Economics Letters* 57 (December): 245–53.

Haque, Nadeem Ul, Manmohan S. Kumar, Nelson Mark, and Donald J. Mathieson. 1996. The Economic Content of Indicators of Developing Country Creditworthiness. *International Monetary Fund Staff Papers* 43 (December): 688–724.

Harrod, Roy F. 1951. *The Life of John Maynard Keynes*. London: Macmillan.

Hatton, Timothy J., and Jeffrey G. Williamson. 1994. *Migration and the International Labor Market, 1850–1939*. London: Routledge.

Haupt, Ottomar. 1894. *Arbitrages et parités*. 8th edition. Paris: Librairie Truchy.

Hausman, Jerry A. 1978. Specification Tests in Econometrics. *Econometrica* 6 (November): 1251–71.

Hawke, Gary R. 1975. Income Estimation from Monetary Data: Further Explorations. *Review of Income and Wealth* 21 (September): 301–7.

Hawtrey, Ralph G. 1947. *The Gold Standard in Theory and Practice*. 5th edition. London: Longmans Green.

Helleiner, Eric. 1994. *States and the Reemergence of Global Finance: From Bretton Woods to the 1990s*. Ithaca: Cornell University Press.

Henry, Peter B. 2000a. Stock Market Liberalization, Economic Reform, and Emerging Market Equity Prices. *Journal of Finance* 55 (April): 529–64.

Henry, Peter B. 2000b. Do Stock Market Liberalizations Cause Investment Booms? *Journal of Financial Economics* 58 (October-November): 301–34.

Higgins, Matthew D. 1993. Why Capital Doesn't Flow From Rich to Poor Countries. Harvard University. Photocopy.

Higgins, Matthew, and Egon Zakrajšek. 1999. Purchasing Power Parity: Three

Stakes Through the Heart of the Unit Root Null. Staff Report no. 80, Federal Reserve Bank of New York (June).

Hjerppe, Riitta. 1989. *The Finnish Economy 1860–1985: Growth and Structural Change*. Translated by Richard Walker. Helsinki: Bank of Finland.

Horsefield, J. Keith, ed. 1969. *The International Monetary Fund 1945–1965*, vol. 3. Washington, D.C.: International Monetary Fund.

Houghton, John. 1681. *A Collection of Letters for the Improvement of Husbandry & Trade*. London: Printed for John Lawrence.

Hsieh, Chang-Tai, and Peter J. Klenow. 2003. Relative Prices and Relative Prosperity. Working Paper Series no. 9701, National Bureau of Economic Research (May).

Hughes, Jonathan R. T. 1991. *The Governmental Habit Redux: Economic Controls from Colonial Times to the Present*. 2nd edition. Princeton, N.J.: Princeton University Press.

IBGE (Fundação Instituto Brasileiro de Geografia e Estatística). 1990. *Estatísticas históricas do Brasil: Séries econômicas, demográficas e sociais de 1550 a 1988*. Rio de Janeiro: IBGE.

INEGI. 1994. *Estadísticas históricas de México*. INEGI: Aguascalientes, México.

International Monetary Fund. 1998. The IMF's Response to the Asian Crisis. Washington, D.C.: International Monetary Fund (June 15). http://www.imf.org/External/np/exr/facts/asia.HTM.

International Monetary Fund. Various dates. *World Economic Outlook*. Washington, D.C.: International Monetary Fund.

International Monetary Fund. Various dates. *Annual Report on Exchange Arrangements and Exchange Restrictions*.

Irigoin, Maria Alejandra. 2000. Inconvertible Paper Money, Inflation and Economic Performance in Early Nineteenth Century Argentina. *Journal of Latin American Studies* 32 (May): 333–59.

Irwin, Douglas A. 1996. *Against the Tide: An Intellectual History of Free Trade*. Princeton, N.J.: Princeton University Press.

Isserlis, L. 1938. Tramp Shipping Cargoes, and Freights. *Journal of the Royal Statistical Society* 101, no. 1: 53–146.

Ito, Takatoshi. 1992. *The Japanese Economy*. Cambridge, Mass.: MIT Press.

James, Harold. 2001. *The End of Globalization: Lessons from the Great Depression*. Cambridge, Mass.: Harvard University Press.

Jansen, W. Jos. 1996. Estimating Saving-Investment Correlations: Evidence for OECD Countries Based on an Error Correction Model. *Journal of International Money and Finance* 15 (October): 749–81.

Jansen, W. Jos. 1997. Can the Intertemporal Budget Constraint Explain the Feldstein-Horioka Puzzle? *Economics Letters* 56 (September): 77–83.

Jansen, W. Jos, and Günther G. Schulze. 1996. Theory-Based Measurement of the Saving-Investment Correlation with an Application to Norway. *Economic Inquiry* 34 (January): 116–32.

Johnson, David R. 1990. Cointegration, Error Correction, and Purchasing Power Parity Between Canada and the United States. *Canadian Journal of Economics* 23 (November): 839–55.

Johnson, Simon, and Todd Mitton. 2001. Cronyism and Capital Controls: Evidence from Malaysia. Working Paper Series no. 8521, National Bureau of Economic Research (October).

Jones, Charles I. 1994. Economic Growth and the Relative Price of Capital. *Journal of Monetary Economics* 34 (December): 359–82.

Jones, Matthew T., and Maurice Obstfeld. 2001. Saving, Investment, and Gold: A Reassessment of Historical Current Account Data. In *Money, Capital Mobility, and Trade: Essays in Honor of Robert Mundell*, edited by Guillermo A. Calvo, Rudiger Dornbusch, and Maurice Obstfeld. Cambridge, Mass.: MIT Press.

Kalemli-Ozcan, Sebnem, Bent E. Sørensen, and Oved Yosha. 2003. Risk Sharing and Industrial Specialization: Regional and International Evidence. *American Economic Review* 93 (June): 903–18.

Kaminsky, Graciela L., and Carmen M. Reinhart. 1999. The Twin Crises: The Causes of Banking and Balance-of-Payments Problems. *American Economic Review* 89 (June): 473–500.

Kaminsky, Graciela L., and Sergio L. Schmukler. 2003. Short-Run Pain, Long-Run Gain: The Effects of Financial Liberalization. Working Paper Series no. 9787, National Bureau of Economic Research (June).

Kaplan, Jacob J., and Günther Schleiminger. 1989. *The European Payments Union: Financial Diplomacy in the 1950s*. Oxford: Clarendon Press.

Kapstein, Ethan B. 1994. *Governing the Global Economy: International Finance and the State*. Cambridge, Mass.: Harvard University Press.

Kaufmann, Daniel, Aart Kraay, and Pablo Zoido-Lobaton. 2002. Governance Matters II: Updated Indicators for 2000–01. World Bank Policy Research Department. Photocopy.

Keynes, John Maynard. 1971. *The Economic Consequences of the Peace. The Collected Writings of John Maynard Keynes*, vol. 2, edited by Donald E. Moggridge. London: Macmillan.

Keynes, John Maynard. 1978. *Activities 1939–1945: Internal War Finance.*

The Collected Writings of John Maynard Keynes, vol. 22, edited by Donald
    E. Moggridge. London: Macmillan.

Keynes, John Maynard. 1980a. *Activities 1940–1944: Shaping the Post-
    War World: The Clearing Union. The Collected Writings of John Maynard
    Keynes*, vol. 25, edited by Donald E. Moggridge. London: Macmillan.

Keynes, John Maynard. 1980b. *Activities 1941–1946: Shaping the Post-
    War World: Bretton Woods and Reparations. The Collected Writings of
    John Maynard Keynes*, vol. 26, edited by Donald E. Moggridge. London:
    Macmillan.

Keynes, John Maynard. 1982. *Activities 1931–1939: World Crises and Policies
    in Britain and America. The Collected Writings of John Maynard Keynes*,
    vol. 21, edited by Donald E. Moggridge. London: Macmillan.

Kim, Yoonbai. 1990. Purchasing Power Parity in the Long Run: A Cointe-
    gration Approach. *Journal of Money, Credit and Banking* 22 (November):
    491–503.

Kindleberger, Charles P. 1965. Balance-of-Payments Deficits and the Inter-
    national Market for Liquidity. *Princeton Essays in International Finance*
    46.

Kindleberger, Charles P. 1978. *Manias, Panics, and Crashes: A History of
    Financial Crises*. New York: Basic Books.

Kindleberger, Charles P. 1984. *A Financial History of Western Europe*. Lon-
    don: George Allen & Unwin.

Kindleberger, Charles P. 1986. *The World in Depression, 1929–1939*. Revised
    edition. Berkeley and Los Angeles: University of California Press.

King, Robert G., and Ross Levine. 1993. Finance and Growth: Schumpeter
    Might Be Right. *Quarterly Journal of Economics* 108 (August): 717–38.

Klein, Michael W. 2003. Capital Account Openness and the Varieties of Growth
    Experience. Working Paper Series no. 9500, National Bureau of Economic
    Research (February).

Klein, Michael W., and Giovanni Olivei. 2000. Capital Account Liberaliza-
    tion, Financial Depth, and Economic Growth. Fletcher School of Law and
    Diplomacy, Tufts University. Photocopy.

Klenow, Peter J., and Andrés Rodríguez-Clare. 1997. The Neoclassical Revival
    in Growth Economics: Has It Gone Too Far? In *NBER Macroeconomics An-
    nual 1997* 12, edited by Ben S. Bernanke and Julio J. Rotemberg. Cambridge,
    Mass.: MIT Press.

Klug, Adam, and Gregor W. Smith. 1999. Suez and Sterling, 1956. *Explo-
    rations in Economic History* 36 (July): 181–203.

Kraay, Aart, and Jaume Ventura. 2000. Current Accounts in Debtor and Creditor Countries. *Quarterly Journal of Economics* 115 (November): 1137–66.

Krueger, Anne O. 2002. Sovereign Debt Restructuring Mechanism: One Year Later. http://www.imf.org/external/np/speeches/2002/111202.htm.

Krugman, Paul R. 1991. Target Zones and Exchange Rate Dynamics. *Quarterly Journal of Economics* 106 (August): 669–82.

Krugman, Paul R., and Maurice Obstfeld. 2000. *International Economics: Theory and Policy.* 5th edition. Reading, Mass.: Addison Wesley.

Lane, Philip, and Gian Maria Milesi-Ferretti. 2001a. The External Wealth of Nations: Measures of Foreign Assets and Liabilities for Industrial and Developing Countries. *Journal of International Economics* 55 (December): 243–62.

Lane, Philip, and Gian Maria Milesi-Ferretti. 2001b. Long-Term Capital Movements. In *NBER Macroeconomics Annual 2001* 16, edited by Ben S. Bernanke and Kenneth S. Rogoff. Cambridge, Mass.: MIT Press.

Leachman, Lori. 1991. Saving, Investment and Capital Mobility among OECD Countries. *Open Economies Review* 2, no. 1:137–63.

League of Nations. 1938a. *Report on Exchange Control.* Geneva: League of Nations.

League of Nations. 1938b. *World Production and Prices, 1937/1938.* Geneva: League of Nations.

Lee, Moon H. 1978. *Purchasing Power Parity.* New York: Marcel Dekker.

Lester, Richard A. 1939. *Monetary Experiments: Early American and Recent Scandinavian.* Princeton, N.J.: Princeton University Press.

Levine, Ross, and David Renelt. 1992. A Sensitivity Analysis of Cross-Country Growth Regressions. *American Economic Review* 82 (September): 942–63.

Levy Yeyati, Eduardo, and Federico Sturzenegger. 2000. Classifying Exchange Rate Regimes: Deeds vs. Words. Universidad Torcuato Di Tella. Photocopy.

Levy, Maria B. 1995. The Brazilian Public Debt: Domestic and Foreign, 1824–1913. In *The Public Debt in Latin America in Historical Perspective,* edited by Reinhard Liehr. Frankfurt: Vervuert.

Lewis, Cleona. 1938. *America's Stake in International Investments.* Washington, D.C.: The Brookings Institution.

Lewis, Cleona. 1945. *Debtor and Creditor Countries: 1938, 1944* (August). Washington, D.C.: The Brookings Institution.

Lewis, Karen K. 1999. Trying to Explain Home Bias in Equities and Consumption. *Journal of Economic Literature* 37 (June): 571–608.

Lindert, Peter H. 1994. The Rise of Social Spending, 1880–1930. *Explorations in Economic History* 31 (January): 1–37.

Lindert, Peter H. 2004. *Social Spending and Economic Growth since the Eighteenth Century.* 2 vols. Cambridge: Cambridge University Press. Forthcoming.

Lindert, Peter H., and Jeffrey G. Williamson. 2003. Does Globalization Make the World More Unequal? In *Globalization in Historical Perspective*, edited by Michael D. Bordo, Alan M. Taylor, and Jeffrey G. Williamson. Chicago: University of Chicago Press.

Lindsey, Brink. 2002. *Against the Dead Hand: The Uncertain Struggle for Global Capitalism.* New York: Wiley.

Lineham, B. T. 1968. New Zealand's Gross Domestic Product, 1918–1938. *New Zealand Economic Papers* 2, no. 2:15–26.

Lloyd Prichard, Muriel F. 1970. *An Economic History of New Zealand to 1939.* Auckland: Collins.

Lothian, James R. 1990. A Century Plus of Yen Exchange Rate Behavior. *Japan and the World Economy* 2 (March): 47–70.

Lothian, James R. 2002. The Internationalization of Money and Finance and the Globalization of Financial Markets. *Journal of International Money and Finance* 21 (November): 699–724.

Lothian, James R., and Mark P. Taylor. 1996. Real Exchange Rate Behavior: The Recent Float From the Perspective of the Past Two Centuries. *Journal of Political Economy* 104 (June): 488–509.

Lucas, Robert E., Jr. 1990. Why Doesn't Capital Flow from Rich to Poor Countries? *American Economic Review* 80 (May): 92–96.

Macaulay, Frederick R. 1938. *Some Theoretical Problems Suggested by the Movements of Interest Rates, Bond Yields and Stock Prices in the United States Since 1856.* New York: National Bureau of Economic Research.

MacDonald, Ronald, and Jun Nagayasu. 2000. The Long-Run Relationship Between Real Exchange Rates and Real Interest Rate Differentials: A Panel Study. *International Monetary Fund Staff Papers* 47 (November): 116–28.

Maddison, Angus. 1991. *Dynamic Forces in Capitalist Development: A Long-Run Comparative View.* Oxford: Oxford University Press.

Maddison, Angus. 1995. *Monitoring the World Economy.* Paris: OECD.

Maddison, Angus. 2001. *The World Economy: A Millennial Perspective.* Paris: OECD.

Mamalakis, Markos J. 1978–89. *Historical Statistics of Chile.* 6 vols. Westport, Conn.: Greenwood Press.

Mankiw, N. Gregory, David Romer, and David N. Weil. 1992. A Contribution to the Empirics of Economic Growth. *Quarterly Journal of Economics* 107 (May): 407–37.

Margraff, Anthony W. 1908. *International Exchange: Its Terms, Parts, Operations and Scope*. 3rd edition. Chicago: Privately printed.

Marion, Nancy P. 1999. Some Parallels between Currency and Banking Crises. In *International Finance and Financial Crises: Essays in Honor of Robert P. Flood, Jr.*, edited by Peter Isard, Assaf Razin, and Andrew K. Rose. Boston: Kluwer.

Marshall, Monty G., and Keith Jaggers. 2002. Polity IV Project: Political Regime Characteristics and Transitions, 1800–2000, Dataset and User's Manual. University of Maryland, Center for International Development and Conflict Management, College Park, Md.

Marston, Richard C. 1995. *International Financial Integration: A Study of Interest Differentials Between the Major Industrial Countries*. Japan-U.S. Center Sanwa Monographs on International Financial Markets. Cambridge: Cambridge University Press.

Martín Aceña, Pablo. 2000. The Spanish Monetary Experience, 1848–1914. In *Monetary Standards in the Periphery: Paper, Silver, and Gold, 1854–1933*, edited by Pablo Martín Aceña and Jaime Reis. New York: St. Martin's Press.

Matsukata, Masayoshi. 1899. *Report on the Adoption of the Gold Standard in Japan*. Tokyo: Government Press.

Mazumdar, Joy. 1996. Do Static Gains from Trade Lead to Medium-Run Growth? *Journal of Political Economy* 104 (December): 1328–37.

McCloskey, Donald N., and J. Richard Zecher. 1984. The Success of Purchasing Power Parity: Historical Evidence and its Implications for Macroeconomics. In *A Retrospective on the Classical Gold Standard, 1880–1913*, edited by Michael D. Bordo and Anna J. Schwartz. Chicago: University of Chicago Press.

McKinnon, Ronald I. 1979. *Money in International Exchange: The Convertible Currency System*. New York: Oxford University Press.

McLean, Ian W. 1994. Saving in Settler Economies: Australian and North American Comparisons. *Explorations in Economic History* 31 (October): 432–52.

Meese, Richard A., and Kenneth S. Rogoff. 1988. Was It Real? The Exchange Rate-Interest Differential Relation over the Modern Floating-Rate Period. *Journal of Finance* 43 (February): 933–48.

Meissner, Christopher M. 2002. A New World Order: Explaining the Emergence of the Classical Gold Standard. Working Paper Series no. 9233, National Bureau of Economic Research (October).

Mikesell, Raymond F. 1954. *Foreign Exchange in the Postwar World*. New York: Twentieth Century Fund.

Miller, Stephen M. 1988. Are Saving and Investment Cointegrated? *Economic Letters* 27, no. 1:31–34.

Mitchell, Brian R. 1992. *International Historical Statistics: Europe, 1750–1988*. New York: Stockton Press.

Mitchell, Brian R. 1993. *International Historical Statistics: The Americas, 1750–1988*. New York: Stockton Press.

Mitchell, Brian R. 1995. *International Historical Statistics: Africa, Asia & Oceania, 1750–1988*. New York: Stockton Press.

Mitchell, Wesley C. 1908. *Gold, Prices, and Wages under the Greenback Standard*. Berkeley, Calif.: The University Press.

Moggridge, Donald E. 1971. British Controls on Long Term Capital Movements, 1924–1931. In *Essays on a Mature Economy: Britain after 1840*, edited by Donald N. McCloskey. London: Methuen.

Morgenstern, Oskar. 1959. *International Financial Transactions and Business Cycles*. Princeton, N.J.: Princeton University Press.

Morris, Stephen, and Hyun Song Shin. 1998. Unique Equilibrium in a Model of Self-Fulfilling Currency Attacks. *American Economic Review* 88 (June): 587–97.

Muller, Jerry Z. 2002. *The Mind and the Market: Capitalism in Modern European Thought*. New York: Alfred A. Knopf.

Mundell, Robert A. 1957. International Trade and Factor Mobility. *American Economic Review* 47 (June): 321–35.

Nakamura, Leonard I., and Carlos E. J. M. Zarazaga. 2003. Banking and Finance, 1900–35. In *A New Economic History of Argentina*, edited by Gerardo della Paolera and Alan M. Taylor. Cambridge: Cambridge University Press.

Neal, Larry. 1990. *The Rise of Financial Capitalism: International Capital Markets in the Age of Reason*. Cambridge: Cambridge University Press.

Neal, Larry. 2000. How It All Began: The Monetary and Financial Architecture of Europe during the First Global Capital Markets, 1648–1815. *Financial History Review* 7 (October): 117–40.

Neal, Larry, and Marc Weidenmier. 2003. Crises in the Global Economy from Tulips to Today: Contagion and Consequences. In *Globalization in Historical Perspective*, edited by Michael D. Bordo, Alan M. Taylor, and Jeffrey G. Williamson. Chicago: University of Chicago Press.

Nelson, Richard R., and Gavin Wright. 1992. The Rise and Fall of American Technological Leadership. *Journal of Economic Literature* 30 (December): 1931–64.

Ng, Serena, and Pierre Perron. 2001. Lag Length Selection and the Construction of Unit Root Tests with Good Size and Power. *Econometrica* 69 (November): 1519–54.

Nugent, Walter T. K. 1992. *Crossings: The Great Transatlantic Migrations, 1870–1914.* Bloomington, Ind.: Indiana University Press.

Nunes, Ana Bela, Eugénia Mata, and Nuno Valério. 1989. Portuguese Economic Growth 1833–1985. *Journal of European Economic History* 18 (Fall): 291–330.

Nurkse, Ragnar. 1944. *International Currency Experience: Lessons of the Inter-war Period.* Geneva: League of Nations.

Nurkse, Ragnar. 1954. International Investment Today in the Light of Nineteenth-Century Experience. *Economic Journal* 64 (December): 744–58.

Obstfeld, Maurice. 1982. Can We Sterilize? Theory and Evidence. *American Economic Review* 72 (May): 45–50.

Obstfeld, Maurice. 1986. Capital Mobility in the World Economy: Theory and Measurement. *Carnegie-Rochester Conference Series on Public Policy* 24.

Obstfeld, Maurice. 1993a. Model Trending Real Exchange Rates. Working Paper no. C93-011, Center for International and Development Economics Research (February).

Obstfeld, Maurice. 1993b. The Adjustment Mechanism. In *A Retrospective on the Bretton Woods System: Lessons for International Monetary Reform*, edited by Michael D. Bordo and Barry J. Eichengreen. Chicago: University of Chicago Press.

Obstfeld, Maurice. 1994a. Risk-Taking, Global Diversification, and Growth. *American Economic Review* 85 (December): 1310–29.

Obstfeld, Maurice. 1994b. The Logic of Currency Crises. *Cahiers Economiques et Monétaires*, no. 43: 189–213.

Obstfeld, Maurice. 1995. International Capital Mobility in the 1990s. In *Understanding Interdependence: The Macroeconomics of the Open Economy*, edited by Peter B. Kenen. Princeton, N.J.: Princeton University Press.

Obstfeld, Maurice. 1996. Models of Currency Crises with Self-fulfilling Features. *European Economic Review* 40 (April): 1037–47.

Obstfeld, Maurice. 1998. The Global Capital Market: Benefactor or Menace? *Journal of Economic Perspectives* 12 (Fall): 9–30.

Obstfeld, Maurice. 2002. Concluding Panel Discussion: The Role of Central Banks in Exchange Rate Regimes in the 21st Century. Panelists' Remarks. *Monetary and Economic Studies* 20 (December): 251–5.

Obstfeld, Maurice, and Kenneth S. Rogoff. 1995. The Mirage of Fixed Exchange Rates. *Journal of Economic Perspectives* 9 (Fall): 73–96.

Obstfeld, Maurice, and Kenneth S. Rogoff. 1996. *Foundations of International Macroeconomics.* Cambridge, Mass.: MIT Press.

Obstfeld, Maurice, and Kenneth S. Rogoff. 2000. The Six Major Puzzles in International Macroeconomics: Is There a Common Cause? In *NBER Macroeconomics Annual 2000* 15, edited by Ben S. Bernanke and Kenneth S. Rogoff. Cambridge, Mass.: MIT Press.

Obstfeld, Maurice, Jay C. Shambaugh, and Alan M. Taylor. 2003. The Trilemma in History: Tradeoffs among Exchange Rates, Monetary Policies, and Capital Mobility. University of California, Berkeley (March). Photocopy.

Obstfeld, Maurice, and Alan M. Taylor. 1997. Nonlinear Aspects of Goods-Market Arbitrage and Adjustment: Heckscher's Commodity Points Revisited. *Journal of the Japanese and International Economies* 11 (December): 441–79.

Obstfeld, Maurice, and Alan M. Taylor. 1998. The Great Depression as a Watershed: International Capital Mobility in the Long Run. In *The Defining Moment: The Great Depression and the American Economy in the Twentieth Century,* edited by Michael D. Bordo, Claudia D. Goldin, and Eugene N. White. Chicago: University of Chicago Press.

Obstfeld, Maurice, and Alan M. Taylor. 2003. Globalization and Capital Markets. In *Globalization in Historical Perspective,* edited by Michael D. Bordo, Alan M. Taylor, and Jeffrey G. Williamson. Chicago: University of Chicago Press.

O'Connell, Paul G. J. 1996. The Overvaluation of Purchasing Power Parity. Harvard University (January). Photocopy.

O'Connell, Paul G. J. 1998. The Overvaluation of Purchasing Power Parity. *Journal of International Economics* 44 (February): 1–19.

Officer, Lawrence H. 1982. *Purchasing Power Parity and Exchange Rates: Theory, Evidence and Relevance.* Greenwich, Conn.: JAI Press.

Officer, Lawrence H. 1996. *Between the Dollar-Sterling Gold Points: Exchange Rates, Parity, and Market Behavior.* Cambridge: Cambridge University Press.

Officer, Lawrence H. 2001. Gold Standard. In *EH.Net Encyclopedia,* edited by Robert Whaples. October 1, 2001. http://www.eh.net/encyclopedia/-contents/officer/gold.standard.php.

Oppers, Stefan E. 1993. The Interest Rate Effect of Dutch Money in Eighteenth-Century Britain. *Journal of Economic History* 53 (March): 25–43.

O'Rourke, Kevin H., Alan M. Taylor, and Jeffrey G. Williamson. 1996. Factor

Price Convergence in the Late Nineteenth Century. *International Economic Review* 37 (August): 499–530.

O'Rourke, Kevin H., and Jeffrey G. Williamson. 1994. Late-Nineteenth Century Anglo-American Factor-Price Convergence: Were Heckscher and Ohlin Right? *Journal of Economic History* 54 (December): 892–916.

O'Rourke, Kevin H., and Jeffrey G. Williamson. 1995. Education, Globalization and Catch-Up: Scandinavia in the Swedish Mirror. *Scandinavian Economic History Review* 43, no. 3:287–309.

O'Rourke, Kevin H., and Jeffrey G. Williamson. 1999. *Globalization and History: The Evolution of a Nineteenth-Century Atlantic Economy.* Cambridge, Mass.: MIT Press.

Padoa-Schioppa, Tommaso. 1988. The European Monetary System: A Long-Term View. In *The European Monetary System,* edited by Francesco Giavazzi, Stefano Micossi, and Marcus Miller. Cambridge: Cambridge University Press.

Paish, George. 1914. Export of Capital and the Cost of Living. *The Statist* (Supplement) (February 14, 1914): i–viii.

Pallage, Stéphane, and Michael A. Robe. 2003. On the Welfare Cost of Economic Fluctuations in Developing Countries. *International Economic Review* 44 (May): 677–98.

Papell, David H. 1997. Searching for Stationarity: Purchasing Power Parity Under the Current Float. *Journal of International Economics* 43 (November): 313–32.

Parente, Stephen L., and Edward C. Prescott. 2000. *Barriers to Riches.* Cambridge, Mass.: MIT Press.

Parsley, David C., and Helen A. Popper. 2001. Official Exchange Rate Arrangements and Real Exchange Rate Behavior. *Journal of Money Credit and Banking* 33 (November): 976–93.

Pedroni, Peter. 1995. Panel Cointegration: Asymptotic and Finite Sample Properties of Pooled Time Series with an Application to the PPP Hypothesis. Working Papers in Economics no. 95-013, Indiana University (June).

Peel, David A., and Mark P. Taylor. 2002. Covered Interest Rate Arbitrage in the Inter-War Period and the Keynes-Einzig Conjecture. *Journal of Money, Credit, and Banking* 34 (February): 51–75.

Penso de la Vega, Josef. 1688 [1957]. *Confusion de confusiones.* Translated by Hermann Kellenbenz. Cambridge, Mass.: Harvard University Printing Office.

Perkins, Edwin J. 1978. Foreign Interest Rates in American Financial Markets:

A Revised Series of Dollar-Sterling Exchange Rates, 1835–1900. *Journal of Economic History* 38 (June): 392–417.

Pesaran, M. Hashem, Yongcheol Shin, and Richard J. Smith. 2001. Bounds Testing Approaches to the Analysis of Level Relationships. *Journal of Applied Econometrics* 16 (May/June): 289–326.

Phillips, Peter C. B. 1988. Regression Theory for Near Integrated Time Series. *Journal of Econometrics* 56 (1988): 1021–43.

Platt, D. C. M. 1986. *Britain's Investment Overseas on the Eve of the First World War: The Use and Abuse of Numbers.* New York: St. Martin's Press.

Polanyi, Karl. 1944. *The Great Transformation.* New York: Rinehart.

Posen, Adam S. 1995. Declarations Are Not Enough: Financial Sector Sources of Central Bank Independence. In *NBER Macroeconomics Annual 1995* 10, edited by Ben S. Bernanke and Julio J. Rotemberg. Cambridge, Mass.: MIT Press.

Prados de la Escosura, Leandro. 2002. *El progreso económico de España, 1850–2000.* Madrid: Fundación BBVA.

Prasad, Eswar, Kenneth S. Rogoff, Shang-Jin Wei, and M. Ayhan Kose. 2003. Effects of Financial Globalization on Developing Countries: Some Empirical Evidence. International Monetary Fund (March). Photocopy.

Quinn, Dennis P. 1997. The Correlates of Change in International Financial Regulation. *American Political Science Review* 91 (September): 531–51.

Quinn, Dennis P., and A. Maria Toyoda. n.d. *Global Finance and Democracies.* Book manuscript.

Rajan, Raghuram G., and Luigi Zingales. 2003. The Great Reversals: The Politics of Financial Development in the 20th Century. *Journal of Financial Economics* 69 (July): 5–50.

Rees, David. 1973. *Harry Dexter White: A Study in Paradox.* New York: Coward, McCann & Geoghegan.

Reinhart, Carmen M., and Kenneth S. Rogoff. 2002. The Modern History of Exchange Rate Arrangements: A Reinterpretation. Working Paper Series no. 8963, National Bureau of Economic Research (May).

Reserve Bank of India. 1954. *Banking and Monetary Statistics of India.* Bombay: Reserve Bank of India.

Rifaat, Mohammed Ali. 1935. *The Monetary System of Egypt: An Inquiry into its History and Present Working.* London: George Allen & Unwin.

Rippy, J. Fred. 1959. *British Investments in Latin America, 1822–1949: A Case Study in the Operations of Private Enterprise in Retarded Regions.* Minneapolis: University of Minnesota Press.

Rodriguez, Francisco, and Dani Rodrik. 2001. Trade Policy and Economic

Growth: A Skeptic's Guide to Cross-National Evidence. In *NBER Macroeconomics Annual 2000* 15, edited by Ben S. Bernanke and Kenneth S. Rogoff. Cambridge, Mass.: MIT Press.

Rodrik, Dani. 1998. Who Needs Capital-Account Convertibility? In *Should the IMF Pursue Capital-Account Convertibility?* by Stanley Fischer et al. *Princeton Essays in International Finance* 207.

Rodrik, Dani. 2000. How Far Will International Economic Integration Go? *Journal of Economic Perspectives* 14 (Winter): 177–86.

Rodrik, Dani, Arvind Subramanian, and Francesco Trebbi. 2002. Institutions Rule: The Primacy of Institutions over Geography and Integration in Economic Development. Working Paper Series no. 9305, National Bureau of Economic Research (November).

Romer, Christina D. 1992. What Ended the Great Depression? *Journal of Economic History* 52 (December): 757–84.

Rose, Andrew K. 1996. Explaining Exchange Rate Volatility: An Empirical Analysis of "The Holy Trinity" of Monetary Independence, Fixed Exchange Rates, and Capital Mobility. *Journal of International Money and Finance* 15 (December): 925–45.

Rousseau, Peter L., and Richard E. Sylla. 2003. Financial Systems, Economic Growth, and Globalization. In *Globalization in Historical Perspective*, edited by Michael D. Bordo, Alan M. Taylor, and Jeffrey G. Williamson. Chicago: University of Chicago Press.

Royal Institute of International Affairs. 1937. *The Problem of International Investment*. London: Oxford University Press.

Sachs, Jeffrey D., and Andrew M. Warner. 1995. Economic Reform and the Process of Global Integration. *Brookings Papers on Economic Activity*, no. 1: 1–118.

Sala-i-Martin, Xavier. 2002. The Disturbing "Rise" of Global Income Inequality. Working Paper Series no. 8904, National Bureau of Economic Research (April).

Salera, Virgil. 1941. *Exchange Control and the Argentine Market*. New York: Columbia University Press.

Samuelson, Paul A. 1964. Theoretical Notes on Trade Problems. *Review of Economics and Statistics* 46 (May): 145–64.

Sargent, Thomas J. 1993. Stopping Moderate Inflations: The Methods of Poincaré and Thatcher. In *Rational Expectations and Inflation*. 2nd edition. New York: HarperCollins.

Sarkees, Meredith R. 2000. The Correlates of War Data on War: An Update to 1997. *Conflict Management and Peace Science* 18 (Fall): 123–44.

Sayers, R. S. 1976. *The Bank of England 1891–1944*. Cambridge: Cambridge University Press.

Schenk, Catherine. 1998. The Origins of the Eurodollar Market in London, 1955–1963. *Explorations in Economic History* 35 (April): 221–38.

Schulze, Max-Stephan. 2000. Patterns of Growth and Stagnation in the Late 19th Century Habsburg Economy. *European Review of Economic History* 4 (December): 311–40.

Shah Mohammed, Saif I., and Jeffrey G. Williamson. 2003. Freight Rates and Productivity Gains in British Tramp Shipping 1869–1950. Working Paper Series no. 9531, National Bureau of Economic Research (February).

Shambaugh, Jay C. 2004. The Effects of Fixed Exchange Rates on Monetary Policy. *Quarterly Journal of Economics*. Forthcoming.

Shaw, George Bernard. 1930. *The Apple Cart: A Political Extravaganza*. London: Constable and Company Ltd.

Shearer, Ronald A., and Carolyn Clark. 1984. Canada and the Interwar Gold Standard, 1920–35: Monetary Policy Without a Central Bank. In *A Retrospective on the Classical Gold Standard, 1821–1931*, edited by Michael D. Bordo and Anna J. Schwartz. Chicago: University of Chicago Press.

Sinn, Stefan. 1992. Saving-Investment Correlations and Capital Mobility: On the Evidence from Annual Data. *Economic Journal* 102 (September): 1171–83.

Skidelsky, Robert. 2001. *John Maynard Keynes: Fighting for Freedom, 1937–1946*. New York: Viking.

Smith, Gregor W., and R. Todd Smith. 1997. Greenback-Gold Returns and Expectations of Resumption, 1862–1879. *Journal of Economic History* 57 (Septemebr): 697–713.

Solomon, Robert. 1982. *The International Monetary System, 1945–1981*. New York: Harper & Row.

Spalding, William F. 1915. *Foreign Exchange and Foreign Bills in Theory and in Practice*. London: Sir Isaac Pitman & Sons.

Stewart, Robert B. 1938. Great Britain's Foreign Loan Policy. *Economica* 5 N.S. (February): 45–60.

Stiglitz, Joseph E. 2002. *Globalization and its Discontents*. New York: Norton.

Stone, Irving. 1999. *The Global Export of Capital from Great Britain, 1865–1914: A Statistical Survey*. New York: St. Martin's Press.

Stulz, René M. 1999. International Portfolio Flows and Security Markets. In *International Capital Flows*, edited by Martin Feldstein. Chicago: University of Chicago Press.

Summers, Lawrence H. 1988. Tax Policy and International Competitiveness.

In *International Aspects of Financial Policies*, edited by Jacob Frenkel. Chicago: University of Chicago Press.

Sussman, Nathan, and Yishay Yafeh. 2000. Institutions, Reforms, and Country Risk: Lessons from Japanese Government Debt in the Meiji Era. *Journal of Economic History* 60 (June): 442–67.

Svensson. Lars E. O. 1991a. The Simplest Test of Target Zone Credibility. *International Monetary Fund Staff Papers* 38 (September): 655–65.

Svensson, Lars E. O. 1991b. The Term Structure of Interest Rate Differentials in a Target Zone: Theory and Swedish Data. *Journal of Monetary Economics* 28 (August): 87–116.

Svensson, Lars E. O. 1994. Why Exchange Rate Bands? *Journal of Monetary Economics* 33 (February): 157–99.

Sylla, Richard E. 1975. *The American Capital Market, 1846–1914: A Study of the Effects of Public Policy on Economic Development.* New York: Arno Press.

Sylla, Richard E. 1998. U.S. Securities Markets and the Banking System, 1790–1840. *Federal Reserve Bank of St. Louis Review* (May/June).

Taylor, Alan M. 1992. External Dependence, Demographic Burdens and Argentine Economic Decline after the *Belle Époque*. *Journal of Economic History* 52 (December): 907–36.

Taylor, Alan M. 1994. Tres fases del crecimiento económico argentino. *Revista de Historia Económica* 12 (Otoño): 649–83.

Taylor, Alan M. 1995. Debt, Dependence, and the Demographic Transition: Latin America into the Next Century. *World Development* 23 (May): 869–79.

Taylor, Alan M. 1996a. International Capital Mobility in History: Purchasing Power Parity in the Long-Run. Working Paper Series no. 5742, National Bureau of Economic Research (September).

Taylor, Alan M., 1996b. International Capital Mobility in History: The Saving-Investment Relationship. Working Paper Series no. 5743, National Bureau of Economic Research (September).

Taylor, Alan M. 1998a. Argentina and the World Capital Market: Saving, Investment, and International Capital Mobility in the Twentieth Century. *Journal of Development Economics* 57 (October): 147–84.

Taylor, Alan M. 1998b. On the Costs of Inward-Looking Development: Price Distortions, Growth, and Divergence in Latin America. *Journal of Economic History* 58 (March): 1–28.

Taylor, Alan M. 2001. Potential Pitfalls for the Purchasing-Power Parity Puzzle? Sampling and Specification Biases in Mean-Reversion Tests of the Law of One Price. *Econometrica* 69 (March): 473–98.

Taylor, Alan M. 2002a. A Century of Current Account Dynamics. *Journal of International Money and Finance* 21 (November): 725–48.

Taylor, Alan M. 2002b. A Century of Purchasing Power Parity. *Review of Economics and Statistics* 84 (February): 139–50.

Taylor, Alan M. 2003. Foreign Capital in Latin America in the Nineteenth and Twentieth Centuries. Working Paper Series no. 9580, National Bureau of Economic Research (March).

Taylor, Alan M., and Jeffrey G. Williamson. 1994. Capital Flows to the New World as an Intergenerational Transfer. *Journal of Political Economy* 102 (April): 348–71.

Taylor, Alan M., and Jeffrey G. Williamson. 1997. Convergence in the Age of Mass Migration. *European Review of Economic History* 1 (April): 27–63.

Taylor, Bryan. 2000. *Encyclopedia of Global Financial Markets*. Global Financial Database. http://www.globalfindata.com.

Taylor, Mark P. 1995. The Economics of Exchange Rates. *Journal of Economic Literature* 33 (March): 13–47.

Taylor, Mark P., and Patrick C. McMahon. 1988. Long-Run Purchasing Power Parity in the 1920s. *European Economic Review* 32 (January): 179–97.

Taylor, Mark P., and Lucio Sarno. 1998. The Behavior of Real Exchange Rates During the Post–Bretton Woods Period. *Journal of International Economics* 46 (December): 281–312.

Temin, Peter. 1989. *Lessons from the Great Depression*. Cambridge: MIT Press.

Tesar, Linda L. 1991. Savings, Investment and International Capital Flows. *Journal of International Economics* 31 (August): 55–78.

Tezel, Yahya Sezai. 1986. *Cumhuriyet döneminin iktisadi tarihi, 1923–1950*. 2nd edition. Ankara: Yurt Yayınları.

Thomas, Brinley. 1954. *Migration and Economic Growth: A Study of Great Britain and the Atlantic Economy*. Cambridge: Cambridge University Press.

Tirole, Jean. 2002. *Financial Crises, Liquidity, and the International Monetary System*. Princeton, N.J.: Princeton University Press.

Tommasi, Mariano. 2002. Crisis, Political Institutions, and Policy Reform: It's Not the Policy, It Is the Polity, Stupid. University of San Andrés. Photocopy.

Tomz, Michael. 2001. How Do Reputations Form? New and Seasoned Borrowers in International Capital Markets. Paper presented at the 2001 Annual Meetings of the American Political Science Association, San Francisco.

Tortella, Gabriel. 2003. Democracy and Gold. Universidad de Alcalá and Columbia University. Photocopy.

Trehan, Bharat, and Carl E. Walsh. 1991. Testing Intertemporal Budget Constraints: Theory and Applications to U.S. Federal Budget and Current Account Deficits. *Journal of Money, Credit, and Banking* 23 (May): 206–23.

Triffin, Robert. 1957. *Europe and the Money Muddle: From Bilateralism to Near-Convertibility, 1947–1956.* New Haven, Conn.: Yale University Press.

Twomey, Michael J. 1998. Patterns of Foreign Investment in Latin America in the Twentieth Century. In *Latin America and the World Economy Since 1800*, edited by John H. Coatsworth and Alan M. Taylor. Cambridge: Harvard University Press.

Twomey, Michael J. 2000. *A Century of Foreign Investment in the Third World.* London: Routledge.

United Nations. 1948. *Public Debt 1914–1946.* Lake Success, N.Y.: United Nations Publications.

Urquhart, Malcolm C. 1988. Canadian Economic Growth 1870–1980. Discussion Paper no. 734, Institute for Economic Research, Queen's University, Kingston, Ontario.

Valério, Nuno, ed. 2001. *Estatísticas históricas portuguesas.* Lisbon: Instituto Nacional de Estatística.

van der Wee, Herman. 1963. *The Growth of the Antwerp Market.* 3 vols. The Hague: Nijhoff.

van Wincoop, Eric. 1999. How Big Are the Potential Gains from International Risksharing? *Journal of International Economics* 47 (February): 109–35.

Vázquez-Presedo, V. (1971–76). *Estadísticas historicas argentinas.* 2 vols. Buenos Aires: Ediciones Macchi.

Velasco, Andrés. 1987. Financial Crises and Balance of Payments Crises: A Simple Model of the Southern Cone Experience. *Journal of Development Economics* 27 (October): 263–83.

Ventura, Jaume. 2002. Towards a Theory of Current Accounts. Working Paper Series no. 9163, National Bureau of Economic Research (September).

Vikøren, Birger. 1991. The Saving-Investment Correlation in the Short and in the Long Run. Working Paper no. 91/7, Norges Bank.

Viner, Jacob. 1943a. Two Plans for International Monetary Stabilization. *Yale Review* 33 (Autumn): 77–107.

Viner, Jacob. 1943b. *Trade Relations between Free-Market and Controlled Economies.* Geneva: League of Nations.

Voth, Hans-Joachim. 2001. Convertibility, Currency Controls and the Cost of

Capital in Western Europe, 1950–1999. Universitat Pompeu Fabra (July). Photocopy.

Warnock, Frank E. 2002. Home Bias and High Turnover Reconsidered. *Journal of International Money and Finance* 21 (November): 795–805.

Wei, Shang-Jin, and David C. Parsley. 1995. Purchasing Power Dis-parity During the Floating Rate Period: Exchange Rate Volatility, Trade Barriers, and Other Culprits. Working Paper Series no. 5032, National Bureau of Economic Research (February).

Weill, Nathan E. 1903. *Die Solidarität der Geldmärkte*. Frankfurt: J. D. Sauerläder.

Wickens, Michael R., and Merih Uctum. 1993. The Sustainability of Current Account Deficits: A Test of the U.S. Intertemporal Budget Constraint. *Journal of Economic Dynamics and Control* 17 (May): 423–41.

Wilde, Oscar. 1899. *An Ideal Husband*. London: Leonard Smithers.

Williamson, Jeffrey G. 1995. The Evolution of Global Labor Markets since 1830: Background Evidence and Hypotheses. *Explorations in Economic History* 32 (April): 141–96.

Williamson, Jeffrey G. 1996. Globalization, Convergence, and History. *Journal of Economic History* 56 (June): 277–306.

Woodruff, William. 1967. *Impact of Western Man: A Study of Europe's Role in the World Economy 1750–1960*. New York: St. Martin's Press.

World Bank. 1994. *World Data 1994: World Bank Indicators on CD-ROM*. Washington, D.C.: The World Bank. CD-ROM.

World Bank. 2000. *Global Development Finance 2000*. Washington, D.C.: The World Bank.

Wyplosz, Charles. 1986. Capital Controls and Balance of Payments Crises. *Journal of International Money and Finance* 5 (June): 167–79.

Yeager, Leland. B. 1976. *International Monetary Relations: Theory, History, and Policy*. 2nd edition. New York: Harper & Row.

Yergin, Daniel, and Joseph Stanislaw. 1998. *The Commanding Heights: The Battle between Government and the Marketplace That Is Remaking the Modern World*. New York: Simon & Schuster.

Yousef, Tarik M. 2002. Egypt's Growth Performance under Economic Liberalism: A Reassessment with New GDP Estimates, 1886–1945. *Review of Income and Wealth* 48 (December): 561–79.

Zevin, Robert B. 1992. Are World Financial Markets More Open? If So, Why and With What Effects? In *Financial Openness and National Autonomy: Opportunities and Constraints*, edited by Tariq Banuri and Juliet B. Schor. Oxford: Clarendon Press.

Index

Fischer, Stanley, 4, 169, 258
Fishlow, Albert, 140
Flandreau, Marc, 25, 93, 126, 172, 199, 206–7, 214, 310–2
float era. See post–Bretton Woods era
foreign investment: historical patterns of, 57–61, 82–3
foreign investment stocks, 48; and equity home bias, 57, 67, 249; historical data on, 51–7; as percentage of world GDP, 55–7; ratio of, to output formula, 49–51;
France: and arbitrage differential, 94; and capital flows, speculative, 157–60; and currency convertibility, postwar, 156; and exchange control, interwar, 132, 135. 137; and foreign investment, 55, 231; and gold standard, 131, 203–4, 208; and interest rates, 96, 191; and transition to post–Bretton Woods era, 160
Frankel, Jeffrey A., 62, 104–5, 121, 161, 173, 177, 192, 273
Frieden, Jeffry A., 34
Friedman, Milton, 147, 152
Friedman, Thomas L., 10
Froot, Kenneth A., 104

Gallman, Robert E., 23, 128, 213
Gardner, Richard N., 155
General Agreement on Tariffs and Trade (GATT): established, 147
Germany: and capital flows, speculative, 157–60; and currency convertibility, postwar, 156; and current account dynamics, 74; and exchange rates, 93–4, 107, 115, 132, 133, 136–7, 138, 139; and foreign investment, 55, 231, 238; and gold standard, 208; and interest-rate convergence, 96; and transition to post–Bretton Woods era, 160
Gerschenkron, Alexander, 34
Giavazzi, Francesco, 62–3, 160
Giovannini, Alberto, 88, 160
Glaeser, Edward L., 249
Glick, Reuven, 287
Global Financial Data (GFD), 197, 208
gold standard era (1870–1914), 25, 34–5, 126–9, 168–9: and arbitrage differentials, 91, 93–4; capital market in, 16; and core-periphery flows, 235–43; and current account dynamics, 72–4; data sources on, 178; and empire as factor in capital flows, 243–9 and exchange rate volatility, 111–12, 117, 120; interest rates in, 98, 121, 181, 183–4,187, 192; net capital stocks in, 231; and PPP, 105–6; saving-investment correlations, 65; and

trilemma, 173–4. See also interwar era; Bretton Woods era; post–Breton Woods era
Gourinchas, Pierre-Olivier, 262–5, 275, 296
Goschen, George J., 87
Great Britain. See Britain
Great Depression: 40, 130, 168; and capital markets, 136–40; impact of, on world capital markets, 15, 16, 24, 61; policy responses to, 141–5. See also crises; interwar era
Greece: and gold standard, 213
Grilli, Vittorio, 31, 165, 274
growth, economic: and financial opening, 271–9

Haberler, Gottfried, 143, 148
Hakkio, Craig S., 68
Hall, Robert E., 248, 261
Hallwood, C. Paul, 88, 224
Harvey, Campbell R., 254
Hatton, Timothy J., 128
Hausman, Jerry A., 65
Hawtrey, Ralph G., 143, 178
Henry, Peter B., 259, 272–3, 278
Hong Kong: and pegged exchange rates, 39
Hopkins, Anthony G., 222
Horioka, Charles Y., 61–2, 253–4. See also Feldstein-Horioka (FH) correlations
Houghton, John, 20
Hsieh, Chang-Tai, 224, 269
Hungary: and exchange controls, Depression-era, 136, 138
Husted, Steven, 104
Hutchison, Michael M., 287
Huttenback, Robert A., 128, 212, 243

IMF. See International Monetary Fund
informational asymmetries: and contract enforcement, 11
institutional strength: and crises, 292, 297; as necessary for economic liberalization, 261, 265, 270 279–82, 288–9 and viability of economic reforms
interest parity, 48
interest rates, 172–4, 192–3; convergence and capital market integration, 96–103; measuring independence, 174–80; individual-country dynamics, 187–92; nominal, 180–7
International Clearing Union, 148
International Monetary Fund (IMF), 168; and Bretton Woods system, 37–8; established, 26,147
interwar era (1914–45), 25–6; and arbitrage differentials, 91, 93–4; and current

Warner, Andrew M., 25, 127, 271, 273
Weidenmier, Marc, 179
Weil, David N., 263
White, Harry Dexter, 41, 142, 147, 149–51
Wickens, Michael R., 68
Williamson, Jeffrey G., 25, 85, 127, 244–6, 248
World Bank: established, 147
World War One: and exchange controls, 130–2
World War Two: impact of, on world capital markets, 16; and intensification of exchange control, 145–7; and Keynes-White plan, 147–51

Yafeh, Yishay, 216

Zecher, J. Richard, 104
Zingales, Luigi, 32, 170